The Military and Politics in Modern Times

Written under the auspices of the
Center for International Affairs
Harvard University

THE MILITARY AND POLITICS

IN MODERN TIMES

On Professionals, Praetorians, and Revolutionary Soldiers

Amos Perlmutter

New Haven and London, Yale University Press

795136

Published with assistance from the foundation established in memory
of Amasa Stone Mather of the Class of 1907, Yale College.

Designed by John O.C. McCrillis
and set in Baskerville type.
Printed in the United States of America by
The Vail-Ballou Press, Inc., Binghamton, New York.

Published in Great Britain, Europe, Africa, and Asia
(except Japan) by Yale University Press, Ltd., London.
Distributed in Australia and New Zealand by Book & Film
Services, Artarmon, N.S.W., Australia; and in Japan by
Harper & Row, Publishers, Tokyo Office.

Library of Congress Cataloging in Publication Data

Perlmutter, Amos.
    The military and politics in modern times.

    "Written under the auspices of the Center for International
Affairs, Harvard University."
    Includes bibliographical references and index.
    1. Sociology, military. 2. Armed Forces—Political activity.
I. Harvard University. Center for International Affairs.
    II. Title.
U21.5.P36   301.5'93   76-45769
ISBN 0-300-02045-7 clothbound
        0-300-02353-7 paperbound

This book is dedicated to
Sam Huntington, who believed;
Marty Lipset, who maintained;
Charlie Hutchinson, who sustained;
and Rosanne, who always was there.
To all, my love and admiration.

Contents

List of Tables and Figures

Foreword

The importance of the book which you are starting to read can only be appreciated by looking at the development of the scholarly literature on civil-military relations during the past two decades. It is, I think, fair to say that prior to World War II civil-military relations received little attention from social scientists and historians, at least in the English-language literature and certainly in American writing. The war experience itself and, even more importantly, the subsequent Cold War, Korean War, and the conflict between President Truman and General MacArthur stimulated in the 1950s a new stream of scholarly analysis of the problems of civil-military relations and military policy-making. By and large these works focused on the American context; I do not think I am immodest or inaccurate in saying that the only effort, at that time, to set forth a general theory of civil-military relations was in *The Soldier and the State*, and even that was illustrated primarily by reference to the American experience. In the following years, however, the studies proliferated on the historical and contemporary problems of civil-military relations in the countries of Western Europe and in Japan. In addition, scholars of communism began to study the issues of party-army relations in the Soviet Union and, eventually, in other communist societies.

The 1960s saw a major blossoming of American academic interest in the politics of the less developed countries. Inevitably, major attention had to be devoted to the role of the military in the politics of those countries and explanations offered as to why that role was so prominent compared to the prevailing pattern in developed Western societies and in communist societies. Different scholars working on different regions advanced theses locating the causes for military political intervention variously in the nature of the military and in the nature of society. Subsequently, attention shifted from the causes of military intervention to its consequences, and scholars in the early 1970s focused on the behavior of military regimes and how it differed or did not differ from that of civilian governments. In these later phases of the exploration of civil-military relations in particular societies, a major contribution was made by the Inter-University Seminar on the Armed Forces and Society under the leadership of Morris Janowitz.

All this activity produced a vast amount of monographic literature dealing with particular countries, particular armies, particular coups, particular military regimes. It also produced a certain amount of comparative quantitative empirical analysis, attempting to relate various economic, social, and political factors to military interventions and the characteristics of military regimes. Left wanting was the imposition of some conceptual order on this material and the placing of it in a broader theoretical perspective.

It is precisely this momentous task which Amos Perlmutter has essayed in this volume, and his effort is precisely the reason for the volume's importance. Perlmutter sets forth a comprehensive general framework for the analysis of modern civil-military relations. On the basis of certain key concepts, he distinguishes three modern types of civil-military relations: the professional, the praetorian, and the professional revolutionary. In effect, his claim is that civil-military relations in any contemporary society can be understood in terms of one or some combination of these models. A stimulating and positive aspect of his typology is that these patterns of civil-military relations do not necessarily coincide with the usual three-way classification of political systems into Western, communist, and developing. Perlmutter treats the Red Army, for instance, along with the French and Prussian armies in the professional category, while the Israeli army is placed in the same category with that of Communist China.

To develop a typology which is both comprehensive and useful is to take the first step toward theory. Perlmutter does not stop there. In addition, he elaborates a central theoretical argument, based on the distinction between professionalism and corporatism. His thesis is that professionalism, as it developed in the West, leads to corporatism, which, in turn, furnishes a motive for political intervention by the military. Although starting from similar concepts, he is, thus, in part challenging my argument that professionalism and political intervention are antithetical. He develops the same point in a different way in his section on praetorianism, in which he argues that modern, as distinguished from historical, praetorianism is also an outgrowth of the professional characteristics of the military in less developed countries. In this connection, he stresses the corporatist, as distinguished from the class or ideological, motivations for military intervention in the politics of less developed countries. All this is extraordinarily suggestive as well as quite controversial. I would, for instance, accept his argument that corporatism can furnish a motive for intervention, but I do not believe that the corporatism which has that consequence is the product of professionalism. Professionalism involves a balance among expertise, responsibility, and corporateness, and the corporatism which leads to intervention represents a perversion of professionalism, in which the corporatist element overbalances the components of expertise and responsibility.

As my remarks illustrate, probably few scholars will accept Professor Perlmutter's argument in toto. But few scholars will also fail to be impressed with the broad research, theoretical originality, and analytical insight displayed in this book. Here is a bold, pioneering, provocative piece of scholarship, setting forth a comprehensive theory of modern civil-military relations. It is a major work of synthesis and interpretation. In the coming years, debates about civil-military relations will be phrased in terms of Perlmutter's categories and will be focused on the theses he has advanced. This book will be read, discussed, and, no doubt, criticized; but it will not be ignored.

SAMUEL P. HUNTINGTON

Preface

Except for the work of a few very talented scholars, an imbalance exists today between the quantity of literature on civil-military relations and its significance. This situation is clearly related to the dynamic but asymmetrical state of the contemporary social sciences, the lack of general agreement on value orientations and research methods, and the absence of governing standards and procedures concerning definitions, conceptualizations, frames of reference, theories, and taxonomies. At the same time, concepts of the military, society, and politics are heavily saturated with ideological orientations that are controversial, even explosive. In the absence of an accepted general theory of conflict, the demarcation lines between order and instability and between politics, society, and the military depend upon such vague or all-inclusive concepts as total war, revolution, dynamic change, and the universal ethic of modernization. Fewer than ten scholars have contributed at least one significant, pioneering study to the field: Samuel P. Huntington, Samuel E. Finer, Morris M. Janowitz, Lucian Pye, Stanislav Andreski, and such earlier scholars as Samuel Stouffer, Hans Speier, Edward M. Earle, and Harold D. Lasswell.

The value orientations and ideological inclinations of social scientists have both impelled and hindered the development of a general theory of civil-military relations. The literature—especially the work of the influential scholars just mentioned—reveals strong ties between the authors' conceptual and analytical positions and the political and ideological climate of their times. In a period of over forty years, at least three different analytical models have been designed, all closely related to the weltanschauung of the writers.

During the 1930s, democratic and liberal political scientists in America reacted against the rise of three totalitarian systems in Europe. From this background emerged Lasswell's construct of the "garrison state," a concept that focused upon the rise of the technician of violence.[1] Thus appeared the model of the garrison officer who would establish the new dictatorship of violence.

After World War II, the monumental research of Samuel Stouffer and others on the American soldier yielded enough material for a new generation of American scholars to re-examine the analytical truisms of

the prewar generation.[2] Naturally, the war resulted in a better understanding of the military and its role. Stouffer's study signified a transition from Lasswell's interpretation to one more modern and less ideological. Huntington and Janowitz (the latter strongly influenced by
Stouffer),[3] have since removed the ideological orientation of anti-
totalitarianism from the study of civil-military relations and begun an
analysis of the modern military, while continuing to focus on the
American military. Thus the model of the totalitarian-oriented garrison
soldier has been replaced by the liberal and civilian-oriented "professional soldier."

The study of the military was further enhanced by the rise of modern
comparative politics. The field of civil-military relations led to new
analyses and to new ideological positions on the military and society.
The spurt of research focused on the developing polities and produced
the model of the "progressive modernizing soldier." Among the first
attempts at a comparative study of the military in developing states was
a work edited by John J. Johnson, a collection of independent essays on
the role of the military in underdeveloped countries that includes
theoretical analyses by several authors.[4] All explain the growing role of
the military in the politics of new states by emphasizing the military's
commitment to modernization and political development. When these
aspirations become operational, they bring about structural and functional differentiation in the modernizing polities. Most of the contribu-
tors consider the military a highly effective instrument of modernization.

My own study draws upon and integrates two basic approaches: a
taxonomic and conceptual analysis of types of civil-military relations
and types and subtypes of professional soldiers and an analysis of
comparative political history. I have rejected a deterministic dichotomy
between "civil" and "military," because in a complex society neither
the military nor the civilian sector can be restricted to its functional
role. What has been functionally known as "the military," or "the
military mind," is often represented by "civilian" groups. "Official"
civilians (such as bureaucrats and politicians) and private social-econom-
ic groups (such as businessmen and industrialists) often perform the
function assigned to the military, that is, the conduct of war. The
military group, which is certainly not of one mind, may also perform
civilian functions and, in fact, often coalesces with other groups to defend
the "civilian" from the "military."[5] No serious student of the modern

military-industrial complex will argue that it is a monolith in the sense of representing a cohesive and centrally programmed system of undivided orientations, behavior, and values. Neither would he argue that this complex is a system directed solely toward the fulfillment of unrestricted militarism, nor that the "civilians" as a whole are relentlessly opposed to "militarism." The types of civil-military relations vary widely, reflecting modern political ideologies, orientations, and organizational structures. The most fruitful explanation of civil-military relations and of military corporatism seems to me, therefore, to be the fusionist theory, which links the professional and bureaucratic modern military.

My work rests on two assumptions. First, the professional soldier is a new social type, a product of postrevolutionary Europe and America, and is the dominant military type of modern times. Second, all forms of political participation by the military in developing as well as developed states involve combinations or modifications of professional military types or orientations.

In this work I offer a theory of military corporate professionalism and praetorianism in modern times and discuss their relationship to society and politics. Military corporatism has appeared in three forms in the modern nation-state. The classical type of professional soldier emerged in Prussia and France in the eighteenth century and held sway in the twentieth century in Japan and the USSR. The second type of corporate professionalism, represented by the praetorian soldier, reached its apex in Latin America in the twentieth century and by the 1970s was the only form of military organizational behavior in the Middle East, North Africa, and sub-Saharan Africa. Finally a third type of professionalism appeared in this century and is represented by the noncorporate revolutionary soldier, who has restored military professionalism to its old glory. Soldiers of this type have ranged from anticorporate romantic revolutionaries at one end of the continuum, through national liberation fighters (Marxist and non-Marxist), to routinized revolutionary professionals. Although in the 1970s the revolutionary soldier is essentially noncorporate, he does exhibit some corporate characteristics. The institutionalization of the revolutionary professional in China and in Israel may orient him more firmly toward corporatism, though it is unlikely that he will ever become "corporate" in the nineteenth-century sense or, for that matter, in the sense of twentieth-century praetorianism.

In analyzing the evolution of these three types of modern military professionals and explaining the rise, decline, and re-emergence of corporate professionalism, my major analytical contention is that the concept of "corporatism" should be extracted from the concept of "professionalism" and treated as an independent variable. I will demonstrate that: (1) military professionalism can be achieved and fulfilled without an exclusively corporate orientation and behavior; (2) the corporate, not the professional, orientation of the modern military determines its objective or subjective political behavior; (3) the degree of commitment to corporatism, rather than to professionalism, determines the level of political intervention by the military; and (4) the military mind—the military's "acceptance" of a specific type of patron and its perception of the power and stability of the political order—determines its clientship orientation. I will also show that a high correlation exists between military praetorianism and corporate professionalism. Finally, I will assess the damage done to military professionalism by praetorianism and intervention in politics, particularly in developing states.

Acknowledgments

No intellectual enterprise, especially one of the scope attempted in this study, is the product of a single scholar. I have long felt that 1,400 items on the military, as recorded in Kurt Lang's bibliography, point out the long-neglected need for a synthesis. The vastness of the literature attests to the cumulative nature of this enterprise. Nevertheless, it is an author's privilege to note the works that have stimulated and impressed him most. I could not have begun this study without the works of Samuel P. Huntington, and his impact is apparent. I single out his *The Soldier and the State* as the most stimulating study on civil-military relations. It influenced my research even if, at times, I chose a different course.

Stanislav Andreski's *Military Organization and Society* is another study that whetted my appetite for further undertakings. S. E. Finer's *Men on Horseback* was a challenge in the sense that I felt that a more comprehensive and, above all, a theoretically rigorous study was imperative. It prompted me to call for a major and revisionist effort to demarcate the study of the military and politics from military sociology.

I must thank persons I know intimately and those whom I have never met who influenced and helped me indirectly. Samuel Huntington and Martin Lipset of Harvard and John Harsanyi of Berkeley were of the greatest intellectual help. Without Samuel Huntington, this study would quite likely not yet have been published. Only he and I know my trials and tribulations, the obstacles laid in the way of an author who dares. We won—as, in the end, truth must.

Next, without the financial support of Charles Hutchinson of the Air Force, Office of Scientific Research, I could not have enjoyed the freedom from economic burdens to start this enterprise. Charlie also provided personal support in critical times.

To my colleagues past and present, Murray Feld, Thomas Schelling, Robert Jervis, George Quester, James Kurth, Dick Betts, Michael Handel, and Judith Hughes of Harvard, I am grateful for their patience in listening to my ideas and in reading several, sometimes incomprehensible, drafts. Thanks also go to Henry Bienen of Princeton, Alfred Stepan of Yale, William Thompson of Florida State University, Liisa North, Jose Nun, Chalmers Johnson, and Aaron Wildavsky of Berkeley. Also, my gratitude goes to H. Stuart Hughes of Santa Cruz; Elie Kedourie of the

London School of Economics; Moshe Maoz, Ellis Joffe, Moshe Lissak, and Yehezkel Dror of the Hebrew University in Jerusalem; Gabriel Ben Dor of Haifa; Eliezer Be'eri of Kibbutz Hazoreah; Charles Moskos of Northwestern University; Claude Welch of SUNY–Buffalo; Valery Bennett, who was always there when needed; and Robin Luckham of the University of Ghana. I owe special thanks to the informal Harvard Center for International Affairs luncheon group for hours of talk and toleration. To Manfred Halpern of Princeton, without whose love of controversy I would not have come to a better understanding of the Arab military, I send special thanks. The intellectual and other dialogues with Benjamin Schwartz of Harvard; John Harsanyi of Berkeley; Reinhard Selten of the Free University of Berlin; Kenneth Waltz of Berkeley; and Bruce Mazlish, Ithiel de Sola Pool, and David Ralston of M.I.T. have widened my historical horizons and sharpened my analytical tools and approach. And, above all, I am grateful for the pleasures of intellectual stimulation all have given me.

To my friends in the Israel Defense Force, I am especially thankful. First, my intimate friend and intellectual companion, Siko (Pinhas Zusmann), presently Director General of the Israeli Ministry of Defense, provided years of stimulation and vast quantities of information. My gratitude also goes to my friend General Mordechai Gur, present Chief of Staff of the IDF, and to the late former Chief of Staff, General David Elazar. To former Chief of Staff Yitzchak Rabin (presently Prime Minister of Israel), to former Defense Minister General Moshe Dayan, to present Defense Minister Shimon Peres, and to Generals Tulkowski, Weizmann, Sharon, Adan, Geva, Zeira, Tamir (Abrasha), Herzog, Harkabi, and Amit—all of the IDF—go my grateful appreciation and admiration.

No scholar can operate without institutional help. The Center for International Affairs at Harvard gave me space, time, and resources for the four years during which I wrote most of this study. To its former director, Professor Robert Bowie, and to its present director, Ray Vernon, go my thanks. For Peter Jacobsohn, present editor, and Murray Feld, librarian, I have special thanks. The Widener Library at Harvard and the Library of Congress proved invaluable.

The Woodrow Wilson International Center for Scholars provided me with a year (1971–72) of most pleasant academic and intellectual atmosphere while I finished the study. My special thanks go to the inspiring former director, Benjamin Read, and his devoted staff. I must thank Edythe Holbrooke, who knows why, and my colleagues at the Center—Alton Frye, Raja Rao, Earl Ravenel, Townsend (Tim) Hoopes, Stuart Lowry, George Reedy, and Chester Cooper—who added to my knowledge. Francis Hunter's help was greatly appreciated.

In my new home at the American University, I have found only good will. Thanks are due Dean Morris Collins for the grant he offered; Dean Lee Fritschler—friend, colleague, and collaborator—for all he did for me; and Coralie (Corky) Bryant, Glynn Wood, and Matthew Bonham for their friendship and help. The many typists who deciphered my incomprehensible handwriting have earned my thanks, especially Mary Wason, Codelle Rosenberg, Tina Taylor, and Betsy Rowe.

To my editors: Dorothy Whitney of the Harvard Center, who assisted in practically rewriting the manuscript; Sally Cox, an unofficial but critical editor; Gale Scott of Princeton; Marya W. Holcombe of Yale; and Karen McPherson, my deep appreciation. I am especially indebted to Marian Neal Ash, social science editor at the Yale University Press, for her dispatch, sympathy, and warmth. Without Marian, I would not have enjoyed so much the privilege of publishing with such a distinguished university press.

I am grateful to the following publishers for permission to use revised portions of material previously published by them: Frank Cass, in *Military and Politics in Israel* (1969); *Comparative Politics*, April 1969; Princeton University Press, in *World Politics*, July 1968 and January 1970; and Transaction, in *Egypt, The Praetorian State* (1974).

I must thank two close friends who long sustained me—Dick Tadjer and Rosanne Ellenbogen of Washington, D.C. The latter deserves more than a dedication.

Needless to say, all errors, vigorous generalizations, and flaws are mine. My colleagues and friends are responsible for the better part of the book.

And finally, if my father, Moshe Perlmutter, were still alive, I know that his happiness that I have completed this book would be boundless. May he rest in peace. I shall never forget what he and my mother, Berta, may she live long, have done for their *enfant terrible*.

Amos Perlmutter

*Cambridge, Massachusetts,
and Washington, D.C.*

1

Professionalism and Corporatism in Military Organizations

A profession is an occupation that requires advanced training in a specialized field. The purpose of long and intensive training is to maintain high levels of achievement and conduct according to standards set either by the rules of the organization or the opinion of peers. The degree of professionalism of a particular occupation is measured by the conduct, method, character, status, and standard of its practitioners. Because of their special status, true professionals possess considerable authority in their relations with "clients."[1]

"The structure of a profession," write Blau and Scott, "tends to make the practitioner's own interests dependent on his serving the interest of his clients to the best of his abilities."[2] This tendency can be traced to the factors that govern professionalism, be it occupational or bureaucratic: (1) universal standards, that is, objective criteria by which to judge a specific case; (2) specificity of professional expertness but no claim to general wisdom; (3) assertion of authority—the confidence of the client in the expertise of the professional; (4) affective neutrality in the client relationship, that is, impersonal detachment; (5) judgment of performance in accordance with principles laid down by professional colleagues; (6) protection of the client that is not based on self-interest but is an end in itself, ensuring protection for even dependent and vulnerable clients.[3]

BUREAUCRACY AND CORPORATISM AND THE MILITARY PROFESSION

The military is an organization that serves the public at large "often, although *not necessarily*, to the exclusion of the very people who are the object of the organization's endeavors."[4] The military profession is a voluntary one since individuals are free to choose an occupation within it, yet it is also coercive in that its members are not free to organize into a voluntary association but are confined to a bureaucratic-hierarchical situation.

The two key qualitative variables of military professionalism are *control* and *skills*.

Control

The military is controlled on two organizational levels. A colleague group oversees the internal cohesion of the officer corps as a professional and social group. This group observes self-imposed standards of personal behavior, and professional conduct. The external source of control and of discipline is the hierarchy of authority. Professional methods and conduct are judged by the faithfulness with which the officer follows directives from above.[5] Professional status and advancement are awarded according to the officer's behavior, both as a professional and as a bureaucrat.

Skills

Historically, the most important attributes of the professional soldier were bravery and discipline. But today's professional must be a bureaucrat as well as a hero. Thus he has needed to acquire the modern skills of management and strategy.[6] Whatever damage it may have done to the romantic image of the soldier, corporate professionalism has widened the military's social and political horizons. As a professional group it must preserve group standards and values. The military weltanschauung is on the whole conservative, protectionist, and exclusive.

As bureaucrats military professionals are closely linked to the modern nation-state, whose technological orientation is revolutionary in both management and strategy. The potential clash is therefore between the self-imposed standards of the military peer group, whose members are generally conservative and exclusivist, and the managerial orientation of the modern nation-state, which is technological, scientific, and revolutionary. Obviously, the technological revolution in management and strategy requires the military to adopt new skills. But this revolution has wrought a more subtle change: it has politicized the military. Integrating new skills is a challenge to the corporate identity of military professionals who espouse tradition and abhor innovation.

The propensity of the military professional to intervene in politics and in policy formation is linked to his corporate and bureaucratic roles and orientations. As a corporate body the military organization strives for internal control of its profession and for protection from external political control (this is Huntington's objective control concept, that is, to

Figure 1.1 Conceptual Linkage of Professionalism and Corporatism

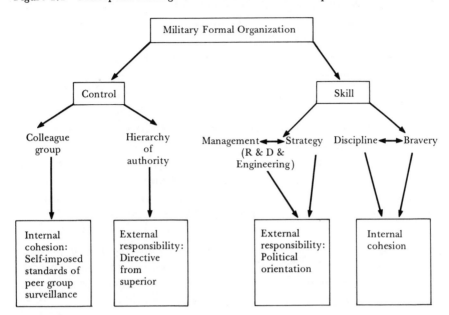

maximize the autonomy of the military organization[7]). Striving to maximize autonomy entails, among other things, exercising influence in politics, both through organizational counterpressures and through political institutions and regimes. As a bureaucratic profession, the military is in politics to the degree that it is a key partner of civilian politicians and bureaucrats in the formation and implementation of national security policy.

The professional and bureaucratic responsibilities of the military establishment converge. As a professional the soldier is responsible to his client, the state, in the sense of a professional "calling." As a bureaucrat he is responsible to the authorities. The modern soldier is corporate (in terms of exclusivity), bureaucratic (in terms of hierarchy), and professional (in terms of sense of mission).

Richard Betts advances an interesting concept of the division between administrative values. In classical administrative theory, the priority is efficiency; the process is command-obedience; and the political behavior is neutral. In revisionist administrative theory, the priority is political control; the administrative process is negotiation; and political behavior displays a high degree of involvement.[8]

The concept that military professionalism removes the military from politics is derived in part from the classical tradition of administrative theory[9] and American public administration. This tradition was built on a premise that politics is separated from administration, that is, that policy making (which is the responsibility of elected officials) is separate from policy implementation (the responsibility of appointed officials). This distinction was advanced to explain the separation of experts from politicians, but it no longer holds. The new administrative theory is fusionist; it recognizes that bureaucracy and politics, as well as government and administration experts and politicians, are all symbiotically connected. The system of hierarchy of authority of the state, that is, the bureaucracy (in this case the military establishment), is *linked* with the skills of the modern military: management and strategy.[10] The fusion of bureaucrat and professional involves the military in policy in non-praetorian states while it propels the military into politics in the praetorian state. Corporate professionalism represents the fusion between the professional and the bureaucrat—a fusion between group exclusivity and managerial responsibility. Inherently the fusionist theory is a pluralistic concept that power in society is diffuse and that advanced societies are characterized by extremely complex and highly differentiated organizations that involve experts and nonexperts, policy makers and policy implementers in the political process.

The authorities of the modern industrial state have imbued the professional military organization with a sense of belonging. The military professional in the state that possesses a nuclear arsenal is highly skilled in the sciences of management and nuclear strategy. He understands that he *shares* with the authorities not only the formulation of strategy and the maintenance of the bureaucratic-hierarchical system but participation in the making of national security policy. Thus, antagonism between professionalism and bureaucracy is mitigated. They become fused. The nineteenth-century discrepancy between the professional and the bureaucrat has almost disappeared. In addition, as we have seen, the virtues of bravery and discipline have now been replaced by the skills of management and strategy.

Thus, the relationship between military and state becomes symbiotic. Two centuries of total war and mobilization of citizen soldiers linked the faith of military establishments to their civilian governments. The two structures became interdependent, influencing each other in war, strategy, and diplomacy. The "civilian" and the "military" could not remain separate bureaucratic structures or "minds" professing different orientations. The cleavage in states where the professional soldier developed was no longer vertical—between "soldiers" and "civilians." The conflict was now horizontal—between and within the "soldier" and "civilian" establishments—over political and ideological orientations as well as a political-bureaucratic struggle over the determination and implementation of national security policy.[11]

Huntington was the first scholar to demonstrate the fusionist theory of military and national security and the emergence of the military as an influential political group in the making of national security policy.[12] In the altered political conditions after World War II, the strategy of deterrence changed both the external and domestic environments of states. Mobilization for deterrence and the strategy of deterrence led to the creation of what some observers, exaggerating slightly, see as the emergence of the national security state.[13] Some claimed that the military's new skills assured its ascendency (despite the fact that Lasswell's 1941 garrison state thesis had been proved wrong by students of modern military organization[14]) and insisted that Lasswell's model had contemporary validity.[15] Nevertheless, strategic decisions brought about structural changes in both the military organization and the organization of security.[16] According to Huntington, national security is primarily a matter of negotiation among executive agencies, in which the actions of the military and other partners in the negotiations (including Congress) can be explained by the fusionist model. It is, therefore, important for students of the modern military to observe the politics of military professionals, also known as bureaucratic politics.[17]

Professionals are judged by their clients, as well as by their peer group, according to standards of knowledge and skill. Bureaucrats are judged according to their orientation toward hierarchy. Professional corporatism among the military expresses the relationship between the officer as professional and the officer as client of the state, or bureaucrat. The problem is one of control and discipline. Who does the military perceive must *control* its organization, the group itself or the authority or both? When professionals accept the dominance of the authorities then civil-military relationships are normal and safe and the military potential for intervention is low. A discrepancy between professional orientation and that of the authorities or a relationship in which the military controls the state could upset civil-military equilibrium. This imbalance would seem to be the cause célèbre for political intervention by the military. That does not mean that a corporate orientation (professional aspirations, group protectionism, and political interests acquired with new skills) provides the only explanation for military intervention. The gaps between the authorities and the professional that are produced by such factors as alienation, misperceptions of each other's role, suspicion, and political ambitions are certainly the dependent variables that explain military interventionism. This study, however, will concentrate on the impact and role of corporate professionalism as the most significant explanation for military interventionism and for the political strains existing between the civilian and the military.

IDEOLOGY AND THE MILITARY ORGANIZATION

The literature on organization theory is replete with analyses of ideologies.[18] In fact, Sheldon Wolin, a noted political theorist, has argued that politics in the age of organization has undergone a significant change. Wolin writes: "Now it is the politics of corporations, trade unions, and even universities that is being scrutinized. This preoccupation suggests that the political has been transferred to another plane, to one that formerly was deemed 'private' but which now is believed to have overshadowed the old political system."[19]

The military organization is a fraternity and a community as well as an instrument of power and a bureaucracy. Thus, military ideology can be analyzed from the organizational perspective of the community of soldiers, the ideological perspective of the military as political bureaucracy, or a fusion of the two.

Much has been written on both the sociology and ideology of the military organization,[20] but clearly the military's political behavior is the most significant variable in explaining civil-military relations, interventionism, and corporatism. Certainly, the corporate orientation of the military is linked to its organizational problems (class origins of officers, officer socialization processes, internal structure of command, the bureaucratic struggle of the officers, organizational expansion and decline). Parenthetically, in the United States context, political ideology should be conceived as (1) *substantive* (conservative, liberal, radical, etc.) and (2) *procedural* (loyalty to Constitution and/or rules of game). For U.S. generals, the second form of ideology serves to neutralize the first in many respects.

In other countries the importance of procedural consensus is linked to the political culture. In the case of several Latin American praetorian states and Kemalist Turkey the national constitutions themselves designate the military as guardians of the constitution. "The military protects the constitution from the barracks."

The emphasis in this study, however, will be on the corporate significance of the military's political orientation. Such topics will be discussed as the weltanschauung of officers and their political aspirations; political procedures and structures created before, during, and after intervention; the consequences of political intervention for the military organization; the political price paid by the interventionist officers who in the end disrupt the very corporate structure they are committed to defend.

"Organizational" ideology will be taken into consideration only as an intervening variable, that is, as a concept devised for the interpretation of functional relationships between independent (professionalism) and dependent (civil-military relations) variables. Class origins, status aspirations, organizational decline, and other elements of military organization will be examined only as they help to explain the conceptual framework of the military's professional-bureaucratic symbiosis and as they impinge upon corporatism, the linkage between the professional and bureaucratic orientations of the officer. Civil-military relations will be studied in an analysis of the relationship between the professional and his client.

Topics such as discipline, cohesion, honor, and hierarchy, although frequently discussed in military sociology, are, in my view, peripheral to any explanation of the military organization as a political actor.[21] Nor are size, internal structure, and budget significant factors in studying motives for intervention. As William Thompson's empirical study clearly demonstrates, none of the following characteristics of political systems show any correlation to frequency of military coup: (1) having a large military establishment; (2) having a relatively large military establishment; (3) having a sophisticated military establishment; (4) allocating a large proportion of the governmental budget for defense.[22] Andreski's military participation ratio (armed forces population) also shows no relationship to frequency of coups. Military ideology therefore is the sum of the orientations of the officer class (whatever its degree of cohesion) toward society, regimes, and politics. It emanates from the relationships between management and strategy, between self-imposed professional standards and responsibility to the client authorities. Huntington prefers to call this orientation of the military mind the "professional military ethic."[23]

The modern military exists because of the primacy of the nation-state, the magnitude of warfare, and the scope of national security goals. Today's military plays an influential role in the making of national security policy. Although it may be that "politics is beyond the scope of military competence"[24] in the sense that the military takes no active role in the electoral system, the military's role in the formation and implementation of national security policy forces it to espouse a political attitude. Because it is in the service of the state and the authorities, the military cannot take a neutral political stance. Of course, officers can be docile or active in their participation in national security policy. Historically, the professional soldier has lacked interest in domestic problems, focusing instead on the external affairs of the state.[25] As studies of the American military have shown, the analyses of the Prussian-German, French, Japanese, Soviet, and Chinese militaries in this study also clearly demonstrate that the typical military attitude toward foreign policy is imperialistic and expansionist; that its orientation toward the community is traditionalist; that the classical professional soldier's ideology is conservative (or what Huntington prefers to call "conservatist realism"). "The military ethic is thus pessimistic, collectivist, historically inclined, power oriented, nationalistic, militaristic, and instrumentalist in its view of the military profession," writes Huntington. "It is, in brief, realistic and conservative."[26]

Among the praetorian soldiers we shall find new types who are both conservative and zealous when it comes to the defense of the corporate group and also liberal, reformist, and progressive in their attitudes toward domestic and foreign policies (compared with their counterparts of the eighteenth and nineteenth centuries). The revolutionary soldier who, like the praetorian, is zealously professional, whose corporate orientation is low, and whose attitude toward internal affairs is radical finds no contradiction in espousing conservative-realistic orientations toward national security policy and foreign affairs. Military ideology thus stems more from the external power role of the military than from the professional's training, which promotes an objective and noninterventionist attitude toward politics. That is, authoritarian-hierarchical behavior on the part of the military does not mean that its political ideology is also authoritarian and imperialistic. The authoritarianism and hierarchical structure of the military organization is no patent for like behavior of the military in domestic or foreign politics. Some of the most corporate-oriented military systems in Latin America and the Middle East produced domestic reformers (though others directed their radicalism to internal repression).

Conversely, some of the most liberal politicians of modern times, for example, the British liberals and the American presidents Woodrow Wilson and John F. Kennedy, were imperialist, and Kennedy supported authoritarian, even neocolonialist, regimes abroad. Furthermore, some of the most illustrious military politicians of modern times were conservatives, realists, and anti-imperialists like Dwight Eisenhower, Charles de Gaulle, and the German generals Wilhelm Groener and Hans von Seeckt.

TYPES OF MILITARY ORIENTATIONS

Three general types of military organization have arisen in the modern nation-state, each as a response to a different type of institutionalized civilian authority. The classical professional soldier is prevalent in stable political systems. The praetorian soldier thrives in an environment of political instability. The revolutionary soldier is linked to a political order that is stable despite its origins in an unstable, decaying, or new political system.

The Professional Soldier

According to Huntington, the modern military is distinguished from the pre-1789 military by its status as a professional corporate group. The professional officer of modern times is a new social type and has the following basic characteristics: (1) expertise ("the management of violence"); (2) clientship (responsibility to its client, the society or the state); (3) corporateness (group consciousness and bureaucratic organization); and (4) ideology (the "military mind"). These characteristics, or independent variables, are found in all modern military establishments in developed and developing politics. It will be demonstrated, however, that two of the variables—corporatism and ideology—are more important than the others and that they may also act as dependent variables. In the late 1960s, Huntington modified his original model to take into account the significant role that military political intervention had come to play in developing nations' revolutionary politics. In *Political Order in Changing Societies* (1968) he relates military political intervention to the conditions of political instability and decay that stem from the politicization of social forces[27] and the absence of institutionalized political parties. Huntington found that the classical professional soldier emerges when a civilian coalition gains supremacy with electoral support and establishes political authority over the military. The soldier, with his professional knowledge and expertise, becomes the single and supreme protector of the state in its military function. The military establishment, which is a corporate unit, is careful to maintain this relationship.

The secularization of society and the economic and legal rationality of market capitalism provided the setting for the professional military organization as well as for the modern bureaucratic state structure with its norms of coercive, legal, and rational order. In most aspects of its development the modern professional military organization has generally emulated modern corporate organizations. The rise of the general staff was contemporary with the rise of the modern corporation and its elaborate system of planning; in fact, the former contributed to the rise of the latter. Feudal patrimonialism had influenced the preprofessional army. The economic captain of industry, not the heroic soldier; the career officer, not the old feudal chief; the rational authoritarian leader, not the feudal warrior—these became the models of the new armies. They were innovative, courageous and ruthless, loyal to the patrimony. Parenthetically, the rank system differentiates the military from business, where promotion and authority is more usually determined by merit than seniority. Huntington's notion that professionalism makes genius superfluous or dangerous could not be applied to business or feudalism.

I am not implying that the modern professional officer type inhabits industrial-capitalist or modern societies exclusively. The general staff was created in feudal Prussia, which later became an agrarian state. The imperial Russian officer class in the nineteenth century borrowed its professional standards from the West (Prussia and France), as did Peter the Great in the seventeenth century. Both the Prussian and the imperial Russian professional officer succeeded in integrating into their respective systems (which were feudal, and, in the case of Russia, bureaucratic and patrimonial) certain characteristics of professionalism that prevailed in the Western armies.

The Ottoman army after 1827 was modernized on the Prussian model; nevertheless it adapted itself to sultanist patrimonialism. The fact that modern professional armies existed in noncapitalist, non-modern states (like Prussia before 1848), however, does not refute the facts that (1) the development of the modern military professional is clearly a modern bureaucratic phenomenon; and (2) the concepts of professionalism, corporatism, and military subservience to the regimes were universally true for capitalist, agrarian, feudal, sultanist regimes and *all* these different military organizations nevertheless espoused the values and norms of modern military professionalism, however modified they might be by different political cultures and environments.

Furthermore, the rise of nationalism, imperialism, and later, total warfare led to an alliance between the military and industrial networks. The German defense ministry under Field Marshal Erich Ludendorff was the prototype of the modern military-industrial complex. "Before the First World War the officer corps and the leaders of heavy industry were mainstays of the authoritarian political and social system of the German empire." World War I demonstrated that war was no longer a matter of military prowess, of blitz, or of tactical maneuverability; in total war the outcome was determined by a nation's economic strength and its political and social stability. The mobilization of resources, human and material, and the active participation of different social groups made for an all-encompassing war machine. The military organization and war machine merged with the grand economic and capitalist corporation. Each emulated the other, consciously or otherwise. The war ministry was both a bureaucratic and a military organization. The German general staff staffed the war ministry and the war ministry patterned itself after the general staff. Several engineers who ran the raw material section of the German defense ministry during World War I, people like Richard von Moellendorff and Walter Rathenau, were devout students of scientific management and American capitalist organization. The contribution of Allgemeine Elektritizitats Geselschaft, (the General Electric Company of Germany), which was one of Germany's greatest industrial concerns and was headed by Rathenau, was decisive in the mobilization of the economy and of labor and industry for total war. Emil Lederer, the German economist, is quoted as follows: "We can say that on the day of mobilization the *society* which existed until then was transformed into a community."[28]

The Praetorian Soldier

Although few military officers choose politics as their vocation, the military profession can serve as a political base. The higher the officer's rank, the more political he becomes—particularly in praetorian and revolutionary situations, which may involve the entire military establishment in political action. Under stable political conditions, few officers are willing to trade their profession for politics, but the role of those few who do is critical to any exploration of civil-military relations and of the role of the modern military. Military praetorianism arises within Huntington's subjective political control systems, often in the wake of a failed social, political, or modernizing revolution. Praetorians certainly emerge in largely agrarian or transitional or ideologically divided societies.* The military potentially and actually is interventionist; its disposition to intervene is permanent; and it has the power to bring about constitutional change. The nature of military clientship shifts when the military "decides" who represents the nation and political order. The locus of authority can also shift from the central government level to regional, tribal, or ethnic levels. On the whole, praetorian conditions affect the military establishment negatively, lowering the standards of professionalism and resulting in fratricide as family feuds break out, coups occur, and officials are assassinated. Officer recruitment, for example, is restrictive and highly competitive in military praetorian regimes. Since the praetorian's mobility is very high compared with that of the classical professional soldier, corporate orientation, status, and military ideology supersede skill and knowledge as professional requirements. Political loyalty and coup-making skill supplant the traditional skills of the professional soldier.

"The first observation of praetorianism," writes Andreski, "is that it is always professional soldiers, never conscripts or militiamen, that are driving forces of praetorianist insurrections." Clearly the officer-bureaucrat, as a client of the state, is the one who revolts against the regime. In praetorian cases, he revolts mainly because the state or regime challenges the military corporate integrity. Loyalty to this entity is obviously lacking among mercenaries, conscripts, or militiamen. "The armed forces," continues Andreski, "are more likely to be arbiters of politics if they are the main pillar of authority, that is to say, if the government

*Chile is a curious and important case. The military there conspicuously did *not* step in for decades following an early (1923) intervention, although coups were common in the rest of Latin America during that period. Only when Allende began to revolutionize Chilean society did the military intervene, and then it did so with a vengeance, adopting Brazil as its model. By 1970, Chile was neither agrarian nor transitional, except in the sense of transition from liberal democracy to socialism. (See chapter 6.)

rests principally on naked force and not on the loyalty of the subjects."[29] The question is one of legitimacy. When the authorities lack support, the chances are that the military will challenge the authorities. It takes the *skill* and *knowledge* of professional officers to engineer the military coup and replace the authorities. The corporate professional in this case, although imbued with a sense of duty to the authorities, champions the cause of interventionism. Officers are not without political ambition. Hence, the military organization becomes the supreme structure, imbued with the values of duty, honor, and country, that is, aspirations for political domination.*

The power of the military praetorian regime stems not just from its professional skill—the use of violence—but also from its inclination to associate the regime that sustains the military with the regime that protects its integrity. The praetorian is the chief defender of corporate autonomy. The military establishment in Egypt, for instance, cognizant that it stood alone in the sense that there was no "state" or "society" that could defend its independence or challenge its existence, became its own client. The praetorian military establishment identifies corporate aspirations with the national interest. The Egyptian army after Nasser (1971) and the Syrian army since 1966 are good examples. By 1973 the militaries of Brazil and Peru had introduced their own rule in the absence of valid and sustaining civilian and political authority to defend the national interest, including the military's corporate integrity.

The Revolutionary Soldier

As an instrument of the revolution, especially before and during the "revolutionary war," the revolutionary military manifests a strong propensity to succumb to political influence. As the revolution becomes institutionalized, the party movement becomes the supreme authority in the state. It then opposes the surrogate role of the military in politics and accepts the rational officer (professional) type of military organization. However, it rejects the premises of military's corporatism and right to intervene in politics. Thus, in the initial stages of the revolution, the military loses its autonomy and modifies some of its professional characteristics in favor of the party or the movement; it becomes an

---

*Huntington disagrees. He claims that the military temperament is antipolitical, and that the military usually wants to divest itself of government once the coup's goals have been attained.

instrument of mobilization for the revolutionary party. In most cases, however, the revolutionary military's tendency toward political intervention is never totally eliminated; the army continues to have at least a latent political role despite its professional orientation.

The revolutionary military type is clearly distinguishable from the professional and praetorian types in its attitudes toward military corporatism and civil-military relations. In contrast to the corporate behavior expected from professional and praetorian soldiers, the revolutionary type prefers comradely nonhierarchical relations between officers and soldiers. Upward mobility for the revolutionary soldier is not the product of military expertise, but of dedication to the revolution and support of the party movement. An elementary practice of revolutionary armies is the formation of cadres. These military cadres are politically indoctrinated and dedicated groups whose expectations reach beyond those of the professional military establishment. Thus, the clear-cut boundary between politics and the military, so well established in the professional army and in the objective-control type of political order, is absent in the revolutionary army and state.

Although conscription, particularly recruitment to the officer class, is restricted for the professional and praetorian types, for the revolutionary type it is universal. A revolutionary army is a mass army, a nation-in-arms. The professional and praetorian military types, on the other hand, maintain a military establishment in which recruitment and promotion are based on membership in a specific and well-marked collectivity, such as class, ethnic group, region, kinship formation, or tribe. Even in highly industrialized polities where the military profession is not high on the achievement and status scale, definite marginal groups or "historical military" groups are recruited (for example, Southerners in the United States).

The most marked distinctions among the revolutionary, the professional, and the praetorian soldier spring from their client relationships and their ideologies.

The client of the professional soldier is clearly the state and, hence, the nation. Praetorian symptoms may occur in the professional soldier, but only when leaders of the military establishment "discover" that there is a "contradiction" between the "state" to which they had pledged loyalty and the "regime" that has taken over. Examples of such discoveries are: Pétain's claim that the Third Republic had betrayed France; de Gaulle's similar condemnation of the Fourth Republic;

Groener's and von Seeckt's understanding that their "right" to intervene in politics stemmed not only from "professionalism betrayed" but also from the belief that Germany was more important than Weimar and that Communists and radicals threatened the nation; and MacArthur's belief that he had sworn allegiance to the Constitution rather than to President Truman and his administration.

The client of the revolutionary soldier changes with each phase of the revolution. The revolutionary professional may be reluctant to come to terms with a new regime, especially if the army has played a decisive role in the revolutionary war of liberation. Before and during the revolution, the soldier is loyal to the party movement. Once the party movement becomes identified with the state or regime, he experiences ambivalance and he may become more loyal to the nation than to the regime. Further confusion over loyalty occurs if the party movement becomes identified with the nation, or the people, or the working class, or one leading figure.

The client of the praetorian army may be any of several entities: the regime, an ethnic group, a tribe, the military. Furthermore, in the absence of a single, mobilizing party movement, the praetorian army, like the revolutionary army, may have several contradictory loyalties. The difference, however, is that the praetorian army does not have to contend with a highly cohesive revolutionary party that dominates the state. Thus, the rise of praetorianism may signify the failure of the revolutionary party to establish domination over national policy. In other words, the breakdown of the revolutionary party or its failure to evolve further may open the door to praetorianism.

Ideology is obviously correlated with clientship. The revolutionary type must, above all, be unswervingly loyal to the revolution and its dogmas. The basic concern of the revolutionary regime is the subordination of all instruments of control to the party movement and its ideology. Thus, revolutionary ideology, contradicting the traditional, professional (and conservative) ideology of the military, comes to embrace the requisites of the professional soldier only at a later time (as in the Soviet Union and Communist China).

The revolutionary soldier turned praetorian may espouse several contradictory ideologies, which are determined by the exigencies of military efficiency and accurately reflect a regime's ambivalent stance. This factor again demonstrates the praetorian nature of the revolutionary military establishment and its society: its first loyalty is to military corporatism, whatever the "ideology" it claims to represent. In the case of the professional soldier, as long as only a small sector of society is recruited to military service and a still smaller sector prefers to follow careers as officers, the professional's fundamental military conservatism blends with the ideologies of certain social groups, and these ideologies do not contradict and may even be compatible with the conservative ideology of the military establishment. If and when a state of war with an external enemy becomes total, it is likely that the military praetorian will harness or suppress any liberal-democratic or communist ideologies. Friction between the army and society will thus become less intense, and the conflict between the conservative and rational officer orientations of

Table 1.1 Military Types and Orientations

Characteristics	Professional	Praetorian	Revolutionary
Expertise	Specific knowledge based on objective standards of professional competence; High	Professional knowledge not very strictly observed	Professional knowledge oriented to social-political values
Client	State	Any of these: Nation Ethnic group Tribe Military State	Party-movement
Corporateness (Type of authority)	Hierarchical, cohesive-organic, collective, subordinate, automatic/manipulative narrow	Hierarchical, noncohesive, collective, shifting subordination, narrow	Before and during revolution: Egalitarian, highly mobile, cadres, manipulative, wide
Conscription	Restrictive; universal only in war	Restrictive	Universal
Ideology	Conservative	Traditional, materialist, antisocialist, praetorian	Revolutionary; party-movement
Disposition to Intervene	Low	Permanent/ continued	High before and during revolution; low after revolution

the military will be confronted directly by the ideology of society's most prevalent civilian-political groups. If all three conditions persist, the chances are that the professional soldier type will degenerate into the praetorian type.

Is the Military a Cohesive and Monolithic Group?

Nowhere in this study will I imply that the military—or, for that matter, the bureaucracy—is a cohesive-coherent, monolithic, elite group. There were and will be divisions between and within military ranks and hierarchies, as well as disputes among individual officers. When I speak of the "military," I have in mind the following: (1) mostly senior officers (above the rank of colonel); (2) corporate-oriented officers (any rank); (3) professional officers (any rank); (4) officers whose rank, status, position, and orientation *link* them to the civilian sector in matters of policy and of politics. A routine senior officer, a general commanding a corps, is of less concern for this study than would be, for instance, a scheming staff officer who may rank anywhere between captain and colonel but whose political ambition and, eventually, influence is *not* equal to his rank. In short, this study focuses on those officers (1) whose rank and role place them in a position where they have to manifest political skills not required of other professionals; (2) whose political skill outweighs their rank, position, and role; (3) whose aspiration is to protect corporate integrity; and (4) whose ambitions are political.

Membership in these categories requires no group, class, or bureaucratic cohesiveness. As this study will demonstrate, the politically oriented officers in the first category represent a small minority of the senior officer class and are even smaller in numbers than those in the second category. Nevertheless, when we speak of civil-military relations, we speak of the hyphen between the two. The "hyphenated" officers are corporate, as are the managerial-strategic officers; they are ipso facto leaders. The number of professional officers is certainly larger than the number of military politicians, but the number of their leaders is not necessarily smaller. Thus, I do not speak of *the* military, *the* military establishment, or *the* senior officers. To understand the hyphen between civil and military is to analyze the conditions, circumstances, roles, and opportunities under which the hyphenated relationship creates politically significant and relevant leaders among the military.

Part I

The Professional Soldier

Character mattered more to an officer than intellect . . . character was of course an essentially aristocratic virtue, whereas intellect was the mark of the *bourgeois*. [Colmar von der] Goltz in his book *The Nation in Arms* stressed that too much intelligence was a bad thing for an officer, because it could lead to doubt and hesitation in giving an order. Heart and character should be decisive in selecting officers, not intellect and scientific attainment.

Martin Kitchen, *The German Officer Corps, 1890–1914*

2

The Modern Nation-State and Its Military Organizations

One outstanding characteristic of the contemporary nation-state is that its citizens belong to one political community, under a single regime whose area of control has defined territorial boundaries, governed by a bureaucracy and a central political order. This organization of public authority has made it impossible for the military establishment to "opt out" and act in isolation from the political system, a choice open to the military in the past under the imperial, patrimonial, or feudal political systems. In the modern state, both civil and military authority structures are civilian-oriented, for both are dependent on and responsible to the political community and must seek its support. Modern regimes are legitimized by the fact of their belonging to a political community. Political structures and military organizations are dependent, therefore, on the consent of the political community, the citizenry, or the governed. This orientation may be challenged, however, when the military, which is naturally oriented toward authority rather than the community, submits itself *only* to the central authority—the regime.

The relationship between political community and political order strongly influences civil-military relations. A stable interaction between the community and the political order, however dynamic or disagreeable that interaction may be, guarantees what Huntington calls "objective" civil-military relations. Unstable interaction between the community and the political order produces "subjective" civil-military relations,[1] which could lead to military intervention and praetorianism.

In modern civil-military relations there is a high correlation between the type of nation-state and the type of military organization. The classifications of nation-states and military organizations used here combine the conceptual framework of social science and that of comparative history.

The nation-state is the ideal form of political organization in modern times. It is a secular organization and has a legal-rational administrative staff system. The two key characteristics, or variables, of the modern nation-state are the efficiency with which it uses rational administrative procedures and its possession of a legitimate authority oriented toward a bureaucratic, stable political order. (An orientation, in Weber's terminology, is a dynamic condition or state of mind, a mood, an expectation, or a system setting a moral and societal direction, such as a value system.)

Legitimacy is the foundation of governmental power. It is a source of support, exercised universally in modern times by rational and complex bureaucratic organizations. The regime that elicits obedience is an organization that regulates its authority relationships, that is the system which causes the people to accept the regime. Modern regimes are rationally oriented and are confined to the nation-state; relations beyond the territorial nation-state do involve the authority or legitimacy of the regime.

The nineteenth-century Prussian court, with its bureaucracy, military, and autocracy, illustrates how closely the modern nation-state, the regime, and its mode of administration are connected. Nineteenth-century France illustrates a similar set of close relationships. Prussia-Germany was a monarchical autocracy, while France was a republican democracy. In the former, however, the military became the preserve of the patrimon, in the latter, an instrument of state. The administrative machinery—military, bureaucratic, and diplomatic—in both France and Germany was rational, secular, and obedient. It did not depend on the support of the population, but on legitimacy (i.e., the authorities' acceptance of the regime).

The modern nation-state is under the command of a regime—that is, when through the regime it is allowed the rational and legitimate use of force in maintaining control over a population and compulsory jurisdiction over a territory. The regime is the highest authority structure (the lowest unit is the individual citizen), as well as the regulator of expectations. The inculcation of the sense of legitimacy, along with the extension of its acceptance, is the most significant function of the regime. Analytically, the regime is composed of values, norms, and structures of authority.[2]

According to Weber, the structures of authority "designate the formal and informal patterns in which power is distributed and organized with regard to the authoritative making and implementing of decisions—the roles and relationships through which authority is distributed and exercised." The norms and the structure of authority limit and legitimate political actions. Therefore, the arena or context of political actions and interactions changes according to changes in the kinds of political relationships allowed, which depend in turn upon changes in values, structures, or roles. In analyzing civil-military relations, it is vital to observe these factors and their relation to the interaction between the modern nation-state and its military organization. When civil and military groups compete for domination of the regime, its normative and authoritative structures constitute the arena.[3]

Legitimacy is a condition of validity and acceptance enjoyed by systems of authority. In the Weberian sense, legitimacy is a system of normative domination, "regulating the flow of diffused support in favor of both the authorities and the regime." Authority has always had an institutional basis. The authority relationship is one of superordination and subordination. Thus an authority relationship is not a personal relationship (as the relationship between a leader and his followers is), but instead resembles relations in a military organization, where soldiers and officers obey authorities they have never met. The authority relationship is a property of organization, transforming norms into statutes. Here the military, as well as bureaucracy in general, is invited to "actively participate in politics." According to Weber, legitimacy is an authoritative orientation only if it can enforce obedience or establish compliance, and his concept of domination requires an administrative staff to execute commands.[4]

Stability in the modern nation-state is an equilibrium or balance of power between the regime (the authorities) and the population (the community). One of the key operating values of the modern nation-state is "civility"—a political order whose ethical principles, orientations, and structures are dominated by a civic spirit. The goal is civilian (nonmilitary) authorship of values, as well as civilian normative inculcation of values into authority roles. Political stability in the modern nation-state requires civility; conversely, the existence of a noncivilian order, an order whose operative ideals are not civic-oriented, leads to instability.[5] The military, however, can play a considerable role in the protection of a civic order. But the military could also do just the opposite when it intervenes. Civilian orientation also means popular support, an area in which the military have little experience and in most cases no interest.

One essential characteristic of the nation-state is that it tends to monopolize the normative use of force. At the same time, bureaucratic and corporate autonomy is the chief characteristic of the modern military organization. The linkage between the modern nation-state and its military organization is high. The development of modern forms of organization in all fields is almost identical with the development and spread of bureaucratic administration. This is true of "church and state, of *armies*, political parties, economic enterprises, interest groups, endowments, clubs, and many others. Its development is, to take the most striking case, at the root of the modern Western state."[6]

The modern army is a bureaucratic army, just as the modern nation-state is a bureaucratic state. The major characteristics of modern bureaucracy have been established by Weber's classic formula: (1) rationality in decision making: a style of behavior that is appropriate to the achievement of certain goals within limits imposed by given constraints; (2) impersonality in social relations: operation through impersonal application of rules; (3) centralization of authority: superordination/subordination relationship subject to impersonal rules; and (4) routinization of tasks through rules, roles, and files. "Only the bureaucratic army structure allows for the development of the professional standing armies which are necessary for the constant pacification of large territories as well as for warfare against distant enemies, especially enemies overseas. Further, military discipline and technical military training can normally be fully developed, at least to its modern high level, only in the bureaucratic army." On the whole, the two salient components of the modern nation-state—mass armies and parties—have both developed complex and rational bureaucracies. "In most cases the bureaucratic tendency has been promoted by needs arising from the creation of standing armies . . . "[7]

Weber makes no distinction between bureaucracy and organization. (In fact, what we today call bureaucracy Weber called administration or the technical quality of bureaucratic organization.[8]) Because both the nation-state and the modern military organization are organization-bureaucracy types, both represent the legal-rational form of domination, and both are professional (that is, both have professional expertise or authority). "Bureaucratic administration means fundamentally domination through knowledge. This is a feature of it which makes it specifically rational." The military and the modern nation-state are also hierarchical, rational, and legal in orientation. A profession of office (role) and a pursuit of exclusive and specialized careers—in other words, *corporate* professionalism—are the fundamental characteristics of both the modern bureaucracy and the modern army. The modern official, according to Weber, always strives for a high salary and for a distinctly elevated social status.[9] Here the aspirations of the modern bureaucrat and the modern military professional converge; both are searching for social esteem and corporate endowment.

The officer's only "life" is his profession. Except for veterans' organizations and groups supporting promilitary politicians (whose power or influence cannot be compared with that of the multitude of private interest groups, business groups, and so forth), the officer has few interest groups to further his cause. (This situation changes, however, if militarists and imperialists attain high political office.)

More than any other professional, the military officer operates only in the interest of his "chosen" clients. He is totally subservient to the state, the patrimon, the province, the party, the movement, or whatever political authority is most powerful at any given time. Yet, paradoxically, the officer's client relationship also helps to explain military intervention in affairs of state. The seeming contradiction whereby the military that is supposed to serve the political authorities instead interferes with them can be traced to Weber's failure to differentiate between the officer's technical proficiency and his orientation toward discipline. For while the officer as an "expert" is expected to act as a "serving" bureaucrat, as a disciplinarian he is expected to act as a ruler. In fact, corporatism among the military is based on the image of the officer as ruler as much as on his image as an expert.

Like Janus, the god of gates, the military professional looks in opposite directions. He is both an expert and a bureaucrat. As a professional he must be dedicated to the universal standards of expertise that are acquired within the organization and set by the collegial community. In their dedication to protecting the organization, officers develop corporate orientations. As a client of authority the officer's corporate orientations are further institutionalized by his role as a bureaucrat. But the military organization is not simply an elite of the state; it is also the state's major defender. Thus, the professional is permanently on guard concerning the stability and sustenance of the state, the military's client. Perceived and actual inefficiency, corruption, instability, or radical tendencies reflect on the professional corporate and organizational integrity and on the military's inclination to intervene. Thus, the propensity to intervene stems from the *same* corporate orientations of the professional that under normal conditions (i.e., a stable, efficient, and nonradical regime) makes him a loyal noninterventionist and in most cases makes the military a subservient organization.

The link between the professional and the bureaucrat, to reiterate, is the dependent variable that explains military interventionism or non-interventionism, and it will be used here to explain the relationship between authority, regimes, and the military organization; the civil-military relations that emerge from these relationships; and professional, praetorian, and revolutionary military orientations. In sum, military corporatism is both a bulwark against intervention and, in different times and regimes, a stimulant for it.

The military establishment, like any other instrument of the state, has no autonomous reason to exist. It can exist only if its client defines its functions, expectations, and behavior. When the soldier delves into politics, he (unlike laborers, farmers, and industrialists) threatens the very reason for his corporate existence, becoming a political master instead of a political instrument. Nevertheless, when the corporate role and conception of the military establishment is challenged or there is a threat of domestic or external violence, the military will contemplate intervention in the absence of a stable, legitimate political authority.

HISTORICAL TYPES OF THE MODERN NATION-STATE

In modern times (since 1789) there have been four historical models for the nation-state: the classical nation-state, the colonizing nation-state, the colonial nation-state, and the revolutionary nation-state (the national liberation movement state).

The Classical Nation-State

The classical nation-state is a political system that has achieved the highest degree of institutionalization and social cohesion. It has three major characteristics: a mature regime buttressed by an institution-alized legitimate authority; a stable, integrated, culturally homogene-ous population; and undisputed territorial boundaries. Furthermore, the classical nation-state has an operating ideological system, and political expectations and aspirations on the part of the majority of the politically mobilized population fall into a fairly stable pattern. Because of the state's internal stability, the military functions mainly to control external enemies.

Civil-military relations are based on the objective control model, which presupposes a sharp line between the military and society. Objective civilian control maximizes military professionalism and civilian influence. The greater the civilian control over the military, the more conducive are conditions to the emergence of professional ethics and behavior among the officer corps, and the lower is the possibility of military intervention.[10] The military self-image is managerial or organizational-technical, subordinate to high political authority. This ideal type, however, has been modified by the political behavior of the military in the classical modern nation-state as well as in the twentieth-century totalitarian nation-state. The values of the military establishment are clearly professional and subordinate, and the supremacy of civilian authority is seldom challenged. Technical proficiency is judged on the open market; the social system is proclaimed to be one of equality.

The Colonizing Nation-State

This type of state is a dynamic system oriented toward political institutionalization and cultural pluralism. Marked by a high degree of social mobilization, this system has been removed from its old environment and transported to a new territory. The United States, Canada, Australia, New Zealand, Israel, and the Latin American states represent this type. They are "the fragments," pieces of Europe that have become whole new nations and are thus no longer recognizable in European terms.

> We know the European ideology, indeed we name it, in terms of its enemies, in terms of the whole of the classical European social struggle. When fragmentation detaches it from this context, and makes it master of a whole region, all sorts of magic inevitably take place. First of all it becomes a universal, sinking beneath the surface of thought to the level of an assumption. Then, almost instantly, it is reborn, transformed into a new nationalism arising out of the necessities of fragmentation itself. Feudalism comes back at us as the French-Canadian Spirit, liberalism as the American Way of Life, radicalism as the Australian Legend.[11]

Colonization entails one group's acquisition of territorial units from a less powerful group, either by conquest, bargaining, squatting, better exploitation of resources, or all these combined. The major tasks of a colonizing nation-state are the conquest of land, the stabilization of

population, and the legitimation of boundaries. The values of the fragment are mission-oriented, pioneering, and liberal. In North America,
Australia, and Israel the ideals that eventually went sour in Europe
flourished anew and became highly productive, contributing to the
achievement of a stable political order in the new environment.

The military establishment plays an important role in the first phases
of nation building (for example, in the United States, Israel, and Latin
America during the wars of liberation) and in the social and political
integration of the population (as in Israel).[12]

In colonizing states, force is generally used only to meet serious threats
and, of course, to uproot the natives from the newly conquered land.
Mission-oriented values in the colonizing society become less dominant
with the development of a complex economic system, because such a
system is highly stratified and requires a complex political network. The
process of normalization (which takes place after the era of role-expan-
sion in society and politics) dictates the formation of a highly professional
military establishment and the demobilization of social-political forces.
Political intervention is rare except in times of extreme crisis, such as a
civil war, internal upheaval, or severe foreign threat.

The military establishment in this type of nation-state draws its
members from the periphery. Soldiers in the United States, Canada,
and Australia tend to be frontier, rural, southern, or small-town men:
in Israel they come from rural cooperatives, collective settlements, the
frontier, and the farms. The fact that this military is noninterventionist
does not stop it from playing an effective and influential role in politics,
particularly in the United States and Israel.

The Colonial Nation-State

This is the most unstable form of modern nation-state. Here central
powers have meager legitimacy, and structures of authority are not
universal. Typically, the center will make an unsuccessful effort to subordinate peripheral ethnicity and cultural pluralism. Support for the
regime and the authorities is weakened by the conflict and separation
between center and periphery. The frontiers of the colonial states were
defined by conquest and guaranteed by the imperial powers, in accordance with the classical nineteenth-century balance-of-power concept.
Once the imperial powers withdrew, the colonial boundaries did not
prove to be viable. The struggle over the frontier was mainly internal—a
struggle over central authority, ethnicity, cultural pluralism, and the
control of the military establishment.

The function of the military in the colonial state is exclusively internal: violence becomes a surrogate for legitimacy, and the regime stabilizes the population by oppression, controls social mobilization, protects the center from the periphery, and stabilizes the state's frontiers as delineated by the departed imperialists. In addition, when one ex-colonial state is in conflict with another over these frontiers it will employ the military for external protection of the state's security. But the most prominent security arrangement is still the buttressing of internal control, and here the military function is crucial. Often the police act as the military's accomplice, and they perform many of the police functions of the military as well.

The National Liberation Movement Nation-State

An ex-colonial, modern nation-state may become a national liberation movement state, led by a party-military alliance that overthrows imperial rule or is forged during a national war of liberation, as in North

Table 2.1 Types of Modern Nation-States and Military Organizations

Type	Regime	Population	Frontiers	Type of Military	Type of Security Orientation
Classical	Institutionalized; cultural homogeneity	Stablized and integrated	Well defined	Professional subordinate	External
Colonizing	Dynamic; oriented toward institutionalized cultural pluralism	Highly mobilized	Stabilized by conquest	Professional or revolutionary	External or internal
Colonial	Unstable; praetorian; subordination of cultural pluralism	Crisis in social mobilization	Defined by conquest	Professional or praetorian	Internal or external
National Liberation Movement	Stable, organizational ideology movement	Mass mobilization liberation	Defined by the war of liberation	Revolutionary, which may turn praeforian or professional	External or internal

and South Vietnam, or takes over after the settlement of a civil war, as in China. Such a regime is ideological and advocates the drastic overthrow of the old elite. Elite circulation is accelerated in proportion to the intensity of the war of liberation. Once in the saddle, the new revolutionary elite is characteristically sustained for an indefinite period (China, North Vietnam, and Cuba). The country's frontiers are defined by the achievements of the national liberation army. The system of compliance is highly normative.

THE PROFESSIONAL REVOLUTION AND MILITARY CORPORATISM

The most significant contribution of scholarship to the study of modern civil-military relations is the recognition that, as Huntington states, "the modern officer corps is a professional body and the modern military officer a professional soldier." From the viewpoint of comparative history, today's military has evolved in five structural stages: (1) the emergence of mass armies, a Napoleonic innovation; (2) the professional revolution; (3) the disbanding of mass armies by the professionals; (4) the incorporation of the military professional; and (5) the institutionalization of professionalism by an academic dogma called "grand strategy," which became the ideology of the corporate professional officer.[13]

The revolutions of the eighteenth and nineteenth centuries led to the democratization of the armed forces; the wars of national liberation converted peasants and urban dwellers into citizens of the nation-in-arms. "The mass army was therefore the expression of an ideological revolution," and higher military ranks were thrown open to all. As Rapoport has written, military service became the vehicle for the attainment of *virtu* (citizenship). But soon—no later than the 1820s—antidemocratic regimes in France and Germany abandoned the concept of nation-in-arms and universal military training. With the rise of conservative regimes, the armies of "revolutionary circumstance" withered away.[14]

The second structural phase in the evolution of the professional soldier, the development of the professional revolution, led inexorably to the next three stages. Postindependence wars were not waged by mass armies but by small, disciplined, skilled military units. Sweeping technological changes in methods of warfare made it possible for a new class of military professional to emerge. This class was trained in the academies in the modern sciences, including military science, which began with Scharnhorst and Clausewitz and was taught by their successors in Prussia and France. The officers could now mobilize, supply, and move troops efficiently. Hence the professional officer did not seek merely to abandon the nation-in-arms concept and its nonskilled, undisciplined military structure; he was dedicated to destroying it. The professional changeover constituted the third structural phase.[15]

In the fourth and longest phase, professionalism, training and expertise were incorporated into the academies. Norms of military conduct were now institutionalized. Professionalism revolutionized the substance of the military organization.

In the fifth phase a new doctrine, called strategy, came to be taught in the academies. The Prussian army successes in 1867, 1868, and 1871 enhanced the reputation of the new science. Planning and technical mobilization became an irrefutable and dogmatic military science throughout Europe, although it proved futile in World War I. Yet until 1914 the "secular clergy"[16] (the officers of the new nation-states) dominated military affairs by reason of their mastery of strategy. These professionals increased their status and influence to the point where they became autonomous—a state that may properly be called corporatism.

The ideology of the military, as Huntington has demonstrated, was originally conservative. The autonomy that the officers' corps gained in professional revolution further enhanced the military's political, corporate conservatism by isolating it from the political community. Professional ideology was buttressed by the dogma learned in the academy, and corporatism enhanced the power and influence of the secular clergy, which could not be challenged by competing elites who had not attended the *Kriegsakademie*. As Feld has pointed out, "The primary allegiance of the military professional transferred itself to the corporate body of which he was a member."[17]

The professional soldier type, as distilled from historical and empirical military literature, can be conceptualized on the basis of two sets of independent variables—the nature of the modern nation-state and the general characteristics of modern professionalism—and understood on the basis of the relationships between them.

Carr-Saunders and Wilson explain the rise of modern professionalism in terms of the convergence of four characteristics: corporate spirit, secularization, skill, and a structure for social mobility. Corporate spirit, the sense of vocational cohesion and self-awareness, arose with "the formation of associates around many aspects of social life, among them the performance of specialized functions and the carrying on of specialized crafts." Secularization accompanied the breakup of medieval corporations and the development of trades into independent professions that were no longer considered primarily as functions of a universal scheme but as rational occupations founded on impersonal and utilitarian values. Skill, "the possession of a specialized intellectual technique," came to be seen as the distinguishing characteristic of the professional regardless of his social position. Finally, a structure for social mobility appeared when emphasis shifted from tradition to quality of performance, and professional status was offered to all who were able to learn and exercise the necessary techniques. The intermingling of classes that resulted from these new opportunities lessened or broke down many barriers, generally encouraging social mobility within the state.[18]

Military professionalism, which is omitted from Carr-Saunders's and Wilson's discussions of the professions since the industrial revolution, has been most comprehensively analyzed in Huntington's *The Soldier and the State*.[19] According to Huntington, the evolution of military professionalism in Prussia-Germany, France, England, and the United States was encouraged by four factors: the development of technology and an increased functionalization of war; the growth of the nation-state as a source of support for independent military professionalism; the rise of democratic ideals; and a tradition of clientship, based on responsibility to the modern state.

Modern professionalism is corporate; that is, it includes group consciousness and a tendency to form corporate professional associations. Such voluntary, rational, exclusive associations of experts have two purposes: first, to maintain the integrity of the profession's expertise and to protect its norms, standards, and values; and second, to defend its exclusivity principle (its organizational autonomy, the homogeneous composition of its membership, and its distinctiveness and distance from other associations, the society, and the state).

To achieve the first purpose, maintaining rational and secular expertise, standards and values are formulated with the approval of an elite that is chosen, ideally, for its integrity and its high standards of professional norms and values. An organization is also created to manipulate the environment for the benefit of the association of experts, controlling the diffusion of new generations of experts and attending to their training. Finally, specialized educational organizations control the curriculum, set examinations, establish boards of judgment and skill, and thus institutionalize orientations and standards.

The second purpose, defense of the exclusivity principle, requires the military elite to exercise veto power over the sources of recruitment of experts and over expulsion of violators of the corporate ethic of the profession. A sense of caste and a system of self-preservation are developed through social activities represented by codes of honor, special clubs, and professional conferences and festivities. In defending exclusivity the elite tries to dominate the career patterns of its experts. Furthermore, it attempts to influence whatever political bodies distribute recognition, titles, and confirmations, and to control boards of examiners and professional schools. Lobbies are also maintained to enhance the exclusivity principle and to sustain a public image under the stress of a corporate ideology specifically designed to fit the profession.[20]

The military profession is an outstanding example of modern corporate professionalism. Like the other modern professions, it is an expression of a new "social type," a conspicuous cultural and social grouping made up of individuals who are "neither 'capitalists' nor 'workers' nor are they typically governmental administrators and 'bureaucrats.'" "This new type is a rational organization."[21] Huntington argues that the military profession, which scholars have largely ignored, is probably the oldest modern professional association. Huntington's major thesis, however, is that the greater the rationalization of the military profession and therefore the greater its "professionalization," the more politically "responsible" it becomes—the more oriented toward a role subordinate to the civil authorities or regime. Thus there are two basic types of civilian control: (1) the maximization of military professionalism (objectivity principle), when the potential for military intervention is low; and (2) the maximization of civilian control (subjectivity principle), when the potential for military intervention is high. In both the military profession is subordinate to civilian authorities. This calls for two levels of analysis of civil-military relations: one, subordination to authority; the other, compatibility of the professional military ethic with the prevailing political ideology in society.[22]

This thesis has become a source of serious controversy, and Huntington's critics have attempted to demonstrate that the military's corporate professionalism is a source of challenge to civilian authority. In my view, this controversy can be resolved by emphasizing the two key concepts of corporate professionalism—the maintenance of expertise standards and the defense of corporateness or exclusivity. The maximization of civilian rule and the minimization of the military motivation to intervene must be analyzed not just in terms of the professionalization of the military establishment (which in itself is the orientation to maximize the rationality factor) but also in relation to the military profession's corporate orientation and exclusivity.[23] It is clear that the military's corporate orientations have strong, and sometimes organic, ties to a specific political arrangement or type of regime. A corporate orientation can motivate the military to either protect a stable regime or to challenge an unstable regime. A military that intervenes does so at the expense of its corporate integrity and in violation of its historically conservative ideology. Furthermore, in the act of coming to power the military may and often does sacrifice its existence, because the military organization, alone among modern professional associations, depends on the political order. I concur with Huntington that corporatism and responsibility are components of modern military professionalism, but I also maintain that corporate orientations are not always positive contributions to the maximization of rationality (or political objectivity) of the modern military profession.

The military on the whole demonstrates little skill or imagination in seeking and manipulating popular support. Instead it weighs the consequences in terms of the conflicts concerning professionalism versus clientship and corporate orientation versus autonomy and decides whether or not to intervene. A legitimate and popular political order will generally not be challenged by the military, because the government will be able to mobilize popular support and defeat any such move. The objectivity dictum in civil-military relations depends not so much on the degree of fulfillment of military corporatism as on subordination to the client, and acceptance of the popularity of the regime, which makes commitment to professional values irrelevant.

Corporate military professionalism is not an abstract ideal. It is a value-laden normative orientation that is organically linked to the historical development of the modern nation-state. In the West the military was the mailed fist for independence, the guarantor of territorial integrity, and the protector of the new national regime. Once order was established, the military organization demanded primacy and organizational integrity. It expected certain norms of behavior, which over time became institutionalized in its relationship with the state.

The modern military establishment patterned its organizational structure after that of the nation-state, and its corporate orientation was designed to perpetuate and preserve the nation-state's integrity. The crisis of corporatism versus professionalism was only precipitated when the growing complexity of society began to invalidate certain concepts, leaving the military to champion the traditional patriotic fundamentals of "duty, honor, country."

The integrity of military corporatism was subjected to severe stress when the following conditions, in combination or alone, appeared in the modern state: the rise of competing socioeconomic elites; the growing marginality of the military profession as a result of either prolonged peace or organizational decay; the decline of officer status: apprehension that "civilians" or "politicians" might bring about reform and change in the military organization; defeat in war; the rise of a radical movement (left or right). Not stress between the military and the state but a positive correlation between the military's expertise and its responsibility to the state is needed to ensure the integrity of military professionalism. The most crucial variable is the degree of the military's subordination to its sole client, the nation-state.

PROFESSIONALISM, CORPORATISM, AND THE MODERN NATION-STATE

If the models of professionalism proposed by Carr-Saunders and Wilson and by Huntington incorporate the basic and natural conditions for the rise of an objective military profession and a civic-dominated political order, the best way to study the vicissitudes of civil-military relations in various political systems is by identifying and explaining the strains, contradictions, and negative correlations of these models. Similarly, if this book's integrative model is to be useful in a wide range of historical situations, it must account for the possibility that military corporatism may challenge the democratic ideals of the nation-state. Close attention must therefore be paid to the nature of the state as a client of the army and to the type of authority that the military is inclined to defend as legitimate.

To clarify the analytical model of the professional soldier, a series of continua for the variables of professionalism should be set up. The particular manifestations of each variable can be arranged along a continuum, with professional efficiency in the military at one end and corporate decay at the other. Points along this continuum can then be correlated with the attitudes of the states that nurture such conditions in order to demonstrate what happens to professional military characteristics as they are affected by various types of client states.

Corporate Spirit

On the corporate level of the military professional continuum, the phenomena of group spirit—collective self-confidence and intragroup competitiveness—are positive aspects of military coordination. The quality of corporate feeling may vary greatly, however, with the nature, history, and intentions of the state in question. Under the influence of the state's encouragement or indulgence, the corporate spirit may be transformed into a jealous tradition of rigid exclusivity, depending not on a commonality of interests and skills for its vitality but on rules of conformity, ceremony, and class restriction. The incentive for improvement may be suppressed by a system of advancement based on hierarchy rather than on merit and by the fear of change that always characterizes a petrified structure. Secrecy and intrigue may take the place of originality and zeal. In general, organic solidarity will no longer be treated in terms of performance, flexibility, and innovation, but will be harnessed to the principle of exclusivity.

Secularity

Because secularity—independence from church, class, and caste, and the maintenance of an organization based on rational principles—will be most likely to foster an objective and professional military establishment, it should be placed at the positive end of the continuum. To the extent that the corporate structure is characterized by an exclusivity controlled and approved by the state, however, it comes naturally under the influence of the prejudices of its military arbitrators. Initiative and rational criticism are thwarted by the limitations of the extraneous system that has been imposed on the profession. If the profession is required only to satisfy superficial forms to maintain the status quo, it will soon fall prey to intellectual stagnation. Even the system of examinations in military colleges can be used to force prospective officers into the desired mold.

Skill

Since the acquisition and maintenance of skill are of fundamental importance to the performance of the specialist, they must be placed at the positive end of the continuum of professionalism. The officer's peculiar expertise is in the management of violence; and the quality of this expertise can be radically affected by the relationship between state and military. The proliferation and sophistication of military education becomes a hallmark of high professional standards as long as that education is conducted and determined by men who are themselves highly proficient in military affairs. An overbearing emphasis on ideology, however, may detract from or even contradict utilitarian teachings. The development of universities at the expense of military academies will also lessen the opportunities for acquiring concentrated expertise in military techniques and must, therefore, be considered detrimental to military professionalism. Bad training, supplying, and direction can all contribute to the degeneration of the officer's skill. The management of these functions may even be appropriated by unqualified civil authorities who wish to show that they dominate the military.

Social Mobility

If a characteristic of military professionalism is the selection and advancement of officers on the basis of skill rather than according to class or other caste distinctions, then the most objective recruitment standards will be most efficient and will, therefore, find the most positive place on the social mobility level of the professional continuum. With the growth of a complex industrial and technological society, however, there will be increasingly intense competition for able personnel, and the military may be forced by cultural as well as professional contingencies to draw from classes that it has not formerly considered particularly eligible. Rather than taking advantage of talent among elements of the population that may be considered dangerous or unpredictable, or whose interests are viewed as conflicting with those of the ruling power, a state that controls its military but whose domination of its civilian population is insecure may choose to limit its military establishment to recruiting citizens whose class and ideology ensure their loyalty, regardless of their skill. General Colmar von der Goltz of Prussia expressed this view when he noted in *The Nation in Arms* that "heart and character should be decisive in selecting officers, not intellect and scientific attainment." Such an orientation obviously tends to limit social mobility and increase the chances that a vigorous professional organization will eventually stagnate.[24]

Ideology and Clientship

The military's ideology, or the "military mind" (which is closely related to that of its client), can be judged in terms of the military's ability, characteristics, and attitudes. An appraisal of the particular manifestations of this variable depends upon its relationship to military professionalism as well as upon the harmony or alienation that exists between the military establishment and its client state. The officer can espouse any ideology and still maintain his professionalism. He can also use any ideology to support his resort to political intervention (or military praetorianism). It is the interaction among power, corporatism, and ideology that is the crucial factor in deciding which alternative the military will adopt. [25]

In the modern nation-state the officer corps and the government bureaucracy as a whole are dependent on and responsible to their client, the regime. There is no reason to assume that the military is more "dedicated" to the regime or its political ideology than is the civilian bureaucracy. Like the rest of the bureaucracy, the military's client orientations are influenced more by its corporate than by its bureaucratic orientation. It has been known to modify its ideological positions in order to protect its corporate autonomy; it has also been known to adjust to regimes it abhors. Consider, for example, the French military between 1789 and 1940 and the Nazi military between 1933 and 1945. The military prefers regimes that are stable because they provide a better guarantee of corporate autonomy. The military is no monolith, and the officer corps can be divided. In actuality the military's overriding responsibility is not, as Huntington argues, to society, or even to an ideology, but to the regime, as long as the latter is legitimate.[26] The Red Army supported a hostile regime, while the soldiers of Japan were loyal to the eternal fountainhead of power—the emperor—rather than the regime. Neither army really challenged the regime. Like the rest of the bureaucracy, the military's corporate identity depends upon its loyalty to the group in power.

The possible negative condition of each of these five variables indicates that extreme civilian domination could produce a military establishment so devoid of vitality, skill, and efficiency that it would not only be unable to perform the minimum barracks functions but could also be shattered by engaging in actual war. Its collapse and the accompanying recognition of its impotence might evoke a strong reaction from the remnant that survived, perhaps in the direction of a determination to reform. More likely, however, the angry military corps would be politicized, and follow its inclination to weaken the authority of a client that had brought upon it such humiliation.

The growth of the modern nation-state in Western Europe and the United States has corresponded with the proliferation of democratic ideals, the rise of industrial societies, and the development of the military profession. Not only can military professionalism be affected by the attitudes of the state, but the position of the military establishment within the state, and therefore its social status, will vary with society's conception of the military's function and with the extent and nature of the military's identification with the society or government of its client state. An alienation of the military in its professional capacity from the general moral orientation of the state can lead to severe tension.[27]

The secularization of modern society has improved the standard of living of almost all its citizens. Furthermore, the rapid expansion of industrial technology has created a value system in which productivity and the material gains are the main goals. In such a context, the contrasts between the military officer as a nonproducer and the citizen as a superproducer are highly visible and irksome to both. Perceiving himself as alienated from prevailing values, the officer may react defensively with a stronger assertion of his own particularity than society demands of him. He thus may cut himself off from the society that he has vowed to defend. The soldier's vital interest in maintaining professional standards in a society based on materialism may turn him against secular nationalism with its emphasis on general welfare. And once the dedication of the officer corps is in question, the sovereign authority may find itself having to choose between the well-being of the state and the security of the regime.[28]

The feeling of the professional soldier toward his state will, of course, be partly determined by the esteem that his profession commands in relation to others. Presumably, the higher his social standing, the more strongly he will identify with the state. In any case, his place vis-à-vis other professionals will certainly reflect the history of his state as well as its particular circumstances at a given point in time.[29] In England, for example, the people have insisted upon their ascendancy over the military since the 1688 revolution; the social status of the military officer has been deliberately minimized. Nor has the fact that most British officers belong to the aristocracy been sufficient to elevate the status of the profession. "The history of the British army . . . is the history of the institution that the British have always been reluctant to accept they needed." The army's institutional growth has been a lengthy process, "a series of *ad hoc* expansions and reforms tenuously connected by the residual life and organization of the army in peace time."[30] Even in the nineteenth-century era of mass armies, the British military establishment remained a pre-Bonapartist, emergency institution, rising to the occasion in times of crisis.

The constitutional development of Britain after 1688, its dependence on the navy, and absence of land wars help explain the country's neglect of the institutional and professional reforms made by the French, German, and imperial Russian armies, the Continent's most important mass armies. In Britain the national army grew out of a system in which peers mustered their tenants to fight in volunteer military groups. The standing army was a professional organization loyal to the crown, and as such was regarded as dangerous to British society after 1660. The officer-aristocrats and the people's militia were actually two different armies. Constitutional crises, particularly the struggle over the subordination of the military and its consequent administrative reform by Lord Marlborough in the early 1700s, sharpened this division.[31] Not until the end of the nineteenth century were the two armies integrated.

In England, the professional army was not autonomous—it was not independent of class, regime, or authority. The officer class was exclusivist by virtue of class and position, not by virtue of profession. Unlike its Prussian and French counterparts, the British military establishment did not bestow social rewards on the ambitious. Whereas in Prussia and France the principle of exclusivity protected and preserved what one achieved, in England it merely saved the aristocrat who "chose" the military as an avocation from a decline in status. The British army was in fact usually the preserve of third sons and aristocratic failures.

It has been argued that Mosca's prescription for protecting society against its soldiers involves thwarting the growth of a self-conscious military profession. The application of this principle in Great Britain may have been one of the reasons why the British military never threatened the state's authority.[32] Another explanation may be that, as a compensation for its sacrifice of social influence, the British military was granted a degree of corporate exclusivity that, though costly to both military efficiency and the egalitarianism of the state, appeased their sense of professional marginality.

Unlike their counterpart in Great Britain, the professional militaries in Prussia-Germany, France, Japan, and the USSR (since 1953), have achieved high social status and influence. An analysis of corporate professionalism and a classification of its types in these countries will illuminate the changing role of the professional soldier, the way an officer functions as both a professional and a bureaucrat, and civil-military relations.

3

The Professional Soldier in Prussia-Germany, France, Japan, and the USSR

Case studies of Prussia-Germany and France provide examples of modern civilian control of the military and indicate the ways military professionalism can be subverted. The history of Prussia also demonstrates that the professional nature of a military establishment can be so corrupted by the state's policies or by the dominant political leaders that it may eventually lose its impartiality and become a threat to the society and to its own establishment. The German army's loss of integrity and its abortive revolts during the Hitler era show the impotence of professionals in the face of ruthless political power. France's army between 1789 and 1940 presents the classical case of modern military noninterventionist corporatism and its Janus face which was also exemplified in the French army revolts of 1940 and 1958. In Japan, military corporatism developed without state interference, because there was no centralized authority to challenge the corporate military groups that grew up after 1867. In the USSR, on the other hand, corporate professionalism developed in the shadow of the centralized Stalinist state. Never equal to the party, the military did not emerge until the end of the Stalin regime. In all four cases military corporatism prevailed over other orientations. Furthermore, in all four cases, the political influence and/or importance of the military grew concomitantly with its corporate autonomy, rather than with its proficiency.[1]

PRUSSIA: THE SWORD ON HORSEBACK

Theorists of modern civil-military relations agree that the Prussian model provides the most fertile field for analysis. The history of nineteenth- and twentieth-century Prussia, from Scharnhorst to Hitler, demonstrates the whole range of the variables proposed in this study.[2]

Army Reform and Military Professionalism

Between 1808 and 1813, after the humiliations of Jena and Auerstädt, a trio of reformers—Boyen, Gneisenau, and Scharnhorst—reacted against (1) the principle of exclusivity (limiting recruits to Junker aristocrats) and the amateurism of an officer corps drawn from the ranks of unskilled gentlemen; (2) nonfunctional training; (3) a hierarchical and rigid ranking system based on seniority; (4) a policy of discrimination against the bourgeoisie and others outside the nobility; and (5) lack of integration between Junker with peasant soldiers, along with a general association of nobility with officership. Instead, these reformers created the modern professional army par excellence—a centralized, rational, efficient, and highly skilled officer corps, loyal to the dynasty and its national ideals. They also instituted a policy under which recruitment from meritorious, nonaristocratic Prussian sources was encouraged.[3]

Resistance to the reforms was considerable, for they demanded new social and political relationships, not only between officer and crown but also between the crown and the lower social strata. The reforms were most successful and made the most significant contribution to modern military professionalism in the field of military education. The Prussians created better schools for officers by upgrading the general education courses and demanding rigorous technical training as well. Knowledge of military science and the acquisition of skills replaced nobility and status as criteria for recruitment. The Kriegsakadamie (war academy) became an extremely important tool of modernization in Prussia, although its influence was not limited to that state. It affected the American scientific management school and the Ottoman Empire's educational system, leading to the Tanzimat reforms. Prussian instructors also influenced the military of Argentina, Chile, and Peru in the nineteenth century.[4]

The powerful influence wielded by the old army loyalists and their supporters, as well as the persistence of the nobility principle and the intimacy between Junker and crown, exerted pressure against the professionalization of the Prussian army from the very beginning. The social and educational reforms began to lose force after 1819, when, in order to maintain the aristocratic character of the military, deliberate evasion of the examination system was widely practiced. As younger officers failed to maintain the interests and ideals of the reformers, the army was "de-Boyenized." The concept of an enlightened citizen soldier fully active in society disappeared, and "in its place there grew the concept of the army as a special calling followed by technicians who were essentially separate from civilian society." The 1870 victory over

Napoleon III strengthened the army's corporatist and militarist tendencies, instead of legitimizing the cherished rules of military professionalism—secularism, objective recruitment, and dedication to the ideals of the nation-state,[5] while the reform era underlined national liberation.

Clientship and Conservatism

One of the crucial variables on the continuum of military professionalism is the principle of clientship, seen in terms of the relationships among military professionalism, secularism, and nationalism. It has been argued that the merger of these three factors enhances the political objectivity of the military. But an examination of the Prussian experience, from which sprang the best professional army in the West, demonstrates that when military professionalism, nationalism, and secularism converge with monarchical absolutism, the principle of clientship may no longer be a guarantee against military interventionism. In fact, the union of the military and the regime in Prussia took place at the expense of the growth of a civic society. The effectiveness of the principle of clientship depends upon the nature of the client as well as upon the military's relationship to it. The concept of the army as a profession does not follow inevitably from a separation of the military and civilian society.[6]

Such separation was not even the intention of the reforms of 1807–08 and 1813. The reformers strove for a happy union of the warrior with civilian society, viewing the Landwehr (the territorial army) as the link between the civilian amateur and the military professional. Here they were completely defeated, however, for corporatism in Prussia developed not from the secular values of a liberal society but from tribal Junkerdom. Although the reformers succeeded in institutionalizing military professional rules—corporatism, administrative autonomy, a high level of education for officers, and loyalty to a central source of legitimacy and to Prussian nationalism (all presumably rational and liberal standards)—the foundations of the state and of monarchical legitimacy oriented the officer class toward the monarch, transformed administrative autonomy into a principle of exclusivity, made the military colleges elitist institutions, and dedicated the officer corps to conservative nationalism. The monarch, preferring Junkers and noblemen as officers, continued to discriminate against the bourgeoisie. Although the army and the monarch supported the professional military principle of separating warriors from nonprofessionals, their reasons were political and ideological; they did not desire to foster an "objective" civic society. Because of the organic ties between crown and army the Junkers became the most favored and prominent class of bureaucrats. The administrative, technical, and organizational aspects of the military were improved by the reforms, but its social consciousness and intellectual orientation remained traditional, particularist, and conservative.

The Prussian army was thus a remarkable contradiction: it had the most efficient bureaucratic organization in Europe, but it espoused preindustrial values and defended anachronistic traditions. The progressive policies of recruitment, examination, and promotion introduced by Scharnhorst and Gneisenau were undermined between 1815 and 1860 despite the ostensible persistence of the cardinal principle of professionalism: a secular, open system of recruitment and skill acquisition.

The military in Prussia was above the political battle in the sense that it was an arm of the crown, not a creature of the constitutional state. For close to two centuries, despite reform, bureaucratic expansion, growing complexity, and setbacks, the Prussian (and later German) military establishment was the private preserve of the Hohenzollern dynasty.[7] Civil-military relations in Prussia-Germany demonstrated an unbroken continuity between the monarch as warlord, authoritarianism and conservatism.

In Prussia, the professional army, as defender of the monarchical principle, was pitted against the liberals as champions of social ideals and the constitutional and representative system of the modern nation-state. The contest began in 1815 and climaxed with a bitter clash in the late 1860s over military budget and parliamentary responsibility, as the military sought freedom from parliamentary control. In halting the dispute, Bismarck succeeded in rescuing the army from exclusivity and reaction. By turning the office of chancellor into a buffer separating the army, the monarchy, and the liberals, he "saved" the army from excessive conservatism, but he also shielded it from liberalism. Although the crown delegated to the chancellor the duty of overseeing civilian domination of the military, the organic ties among crown, Junkers, and conservatism were not impaired and the army was protected from control by the liberal middle classes.[8]

Detachment from modern civil society, a secularist stance, and ideological conservatism were closely correlated in the Prussian professional officer corps throughout the nineteenth century. These attitudes become even more strongly connected in the twentieth century and eventually produced a conservative military mind imbued with a desire for autonomy and a rationale for political interventionism.

The rapid decay of the army reforms in Prussia suggests that military professionalism does not grow deep roots merely by virtue of bureaucratic reform and reorganization. The facts that Prussia remained a conservative (and sometimes reactionary) state until 1919 and that the crown remained virtually the only fountainhead of legitimacy militated against the forging of a liberal nation despite the existence of a professional army.

Military Corporatism, Authoritarianism, and Social Change

The transformation of the German economy affected the pattern of German society during the early period of industrialization. Population rose from 25 to 40 million in four decades (1815–58), an increase of close to 40 percent. Yet the demographic expansion was uneven. As a result of the imbalances in economic growth among German states and classes the bourgeoisie became a creative force in economics but accepted a subservient role in national and political affairs.[9]

The social structure remained intact even as the middle classes emerged.[10] The middle classes were co-opted to staff the state bureaucracy and began to evidence the authoritarianism of the ruling Junkers. Thus shift in distribution of wealth did not reflect a shift in distribution of power. "Here was the heart of the political conflict of the mid-century which found its resolution in the achievement of national unification."[11] Thus, national unification under Prussian monarchical and conservative hegemony stabilized class structure and muted social conflict.

The relationships between the military and the bourgeoisie were one-sided. The military made concessions to the bourgeoisie partly because of the need for a larger army but "more important as a means of building up a bloc of influential supporters for [the army's] reactionary views."[12] Dominating the state, influential with the powerful bureaucracy, dedicated to authoritarian rule, the army provided a model for the bourgeoisie. "The bourgeois was only too anxious to share something of the glamour and glory of the army, and a lieutenant's epaulettes or an invitation to the mess was a low price for the army to pay for loyal support against liberalism and democracy."[13] The civilian gained status at the price of accepting the military ethic and orientations. "Service in the armed forces was part of an educational process which tended to make the lower classes politically submissive,"[14] writes Hamerow. In a state excessively influenced by the army, bureaucracy, and authoritarians, "the influence of the army could only be maintained with the active support of a wide section of the bourgeoisie."[15] The military pre-empted social change; it made the middle class the clients of the patrimonial-authoritarian state. The military, the system of education, and the instruments of political power all were linked to arrest social change and channel the bourgeoisie's aspirations toward Junkerdom rather than autonomy. Still, like the monarchy, the bureaucracy, and the military, the civilian section became corporate and civic organizations became instruments of authority incorporated into the Reich, but *unequal* in status, power, and influence with the military and the senior civil service. Education, the conspicuous property of the middle class, was geared to "ultimately find employment in the bureaucracy, the armed forces, the skilled professions, and important industrial and agricultural enterprises."[16] "Political pressure groups in central Europe reflected the oligarchic character of public life; since there was no mass electorate, there could be no mass parties."[17] Thus, political power was masked and at the disposal of bureaucratic and military corporatists who were unswervingly loyal to the monarchy. The army was not called to protect the civil rights of the struggling bourgeoisie but to act as its police force.[18]

The Nation-in-Arms and Corporate Exclusivity

The most serious challenge to professionalism was the military's policy toward recruitment. The complexity of warfare demanded officers skilled in industrial arts. Selection on that basis, however, would violate the exclusivity principle, and middle-class officers and Jews would be able to challenge the Prussian and aristocratic criteria for advancement. This conflict was the army's fundamental problem during the period of William II (1888–1918). The dictum that heart and character should be the principle of recruitment for officers forced the army to turn the clock back to the days of Frederick the Great, when nobility, both military and political, as the natural basis of political authority stood unchallenged. This frustrated not only the officers but many German bourgeois patriots as well. The reserve system, a separate and lesser branch of the military, was not a civilian-inclined military structure but "an effective and popular way of assimilating the *bourgeoisie* into an aristocratic and monarchical state." The army used its power to dominate and influence the youth, to secure choice civil service jobs by reserving senior positions for veterans, to distribute social and status privileges, and to bestow military titles on professors.[19]

The controversy over the nation-in-arms concept bears witness to the tension existing between the idea of a mass citizens' conscription army and that of an elitist army restricted to aristocratic class and professional standards. The components of the nation-in-arms varied depending on the historical and political dynamics of the country in question. In France, it was an outgrowth of the Revolution, when the citizen turned soldier and the bourgeois became his officer. The German nation-in-arms was quite different. It was designed to militarize the middle classes by making the general staff, Junkerdom, and the crown the fountainhead of *virtu* (valor, moral excellence). Highly developed military competence and a high ratio of citizens with military training did not bring about a popular or bourgeois army. In fact, the Prussian nation-in-arms was designed to protect the military from a populist challenge. Conservative patriotism, stimulated and encouraged by the *Kriegerverein* veterans' organization, diffused Prussian absolutist and professional military values into society, and virtu became a combination of monarchical legitimacy, Prussian conservatism, and military exclusivity.[20]

The army was expected to function as a laboratory for national integration. According to General von der Goltz, it was to be a system protecting heart and character from the onslaught of science, industry, intellectualism, and populism. Both he and General Bernhardi, a chief propagandist of the theory of preventive war, espoused a militant pan-Germanism. Bernhardi spoke of the Prussian historical mission as a racial crusade against Slavs, an antiliberal Weltpolitik, and von der Goltz echoed him. Von der Goltz equated the officer's professional responsibility to the state and its ideals with devotion to absolutist Prussian patriotism, and considered liberal republicanism anti-Prussian and antihistorical in spirit. Thus, the special bond between the officer corps and the legitimate source of authority in Germany created a particularist military professionalism, not the model of modern military professionalism it is generally believed to be. As military and political institutions became inseparable, they acted in society as mutually dependent variables.

In Prussia-Germany, a bureaucratic state with a weak middle class, the professional soldier became wedded to the antiquated but powerful monarchical system of legitimacy; in the absence of a liberal society, he was the servant of Prussian absolutism. The aristocratic professional was naturally tied to the state; and the upstart who chose the military profession as a vehicle for mobility also became a defender of the dynasty. The nationalism of the professional soldier, buttressed by a strict concept of virtu, was the despair of the liberals, the bourgeoisie, the advocates of representative government, and the rising socialists. Conversely, the military was convinced that in its struggle against social democracy it was defending its state, the Prussian monarchy, against dangerous men who sought to abolish the Prussian army.

Even in 1815–58 German society was characterized by a marked indifference to politics. This attitude was most pronounced among the peasantry,[21] since co-optation of middle and artisan classes had made them muted legitimists. The struggle of social democracy in Germany also demonstrates the working classes' incorporation into the legitimate system. The working classes were politically active, but they were oriented toward legitimacy and authoritarianism.

"What the working classes needed above all was protection against laissez-faire capitalism. Yet this protection could not be found in corporative regulation of industrial production."[22] Lassalle's program was "dependent on the willingness of the government to support producer associations organized by the workers which could compete with capitalist establishments";[23] in other words, he "hoped to enlist the Hohenzollern dynasty itself in his crusade for a socialist economy."[24] Lassalle was a preacher "on the high mission of the state."[25]

Lassalle's successor, Liebknecht, "obsessed by the new order, which to him was only a tool of a despotic and militaristic Junkerdom."[26] clashed with the regime. Opposing military victory and national unification, the leaders of social democracy were sent to prison and the movement was crushed.[27] Thereafter, with the exception of a minority of working-class intellectuals and unionists, political servility, placidity, and conformity was the rule.

Fritz Stern, following Ralf Dahrendorff, succinctly depicts imperial Germany as Bonapartist, conservative, and authoritarian.[28] Its character can be best caught by the term illiberal. "By illiberalism," writes Stern, "I mean not only the structure of the political regime, suffrage restrictions, or class chicanery, but *a state of mind*."[29] (Italics mine.) "Illiberalism first of all constituted a commitment of mind and policy against any further concessions to democracy, even at the price of one's political independence. Any concession in any realm might undermine the authority, prestige, and status of the entire system."[30] The role of military corporatism in Prussia-Germany was to foster illiberalism as a habitual response.

Military Corporatism and Political Power

Nevertheless, reforms concerning organizational efficiency, bureaucratic centralization of the armed forces, and officer education culminated in the creation of one of the most powerful military institutions of the nineteenth century, the German general staff. This highly specialized group, nurtured on conservative values and trained in modern rational and secular science, became a political institution bent on defending dynastic rule. Its function, privileges, and bureaucratic cohesiveness raised the Prussian army to a position of political primacy. As the guardian of the fountainhead of power, its constitutional role was undefined. However, the rivalry between Bismarck and the high command indicates the general staff's extraconstitutional capacities.[31]

After the 1860s, General Helmuth von Moltke, through his favored position with King William I, succeeded in making the general staff the dominant agency, superseding the war ministry, and its chief became the king's military adviser. Even the mighty Bismarck encountered serious opposition and interference from this unique agency. Here again, he saved the principle of civilian predominance over the military, this time by opposing Moltke's demands for a war of extermination with France.[32] However, the integrity of military professionalism, its very separation from society, was constantly challenged by the central edifice of military professional corporatism—the general staff. One of Scharnhorst's supreme contributions to the rationalization of the military profession was the creation of the Allgemeine Kriegsdepartment, a military cabinet run by an Oberkriegskollegium, a small group of officers serving as personal aides to the king. It was an early version of a ministry of war. When the general staff achieved autonomy from the ministry of war, however, it clearly violated the cardinal principle of the unity of command established by Scharnhorst, and after Bismarck it came to dominate the war ministry. Thus "the way was now open for the tensions and divisions between the three highest military institutions. . . . This was to weaken the unity of command within the army."[33] Here is a prime example of correlation between military professional corporatism and political interventionism.

In Prussia-Germany the principle of objective political conduct was flagrantly violated in defense of monarchical conservatism. Until 1945, during periods of war, social revolution, and political violence the military generally opted to defend the king rather than the nation-state and its ideals. The legacy of Moltke prevailed over that of Bismarck. In fact, Moltke's distrust of diplomats and politicians was an inheritance the general staff never renounced.[34]

The officer corps became progressively alienated from both politicians and society after the victory of Sedan in 1870; and the mushrooming growth of German industry resulted in social changes that further widened the gulf between the professional soldier and the civilian. When society craved reform, the officer corps stood firm against political and social change. The military successes of the Austrian and French campaigns, the politics of unification, and the decline of Bismarck led to the increased organizational and political autonomy of the general staff and the military. The success of the Prussian military principle that resulted in the unification of Germany in 1871 was a victory for organization and centralization of authority, cultivated by the Prussian general staff, which considered itself the champion of German unification, of defeat of Germany's eternal foes in Europe, of German imperialism, and of dynastic legitimacy.

Without doubt the Prussian general staff perceived itself as the quintessence of Germanism. Its brilliant military victories were the product of national and secular organization, but they paradoxically increased Prussian patrimonial arrogance and extended bureaucratic authoritarianism. The success of the army enhanced Prussian hegemony over the Germanies and signified the victory of Junkerdom and all it stood for. "Absolute government ushered in a more advanced stage in organized coercion."[35] This had been as true of the Great Elector, Frederick William I, as it was of his descendant William I. Now the holy trinity of kaiser, general staff, and Junkerdom prevailed. Its ascendancy was exhibited in the recruitment policy, which encouraged the predominance of Prussian officers and members of the Prussian nobility; in the diminished influence of the war ministry; in weakening parliamentary control over the military; and in the protection of the army's social structures from liberal, bourgeois, and Jewish elements.

Furthermore, the corporate officer's code of honor was institutionalized as an essential condition for retaining the caste status and privileges of the military. The preservation of the custom of dueling underlined the corporate orientation of the Prussian officer class. General Von Loe writes (as quoted by Kitchen):

> The strength of the Officer Corps lies in its homogeneous composition and in its exclusiveness. Neither a title nor riches give one the right to hope to become an officer, but an innate feeling for duty, education and the aristocracy of character. The more exclusively we concentrate on that section of the community from which we wish to draw out recruits, the more certain we are to be able to protect our profession from alien elements, in spite of the general mania for equality . . . the duel must not be thought of as an act of revenge, but as a confession of faith . . . an act that shows fidelity to one's beliefs and also an act of justice, the necessity and moral justification of which lies deep in noble human feelings.

And Kitchen concludes:

> The rigorous code of honor and the duels formed part of an attempt by the army to preserve its exclusive position in the state by underlining the differences between the military and the civilian population, by claiming for itself a higher sense of values, and by dinding the members of the Officer Corps closer together in a corporate attitude to life that remained distinct from, and in many ways opposed to, the generally accepted ideas of the day.[36]

World War I

German society at the turn of the century was polarized. The army was left to defend the regime. The opposition rejected Prussian values, most of which were identified with the military. The army entered World War I alienated from the society it presumably was fighting to defend. Though the bourgeoisie were swept along into supporting the war effort, the gap between the officer corps and the civic code widened. Under the silent dictatorship of Ludendorff and von Hindenburg in 1916 the officer corps became increasingly estranged from society. In upholding one cardinal rule of professionalism by remaining an autonomous class, the officers violated another, commitment to the nation-state and all its classes. But this conflict was short-lived. The general staff was forced to broaden the ranks of the officers, and non-Prussians and nonaristocrats, men like Ludendorff, Groener, and Hoffmann, penetrated the bastion of the Prussian army.

The general staff was actually less ready for total war than were German civilians. Appointed chief custodian of citizens' preparedness, the army, one of the most efficient military organizations of the nineteenth century, failed to mobilize the country for war. "While the army made use of the technological discoveries of modern science and employed the products of modern industry, the officer corps was by no means imbued with their spirit."[37] Indeed, the general staff proved to be a haven for nostalgic Prussians whose contempt for science and industry was matched only by their rigid ceremonial spirit and reactionary outlook. In this situation "militarism" and martial and aristocratic values had to be utilized by the military in its own defense. Militarism became the defense mechanism of the intellectually backward military caste, increasingly lost in a complex industrial society. When it became apparent that the war could not be won through a blitz strategy, military organizational stagnation became more noticeable. Militarism was "above all a social phenomenon whose fundamental characteristics were the preservation of those retarded social attitudes and authoritarian institutions associated with the officer corps and the development of a feeling of respect and admiration for those attitudes and institutions in the public at large."[38]

The total defeat of the German army in the war seemed a coup de grace for the general staff. Yet it emerged in 1918 "with most of the fondest prejudices of the Wilhelmine period unchanged." Paradoxically, the more political the professional Prussian soldier became, the brighter were his memories. Because of the incompetence of various civilian bureaucrats (in contrast to the efficiency of private industry and the industrialists recruited to the war effort), the mobilization of resources and the war effort gave the army a new political impetus. Thus the military command became the dominant political force in postwar Germany,[39] the arbiter in disputes between political radical and moderate forces.

The Weimar Republic

The successors to the ambitious Ludendorff and the politically naive von Hindenburg were two generals, Groener and von Seeckt, who not only determined the rules of behavior for the military and the general staff between 1919 and 1933 but also helped to lay the foundations of the Weimar Republic. Although the war had clearly been lost by the army, the high command was shrewd enough to pass the onus of defeat to the civilians. Thus, a center party (Catholic) politician, Matthais Erzberger, conducted the humiliating negotiations for the armistice. Groener reminisces: "The High Command deliberately adopted the position of refusing the responsibility for the armistice and all the later steps. Strictly legally seen, it did so without justification, but to me and my associates it was vital to keep the armor shining [*die Waffe blank*] and the General Staff free of burdens for the future."[40] At Versailles was launched the Reichswehr, beginning the last phase in the glorious history of the Prussian army and its general staff.

The corporate orientation of the German military complemented the Versailles conception of a limited Reichswehr. Not unlike the reformers of 1808, von Seeckt was unwilling to be a surrogate for the kaiser or to "surrender" the army to the new legitimacy, Weimar, viewed as at best a Vernunftrepublik ("republic of convenience"). The general philosophy of the Heeresleitung (army command), he felt, should be to maintain a reliable, efficient, strong army and, to this end, corporate autonomy was necessary. "The Reichswehr must obey the orders given to it by the duly constituted authority, but General von Seeckt and the Heeresleitung bitterly resented any attempt by these authorities to interfere with the internal functioning of the Reichswehr."[41] Thus the correlation between corporatism and professionalism was high when the military became politically involved.

With military defeat and the Weimar Revolution of 1918 came a general shift to the Left in Germany. In the officer corps, where corporate feeling was threatened by the disintegration of the Empire, fear of the Bolshevik menace spread from the high command to the lowest subaltern. Hoping to stem the tide of socialism, the leaders of the Reichswehr plunged into politics.[42]

Both Groener and von Seeckt had faith that they could protect military corporatism by undertaking their own form of political intervention, and, as General Groener phrased it, "politics must be conducted by a few only—tenaciously and silently."[43] At best, the generals could only tolerate Weimar, which they considered incapable of protecting corporatism and legitimacy from leftist insurrection. The very weakness of the civilian authority, in fact, led the military to conceive of the Reichswehr as an independent suprapolitical national organization. In

1918–19 von Seeckt and Groener allied with Ebert's Right Socialists in order to defend—not the republic—the military organization from a threatened Communist takeover. During the 1920s von Seeckt instilled in the army command its praetorian role, which contributed to republican stability even though it proved unable to provide a permanent support.

HITLER AND THE ARMY

Ultimately, the Reichswehr fell victim to its own stubborn corporatism and its principles of organizational autonomy.

> A Reichswehr which in the hour of peril would have cooperated with the Prussian police and the republican organizations, instead of intriguing against them, could have been the rock on which the waves broke. But the policy of the army command prevented such a cooperation and led to a weakening of the Republic and of the organizations willing to defend it. In so doing, however, the army command also undermined the foundations of its own power. The position it had acquired could only be held while the government remained weak. If a really strong government supplanted it, the autonomy of the Reichswehr would come to an end, and with it the strong influence which it wielded in the political sphere.[44]

In fairness to some of the leaders of the Reichswehr, the members of Hitler's general staff were not necessarily political simpletons or arrogant professionals or subservient corporatists. In fact, the revisionist study of party-army relationships by Robert O'Neill clearly demonstrates that the high command was not monolithic.[45] General von Hammerstein-Equord—a man of great courage and initiative, chief of the high command—had labored hard to keep the Reichswehr's neutrality in 1933 and to protect the army from the Nazi party.

The high command after Hitler's first reorganization (1934–35) continued to seek the goal of the classical professionals—separation of military from politics. Nevertheless, the four most important positions within the German high command between 1934 and 1938 were occupied by four individuals who represented two schools of thought. The traditionalists were led by von Fritsch, chief of the high command, and von Beck, his chief of staff. They aspired to continue in the spirit of von Hammerstein-Equord. The second school, representing the New Era, was led by General von Blomberg, the new Reichswehr minister and the head of the Wehrmachtamt (Armed Forces Office), and General von Reichenau.[46] The first group wanted "to increase greatly the size and standard of efficiency of the army." The second group "were concerned with the adaptation of the Reichswehr to the Nazi government, the Nazi party, and Nazi ideology; so that political-military relations ran as smoothly as possible."[47]

Disputes within the high command, the army's failure to oppose Hitler's militaristic policies, and the von Fritsch crisis led to the second reorganization of the Reichswehr in 1938. Now Hitler took direct command. He appointed himself supreme commander, purged the most senior officers—von Blomberg and von Fritsch—and appointed his creature General Keitel head of the Oberkommando der Wehrmacht (OKW), the new Armed Forces High Command, which replaced the 1934 Armed Forces Office with functions of a military staff under the führer as supreme commander. Hitler then appointed General von Brauchitsch, of the old school (his inclinations were those of a pre-Nazi Prussian officer), as head of a new office, the Oberkommando des Heers (OKH), the Army High Command, the functional-professional chief officer of the Reichswehr. Thus the führer gradually assumed personal control of the army and purged the professional officers who opposed him. O'Neill's revisionist analysis does not refute my argument that professionalism is neither a buttress against the army's politicization nor a buffer against its domination by authoritarian politicians and parties. In fact, O'Neill's study clearly demonstrates that many factors —the army's role in formulating military policies, its anxiety to attain military goals, its desire to compromise with the party for the sake of national security, its exploitation of the new atmosphere of rearmament, induced by the führer to further Nazi military aims—created exactly the opposite situation from the neutrality to which the traditional-professional officers aspired.[48] Their disunity reduced their ability to oppose Hitler, but so, to reiterate O'Neill, did "their lack of political consciousness" and overabundant concern for the "defense" of Germany. "The majority of officers averse to Nazism were like rudderless ships amidst swift currents."[49]

Corporatism is certainly Janus-faced. "Their education and traditions had kept them apart from politics, and so their realization of the significance of events taking place around them was, at best, slow."[50] What was their "education"? Subservience to Prussian warlords. What were their traditions? Those of the spoiled elite culture of the Hohenzollerns. What kept them apart from "politics" and "events"? Their cognition that "politics" is managed by their warlord, that "events" will be handled by the state, that is, the traditional Prussian system. Thus, their professional commitment under Hitler, their lack of activity in anti-Nazi politics, cost them their lives and reputations and eventually their cherished Prussian general staff. The Hitler officers were remarkably different from their Weimar seniors, von Seeckt, Groener, and von Schleicher, who were interventionists. The Hitler officers made, in the end (1944), merely a fragile and futile coup. Certainly the reasons why von Seeckt and his colleagues could assert political influences lay in the nature of the politically precarious Weimar regime. Under the Hilter regime, von Blomberg and the traditionalists could not intervene politically. Von Blomberg's efforts to ensure the Reichswehr's integrity through faith in Hitler and his dedication in bringing the army and the party into intimate union produced totally contrary results. The army became subservient to Hitler.[51]

This subservience was not, as O'Neill contends, the result of the military's "lack of political consciousness." More accurate is Bracher's argument that it resulted from "political ineptitude and unpolitical arrogance." O'Neill himself argues that "when this outlook [man's honor and his pledged loyalty to Hitler] has combined with the strict code of military obedience which inhibits protest against orders, the Nazi Party was given a degree of control over the German army quite unknown to the armies of Western democracies."[52] The Prussian officer corps from Moltke to von Blomberg (although it always contained dissenters) contributed (as the interventionist von Schleicher and the "neutral" von Hindenburg in Hitler's time certainly did) to the demise of democracy in Germany. This is not true of other Western countries, including France.

In fact, O'Neill admits that "the greater availability, compared with the days of the Weimar Republic, of materials, men, and finance, the improved conditions of service, the modernization of the Army, the fascination of new work and the emphasis on professional proficiency were associated in the minds of many soldiers, and with considerable justification, with the National-Socialist government. Apart from local friction with minor Party officials which was often rationalized in terms of the Führer's ignorance of the misconduct of his juniors, there was much about the Third Reich in its pre-war years which seemed to the German Army at large to be wholly right and proper. The overall system had provided the good things—it only remained for Hitler to clean up the defects on the lower levels, when he had time, for Germany to be put back on her feet again as a healthy and vigorous nation which had cast off the gloom and shame of the 'twenties. It was only too easy for the Party propaganda machine to impress this sort of thinking upon the receptive minds of many soldiers and to make others, who were less credulous, more hesitant in criticizing the Party.

"Thus the German Army came to be dominated by Hitler. The forces acting on the Nazi Party enabled it to pursue its own policy with little need for compromise with the Army, while the Army was subject to an overwhelming number of influences which combined on many levels to make it subservient to its political master."[53]

The high command moved from wavering cooperation with the Weimar Republic between 1918 and 1926 to surrender to the totalitarian state after 1938.[54] All the while the corporate entity of the military remained its chief concern. But "politics" caught up with the Reichswehr. A century of silence, of monarchical subordination, and of equality at the royal court had blinded the gray-uniformed elite to the reality of politics under any other regime than a benevolent dynasty. In the long run, even the most politically minded officer of Weimar, General Kurt von Schleicher, who was highly skilled in political deception, proved to be no match for Adolf Hitler. By manipulating the conservative and nationalist politicians, parties, and groups, von Schleicher rose meteorically to become the éminence grise of the aging, politically inept "wooden titan," Field Marshal von Hindenburg. Von Schleicher made himself head of the war ministry, and as a result of his intrigues Groener was appointed to the ministry of defense in 1928.

Von Schleicher's appeasement policy was based on the hope that he "could guide the German ship of State into safety . . . by means of clever and devious maneuvers calculated either to beguile or to divide the enemy." But he was outflanked by Hitler in 1933 and assassinated by Nazi henchmen in 1934, leaving the republic, the military, and the conservative nationalists at the mercy of a mercurial déclassé corporal.[55]

It is one of the most curious paradoxes of modern history that a political man like Hitler was able to subdue the independent corporate spirit of the German officer corps and that he also succeeded in "civilianizing" the German state and providing for political legitimacy, even though it was not a legitimacy supported by the officer corps. The military never saw in Hitler a real replacement for monarchical legitimacy, but in the king's absence, it preferred the legitimacy of the state and favored the ideals of the Right over those of the Left. Supporting the moderate and conservative parties in the hope that they could defend historical legitimacy, under Hitler the army as an autonomous corporate group slowly disintegrated. Hitler returned the army to its strictly "professional" role as an instrument of violence. The Nazi party, a tremendous political machine, acted as a counterbalance to the military, and Hitler's paramilitary structures inherited its political-ideological functions. Above all, Hitler took advantage of the weakness, naiveté, and timidity of members of the high command. He used his own Reichswehr appointments to bring about the end of one of the most successful professional officer systems of modern times.

France: From La Grande Muette to Insurrection

If the Prussian army was the archetype of modern military professionalism as a subservient instrument of the state, the French military during almost a century and a half (1789–1870, 1890–1940) is a prime example of modern military corporatism. "To protect the army against the perils of French political life in the nineteenth century required that the soldiers themselves revise, consciously or unconsciously, certain of their fundamental assumptions with regard to such matters as discipline, obedience, loyalty, and military honor."[56]

The military had to adapt to survive in the bitter struggle between authority and society in France between 1789 and 1870. It resorted to corporate autonomy in order to prevent the destruction of its organization and tradition by the conflicting regimes—constitutional monarchies, empires, republics—that held sway during that period. The military was loyal to most regimes and unperturbed by the different ideologies espoused by their governing elites. It was loyal ultimately to a single authority, its only client—the state of France. This corporate orientation made the military a silent partner of the rapidly changing regimes and kept it uncompromised. The historian of the French army, Raoul Girardet, writes: "The revolutions of the nineteenth century were too numerous and too varied for the army to have let itself be drawn into them, without running the risk of complete and rapid disintegration. To assert its absolute disinterest with regard to political matters was doubtless the only way in which the army could be certain of preserving its coherence and even of continuing to remain in existence."[57]

From the time of Cardinal Richelieu the concept of a dynastic army had been instilled in the French officer corps, then an unruly and semi-autonomous body within the state."[58] By 1660 (during the reign of Louis XIV), Minister Cardinal Mazarin and Marshal Le Tellier, his most able military adviser, had succeeded in impressing upon the French military the basic rules of behavior—loyalty to the dynasty, skill, and high morale—that were the antecedents of modern military professionalism. But the dynastic army, depleted and demoralized by a long series of fruitless wars, was to be fundamentally challenged by the French Revolution. That the collapse of legitimate authority after 1789 did not give rise to a praetorian civil-military relationship must be attributed to the strength of the army's corporate tradition.

The Nation-in-Arms

The French nation-in-arms was conceived during the Revolution—not by the early leaders, but by their immediate successors, the radical Jacobins, who came to power in 1792. To accomplish the Jacobins' planned fundamental reform of French society and politics, it was necessary to revolutionize the army, which was still loyal to a fallen legitimacy. Hoping to integrate the army with society, the Jacobins established the Paris Commune of 1792 and passed the decree of the levée en masse in 1793.

The Paris Commune represented the revolt of an urban proletariat against the rural rentiers who dominated the city. The Babeuf concept was to "Parisify" France—achieving autonomy for the proletariat and establishing a national guard under the Comité Central de la Garde Nationale, an institution formed to coordinate the political activities of the Commune. The military vision of Robespierre and Saint-Just provided a model for the new army, which was to be a patriotic, egalitarian, highly politicized people's militia. Its politicized officers called for the abolition of officership as a privilege of nobility and of military discipline based on class and status, and they demanded greater participation of the people in military decision making. "Unruly but patriotic, undisciplined but enthusiastic, discouraged by defeat and by the ineptitude and colorlessness of its generals, extremely political but inclined to take a low view of politicians, the army in August, 1792, like France itself, was a formless and fluctuating mass."[59]

The nation-in-arms was an effort by the Jacobins to supplant the newly created professional soldier by initiating an organizational revolution: universal conscription. The principle of exclusivity was to be modified by a new mass conception: above all, by the promotion and recruitment of officers from social and professional classes never tapped before. The nation-in-arms in France not only involved a different type of military professional, but it was also designed to deal with new types of warfare. In fact, one could argue that post-Napoleonic warfare required such a modification of military organizational structure. Widening the scope of warfare permitted the integration of the masses with the military. The nation-in-arms was the French contribution to popular and often totalitarian democracy.

Mobilization is a military concept, a form of social ordanization that corresponds to a specific time in history. Its purpose is to fuse the civilian and military functions, thereby producing a nation-in-arms. If the professional soldier can be called the handmaiden of modern state bureaucracy, the mobilizing officer is the handmaiden of the populist democracy forged in the West by war. The nation-in-arms type of military organization has four essential characteristics. (1) Its dominant feature is public service—virtu—which is best expressed in military duty. It is a personal burden, and its weight cannot be lifted by either economic or social influence. (2) An egalitarian sentiment is manifested in the military posture as well as in the political and economic institutions of the nation. The government can be radically democratic or radically despotic, but public authority must be stable in order to pursue consistent educational policies and to keep alive the popular will to participate in state-sponsored activities, including the military. (3) The nation-in-arms has a high degree of military competence, excellent fighting qualities, dedication, responsible citizenship, and, above all, superior human beings with a superior military organization. (4) Military morale, which is infused with public virtue, is exceptionally high; paramilitary organizations are linked to paracivic training and organization. The military establishment of the nation-in-arms constitutes the universal testing ground for public-spirited citizens.

The concept of the citizen-soldier plagued French politics and the French military throughout the nineteenth century. Political philosophers of that century wrongly believed that because the French army took a more active political role after the Revolution than it had during the monarchy, the nation-in-arms and the concept of democracy were linked with militarism (later to be called praetorianism). Democracy was identified with military revolutions. To quote de Tocqueville: "Military revolutions which are scarcely ever to be apprehended in aristocracies are always to be dreaded among democratic nations. These perils must be reckoned among the most formidable which beset their future fate, and the attention of statesmen should be sedulously applied to finding a remedy for the evil." Sir Henry Maine also tried to link popular governments and praetorianism. Democracy, he said, would have difficulty in controlling the sort of standing army that was necessary in a commercial state:

> The maxims of the two systems (democracy and standing armies) flatly contradict one another and the man who would loyally obey both finds his moral constitution cut into two halves. It has been found by recent experience that the more popular the civil institutions, the harder it is to keep the army from meddling with politics. Military insurrections are made by officers, but not before every soldier has discovered that the share of power which belongs to him as a unit in a regiment is more valuable than his fragment of power as a unit in a constitution.[60]

The professional military organization and the nation-in-arms or mobilizing organization are historically parallel, as are their clients, the bureaucratic modern nation-state and the modern political community. The professional soldier established the model for a rational legal authority and eventually became the champion of the *Rechtsstaat* (constitutional state) and the bureaucratic ideology. The mobilizing, nation-in-arms state—the collectivity—was the structural expression of commitment to the political community. Whereas in pre-1789 political systems religious mobilization had transformed prepolitical societies into political communities, after 1789 the Bonapartist military type mobilized the individual will into the general will.

The legacy of the Revolution proved as great a problem to Napoleon as it was to the traditional French officer corps. Failure of discipline, lack of skill, high politicization, inefficiency, and the total absence of what later came to be known as military professionalism prevailed. But in spite of the fact that the nation-in-arms concept inflicted serious damage on the efficacy and capability of the French army, once the Revolution foundered, the army under Napoleon's leadership did fill the political vacuum. Consequently, the concept of the nation-in-arms has been incorporated into the French military heritage, becoming a focus for military organization and the conduct of warfare.[61]

The Faces of Janus: Corporatism and Professionalism

Loyalty to France ultimately linked the professional to the soldier as bureaucrat-ruler. The army was dedicated to national glory and (before 1848) to the achievements of the Revolution, although as a corporate group it was not ideologically oriented. The army was further dedicated to the affirmation of the principles of order and authority. Thus, Bonapartism (which is commonly misinterpreted as militarism and military interventionism) "reconciled democracy and authority in a way which was neither reactionary on the one hand, nor nonparliamentary on the other. It offered itself as an answer to the rule of anarchic and discredited parliaments—unlike Royalism . . . Bonaparte aspired to preserve the work of the Revolution . . . [62]

The professional revolution orientation, antagonistic to the concept of mass armies and to anarchy and lack of authority, accepted the nation-in-arms only because it represented the affirmative principles of the revolution, the equality of men, and careers open to talent.[63] Structurally, however, the military profession became corporate, restrictive, and exclusivist. "Militarism, the passion for glory and foreign adventures was, before 1848, essentially a characteristic of the republicans."[64] The military during the Second Empire (1852–70) did not run the country or aspire to imperial grandeur. The national guard, acting as nation-in-arms, kept the peace at home after 1815, and by 1848 it had become a police system.[65] Thereafter, when it proved ineffective in protecting political order, it decayed, and the military became the guarantor of political and social order, a situation the Bonapartists preferred. "When the army, like the notables, developed an independent *esprit de corps*, it forgot its revolutionary origins, and became the defender of hierarchy and order."[66] Bonapartism turned the revolutionary aspirations and ideals of the military upside down, and corporate professionalism became the ally of the Empire. "The Imperial Guard with its splendid uniforms appeared as a new praetorian bulwark of the regime."[67]

Only the Third Republic and adoption of the Prussian system of conscription would turn the professional back to the concept of nation-in-arms. But, in order to build the army of *La Revanche*, Napoleon III, very conscious of the defects of his army, wanted to establish universal military service, copying the Prussians.[68]

France and Prussia

The roads France and Prussia took to modern military professionalism were as different as the countries themselves. Modern professionalism emerged in Prussia in response to the disasters of Auerstädt and Jena. French military professionalism appeared in reaction to the perils of the Revolution.[69] The French officer became a politically passive civil servant, loyal to the regime of the moment; he was devoted to the nation, but separated from society. The nineteenth-century French army, in fact, followed the Prussian professional model invented by Scharnhorst and Gneisenau but abandoned by their successors.

The history of French civil-military relations between 1815 and 1940 indicates that the military's political objectivity may be purchased at the price of total separation from society. "The condition of a soldier's existence—the distinctive uniform, the low scale of pay, the constant changes of garrison, the special code of justice and discipline—all conspired to keep him on the margin of French society in the nineteenth century."[70] An army shorn of émigré aristocrats and lacking a sizable middle-class contingent was bound to exist on the edge of a modern market society. The French army, however, was completely dedicated to its professional and corporate tasks.

Occasionally the military did succumb to the temptations of political activism. For example, beginning in 1866 under the stress of conflict and ending in 1870 with defeat by Germany, the nation-in-arms controversy resurfaced. The officers lacked faith in the conscript soldier. Their mistrust of Jacobinism hindered the recruitment and especially the training of skilled fighting men. At the same time, the French people opposed compulsory military service. Thus the nation-in-arms concept had a catastrophic impact. In 1914 and again in 1939, it "led the French to expect and plan for a particular type of warfare, which never materialized and thus had a marked effect upon the military outcome."[71] The Jacobin theory of a conscript army created a wedge between the republic and the army. Espousing a professional army resulted in several serious challenges to civilian supremacy in nineteenth-century France. Republican regimes and ideologues tried unsuccessfully to foist a democratic ideology on the French military. Even defeat did not change the corporate and restrictive concepts of the French military establishment. In flagrant violation of professional "responsibility" to the state, the military preferred corporatism to obedience to republican and (in their view) temporary regimes.

After suffering defeat in the Franco-Prussian War of 1870–71, the French attempted to improve the corporate structure of the army by strengthening the military establishment and emulating the Prussian general staff. But the doctrines of mass warfare and total war were more acceptable to Prussia-Germany than to France, as were the bureaucratic reforms that had strengthened and centralized the Prussian military establishment at the expense of the civilian authorities.[72] In the patrimonial Prussian political system, the powerful military machine led by the general staff could easily supplant the civilians (with the exception of Bismarck, who essentially assumed the leader's role). In the context of the legal-rational authority relations of republican France, the same pattern could not be achieved. However, Bonapartist authoritarianism and centralism modified republicanism and eventually enhanced the political influence of the professionals.

In addition, in Prussia the army, nation, and regime merged to bring about total mobilization and domination. In contrast, republican France suffered from the fact that the Jacobin nation-in-arms doctrine, the general staff concept, and the nature of representative government were irreconcilable. This conflict, however, did not prevent the enactment and implementation of military reforms, for the army and the regime respected each other's sphere of competence. The essential political interests of the regime were not involved in the organization or functioning of the army, and the military only occasionally took note of political developments under the republic, at least until the turn of the century.[73] Corporate noninterventionism prevailed during the republic with the exception of the Dreyfus period, and even then support for nonintervention was strong.

Civil-military relations in France did change somewhat with the implementation of the reforms in the 1870s and 1880s. The introduction of the general staff concepts strengthened the political authority of the high command, which had lacked a central institution, at least in a technical sense. The high command challenged the civilian government over defense policy and the conduct of war; and the army began to conceive of itself as the client of the nation. It is true that the civilian government, dominated by republican politicians who were antagonistic to the high command concept of war and society, had modified the Prussian model by curtailing the powers of the chief of the general staff and limiting his tenure. Nevertheless, because of perennial governmental changes, the tenure of the minister of war was generally shorter than that of the chief of the general staff.[74]

La Grande Muette

These structural differences and the crises of the 1880s and 1890s widened the gaps between the military and society at large (as they would again in the 1940s). Although the republicans accepted the general staff concept, inevitably an antirepublican instrument, as a necessary evil, rivalry between the army and the republic over who would represent France and its institutions threatened the delicate structure of the French polity. Despite antagonism and distrust, however, and "for all the structural and spiritual incompatibility between the Republic and the army, they managed to live together over the years between 1871 and 1914 and to evolve a satisfactory, but thoroughly pragmatic, relationship."[75]

During the Dreyfus affair the army seemed to desert its traditionally nonpolitical role and to join those who were attacking the republic, but the defection was only temporary. "In effect, the opponents of the regime seized upon an issue that directly concerned the right of the military to manage its own internal affairs and used it as a chief weapon in their campaign to overthrow the Republic." Ultimately the French antirepublican politicians failed in their efforts to recruit the military to their cause.[76]

The Prussian model was so thoroughly institutionalized by the post-Napoleonic French army that its political docility and obedience earned it the nickname "La Grande Muette" (the army of silence). "La Revanche [World War I] was a tribute to the soundness and the efficacy of the military institutions of France under the Third Republic."[77]

Because it required legitimacy, the army was reconciled to the republican regime, though not to its ideals. The civilians, for their part, wanted a better army. All were working toward La Revanche. As a result the generals' adaptations to republicanism were various and interesting, while the civilians kept a wary eye on the army but also nurtured it. During the era of political crisis and polarization that followed World War I, the military was still subservient to the civilian government. The attitude of General Maxime Weygand provides an example. He was a conservative realist who subscribed to the principles of professionalism. Although he was opposed to socialism, he supported the socialist regime of the Popular Front.[78]

The Third Republic and Vichy

The corporate tradition survived the hardships of World War I, but the confidence and exuberance of the era of La Grande Muette had disappeared. The French military was eager to adjust to the politics of peace and acquiesced to the pusillanimous civilian response to international challenge. The condition thus created is commonly called *la malaise militaire*—the dislocation of the French military establishment resulting from a reduction in the length of military service and an inadequate defense budget.[79]

Responsibility for the broad framework needed to enforce the Versailles treaty was shared by both civilian and military establishments. The tradition of La Grande Muette, however modified, prevailed, and the country's defensive posture was mirrored by the military. The professionals reinforced both the fortifications of the Maginot Line and corporate professionalism. "France's *défaillance* [exhaustion] came as a culmination of more than a decade of military and diplomatic weakness." Corporate impotence combined with political indolence brought about the strange and psychologically devastating capitulation of 1940.[80]

That defeat was catastrophic for both the French army and the republic. Yet the army supported the republic to the end and accepted the rule of Vichy, which failed in the end to sustain the army. In the best professional tradition, the army upheld the republic to defend its own corporate interest and preserve its institutional continuity. The French Armistice Army of 1940–42, approved by Hitler to guard France, attests to the remarkable resiliency of the dictum that corporate interest is identified not with the regimes of France, but with France the eternal.

The military's attitude toward the Third Republic was as lukewarm as had been its attitude toward earlier republics, or, for that matter, any of the numerous regimes France had known since 1789. When Pétain claimed that the military was not political, he implied that the military was not the guardian of democracy or the Popular Front, but of France. France was perceived by the Vichy army to be the guardian of *travail*, *famille*, and *patrie*—not *liberté*, *egalité*, and *fraternité*. The first set of values was considered by several traditionalist officers to be a guarantee of military corporatism. The military did not take the initiative in substituting traditional values for republican-democratic ones. However, when it had the opportunity to choose between regimes and remain intact, it opted to collaborate with the regime that promised to protect the old value system, which in 1940 was Vichy. The army, according to Pétain and Weygand, was therefore the essence of the country.[81]

But the military's subservience to the regimes from 1789 to 1940 had an unexpected by-product, a succession of insurrectionary officers, beginning with de Gaulle in 1940 and ending with his implacable foes on the steps of the government house in Algeria. The Hitler-Abetz plan to permit the French army to maintain its corporate autonomy and organizational integrity was a devilish creation, "one that deprived Germany of the immediate advantages of total occupation, yet provided the Nazis with countless opportunities for exploiting French weaknesses." The Armistice Army represented the mainstream of the professional tradition—gallant, obedient, politically docile, and civilian-oriented—and the enemy of this tradition was de Gaulle![82]

Military indiscipline followed La Grande Muette. The composition of the 1945 army was essentially that of the Armistice Army. Despite a purge of some 13,000 Vichy officers, the regular army prevailed over the Resistance and Gaullist divisions, demonstrating once again the superior adaptability of the professionals over the Jacobins. The upper echelons of the army of 1945 were still St. Cyrian; in fact, the 1944 Liberation army had numerous Armistice Army officers. Every chief of staff of the army and of National Defense after the war had served in the Armistice Army.[83] But the postwar army revolted. Why?

The democratization of the army after 1945 provides one reason— it became insurrectionist. The flood of new officers from the ranks, especially the sons of noncommissioned officers, precipitated the decline of St. Cyrians and Polytechniciens, the graduates of the *grandes écoles* (elite schools).[84] The resulting proletarianization of the officer corps was an important factor in the orientation of the officers toward the colonies.

Inhibited by the Vichy experience, the French officer corps in the 1950s was profoundly concerned with the colonies and France's imperial role. In fact, the officers were more deeply shocked by the crisis of decolonialization than by Vichy. "If the colonies seemed so much more vital than ever, it was in part because the American, British, and German threats to the French Empire had been so real a danger for Vichy." The example of the June 15, 1940, insurrection led by de Gaulle was the model for the military's non-Jacobin revolt of the 1950s, betraying the tradition of the proud resignation of the army of silence.[85] The bitter fruits of obedience, of corporate insularity, and of civilian domination resulted in a revolt against docile professionalism. Again, as in Prussia-Germany, the highest correlation between a professional orientation and military politicization occurred in a time of acute political crisis, exactly when professionalism was expected to hold back the flood.

Japan: Soldiers without a State

To Harold Lasswell, Japan of the 1930s was the epitome of military totalitarianism, the garrison state par excellence, the "state within the state" of the technician of violence.[86] Yet most, if not all, of the recent studies of Japan's so-called fascist and militarist epoch conclusively demonstrate both the conceptual and the empirical fallacy of the garrison-state idea when deduced from or applied to Japan. The fact is that Lasswell mistakenly identified the technician of violence as the high priest of totalitarianism. A careful analysis reveals that the grand inquisitors and villains of the garrison state were actually the civilian ideologues and demogogues, the romantic primitivists of Japan (and of Nazi Germany, for that matter).

The history of modern Japan began with two fundamental transformations: the emergence of centralized feudalism (the Tokugawa shogunate, 1600–1867) and the response to the challenge of foreign stimuli (the Meiji Restoration, 1868–1912).[87]

Hideyoshi had begun to unify Japan in the late sixteenth century, and his efforts were continued by his adopted son Ieyasu, who founded the Tokugawa shogunate in 1600. The shogun ruled through a central administration, the Bakufu, a superfeudal state. During the Tokugawa period, which was one of prolonged peace, the military class, the samurai, developed new bureaucratic, administrative, and commercial talents. The rise of *Bushido* (swordsmanship) and Confucianism and the decline of Buddhism were contemporary with monetary and administrative reforms. Urbanization, the growth of a money economy, and the rise of "Dutch" and "Portuguese" schools—in other words, the stimuli of rationalism and the Western style of administrative organization—resulted in the Meiji Restoration of 1868. The Meiji Restoration represented the end of military feudalism and the beginning of the development of a centralized, modern nation-state.

Civil-military relations after the Meiji Restoration can be explained by two related factors : (1) the unsuccessful efforts of alienated and declining segments of the samurai to re-establish themselves as the leading political elite, and (2) the failure to create a strong and centralized state. As Meiji Japan moved away from feudalism, the military class became even more alienated. Although the bulk of the Meiji modernist elite was recruited from the samurai class, the samurai traditionalists were persistently antireformist. The friction between the founders and followers of the Meiji system and their radical, rural, and xenophobic opponents ended in the 1930s in an unholy alliance between the mystical nationalists and the alienated military class, a coalition that perpetrated the calamity of the China War of 1937 and the attack on Pearl Harbor.

Emergence of an Alienated Class

The outstanding fact about Tokugawa Japan had been its inability to resist the threat of Western influence. This failure was charged against the weak military class, which was already declining in the last decades of the shogunate. Commerce thrived (although participation in it was not socially esteemed or politically rewarded) but the agricultural class ruled by the samurai lacked the impetus to reform its techniques and organization. Thus the warrior class became economically dependent, spiritless, and uninterested in reforming its own degenerate military arts. "Under the spell of urban influence they had lost their martial vigor to the pleasures of peace."[88]

It was this military class, however, which reacted first and most conspicuously to the Western challenge. What seemed a remote danger in 1830 when the West won the Chinese Opium War became a direct threat after Perry's 1853 expedition, which was designed to force open the gates of Japan to Western commerce and influence. To the material and technological challenge of the West the samurai responded vigorously by modernizing and professionalizing its military arts and techniques, including the rise of modern military academies in the middle of the nineteenth century, the acceptance of the science of ballistics and engineering, and the study of foreign languages—Dutch, Portuguese, and English.[89] The defeats of Jena and Auerstädt had stimulated the development of the modern military professional in Prussia; the challenges of the Opium War and the Perry expedition elicited the organizational, technical, and educational reforms of the samurai.

The Meiji program for modernization created the best professional military establishment in Asia. The army served as a major instrument for inculcating the national values and Meiji goals of unifying Japan and providing a powerful military force, and it was also regarded as a nation-builder. It would be anachronistic to speak of an industrial-military complex forming in Meiji Japan; however, the growth of a modern military establishment did encourage the growth of specific industries as well as expanding the role of the military interests in the regime. After the victory over China in 1895, General Yamagata, the architect of military modernization and professionalization, initiated expansion of the army and navy through military conscription, thus preparing Japan for a role as a major international power.[90]

But it is significant that while the formal education and expertise of the professional soldier improved considerably, the political and social concepts and values of the military class remained traditionalist and primitivist, as outmoded as the art of swordsmanship. Thus the samurai, the most active participants in the Restoration, which they had hoped would revive their class's martial values, were in the end excluded politically from the Meiji system. Even though most of the Meiji oligarchs were former samurai, the Restoration served largely to encourage the rising mercantile, financial, and industrial classes. "Meiji Japan generated the power to make her economy run uphill, leap unbelievable hurdles, break down centuries-old barriers, and finally arrive at self-sustained industrial growth."[91]

As the samurai originators of the Meiji regime were passed over in favor of merchants, state bureaucrats, entrepreneurs, and industrialists, the professional soldiers' loyalty to the Meiji emperor began to dwindle. The first anti-Meiji rebellion, which occurred as early as 1877, was touched off by Saigo, one of the leaders of the Meiji Restoration. The rebellion represented a protest by the tradition-loving samurai against the military reforms of the Meiji regime. Saigo, a professional soldier, defended the spirit of the samurai tradition of Japan, thus resolving the conflict in favor of traditionalism. Even so, many samurai became resentful and isolated. Economically and politically alienated, they carried antiquarian and racist values into the twentieth century. Lacking the purpose and ability to make Japan a great industrial country, they opted to build an empire, a political lebensraum in which it would no longer be alienated from the center of power.

The "Impotence" of the Meiji State

When the emperor returned to power in 1868, the shogunate was theoretically required to relinquish its political power to him, because legitimacy resided in the imperial institution. However, the Meiji Restoration demonstrates instead the introduction of Weberian traditionalist legitimization for the purpose of organizing, developing, and enhancing a modern, rational, and bureaucratic order. "Surely there is no more amazing instance in world history of the use of traditionalist means to radical ends than when the leaders of early Meiji masked the political changes which they had made with the label of an 'imperial restoration.' " While the Tokugawa concept of the emperor had been one of limitation—a passive figure whose political symbolism masked his impotence—Meiji loyalists symbolically assigned him political power. The *exercise* of that power, however, was entrusted to other agencies, the Genro (an informal group), the cabinet, and the Meiji oligarchs.[92]

To the Meiji oligarchs, harmony between the throne and government was a matter of natural law. The emperor's restoration settled the matter of legitimacy; clearly it rested with the throne. But "if the emperors of late nineteenth and early twentieth century Japan were not merely figureheads, neither were they the actual rulers of the country." The Meiji oligarchs left the question of who was to rule on behalf of imperial authority unanswered.

The Meiji's twentieth-century successors did not accept their organic concept of political behavior. Neither did extreme nationalists, rural radicals, and the alienated military establishment of the late nineteenth century. "The Imperial will then cease to mean merely the ethical axioms of traditional Japanese society, but took on the new meaning of the expressed decisions of the emperor's government," and the nationalists, radicals, and the army dedicated themselves to restoring historical Japanese mores. Also, even if the orthodox Meiji group had wanted to relegate the emperor to symbolic authority, they would have had to contend with the twentieth-century nationalists. This group, bred in the 1920s, raising a challenge in the 1930s, and coming to power between 1937 and 1945 would insist upon one fundamental difference: they, not the Meiji oligarchs, should represent and defend the legitimacy of imperial rule.[93]

Thus the contest for power between the Genro, cabinet, and Meiji successors, on the one hand, and the extreme nationalists, on the other, was essentially a debate over who represented legitimacy. The nationalistic military radicals and their cohorts challenged the government on behalf of the throne—the symbol of Japan, according to all Japanese theorists—seeking to defend it against the disloyal, and thus illegitimate, modernist state. Here the concept of clientship was clearly in question. The client of the military radical (who was a professional soldier) was the emperor as the defender of traditional Japan. The soldier could no longer defend the government and the state, because they were betraying Japanese values. The military, therefore, was prepared to overthrow the "Westernizers" on the emperor's behalf.

Professional Soldiers as Xenophobes and Radicals

National security and the definition of national objectives became primary concerns of Japanese foreign policy in the 1930s. The dynamics of putting into operation a radical security policy gradually became the business of the military, which conceived of itself as the protector of Meiji legitimacy, imperial grandeur, and national defense.[94] To consolidate the empire, according to the army, was to pursue a "Chinese" policy, which involved gaining supremacy in northern China and Manchuria and instituting a planned economy at home. Thus would come into being a Japanese-dominated East Asian sphere of prosperity.

It was significant that the interests of Japanese national security converged with the cause of the alienated military class, for national security concerned the Meiji oligarchs only to the extent that it buttressed the Restoration regime. Certainly there were imperialistic oligarchs, but in their view it was not up to the military to define Japan's national security. The military, on the other hand, challenged the regime's attempt to dominate the army and to formulate foreign policy. This conflict took place after the decline of the traditional political elite and founding fathers' group, the Genro and the party leaders, when the professional officer class set out to become the new and legitimate heirs to state authority.

In the officers' view, their own concept of corporate responsibility did not violate the military professional rule of nonintervention. The officers did not challenge the Meiji doctrine that legitimacy symbolically resided in the emperor. On the contrary, the army's reason for intervention was to defeat the political forces that no longer "protected" the emperor. Intervention thus was actually seen as a corporate duty of patriotic military groups.

This attitude was not peculiar to the military in the 1930s. Nationalists, romantics, bureaucrats, and politicians were also searching for a new definition of Japanese national security. In some ways the extreme nationalists among the civilians were more militant than the military in their desire to protect the legitimacy of the emperor against the politicians. The officers considered themselves to be restorers of imperial grandeur rather than insurrectionists. They saw themselves as the loyal servants of a legitimate and sustaining imperial order. The military (including the officers), however, fell into two groups; one supported a national security policy on behalf of legitimacy and the other challenged the political system because it was an alienated class.

Yet the insurrections of 1931, 1932, 1936, 1937, and 1941 succeeded not because the romantic anti-Meiji primitivists and the alienated class won out, but because they finally succeeded in challenging the political system and twisting the military idea of national security to coincide with the military concept of national security. The military triumphed also when the Genro, the cabinet, and especially the army came to be dominated by militant imperialists. It has been observed that the primacy of the war minister and the cabinet contributed to Taisho democracy, the era of party government in the 1920s. It could equally truthfully be said that when the war ministry and the cabinet were taken over by the military, the result was an imperialist Japan.[95]

The Japanese army, operating under a misguided concept of client-ship, also violated another condition of professionalism—expertise. First, although admission to the academy in the 1880s was supposed to have been based on achievement and competitive exams, members of the traditionally military *hans* (tribes), the Choshu and the Satsuma, were given preference. Second, the ethics of the warrior, the cult of Bushido, was taught as a basic skill after cadres had been admitted on the basis of other value-oriented exams. Third, two different career patterns developed, one for the graduates of the academy and one for graduates of the war college, a small group composed primarily of Satsuma and Choshu officers destined for the high command.[96]

It was not the traditional martial values that made the Japanese army powerful, however, but its militance. In the 1930s Japan's foreign and security policies were the outgrowth of three factors: (1) her changing diplomatic relations with the West; (2) factional conflict over the interpretation of national defense; and (3) struggles among the foreign, war, and naval ministries over the proper objectives of foreign policy. Because Japan's attempt at peaceful expansion, "economic diplomacy," had failed in the 1920s, the pursuit of co-prosperity goals had been turned over to the military. "Militarism triumphed not as a goal but as a means for obtaining the same ends which the diplomacy of the preceding era [the 1920s] had unsuccessfully sought."[97] The degree of civilian control in the 1920s depended upon the extent of cabinet dominance over the political system. "The right of supreme command," promulgated by the cabinet in 1930 and mainly directed against militant nationalists, did preserve for a while civilian supremacy over the military.

The military violated yet another principle of military professionalism, corporate autonomy, in the 1930s. Political intrigues on the part of the field armies, especially the Kwantung army in northern China, succeeded in frustrating the efforts of the military in the foreign office to come to terms with Chiang Kai-shek.[98] The violent struggles between agrarian radicals and other militants also blurred the line between the military and the civilian. The persistence of fascist and fundamentalist ideologues further politicized the army and was a necessary factor in propelling Japan along a militarist course.

Japan was brought to the brink of praetorianism when the state, the society, and the forces of ideology all converged in support of expansionism. The road to militarism was not paved by the army alone, even if it eventually did play a prominent role in subverting the civilian system. Military *pronunciamientos*, far from being autonomous military creations, resulted from the connivance of a number of groups under the influence of a militant weltanschauung.

The formulation of a militant national security policy could not end in the surrendering of political power to the military. Once the officers violated the professional dictum of civilian control, they, like their German counterparts, brought disaster on both their nation and on their own institution. Once again the demise of the cardinal principle of professionalism—nonintervention—coincided with the disastrous end of military corporatism.

The USSR: The Quest for Corporate Autonomy

The Soviet case represents an extreme example of the subjective civilian control model. "Subjective civilian control achieves its end by civilianizing the military, making them the mirror of the state . . . the essence of subjective civilian control is the *denial* of an independent military sphere."[99]

An analysis of civil-military relations in the USSR from Lenin to Brezhnev reveals that the major characteristics of the Red Army are (1) its permanent harness to the party; (2) the permanent political threat by the party to its professional authority; (3) the cycle of development from autonomous leadership in professional military affairs to corporate servility and back to autonomy; and (4) the permanent insecurity and the bitter and unequal rivalry (personal, professional, and political) between the military and the party.[100]

An unsatisfactory and uneasy equilibrium between the party and the military has existed throughout the turbulent half century of Bolshevik ascendancy. At no time would it have been safe to conclude that the conflict between the totalitarian single party system and its huge military establishment could be objectively resolved. "On the one hand they [the party] pursue an ambitious foreign policy, predicated to a large extent on the continued viability of a powerful military capability, and invest a substantial share of their GNP, and large numbers of scarce scientific and technical personnel, in the development and maintenance of this military juggernaut. On the other hand, the Party antagonizes the military leadership and burdens a modern war machine with the archaic impediment of a political control system."[101]

The rivalry and unequal relationships between party and army stem directly from the nature of the Leninist-Stalinist model of the state, society, and regime, which is based on the supremacy of the Bolshevik party of the proletariat, the vanguard of the revolution. According to an extreme interpretation, all other groups, social classes, and organizations are excluded from political power. They are viewed with suspicion, periodically checked, and constantly harassed. If it appears necessary, they are reformed and integrated or, if this fails, annihilated, so that there will be no potential or actual threat to the political supremacy of the party. By the middle 1970s, however, evolution of the Bolshevik model and the trauma of transfer of political power and leadership and of institutional transformation had deeply affected party-army relationships.[102]

The party has become a powerful and complex state bureaucracy, and any challenge to its political autonomy is dealt with severely. Its most serious potential challenger is the military establishment, which, according to Bolshevik doctrines and perceived national interest, must be kept large and aggressive. Military aggrandizement has aways been a goal of the Soviet state, whether it is dedicated to world revolution, as it was in Lenin's time, or to international stability and détente, as in the 1970s, when it had attained global parity with the United States.

The Red Army was the first instrument of the Soviet political system to become professional, modern, and apolitical (in terms of Bolshevik dogma). This was not achieved without bitter political infighting and conflicts between the Red Army and the party, and there were brutal interruptions of the process. The claims of professional autonomy were challenged without mercy by an elaborate network of political controls established by the party to ensure its mastery. Nevertheless, the Red Army developed into a professional military establishment that was essentially apolitical but did not totally lack political ambition. From the outset, in fact, the Red Army had to face a choice between military professionalism and revolution.[103]

The Red Army was created at the end of World War I, out of the demobilizing Czarist army. The new army, forced to organize quickly to fight a bitter and bloody civil war, was initially short of leadership, resources, and drive. Furthermore, the Bolshevik revolutionaries who founded the Soviet state envisaged their army as fundamentally different from bourgeois armies. Trotsky and his colleagues attempted to achieve a combination of the army of the Paris Commune and the Jauresian New Army (L'Armée Nouvelle), derived from Engels and earlier socialist writers. It is not illogical to argue that Trotsky, the most brilliant of the Bolsheviks, who served as commissar of war during the War for Communism (1918–20), was the Scharnhorst of the Red Army. Trotsky mobilized resources, restored morale, recruited skilled officers, and charged the army with drive and determination. His orchestration of the Red Army helped lead it to victory and shaped its institutions for the next several decades.[104]

To keep the Red Army under civilian control required its total loyalty. As it happened, the military establishment never did challange civilian rule nor the legitimacy of the party. The party and the army did carry on a running battle concerning Bolshevik orientations and attitudes toward the army, however. Clearly, although the Bolsheviks required a massive army to carry out their aims, a large, reformed, and professionalized military establishment constituted a threat to party control.

Conflict over Orientation

Acknowledged political control over the military was a cardinal principle of the Leninist party and state. Although the party was (and still is) suspicious of the army, no Bolshevik inside or outside the military establishment even entertained the idea of military supremacy over the party. Czarist and Bolshevik reactions to Bonapartism produced a special antipathy toward the military in Russia. As perceived by the Czarists, Bonapartism was a revolutionary-imperialistic military regime that had threatened the Russian regime's legitimacy. To the revolutionaries, Napoleon's career signified the revolution betrayed. Furthermore, they

saw the Napoleonic type of army, a conservative corporate and autonomous professional army, as a counterrevolutionary military challenge
to Bolshevism. Thus, curiously, Bonapartism's legacy set the stage for
the evolution of subjective civilian control in Russia.[105]

The men who brought about the October Revolution accepted only
one source of legitimacy—the party—as the fountainhead for ideas,
leadership, and structural arrangements. Within the army, political
control was maintained at the expense of corporate professionalism. The
military was subjected to commissars and apparatchiks (Communist
party agents), yet it was expected to maintain an objective professional
stance. Between 1918 and 1920 the conflict between the two elements of
the army, the Red Guard and the professional soldiers (mostly former
Czarist officers, called "military experts") was fierce, but under Trotsky
the army weathered the storm of war, revolution, and Communist
peace. All this, however, took its toll. The Bolsheviks on the whole had
had an unpleasant experience with the military during the civil war.
The distrust felt by the "experts" (Czarist officers) for the Bolsheviks
was compounded by acts of betrayal and the defection of considerable
numbers of Red Army officers to the Whites. In fact, the suspicion
with which Stalin and the other Bolsheviks dealt with the Red Army
originated at least in part in civil war experiences.

The pattern of army-party relations has since become fixed: intraparty rivalries invariably affected the army. But political control of the
army did not turn the officers into interventionists, because the party,
as the stronger of the two, succeeded in programming the military for
absolute subservience to party interests.[106] It balanced military experts
with the Red Guard and fenced off the clique led by Stalin and Voroshilov; it established a coherent policy of centralization and trained a
hard-core military elite that was imbued with Bolshevik ideas but
professionally oriented and politically subordinate. The commissar
system, supposedly an instrument for the inculcation of Bolshevik virtue
and socialist morale, was actually a political weapon to police the army
professionals and to eliminate potential "Bonapartists." Although
Trotsky was accused of building a potential Bonapartist (conservative-
professional) military establishment, in the end he was ousted not
because of the conflict over the structure and composition of the Red
Army and its high command—brutal though that struggle was—but
because he lost the titanic power struggle over who would inherit

Lenin's control of the party. Here the military, along with other structures of the state, was sacrificed to Bolshevik power machinations.

These bitter struggles within the party (only dimly reflected in the army) took place in the 1930s, when the Red Army, aided by the Germans, had already begun to mechanize and professionalize. Modernization triggered serious debates over the highly explosive questions of military strategy and power in the Soviet state. The first modernizer of the Red Army, Mikhail Frunze, and his assistant A.S. Busev insisted on the principle of Communist internationalism, which dictated an aggressive and elaborate military machine. But the Stalinist doctrine of socialism in one country could not tolerate the offensive views advocated by Marshal Mikhail N. Tukhachevsky, the most brilliant Soviet marshal of the 1930s and undoubtedly the most impressive figure in the Red Army after Trotsky. The debates about strategy in that decade were symptomatic of the political tension within the party. Party-army relationships in Stalin's time reflected the essential incompatibility and conflict between military professionals and political apparatchiks[107] and Stalin systematically used terror and recurrent purges of the officer corps in his efforts to eliminate all opposition.

Although the 1937–38 army purge took place several years after the party purge trials following the expulsion of Trotsky and Bukharin, it was equally brutal. Some 30 percent (over 30,000) of the officer corps, from the high command to battalion level, were destroyed. The military craved corporate autonomy, a natural consequence of its professionalization. This desire touched off the action by Stalin, who, after using the military for his purposes of industrialization and modernization, decided he should "curtail" the army's role expansion. "The sacrifice of a command was worth . . . [national] security. . . . Since its early days, the Soviet regime had been forced to balance political reliability and military efficiency most precariously."[108]

From Subordination to Accommodation

According to Kolkowicz, Soviet civil-military relations were shaped by several important systemic, structural, and ideological factors, including: (1) the hegemony of the party, (2) the absence of formal constitutional-legal and traditional provisions for the transfer of power; (3) the presence of powerful security organs within and around the military, including countervailing paramilitary organizations of proven loyalty to the party; and (4) the antimilitaristic tradition of Marxism-Leninism.

Kolkowicz divided the evolution of civil-military relations in the USSR into three phases: (1) Stalinist subordination (1930s to 1950s); (2) Khrushchev's co-optation (1960s); (3) Brezhnev's accommodation (1970s).

The transformation from subordination to accommodation was accompanied by the decay of the totalitarian model, intensive economic development, the substitution of collective leadership for single-person rule, the dismantling of the terror machine, and new global foreign and military policies. Internally quiescent, the military nevertheless became a unified and modernized force, enjoying an autonomy it had never possessed under Stalin.[109]

Autonomy and Political Influence

After the death of Stalin a remarkable revolution occurred in the Soviet military establishment that eventually led to the reshaping of the command structure between 1965 and 1970. The modernization, technocratization, and rejuvenation of that institution gave the Red Army a new dimension.

Khrushchev's "new outlook" policy, followed by Brezhnev's globalism, led the USSR to take a militant imperialistic course in world affairs that Stalin had considered but never embarked upon. The Soviet officer was caught by the technological-strategic revolution. Soviet weltpolitik required the modernization and role expansion of the army, an increase in its status, and the rejuvenation of its officer corps. Between 1958 and 1960, 250,000 officers were forced out and 454 were promoted to the rank of general. This metamorphosis was designed to complement the new "mixed strategy" (nuclear and conventional), which called for a strategic missile command and thus brought engineers and technocrats into the officer corps. The reorganized high command assumed control of appointment and promotion. It also asserted centralized power over the military districts and gained control of the ministry of defense.[110] Thus the high command and the senior officers gained an influence over foreign and security policy that had not been enjoyed by any structure (with the possible exception of the state security police) in the politburo since the death of Lenin.

The institutional expansion of the defense functions, the technological and strategic revolutions, and the growing political autonomy of the highest structures of the military establishment indicate the enormous influence that the military has wielded in policy making. In fact, the "democratization" of the organizational structure of the military and its "civilianization" (making it the partner of the state instead of keeping it in a separate sphere) have enhanced the military's political influence. Civilian-military conflicts are no longer controversies between the "authoritarian" military and the "democratic" civilian institutions, but over ideology, political expectations, and national security. The military's growing role in the policy making of modern warfare have made it a very valuable ally for military-oriented civilians and an influential political elite in the new post-Stalinist collegial politburo.

Although it is like the American military in its orientation toward national security policy, the Soviet military is still the product of Stalinism. The military, in fact, has contributed significantly to the unpredictable actions of the present Soviet political elite. They played a considerable part in the policy making that led to Russia's 1967 Middle East fiasco, to the invasion of Czechoslovakia in 1968, to the missile build-up in Egypt in 1970, to the stationing of a huge Soviet army on the Chinese border, and, above all, to the arms race.

Using concern for strategic considerations as a disguise, the military technocrat supports simultaneously both professional superiority and the use of force and political intervention in foreign countries. Thus leaders divided on the question of strategy in world politics can (and do) ally with technocrats whose advice supports their strategic and political goals. Political leaders in the USSR (and in the United States) make extensive use of military allies whose professional advice may tip the balance in their favor. Thus the technocrat, either directly or indirectly, achieves what the traditional professional failed to attain in the first half-century of civil-military relations in the USSR—corporate autonomy and political influence.

The concept of responsibility helps to explain the orientation toward civilian control and professional autonomy in Germany, France, and Japan, but it does not aid in understanding the situation in the USSR, where party domination has curtailed the professional autonomy of the army. Yet civilian control encouraged the rise of loyalist professionals. Both Stalin and Khrushchev were aided in their rise to power by a group of officers associated with a battle over Stalingrad. Stalin was aided by three generals—Voroshilov, Gusev, and Kirov—who defended Tsaritsyn (later Stalingrad) in October 1918. Khrushchev was helped by generals who had distinguished themselves in the 1942 Stalingrad campaign—Marshals Konev and Vatutin, Malinovsky and Grechko (who later became defense ministers), and Zakharov (who became deputy defense minister).[111] The careers of members of the Soviet high command from Frunze through Tukhachevsky, Shaposhnikov, and the Stalingrad group demonstrate clearly the crucial role played by loyalists in buttressing the Bolshevik concept of military subordination. In the Bolshevik one-party model, loyalist cliques and coteries can act as liaison, intermediary, and support groups for the regime in the army and the bureaucracy.

"Both Stalin and Khrushchev were substantially aided in their rise to power by the support of personal followers in the military, and both used their Trojan horses to control the military." In 1970 Brezhnev's rise to power had similar support, except that professionalism played a key role; Brezhnev's allies were the products of the technological revolution. As a result of traditional, personalist (loyalist) practices, responsibility to the state has been confused with responsibility to the party secretary. In a way, the confusion is also a defense mechanism, a protective device by which the army can assure the party leader(s) of political loyalty without relinquishing professional practices. It is interesting to observe that the professionals resent the limited definition of clientship (under which they may be replaced by "politicals" in crisis situations, as when Malinovsky replaced Zhukov)[112] because the broadest interpretation gives them greater corporate autonomy. Once more the professional ethic and the bureaucratic responsibility of the military establishment are linked.

The system of party control assures the cooperation of loyalists and potential loyalists. For instance, during the defense of Tsaritsyn Stalin exploited the field commanders' dislike for Trotsky and his methods. The political supervisors of the military in two world wars became prominent in the Soviet hierarchy: Voroshilov and Budenny in World War I, Zhdanov and Bulganin in World War II. During World War II, Khrushchev, as a member of Stavka (Supreme Command Headquarters) and a political supervisor, became acquainted with many senior officers, which placed him "in the highly advantageous position of an intermediary between Moscow and the field commanders."[113] Two chief "tamers" of the military, Stalin and Khrushchev, became heads of state and dictators. Brezhnev shows signs of following in their footsteps.

Both the civil war and World War II had a traumatic impact on the Soviet political system, increasing its dependence on the military establishment. Yet the resiliency of the party, the effectiveness of its secret police control mechanism, and its organizational flexibility outweighed the strengths of the military organization, which was shorn of the glories it had won in battle and its best commanders and deprived of the use of a secret police and of ideological legitimacy. Nevertheless, despite the suppression of its institutional values, corporate autonomy, and professional needs, the military establishment has asserted itself more effectively than any other institutional, bureaucratic, or social group in the Soviet system. To deter military professional "separatist" practices, the political integration of the army, and especially of its "free" technocrats, has been imperative.[114] However, the gap between a military stressing professional excellence and a traditionally oriented party, clinging to anachronistic Bolshevik neo-Stalinist principles, is as great in the middle 1970s as it was in the 1920s. Not until the party is truly reformed or a two-party system established will this tension cease. And then, what would stop the military from becoming the predominant force in the party government?

The nature of civil-military relations in the USSR springs from the complexity of the Soviet political, economic, and social system—the party-dominated state—and the distrust of one another generated during the Civil War and World War II. As long as the party dominates, subjective political control over the military is guaranteed. The collapse of the party as the single authoritative political structure of the USSR could change the relationship between the party and the army. Such a shift might be due to either a political struggle within the collective leadership or resentment against the return of a one-man dictatorship (or, although it is very unlikely, to some internal upheaval). The Communist party in the post-Stalinist age has lost its ideological fervor and thus some of its legitimacy. It rules only by virtue of a highly institutionalized social system and a working internal control system. The lessons of Stalin and Khrushchev have apparently permeated the collective leadership since 1965. In addition, the leadership has demonstrated its capacity to absorb the pressure of modernization and growth at home. On the other hand, it has been engaged in a program of militarization and armament coupled with an imperialist foreign policy in the Middle East and the Indian Ocean. Its ruthless suppression of Czech liberal

communism and its aggressive stance toward China have also strengthened considerably the militaristic group in the party (though not necessarily in the army).

In the future, a disaster in foreign and security policy could trigger
the formation of an alliance between civilian and military members of
the politburo and could also lead the USSR toward praetorianism. Such
an event would introduce a totally new relationship between the party
and the army. It could strengthen the leaders of the military, who under
a praetorian rule could finally achieve complete corporate autonomy.
A praetorian army could act as a buffer against a potential militaristic
alliance between civilian and military members of the politburo. It
could also serve as a pressure group, which, through tacit bargaining
(using its potential to intervene as a bargaining point), could tame a
militaristic oligarchy. Another option is military corporate "liberation,"
and the military's integration into the party as its most powerful or veto
elite. In any case, in the absence of Leninist legitimacy and Stalinist
brutality, a future conflict between a single-party system and a huge
military organization may not be resolved without violence, although it
is not a very likely option.

Institutional security depends on stable order and legitimacy, derived
from normative compliance. Not until the problems of legitimacy are
settled and the transfer of power is institutionalized in the Soviet system
can institutional autonomy be achieved for the military or any other
group except the fountainhead of legitimacy—the party.

These four examples of modern civil-military relations have included
three European powers and one Asian power as well as three autocracies
and one democracy. The first nation (Prussia-Germany) moved along a
continuum from aristocratic autocracy to popular tyranny. The second
(France) swung from revoluntionary Jacobinism and democratic-re-
publicanism to Vichy etatism. The third (Japan) evolved from patrimonial to oligarchic autocracy. The last (USSR) changed from monarchical to Stalinist tyranny, and in the middle 1970s it still has a one-
party Bolshevik system. All four nations were or are great powers and
their military establishments were or are among the most professionally
skilled, obedient, powerful, and sizable of all times.

Analysis of the four political systems points to the following general
conclusions: (1) Like all modern, rational, bureaucratic groups, the
military behaves like a corporate group. (2) Professional proficiency is
not necessarily correlated with nor does it guarantee a regime's objec-

tive control. (3) Corporate integrity, not ideology, accounts for the officers' loyalty to the principle of clientship. (4) Like other organized groups in society, different officer groups espouse different ideologies. (5) Although a few prominent officers may prefer one type of regime, at different times they may uphold conflicting types of regimes. (6) Although the officer group as a corporate entity is politically conservative, with most officers preferring a traditional regime, it can adjust to radical regimes in order to protect its corporate integrity. (7) Military corporatism is Janus-faced; instability invites the military to abandon its clientship responsibility and intervene. Intervention bolsters the solidarity of the military as a corporate group. The officer is always responsible to the state (the threatened client) but not to its regimes. (8) If the military becomes interventionist under an unstable regime, it will ultimately lose its autonomy, its corporate integrity, and perhaps even its client—the nation.

These four cases demonstrate the delicate and complex nature of the relationship between independent regimes and autonomous military establishments. In all four states the military was the chief instrument of territorial and political expansion. As empire-builders they constantly challenged civilian control. Obsessed with the desire for corporate integrity, some of them violated the iron law of civilian control—the principle of obedience. Yet in each case, with the exception of France, autocratic civilian control prevailed at the expense of the integrity of the military establishment.

Table 3.1 Types of Professional Orientations, Changes over Time (Approximate) in Europe, 1800–1958

	Corporate Noninterventionist	Corporate Interventionist	Revolutionary	Routinized Revolutionary
Prussia-Germany	1820–60 1914–16 1924–28 1933–44	1860–70 1890–1914 1916–18 1929–33 1944–45	1806–08	1809–20
France	1799–1870 1940–42 1946–52	1870–85 1939–40 1953–58	1789–99	1799–1805
USSR	1920–		1917–18	1918–20
Japan	1867–77 1878–1930	1877 1930–45		

Part II

The Praetorian Soldier

The philosophy of the revolution's purpose is like that of a patrol. To patrol is the true purpose of the [Egyptian military] in the annals of Egypt. . . . We now are to fight the greatest of our wars: the liberation of our fatherland from all its chains.

Gamal Abdel Nasser, *Falsafat al Thawra*
(*The philosophy of the revolution*), translated by Amos Perlmutter

4

The Praetorian Army and the Praetorian State

Considered a deviant phenomenon before 1945, instances in which the military played an increasingly active role in politics became widespread after World War II. An army-dominated government was considered unnatural not because it was perceived as a new phenomenon— it had been recognized by political philosophers from Machiavelli to Mosca—but because some social scientists did not believe military rule was as worthy of study as civilian rule. This prejudice had a variety of causes, ranging from ignorance to antagonism toward war and the military profession. In the 1930s, for example, military government was identified as the ultimate type of totalitarianism.[1]

In the nineteenth and twentieth centuries military political interventionism was prevalent. Coups and countercoups occurred in all Latin American republics, in most independent Arab states, in most African states, in several Southeast Asian polities, in Pakistan, and in Greece and Portugal. These events confirm the historical and political fact that when civilian government is neither effective nor institutionalized the executive is unable to control the military. The collapse of executive power is a precondition for praetorianism. Under praetorian conditions, many civil-military combinations become possible: the army can take over the government with or without the consent of civilian politicians, on their behalf or against them, with the aim of replacing one civilian group with another or with the aim of eliminating rivals in the military.

Frederick Mundell Watkins's classic definition of praetorianism appeared in the 1933 edition of the *Encyclopedia of the Social Sciences*: "Praetorianism is a word frequently used to characterize a situation where the military class of a given society exercises independent political power within it by virtue of an actual or threatened use of force." There is an essential distinction between historical and modern praetorianism.

89

Historical Praetorianism

The Roman Praetorian Guard, the prototype of historical praetorianism, was a small military contingent in the imperial capital that preserved the legitimacy of the empire by defending the Senate against rebellious military garrisons. The influence of the Roman Praetorian Guard was based on three factors: its monopoly of local military power, the absence of definitive rules of succession, and the prestige of the Roman Senate. Though there was no hard and fast rule concerning selection of the princeps, the Senate's decree made him a legitimate ruler acceptable to the provincial armies; and the Praetorian Guard, the sole resident military force, was able to impose its candidate upon the Senate. Thus it was able to manipulate a widely subscribed concept of legitimacy and to attain a degree of political influence disproportionate to its size and military resources. Only when the provincial armies stumbled upon the secret that emperors need not be made in Rome did the legitimizing powers of the Senate as well as the strength of the Praetorians disappear.[2]

Patrimonialism and Praetorianism in Advanced Agricultural Societies

In Weberian theory, praetorianism is defined as domination by *honoratiores* (honorable men, noblemen). It is a type of authority exercised in the manorial or patrimonial group (a more advanced unit than the patriarchal household, which is a relatively small unit based on blood ties). Patrimonialism is manifested in the decentralization of the patriarchal household and the extension of landholding, empire building, and "extrapatrimonial" recruitment (that is, recruitment not based on kinship). In this prebureaucratic political system, the ruler's staff is recruited only to ensure subordination to patriarchal rule, extended in "extrapatrimonial" recruitment to relations based on feudal, bureaucratic, or merely personal rulership. In patrimonialism, as in the patriarchal system, dependent relationships are based on loyalty and fidelity. The chief obligation of the subject is the material maintenance of the ruler. Patrimonial conditions give rise to political domination, for both the military and judicial authorities "are exercised without any restraint by the master as components of his patrimonial power."[3]

Whereas military authority and security arrangements are on an ad hoc basis in patriarchal types of domination, in a patrimonial state the military becomes a permanent establishment as the process of financial rationalization develops. Among the most important tributes which the patrimonial ruler extracts from his subjects are provision of troops or taxes to pay for mercenaries. Patrimonial states have recruited from the following sources: patrimonial slaves, retainers living on allowances (the *coloni* type); slaves completely separated from agricultural production; janissaries and mercenaries, supported by levies from the population but recruited from alien tribes or religious groups (Bedouins, Christians); or manorial peasants substituting military for economic service.[4]

The relationship between the patrimon and his conscripts has two pure forms, clientship and slavery, and various combinations. In the Ottoman Empire, for example, janissaries were recruited from aliens and pariah castes (Druze, 'Alawi, Kurds), while a "citizen" army was recruited from the peasants. The feudal armies of Western Europe, as an outgrowth of increased economic rationalism (with its need for organization, accounting, and planning), developed a group of privileged honoratiores, using peasant soldiers and military technology. As training became crucial, however, the relationship between patrimonial authority and the military was altered. The patrician no longer handled military affairs directly. With the development of military professionalization, it became possible for the military establishment to be used against the patrimonial authority's own political subjects. If a patrimon's political authority rested solely on threats—on the army or "coercive compliance"—his power to dominate might collapse. The Weberian term for the disintegration of the patrimonial system was "Sultanism"; its modern equivalent in social science theory is praetorianism.[5]

Patrimonial power was particularly susceptible to military domination in advanced agrarian societies (historical bureaucratic empires) that had large mercenary armies. "Native or foreign, once regularly organized mercenaries have become the preponderant force in a country, they have normally tried to force their rule upon the rest of society." If the military was not subdued, it became institutionalized as an autonomous group, and with every gain in professionalism its political importance increased. Then when legitimate authority faltered, the military could supplant it and fill the gap. For example, in the Ottoman Empire, the ruling institution became identical with the army during and after the reign of Suleiman the Magnificent in the sixteenth century; the janissaries remained the chief instrument of the sultan until 1827. Gradually they became a formidable and complex bureaucracy, and the introduction of firearms and cavalry increased their effectiveness. As praetorian values were routinized in the new technical units, they ensured the cohesiveness and political loyalty of all branches of the janissaries, the upholders of legitimacy.[6]

The Imperial-Colonial Legacies

In the European colonies during the nineteenth and twentieth centuries, the military was specifically oriented toward external conquest and dominance. External domination provided a vocational ideal, which was expressed in such organizations as the civil and military services in British India, the French Foreign Legion, the French Equatorial Army (the "Africans"), and the Spanish army in Morocco and South America. The values of the system were embodied in "civilization française," Kipling's "white man's burden," and the missionary zeal of General Lyautey (a military administrator of French Africa). The concept of "civilization française" was developed by the military who administered and in fact dominated French imperial policy in Africa and who were dedicated to the expansion of the empire.[7] The mission-oriented military was prone to become interventionist, particularly in the French and Spanish colonies.

This military type represented "the extreme in separation between a military organization and its supporting society." The basis of recruitment was particularistic: the aristocracy served as officers and the minorities as common soldiers. "Officers regard[ed] themselves as agents of a spiritual force, civilization, and view[ed] their service as a mission as well as a profession."[8] Soldiers were recruited from the imperial power's periphery or from the "native" population of the colonies, a procedure that was designed to safeguard imperial rule and loyalty. These natives were generally drawn from ethnic, cultural, and religious minorities (Druze, 'Alawi, and Kurd in the Arab East; Ghurka and Goumi in India; non-Moslems and members of small tribes in French Equatorial Africa). The imperial officer, who was expected to be a model for his colonial subordinate, might gain the reward of political domination through his subordinate capacity for leadership. For the colonizer (the imperial officer), soldiering and service in the empire were either the crucial test of an aristocrat or rungs on the climb up the social ladder for the middle class. The imperial officer was slavishly emulated by his subordinates and this model had considerable influence on modern Arab and African praetorians.

MODERN PRAETORIANISM

In developing polities the military functions somewhat as it did in the patrimonial states, serving as a center for political turmoil, political ambition, and threats to legitimate authority. But modern praetorianism differs from the patrimonial model in two respects. First, the patrimonial military represented and defended legitimacy, but the modern military *challenges* legitimacy and offers a new type of authority.[9] Second (though less important), in historical praetorianism the authority relationship between the military establishment and political order is based on a traditional orientation, but in modern praetorianism authority relationships are based on a legal-rational orientation.[10] Modern praetorianism is the praetorianism of the professional soldier.

A modern praetorian state is one in which the military tends to intervene in the government and has the potential to dominate the executive. Among its characteristics are an ineffective executive and political decay.

The political processes of the praetorian state favor the development of the military as the core group and encourage the growth of its expectations as a ruling class. The political leadership of the state (as distinguished from its bureaucratic, administrative, and managerial leadership) is chiefly recruited from the military or from groups sympathetic to it. Constitutional changes are effected and sustained by the military, which plays a dominant role in all political institutions.

A modern praetorian government is most likely to develop when civilian institutions lack legitimacy; that is, they lack electoral support and effective executive power.* Such governments have often arisen from the ashes of weak republics. The most conspicuous examples have been the nineteenth-century nationalist polities in Spain and Latin America. Spain was the best model of praetorianism in the nineteenth century. Its regime was the handiwork of disgruntled civilians and power-seeking politicians, all groping for ways to dominate central political power. Lacking popular support, liberal and progressive politicians viewed the army as a vehicle of hope and liberation, the

---

*Above all, in illegitimate regimes belief in the stability, credibility, or effectiveness of established authority is lacking. In the Weberian sense, illegitimacy is lack of orientation toward authority. In modern praetorian regimes, the incumbent authorities do not derive their power simply from constitutional and fundamental laws, as Weber would have it. Rather, legitimacy is both a principle of authority and the orientation toward securing political electoral support. Thus, the praetorian condition is identified with the absence of electoral and political support procedures necessary for the establishment of authority.

instrument for gaining power and establishing an effective executive. In seeking military support, however, they threatened the very constitutional and political practices to which they were dedicated. Furthermore, when army officers entered politics, they adopted political behavior (that is, they aspired to rule) thus gradually losing their hold over the army. Their strength was challenged by rivals within the military: professionally oriented officers dedicated to the separation of the military and political spheres; politically oriented officers dissatisfied with their own lack of power or status; a branch, section, or service discontented with its position within the military; or peripheral and fratricidal elements. Officers turned politician were also hurt by the civilian government's failure to supply generals with armies, by soldiers' revolts, or by defeat in war.

In the twentieth century a developing country is ripe for praetorianism when the civilian government fails in its pursuit of such nationalist goals as unification, order, modernization, and urbanization. Various types of praetorianism probably represent specific stages of development. By the 1970s, for example, praetorianism often appeared in states that were in the early and middle stages of modernization and political mobilization.[11] Generally the army is propelled into political action in underdeveloped states when civilian political groups fail to legitimize themselves. The army's presence in civilian affairs is often an indicator of the existence of a corruption that is not expected to disappear in the near future. Modern praetorians are most likely to specify the "betrayal" and "corruption" of civilian politicians, parties, and parliaments as the reason for military intervention. Gamal Abdel Nasser, for instance, stated that the army must patrol society and that military rule is rule by order, shorn of "complicating" (that is independent) political structures and institutions. On the other hand, military intervention may occur when a state's material improvements are not appropriate to its corporate perspectives or when traditional institutions have been unable to produce such gains. Or it may be that, because of the traditional orientation of the people, modernized elites have proved incapable of establishing political institutions that would sustain the momentum of social mobilization and modernization.[12] Whatever the cause, in the ensuing disorganization both economy and ideology suffer setbacks.

TYPES OF MODERN MILITARY PRAETORIANISM

There are three forms (or subtypes) of military praetorianism: autocracy, oligarchy, and authoritarian praetorianism. Autocracy is a simple military tyranny, military rule by one man. In this system, unchecked personal authority is embodied in the single supreme ruler. The second subtype, military oligarchy, is government by the few. The executive is composed primarily of military men. The only intrinsic difference between the military oligarchy and the military autocracy is the number of rulers.

Authoritarian praetorianism, the third subtype, is characterized by military-civilian fusionist rule. Governmental authority, although unchecked politically, is nevertheless a coalition of military and civilian governing with little or no external political control. In the military autocracy the supreme ruler is always a military officer. In the military oligarchy the chief executive is either a former military man, now a civilian, or a civilian whose support comes exclusively from the military. Such a system cannot survive without the support of the military establishment. An authoritarian military regime is almost exclusively composed of military, bureaucrats, managers, and technocrats who restrict political support and mobilization. The majority of the authoritarian military executive body might be composed of military men or civilians, and the head of the government is not necessarily a military man. In fact, he may not possess military skills.

The major source of support in all military praetorian subtypes is the military establishment. In the military autocracy, electoral exercises are not even contemplated. A military oligarchy spends considerable effort to create a facade of electoral support and calls infrequent elections. The authoritarian military regime seeks external (in relation to the military) political support and is sincere in the exercise of restrictive elections, even if the choice is limited to the military-supported executive. However, this type of regime might tolerate political institutions and structures on the national level that are not necessarily oriented toward military rule (for example, parliaments, parties, and pressure groups).*

SOCIAL CONDITIONS CONTRIBUTING TO PRAETORIANISM

The following conditions in a society may contribute to the rise of

---

*Analyzing the military regime in Brazil in 1973, Juan Linz commented: "Power basically remained with the armed forces, except for economic policy making, which is shared between the military, selected technocrats, and, to a lesser extent, businessmen. Institutions outside the armed forces have been created and disregarded constantly, leaving the military with ultimate power" ("The Future of an Authoritarian Situation" in *Authoritarian Brazil*, ed. Alfred Stepan [New Haven, Yale University Press, 1973], p. 235).

praetorianism: structural weakness or disorganization; the existence of
fratricidal classes, including a politically impotent middle class; and low
levels of social action and of mobilization of material resources. The
presence of some of these conditions does not necessarily lead to army
intervention, however. Conversely, intervention may occur even though
some conditions are missing.

In a state that lacks social cohesion, personal desires and group aims
frequently diverge. The formal structure of the state is not buttressed by
an informal structure; institutions do not develop readily or operate
effectively; social control is ineffective; and channels for communication are few. Furthermore, there are no meaningful universal symbols to
bind the society together. This syndrome is typical of a state in which
the traditional patterns of social cohesion have broken down and have
not yet been replaced by new patterns.[13] It may also accompany the
emergence of new patterns of social cohesion in an unstable traditional
society. Only a group separated from the society—a revolutionary
organization, a party, a bureaucracy, or the army—can destroy such a
syndrome of social and economic disorganization. If the ruling civilians
lack political experience and symbols of authority, military personnel
may be able to manipulate the symbols of their institution to rule and to
introduce some social cohesiveness. Although military leaders tend to
have less articulateness and sophistication than civilian leaders, such
attributes as impartiality and courage can make the military leaders
more effective. They are better able to communicate with the people
because they can elicit a psychological response on the symbolic level.
Furthermore, they may be expected to overcome the syndrome of
social disorganization to the extent that they maintain some distance
from the divisions within the politically active population.

The second condition that promotes praetorianism is the existence of
social classes that tend to be fragmented and incapable of mounting
unified action even to achieve benefits for a particular sector. Although
similar differences existed within classes during the developmental
process in Western Europe or North America, such divisions are particularly acute in the underdeveloped countries of the twentieth century,
where social and economic changes have been rapid and many stages
of development have occurred simultaneously. In addition to the natural
polarization between the wealthy few and the many poor in such countries, there are marked gradations and variations (leading to conflicts)
within all three social layers—bottom, middle, and top. The top group

is usually divided between traditionalists and modernists, mostly land-owners who have adopted modern technology. The group at the bottom is also divided—in the case of underdeveloped countries, between the urban worker elite and the less privileged laborers.

Large foreign-owned industrial enterprises may give urban workers special benefits, such as high wages. Therefore this elite group of workers is little inclined to suffer the deprivations that political action designed to help its less privileged brethren may entail. Yet, it is precisely these workers, who are concentrated in large enterprises, who could be most easily organized for revolutionary action.[14]

This phenomenon has appeared throughout the underdeveloped world in the twentieth century. The urban workers in the large enter-prises may be quite well off, as they were in prerevolutionary China, while the conditions under which the masses of workers live are nearly subhuman. In Cuba, too, "permanently employed skilled and semi-skilled workers tended to develop a stake in the existing political and economic order. Even those not organized into unions had their interests carefully protected by labor laws. Although they themselves might be denied opportunities for upward social mobility, skilled workers and those at the foreman level were in a position to provide their sons with an education that would enable them to move ahead."[15]

The absence of a strong, cohesive, and articulate middle class—the class that historically has acted as the stabilizer of civilian government during modernization—is another condition contributing to the estab-lishment of a praetorian government. The middle class in most prae-torian states is small, divided, and politically impotent. In most states of the Middle East, for example, it represents no more than 6 percent, and never more than 10 percent, of the population. Unlike the middle class in the West during industrialization, this class in the Middle East is composed of either bureaucrats or self-employed small businessmen; it rarely includes employers.[16] Since its members occupy different types of economic statuses, their economic interests diverge, as do their political interests. In Latin America (Argentina and Brazil, for instance) the middle class is relatively large and cohesive, comprising between 10 and 20 percent of the population, and sometimes more. And since it has a high percentage of politically active members, it could be the precipi-tator of military intervention because it requires military help to come to power or to retain power if it fails to win electoral support. In the Middle East, on the other hand, the military does not intervene on behalf of the middle class, or any class, for that matter. Thus, there is no conclusive evidence of a casual relationship between the military coup and the middle classes.

The next social condition for praetorianism is a low level of group social action and of mobilization of material resources. A state in the transitional stage of modernization not only lacks a commonly valued pattern of action but also lacks common symbols that aid mobilization for social and political action. The organization that is theoretically the most encompassing—the government—is supported by only a few divided sectors of inchoate social groups. The government thus has difficulty in obtaining support for its activities. Its programs are subverted and development projects fail. This failure in human mobilization results from the differences in the values of groups and members of society. Material resources, needed by the government as much as human resources, are also withheld. Industrialists disguise their profits to cheat the tax collector; bureaucrats take bribes; peasants hoard. The withholding of resources may take many forms, but the result is always the same: the government's development programs are subverted and its ability to remain in power without military support is jeopardized.[17]

MILITARY PRAETORIAN REGIMES: A POLITICAL EXPLANATION

To explain the political conditions for praetorian interventionism, I propose this axiom. *The praetorian army tends to replace weak and unstable political groups and regimes.* The motivation of the military to intervene is clearly political, even if it is triggered by noninstitutionalized social conditions.[18]

Several hypotheses that can be derived from the literature attempt to explain the cause of military coups and praetorianism. Some hypotheses are sufficient; most others are conjectural and/or insufficient.

William Thompson, for instance, examines several hypotheses and causal inferences in the literature relating to military coups and regime replacement. According to him the dominant hypothesis concerns the pull of the system; that is, "much of indirect theorizing on military coups is concerned with the question of regime vulnerability. It is by far the dominant concern in the 'military politics' literature."[19] Since I concur that regime vulnerability is the major, if not the single, condition that propels the military into politics, it is necessary (especially in view of several of Thompson's valid criticisms) to distinguish between sufficient and insufficient explanations for the pull of regimes by military coups.

Insufficient Explanations

1. *The decline of authority*. Almost every student of the military in politics has proposed the decline of authority as an explanation or a cause of military coups. Although the literature is replete with empirical and other "proofs," the fact remains that not *all* declining authorities were pulled down by military coups. Most changes of regimes are neither designed nor initiated by the military. Nevertheless, I propose Portugal and Spain (1975); the People's Republic of China (1949); and the USSR (1917) as cases in which the decline of authority did not make the army overthrow the system. Instead the army did so only as an *instrument* of the regime (China, USSR) or in *coalition* with an established political party or group (Portugal). The fact that all Eastern European regimes (with the exception of Czechoslovakia and, partially, Yugoslavia) were pulled down by military coups between 1919 and 1939 and the new regimes were imposed by native Communist parties and the USSR after 1945 clearly demonstrates the insufficiency of this explanation. Decline of authority only explains the praetorian nature of the political system, that is, regime vulnerability may be exploited by *any* organized political force, including the military.[20]

2. *Historical legacies, failure of democracy*. Thompson also clearly demonstrates that explanations such as historical legacies, the failure of democracy, and the disjointed system[21] are insufficient to explain the rise of military regimes. In my view, the explanation why the military and not another group replaces a "declining authority" does not stem so much from the military's political motivation (which does, indeed, exist) as it does from the *relative* power of the military in regimes whose authority has declined.

3. *The military middle-class coup*. The most pervasive and nonsubstantiated explanation for the military *in* politics is that it is the spear-carrier of the middle class: that the decline of authority is coupled with the absence of a strong, cohesive middle class. The literature is replete with claims of evidence linking the military and the middle class. Essentially, two arguments have been derived from the same hypothesis: first, that the military is the spear-carrier of the middle class, and second, that in the absence of a cohesive or established middle class, the pro-

pensity for military intervention is high. Both propositions are false because:

> a. the military may intervene on behalf of one class, all classes, or no class at all.[22] There is no proof that it is the middle-class spearhead.
>
> b. the political motivation of the military activists, even when it benefits the middle class, is not necessarily generated by the *politics* or *ideology* of the middle classes (see chapter 5).
>
> c. when they lack political power the middle classes search for allies. This is a logical political strategy for any group that seeks political power. In Latin America, for instance, many coups occur that could be properly called "working class coups." Such coups take place because the military finds alliance with labor unions politically rewarding, not because it possesses working-class consciousness. Historically some Latin American militaries have allied with the *caudillo*, some with the aristocracy, some with the liberals.

The next chapter comprises a comparative study of military and politics in praetorian states and will clearly demonstrate that various activist officers have "represented" different classes and sought such disparate allies as aristocrats, autocrats, anarchists, syndicalists, and Maoists. The soldiers of the Ottoman and the Austro-Hungarian empires were no more dedicated to a specific class than the modern Arab.[23]

Sufficient Explanations

Let us now turn to the dynamics of military coups. Again, there are interesting derivations from the proposition that coups are political actions of the military designed to replace rival groups and regimes with their own regime or one dominated by them.

1. I propose, based on the literature, that the military group replaces an existing regime:

> a. when the military is the most cohesive and *politically* the best organized group at a given time in a given political system.
>
> b. when no relatively more powerful opposition exists. The Turkish army between 1961 and 1963 feared to intervene because of the retaliatory capabilities of the country's political

parties. For more than a decade, the Egyptian Free Officers groups hesitated to intervene for fear of a combined forces of the Egyptian court and Great Britain.[24] Some of Hitler's generals, especially the conservatives, planned four coups between 1938 and 1944. Nevertheless, most officers objected to the coups for fear of Hitler's popularity and Nazi-SS retaliatory power. Only in 1944, less than a year before the final defeat, did the military execute an abortive coup. (See chapter 3.)

2. Military coups and military intervention are conducted by:

a. political activists in the military organization.
b. members of political clubs, conspiratorial cabals within the military organization;
c. officers with present or future political ambitions; and
d. officers who do not consider the military as the life career. Political skill and commitment are more significant characteristics of coupmakers than age, rank, and seniority.[25] The argument that coupmakers are, on the whole, young, junior officers does not hold.

3. Officers may be politicized as a result of:

a. infiltration of their ranks by politically or ideologically committed officers or civilians who seek collaborators for a "civilianistic" coup;
b. a new weltanschauung, such as fascism, socialism, or communism; or
c. events—the anticolonial struggle, the coming of independence, economic disaster.

4. Military coups are organized by:

a. a coterie or a loose coalition of the political activists and their allies organized to negotiate their political role within the army, if possible, but if not, by means of the coup. A grievances coup (that is, one based on demands for better wages and working conditions) is a limited political action in the sense that such negotiations do not involve requests for political power and influence (the AFL-CIO president does not attempt to negotiate himself into the presidency of the United States); or

b. a tight conspiracy composed of a few officers. On the whole coups have clandestine *political* support from outside the military. In addition, conspirators against established military regimes *must* join with politically influential individuals, interest groups, parties, or groups *outside* the army).[26]

5. The decision to intervene, that is, to execute the coup, is a purely political decision that involves:

    a. political readiness
    i. the maturation of the cabal
   ii. its political cohesiveness and commitment
 iii. the nature of its leadership
    b. political timing
    i. strength of the authority to be replaced
   ii. the structure of coalition (with outside help)
 iii. political events

6. Coup legitimization, which begins as soon as the old regime is replaced, is a purely political action.

    a. The military, if it has acted alone, searches for political allies and kindred souls among the opposition and, if possible, among the disgruntled elements or opportunists of the deposed regime.

    b. If the coup is the product of a coalition, the political struggle between the military activists and their civilian allies is usually resolved when the military replaces or dominates the civilians.[27] (There are only a few exceptions, such as Portugal in 1975 and Turkey in 1971.)

THE PRAETORIAN ARMY

Political activity is contrary to the professional ethics and standards of the modern military, and the code of the professional army dictates that promotions be determined by ability, expertise, and education. Yet even in a nonpraetorian army such principles are not always accepted or observed. The link between professional and ruler precludes the certitude of professional noninterventionism. Character (that is, class) or political leanings often overrule expertise in the selection and promotion of officers. In some cases, professional standards may not exist at all, either because the army does not have a professional tradition or because the tradition has deteriorated. For example, in Argentina at the end of the nineteenth century, "institutional formal norms were never sufficiently enforced for the maintenance of discipline. Personal relationships and political affiliations remained major factors in the preservation of cohesion within the army and its control by civilian governments." In the imperial German army, as a result of emphasis on aristocracy and distrust of the bourgeoisie, character took precedence over intellect as a criterion for officer selection.[28]

When army affairs have become intertwined with politics, appointments and promotions are made on the basis of the officer's political affiliations rather than on his professional qualifications. In order to advance in the military hierarchy, an officer is obliged to establish political alliances with civilian superiors. Yet, even in praetorian states, the remnants of professionalism may survive to the extent that conflicts arise between political activity and formally adopted professional norms. Often, however, these conflicts deepen the political involvement of the officers by widening the circle of political activists, and the officer corps then tends to divide into factions and cliques. The divisiveness and political involvement of the officers may also be abetted by foreign intervention, such as the United States counterinsurgency training and military aid in Latin America and Nasser's intervention in the internal rivalries of the Syrian, Iraqi, Yemeni, and Jordanian armies.[29]

An army becomes praetorian when a small group of officers, a few key activists, succeed in propelling the military into politics. This group is never more than 5 percent of the total officer corps. In the most extreme form of praetorian army (the "ruler" type) the military establishes an independent executive and a political organization to dominate society and politics. The less extreme "arbitrator" type has no independent political organization and shows little interest in manufacturing a political ideology. To illustrate, the Iraqi military interventions in the late 1930s were carried out by an arbitrator army; those in the late 1950s, by a ruler army. The officers responsible for the first coup d'etat (October 1936), which was led by General Bakr Sidqi, eliminated moderate political leadership and transformed the government into a military dictatorship, but they had no political organization of their own. After Bakr Sidqi's assassination they were left leaderless and divided. The coup was followed by a countercoup, which was followed by several other military coups, until a civilian government was finally established in 1941. Although the army was a decisive factor in the political life of Iraq between 1936 and 1941, it could not serve as an effective and stabilizing alternative to the regimes and cabinets it toppled. Curiously enough, the political failures of the Iraqi army did not discourage Middle Eastern praetorian armies, including the Iraqi army itself. In 1958 another coup was staged by a ruler type of army. This time the army, under the leadership of Abd al-Karim Qassem, was more successful politically. It eliminated civilian politicians of both left and right, pruned its own ranks, and established a praetorian syndrome. By the middle 1970s, there seemed little chance of return to civilian rule.[30]

The actions of both types of praetorian armies—arbitrator and ruler—are affected by the internal structure of the army and the extent to which it has developed an identifiable political consciousness, political organization, and autonomy; by interaction between the army and civilian politicians and structures; and by the kind of political order the army wants to eliminate and the kind it wants to establish. Although the civilian and military spheres are treated here as independent variables in interaction and conflict, the military organization cannot be divorced from its social context. Initially, the political commitments and ideological positions of the military in the praetorian state are sustained either by the civilian politicians who encourage the army to enter politics or by the general sociopolitical context. After a certain level of political involvement has been attained, however, officers can begin to influence the positions taken by civilian politicians. This development occurs when a political group that originally infiltrated the army to avoid losing its support comes to share the goals of the army. The more completely the army is immersed in politics, the greater is its desire to change the sociopolitical context and the greater are the chances for political instability.

The Arbitrator Army

This type of praetorian army has the following general characteristics: (1) acceptance of the existing social order; (2) willingness to return to the barracks after disputes are settled; (3) no independent political organization and lack of desire to maximize army rule; (4) a time limit for army rule; (5) concern with improvement of professionalism; (6)

a tendency to operate behind the scenes as a pressure group; and (7) a fear of civilian retribution.

1. The arbitrator army accepts the existing social order and makes no fundamental changes in the regime or the executive structure.

In an underdeveloped country, where accepting the existing order often implies an antirevolutionary ideology, the arbitrator army may be the instrument of conservative and antiliberal forces. The Ottoman army was a conservative instrument before the coup of 1909, as was the Iraqi army in the 1920s.[31] The Argentine military establishment, which displayed an arbitrating orientation after the fall of Juan Perón in 1955, was antileftist and, specifically, after 1959, anti-Castro. Traditional Latin American caudillos usually have not attempted to change the social order.

2. The officers of the arbitrator army are civilian-oriented. Furthermore, at least in Latin America and Turkey, they are dedicated to protecting and preserving constitutional government. Even when civilian groups are not well enough organized to set up a government, or when officers occupy positions in the government, the officers obey the instructions of civilian political groups. They do not inject their own viewpoint. They want to return to normality, which means acceptance of the status quo. This type of army expects to return to the barracks after political corruption has been eliminated and stability restored, for its officers are aware that they lack the skills to govern and they wish to avoid further political involvement.

The Chilean army of the 1924–33 period expected to return to barracks. Its officers participated in politics because civilian political groups had become disorganized, but the participation was limited and the professional norms of the military establishment were largely retained even during periods of fairly deep involvement. After returning to the barracks this type of army does not necessarily relinquish its political influence. In many cases it has continued to act as guardian of civilian authority and political stability. This is the essence of the Kemalist legacy in Turkey: the army serves as the guardian of the constitution. Until 1964 the army of Brazil played a similar arbitrator part.[32]

3. The arbitrator army has no independent political organization and makes no attempt to maximize army rule. General Nagib of Egypt, for example, who was recruited by Nasser and the Society of Free Officers in 1951 to head the list of Free Officers in the elections for the adminis-

trative committee of the Officers' Club, had no political organization of his own. He was not a charter member of the Free Officers, but was chosen from among three candidates to become the titular head of the 1952 coup. Lacking his own organization, Nagib was obliged to deal with the Free Officers' political organization, the Revolutionary Command Council (RCC).[33] Unfortunately for Nagib, his efforts to maximize civilian participation in the RCC cabinet and to oppose the policy of Nasser and the RCC to legitimize the military dictatorship failed, and he was ousted by the RCC in 1954.

4. The arbitrator army imposes a time limit on army rule and expects to hand the government over to an "acceptable" civilian regime, for it views prolonged rule as detrimental to its professional integrity. Therefore it encourages political groups that are capable of establishing order, preserving stability, and guaranteeing that the new government will not retrogress. The existence of such organized civilian groups has a vital bearing on the army's decision to surrender its rule. When no such groups exist—that is, when there is a state of near anarchy—the arbitrator army, the only organized group in the state, may have to continue governing despite its civilian orientation and its desire to return to its own affairs. Where organized civilian groups do exist, the military as a whole withdraws from the government, although at times a key military figure may continue as chief of state. General Carlos Ibáñez, for instance, was chief of state in Chile in the late 1920s and early 1930s, but the military institution as a whole was not politically involved.[34]

5. Professionalism and corporateness—the collective sense that arises from professional unity and consciousness—are closely related to the political attitude of the military, for unlike such other professionals as lawyers and physicians, soldiers depend upon the state for security. Both the praetorian military and the civil service are sensitive to political change, but the civil service is less affected by it because it has little physical power with which to threaten the regime. In an arbitrator army the officer corps (or important sectors of it) is strongly opposed to political involvement since it may destroy the professional military norms and expertise that provide security and predictability for the officer's career. This type of army tends to defend the existing regime in order to protect its own professional integrity. It may even intervene to defend the military against the threat posed by a disintegrating or unstable regime.

6. Because it fears open involvement in politics, the arbitrator army tends to operate behind the scenes as a pressure group. It influences civilian governments to respond to popular demands, thereby making it unnecessary for the military to intervene openly. However, the military's refusal to take responsibility for its actions creates a situation in which power is divorced from responsibility—a situation that may lead to instability. Moreover, since the arbitrator type of officer corps lacks cohesion, instability may result in factionalism or aggravate existing divisions. This condition may then lead to a pattern of coup and countercoup in which the frequent changes in government are not accompanied by changes in policies but merely reflect personal rivalries. Most of the unsuccessful coups in Syria have been of this type. Civilians usually are involved in these personalistic cliques and attempt to use them for their own ends. Such entanglements may result in a vicious circle: civilian action tends to increase military cliquishness, and vice versa, because the combination of army and civilian motives blurs the separation of the army from the civilian sociopolitical context and results in the army's inability to change the political situation. This pattern has appeared in the Latin American sequences of coups d'etat (*cuartelazos*).[35]

7. The arbitrator army may be afraid of retribution from both civilian politicians and the civilian population. The presence of organized civilian groups may cause the military to fear the future actions of civilian politicians—dismissal of officers, demotion, or peripheral appointments and assignments. Such fears were apparent in General Gursel's attitude during the 1960–61 coup in Turkey and in Portugal in 1975–76.[36] If an army has become unpopular because it has initiated repressive measures, especially if its soldiers have been recruited from the native population, doubts about the civilian population's willingness to follow its orders may cause the army to withdraw because it fears mass violence as well as political retribution.

THE RULER PRAETORIAN ARMY

In its pure form this type of praetorian army has characteristics that are in direct opposition to those of the arbitrator type. It (1) rejects the existing order and challenges its legitimacy; (2) lacks confidence in civilian rule and has no expectation of returning to the barracks; (3) has a political organization and tends to maximize army rule; (4) is convinced that army rule is the only alternative to political disorder;

(5) politicizes professionalism; (6) operates in the open; and (7) has little fear of civilian retribution. In practice, however, an army that displays most of the characteristics of the ruler type, including a well-articulated ideology to which the officer corps adheres, may not actually rule. In such a case—the Peruvian army until 1972 for instance—the military presents a unified point of view and acts as the stabilizer of civilian governments that hold views similar to its own.[37]

1. Officers in developing countries challenge the legitimacy of the existing order, opposing both the political corruption of the traditional parliamentary liberal regimes and some of the modernizing authoritarian one-party systems. In these countries, traditional parliamentary politics and liberalism have become identified with status quo politics. The ruler type of praetorian army increasingly tends to abandon or convert existing institutions, ideologies, and procedures in favor of the institutions for modernization, industrialization, and political mobilization that are proposed by theorists of rapid growth. To nonconservative praetorians, the new theories are more suitable guides for altering traditional institutions than are the old "corrupt" liberal ideologies. However, these praetorians also reject as corrupt those radical-revolutionary civilian regimes that favor rapid modernization under a one-party system. The officers are not revolutionaries. Instead, they tend to be reformers, and any self-proclaimed conversion to revolutionary causes is likely to be much more superficial than their conversion to anticonservatism. Yet, in its reformist role, the army may be adamantly opposed to communism (to Castroism, in contemporary Latin America). In Peru, the military has generally opposed the local revolutionary party (APRA), but this has not prevented the army from adopting a reform orientation since 1973.[38]

The ruler army has at least three subtypes that reject the existing order and challenge its legitimacy: the antitraditionalist radical army, the antitraditionalist reformer army, and the conservative, antiradical army. The term "antitraditionalist" indicates opposition to traditional institutions such as the Sharia (Islamic canon law) and patrimony; "radical" means opposition to party or liberal organizations (parliamentary institutions, multiparty systems, democratic elections); and "reformer" refers to the acceptance of reform parties and parliamentary politics. These types can be placed on a left-right continuum in relation to the political order. Examples of the antitraditionalist radical army are the regimes of Abd al-Karim Qassem in Iraq

(1958–63) and Juan Perón in Argentina (1945–55); the military regimes of Gamal Abdel Nasser in Egypt (1952–70); Houari Boumedienne in Algeria (after 1965); most Syrian and Iraqi regimes since 1963; Portugal (1975); and General Suharto in Indonesia (after 1965). The antitraditionalist reformer army is represented by Mustafa Kemal (Atatürk) of Turkey (1919–23) and Ayub Khan of Pakistan (1958–70). The conservative, antiradical army is exemplified by the anti-Castro, anticommunist military rulers of Brazil and Argentina since 1966, and the regime of Colonel Gadhafi of Libya since 1969. The ruler army chooses the new political order as a reaction to the order that it has replaced. In other words, the ideology of the praetorian army depends on the nature of the ideology it has rejected. Choice here is rather limited; the final selection will depend upon what means the army takes to transform society into "something else," most often into something initially unknown to it. It took Nasser a decade, for instance, to opt for Arab socialism; in that period it was clearer to him what political system to destroy than what political system to create. Nasser was more leftist than the Wafd, just as Ayub Khan was more radical than the old Muslim League party. Boumedienne was to the right of Ben Bella, and Suharto to the right of Sukarno. Sadat moved to the right of Nasser. The Syrian 'Alawi are more radical than the mainstream Sunni Ba'th officers; the Portuguese army is more radical than Salazar.

In Pakistan, Ayub Khan's "basic democracy" developed as an alternative to the regime it replaced. Although the Pakistani army, an offshoot of the British Indian army, had kept aloof from politics, the need for reform and modernization enhanced its propensity for institutional autonomy and made a temporary ruler of Ayub Khan, who had been dedicated to military professionalism and maximizing civilian rule. Imbued with the British civil service tradition, he chose to blend a very modified version of British bureaucracy with the "military mind" and political reality of Pakistan—a coalition of bureaucracy and the military. The resulting mixture of traditional values and professionalism (both bureaucratic and military) created the concept of "basic democracy"—the ideology of the Pakistani army after 1958. In Algeria, Houari Boumedienne did not abandon Arab socialism but merely reduced its ideological intensity and commitments. It the process he became an antiradical type of ruler. Although by the middle 1970s he had not adopted an ideology of his own, by eliminating Ben Bella's legacy he had moved toward the modernization of Algeria without

Ben Bella's radicalism. In Indonesia, after the 1965 Communist coup, the army liquidated the old regime; Sukarno's "guided democracy" had radicalized it. The political evolution of the Indonesian army indicated that, even if it did not offer an alternative ideology, it might proceed along the lines of a modified guided democracy without the vehemence, the radicalism, and the messianism that had marked the reign of President Sukarno.[39]

2. The ruler army has no confidence in civilian rule and makes no provision for returning to the barracks. This attitude may be a consequence of the development by an important sector of the officer corps of an independent political orientation opposed to the ruling civilian groups. Alternatively, civilian disorganization may have reached the point where progressive elements are unable to put their programs into effect. By the time military inervention occurs, civilians have already manifested their inability to control the situation. Civilian failure prompts the officers to feel that they should occupy formal positions in the governmental structure. In Egypt, for example, officers blamed civilians for the Palestinian crisis and for the Cairo riots of January 1952; they did not even trust those civilians—such as the more radical members of the Wafd or the Muslim Brotherhood—who subscribed to political philosophies similar to their own. In the early 1950s, after a number of years of civil war, the Colombian army led by Rojas Pinilla lost confidence in civilian rule, took control of the government, and implemented a Perónist type of developmental program. When this change occurred, only part of the army shared Rojas Pinilla's orientation, but afterwards the army showed an inclination to adopt developmental ideologies based on technological and evolutionary change. By the middle 1970s the army still had no confidence in civilian rule and it seemed likely that it might again take over the government of Colombia. The military of Argentina, Brazil, and Peru also lost confidence in civilian ability to maintain constitutional rule under the pressure of social mobilization.

3. The ruler army has an independent political organization, and it attempts to legitimize and maximize its own rule. Considering itself the one elite group capable of governing, it usually tries to assure the indefinite continuation of army rule by taking advantage of the lack of political and social cohesion and by strengthening its authority. Legitimizing itself through the creation of a radical-nationalist party, the ruler army manufactures or incorporates an ideology to support its

organization. In Syria, for example, Adib Shishakly founded the Arab Liberation Movement in 1952 to legitimize the military dictatorship he had established in 1951.[40] Since then military coups in the Middle East have followed the precedent of establishing a Revolutionary Command Council to legitimize army rule and eliminate civilian and army opposition. While the formation of a RCC does not guarantee a coup's success nor ensure that it will attain legitimacy, it does give the army independence in political action and a means of circumventing whatever strong civilian organizations exist. Where such groups do not exist, the RCC serves to preserve the military dictatorship.

Legitimization of the army as the guarantor of stability and progress does not necessarily imply that its rule will be permanent. In Turkey, the Kemalist legacy served as a watchdog to prevent the civilian regime from returning to corrupt practices. By civilianizing his regime under the auspices of the army, Atatürk also legitimized the army's role in politics as the defender and protector of the constitution and of republican and honest civilian rule; in effect, he maximized civilian rule by legitimizing the army as its sole protector. Nasser, on the other hand, gave a civilian role to political parties and bureaucracies created by the army. Although this practice maximized army domination, it might discourage a return to civilian rule after Egypt has achieved modernization.

An army need not have its own ideology or political organization in order to favor a ruler type of praetorianism; it can take over the established, popular, nationalist-radical party. When the army came to power in Iraq after the 1958 revolution, it participated in the struggle between the oligarchs and the new generation, and many military leaders were closely associated with various ideological groups. Nevertheless, instead of formulating its own distinct set of ideals, it merely carried out the programs of the civilian groups. Its most important step was to take over the Ba'th party and militarize it. In Syria a somewhat different relationship developed between the army and the Ba'th party. Though sharing a common political ideology, the two organizations did not hold the same view of army rule: the Ba'th advocated parliamentary rule, while the army preferred praetorianism. The February 1966 coup indicated the trend in favor of the army rule. An army faction took over the Ba'th party's left wing, signifying further attrition of Ba'thist and civilian groups in Syria. In this case, the ideology of a civilian party served to legitimize the rule of the army; the Ba'th party became a party in uniform.

In Indonesia the evolution of the army as a political organization strengthened its position as a ruler. The political consolidation of the army occurred when many officers, supporting Sukarno's "guided democracy" in order to keep political parties out of power and to weaken the Indonesian Communist party, were absorbed into the national elite. The army participated in civic action and boosted economic development to compete with the Communist party at the grass-roots level. When the Communists attacked the army, the army struck back, and after 1965 it was involved in dissolving the old order and establishing a new one under army rule.[41]

4. The ruler army is convinced that its regime is the only alternative to political disorder and thus does not set a time limit nor search for an acceptable civilian successor government. This attitude is illustrated clearly by Nasser's political philosophy. In *Egypt's Liberation: The Philosophy of the Revolution*, Nasser argues that "only the army" can ameliorate conditions in Egypt and that the army plays the "role of vanguard" in the Egyptian revolution. This attitude also typified some of the extreme radical nationalists in the Iraqi army during the late 1930s, among them Salah al-Din al-Sabbagh, whose xenophobia and anti-imperialist convictions led him to believe that the army was destined to relieve Iraq and Islam of the yoke of external and internal oppressors.[42] In the Middle East most army leaders have tended to espouse the kind of military dictatorships established by Shishakly and Nasser. If an army there still acts as an arbitrator (as it does especially in Syria), it is due more to civilian opposition and intra-army rivalry than to the army's belief in civilian rule.

5. The ruler army sacrifices professionalism to political expediency. Political considerations take precedence over expertise, internal organization, and career security, and a new set of norms is developed. Politicization may destroy professional concepts of status and rank, for in certain situations (for example, in Syria between 1963 and 1966), a low-ranking officer may be politically superior to an officer of higher rank. The Thai army is a striking exception to the thesis that a ruler army's political involvement diminishes its professional integrity, however. Since 1932 the officers of the Thai army, which is rooted in the traditional bureaucracy, "have led the ruling group, dominated

the institutions of government, and set the style of Thai politics."
Apparently the professional norms of the officer class can survive in a
country where politics and social structure are bureaucratic.[43]

6. The ruler army operates in the open because it wants to use
military symbols to gain support for its programs and activities. A
peculiar combination of both traditional and modern components,
the military may be quite acceptable to a population for whom it
represents a technologically advanced organization. For the traditionalists, the military symbolizes heroic leadership and honor, even
though its officers may be "experts" and managers. "The great stress
placed on professionalism and the extremely explicit standards for
individual behavior make the military appear to be a more sacred than
secular institution."[44]

7. By the time the ruler type of praetorianism has developed, the
army already exercises so much power that it does not need to fear
civilians. In Egypt, for example, the emergence of the army as ruler
took place after an extended period of disorganization—growing
violence in urban areas and the manifest failure of civilians to maintain
order or implement development programs. Furthermore, the civilians
were considered incapable of defending Egypt against imperialist
powers.

Military government is government by surrogate. A praetorian
government is one that secures political support without legitimacy.
It is a military stewardship on behalf of absent executive and civilian
political groups, and it results more from the inefficiency of civilian
political organizations than from the political aptitude of the military
interventionists. On the whole the military usurpers prove to be even
greater simpletons in exercising political power than their civilian
predecessors. In the absence of organized, politically articulate groups,
officers who are untrained and unsuited for politics attempt to manipulate power to serve a variety of noble causes, including the elimination of corruption and avarice and saving the nation from foreign
aggression or domination (and such threats have often been invented
by the politically minded military itself). After entering the political
arena, these officers have produced patriotic slogans, ideological pronunciamientos, and promises, rather than practical reforms, revolution,
or counterrevolution. Tanks have replaced cavalry, the television
station the pronunciamento, and the revolutionary command council

the civilian executive. But praetorianism is still government from the turrets. Army control has become the rule, civilian control the exception. Patrolling used to be the function of civilian guards. Now it has become the exercise of praetorians in mufti.

5

The Military That Patrols Society: Evolution and Structural Cleavage in Arab and African Military Regimes

Arab and African military elites have a propensity to intervene in government. This tendency is highly correlated with the military's corporate orientation, the politicization of the army, and political institutional instability and fragmentation in structural and political systems that have arisen from colonial backgrounds. William Thompson's hypothesis that regimes with colonial backgrounds tend to be more prone to military coups is empirically corroborated (Table 5.1). (The era of

Table 5.1 Summary of Military Coup Frequency, 1946–70

Coup Frequency	Number of States	States
1	17	Cambodia, Costa Rica, Equatorial Guinea, Ethiopia, Gabon, Iran, Jordan, Lebanon, Libya, Mali, Nepal, Nicaragua, Oman, Senegal, South Yemen, Uganda, Upper Volta
2	9	Burma, Central African Republic, Egypt, France, Ghana, Greece, Somalia, South Korea, Togo
3	7	Burundi, Congo (Kinshasa) or Zaire, Cuba, Pakistan, Portugal, Sierra Leone, Turkey
4	3	Colombia, El Salvador, Nigeria
5	6	Algeria, Congo (Brazzaville), Dahomey, Indonesia, Panama, Yemen
6	2	Dominican Republic, Honduras
7	2	Haiti, Sudan
8	2	Paraguay, Thailand
9	5	Brazil, Guatemala, Laos, Peru, South Vietnam
11	1	Iraq
12	1	Ecuador
14	1	Syria
16	1	Argentina
18	2	Bolivia, Venezuela

SOURCE: William Thompson, "Explanations of the Military Coup" (Ph.D. diss., University of Washington, 1972), table 1.2, p. 11.

Figure 5.1 Corporate Orientation and Military Interventionism in Non-institutionalized Political Systems

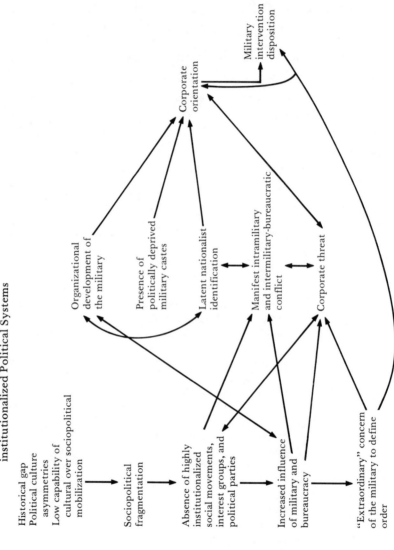

coup-proneness reflects coups occurring both immediately after independence or a short period of, say, five to ten years after independence.)

The argument is clearly this; the propensity to intervene is correlated
with the increased influence of military and bureaucracy in government and the intramilitary conflict connected with the evolution and
organizational and managerial development of the army. Intervention
takes place when the military corporate orientation is being threatened
by fragmented social movements, interest groups, or political parties.
Thus, the propensity to intervene is claimed by the military on behalf
of both corporate integrity and a "well-defined" order. Like classical
professionalism, corporatism is Janus-faced. Although the praetorian's
role is to protect order, more often than not (when his dual role as bureaucrat and professional is threatened) the corporate praetorian challenges order.

Therefore, in an analysis of Arab and African civil-military relations,
these subjects must be considered: (1) the types of military professionalism and corporatism that have evolved in these areas; (2) the evolution of functional political elites and coteries, including the military;
and (3) pattern and structures of the Arab-African military regimes.

Types of Corporatism: Their Nature, Evolution, Posture, and Future

The last vestige of colonial bureaucracy in Africa was the army.
In the evolution of the military there and in the Arab countries, two
types of corporate orientations are evident: a satrapic-sultanist type,
which is noninterventionist, and a modern nationalist and bureaucratic
type, which is interventionist.

Satrapic-Sultanist Noninterventionists

Satrapism implies the aping of a superior, usually external, culture.
It is a process of passive acculturation in which one's own culture and
identity are abnegated. Psychologically, satrapism results from colonial
or patrimonial rule. It is a cognitive subordination to "higher" foreign
values. Socially, it forces subordinate groups to emulate the "superior"
culture and abandon their own mores and values. Politically, satrapism
involves a quixotic, superficial emulation of the so-called superior
culture's procedures, structures, and manifestations. Political satrapism,
in contradistinction to social satrapism, is not restricted to the lower
classes but involves the subordination of all classes to an external culture.
In developing countries, corporate professionalism, which is culturally

and psychologically a product of another culture, is satrapic. The African military, for instance, has modeled itself on that of its former foreign instructors and attempted to follow the teachings of their academies.

"More than any institution left behind by colonialism, the armies of Africa were set in the colonial pattern," writes Ruth First. From the beginning of the twentieth century to the era of African independence in the 1950s, the concern of the British, in addition to using the West African armies for imperial defense, was to organize and train them to maintain internal security. The military concept followed in British India—recruiting from the "warrior race" or "martial people"—was never even attempted in West Africa. Reliability, loyalty, and subordination were the criteria for recruitment into the African armies. "The WAFF [West African Frontier Force] can be described as a European-led colonial army with African infantry soldiers and carriers." The early postindependence African armies were very much like the European colonial armies; the African soldiers, who were now subordinate to the new civilian regimes, were only satraps, and therefore they were professionally inferior.[1]

The most significant factor in the satrapic orientation of the Arab-African military (and to a lesser extent, of the Egyptian military) is that not only were the satraps members of a socially inferior group in their traditional society but their models, the British and French colonial officers, were themselves socially inferior at home and their service abroad was a means of elevating their status.[2] They were the ones who imposed the concept of dominant martial races (i.e., races the colonial administration deemed warlike—Gurkas, Druze, etc.) upon the Arab and especially the African officers. It is essential, however, to note an important difference between Arabs and Africans. While the African officers were trained by and emulated colonial European professionals, Arabs were also influenced by the legacy of the Ottoman Empire.

Sultanism, which Weber identifies with the disintegration of the patrimonial system, became entrenched in the Ottoman Empire during its decline in the sixteenth and seventeenth centuries. Then the janissaries (the imperial praetorian guard), finding it impossible to acquire Christian slaves, were forced to recruit the natives of the Arab provinces.[3] Particularly after 1827 the Ottoman bureaucracy and the military were gradually replenished with native Arabs, workers and soldiers who owed allegiance to the empire and defended the sultanate of Constantinople rather than the vague quasinational entity of the Arab people. The structure of the empire's military organization reflected the rigid class divisions of the sultanate and, in the late years of the nineteenth century, it was also affected by the rigidities of German militarism through German instructors. (Between 1805 and 1880 the Egyptian military, for example, was politically docile owing to the influence of the European instructors who helped build it in 1801–30. Its docility was reinforced by European instructors again after 1865.) The situation began to change with the modernization of the Ottoman Empire. Following the Young Turk revolt of 1908 a Turkish elite emerged and it was determined to replace the Arab natives in the bureaucracy, the military, and the "ruling institution," which was the Ottoman political (rather than religious) organization. After 1914, therefore, the Arab officers in the Ottoman army, purportedly acting to further Arab nationalism, were among the first to betray the empire to the British.[4]

Originating as an instrument of the Ottoman Empire, the Arab officer class did not belong to or owe its emergence to the medieval city. In the Arab East (Iraq and Syria) the military was also sultanist, but less servile than the Egyptians. Composed of the so-called martial races, the Arab officers were the *déclassés* of a Suni Islamic civilization. Everywhere in the Arab lands the sultanist type was subordinate and noninterventionist; yet from it developed the modern interventionist Arab-Egyptian officer, after the empire collapsed.

National and Corporate Interventionists

The sultanist officer was challenged in Egypt as early as 1882. During the Urabi revolt under the khedivate, the Egyptian military made an overt bid for power. The Urabi officers were forced to choose between the khedivate, then subordinate to the British, or the Egyptian nationalist-constitutionalist movement. This was a personal and, above all, a corporate challenge. On the one hand, as patrimonially oriented soldiers, they could not remain loyal to the khedivate because the khedive was under the thumb of the British.[5] On the other hand, to renounce their allegiance would violate the patrimonial code of the officers. The revolt was an attempt to seek corporate autonomy under the guise of Egyptian nationalism. The Urabi officers, however, refused to join the Egyptian nationalists once they had achieved corporate autonomy by collaborating with the khedivate. In the end, the khedive, aided by the British, suppressed the military. As the army declined, the officer class became alienated, lost prestige, and eventually turned unsuccessfully toward the nationalist-radical movement to regain its corporate status.

Just as the praetorian attitudes of the Egyptian officers (which ultimately led to Nasserism) grew out of their position as a politically *déclassé* group that played a junior role in Egyptian nationalism until the 1930s despite its potential power, so in other former colonies military domination tends to be encouraged by the ambitions of politically deprived military castes. The military acquires the disposition to intervene when it reaches the stage of organizational autonomy and feels threatened by the civilian nationalist regime. Then the military and bureaucratic structures become the arenas for political competition among the modern nationalist elites. All over the world military professionals tend to intervene in developing polities. The military's new modern skills of management and organization lead it to increase its political participation and eventually to enhance its political orientation. The raising of its professional level and its emergence as an autonomous bureaucratic organization are also part of the pattern. Thus the "professionalization," that is, the bureaucratization of the military in the Arab Middle East, North Africa, and sub-Saharan Africa, linked to the absence of corporate autonomy, has led to the rise of modern military praetorianism. In the Middle East and particularly in sub-Saharan Africa, however the military organizations that aspired to maintain order actually further fragmented the social system.[6]

To explain military intervention in Africa and the Middle East, one has to consider the politics of development and modernization and its impact on the military establishment. Analyses of the domestic structure of the regimes in these areas are significant because they reveal pertinent centerperiphery, tribal, and ethnic conflicts, as well as the ideological orientations of different military groups, and the military's latent nationalism. Intervention is instigated by organizational and collegial conflict within the army and exacerbated by the political struggle within the military establishment and between the military and the nationalist civilian regime. The new military elites expropriate the instruments of power as a source of support for military corporatism in the absence of stable executive authority.

In the military-bureaucratic axis, there are two kinds of rivalries, one within the military and the other between the military and the civilian bureaucracy. The first centers on office, position, and status. The challenge facing the military bureaucracy became apparent when the newly independent regimes put the army last on the list of social, political, and, above all, economic rewards. The rewards went instead to party politicians, trade union leaders, propagandists, apparatchiks, and civil servants. The rivalry within the military was exaggerated by a class struggle in the postindependence generations of Arab and African military, between the sons of the middle or upper classes, trained in the best military academies in the West, and the satrapic lower class African generals who had risen from the noncommissioned ranks of the colonial army. However, the class struggle played a minor role in the generational struggle within the military praetorians.[7]

The major conflict—that between the military and the civilian bureaucracy—springs naturally from the fact that they occupy similar positions in the political structure:

> Both officers and civil servants are organized in relatively rigid hierarchies with little scope for initiative and relatively ordered promotion, so that they depend upon political competition for office. Although claiming to strive for stability, in most cases, especially in the Middle East, these hierarchies bring about the opposite. Therefore, the site of conflict within the executive is between these two groups which, with sometimes similar social processes, educational backgrounds and political ambitions, are rivals for the control of the instrumentalities of power precisely *because* of their common bureaucratic and corporate orientations.[8]

The corporate orientations of officers thus are an important factor in accounting for the army's interventionism. Colonel A. A. Afrifa states in *The Ghana Coup, 24th February 1966*: "I have aways felt it painful to associate myself with a coup to overthrow a constitutional government, however perverted that constitution may be. . . . It was painful, therefore, to come to the conclusion that the coup was necessary to save our country and our people. We owed allegiance and loyalty to the people of Ghana for their protection and to us it was 'Dulce et Decorum est pro Patria Mori.' "

Speaking as a corporate officer, Afrifa writes that "a coup d'etat is the last resort in the range of means whereby an unpopular government may be overthrown. But in our case where there were no constitutional means of offering political opposition to the one-party government the Armed Forces automatically became the official opposition of the

Government." Only when the officers feared the loss of their political freedom did they resort to the coup in defense of the constitution.[9]

The argument will be further developed in this chapter that the propensity to intervene significantly is correlated with military corporate orientation and overt positions of power and influence in the military-bureaucratic axis and the role of the military among competing modern and nationalistic elites. I hope to have also demonstrated in this chapter that corporate orientation is not only Janus-faced but dichotomous: satrapic praetorians are on the whole noninterventionist, while bureaucratic-nationalist praetorians are interventionist. The propensity to intervene is on the whole increased by corporate threat or deprivation. Intervention nevertheless is linked to the bureaucratic struggle of modern civil-military elites and to nationalist identification, yet the latter factors do not necessarily explain intervention as do corporate orientation and threat to the integrity of the military establishment.

MODERN ELITES AND THE MILITARY

Political changes in the Middle East and sub-Saharan Africa cannot be classified as revolutionary according to Huntington's definition: "Revolution is the extreme case of the expression of political participation. Without this explosion there is no revolution." Huntington also argues that the process of broadening the political community (the political revolution) requires an alienated intelligentsia mobilizing a mass peasantry.[10] Although an alienated intelligentsia and a mass peasantry certainly exist in the Middle East and sub-Saharan Africa, the intelligentsia lacks the necessary orientation. The intelligentsia and the political elites in the Arab world and sub-Saharan Africa are self-indulgent. The members of the intelligentsia, alienated because the colonial powers had kept them from political power, sought to take power to ease their isolation. After assuming power, the members of the intelligentsia were no longer alienated (except for minorities—Christians, Copts, Druze, 'Alawi, in the Arab world, and alienated African tribes), but soon they were challenged by the military. Political change in praetorian polities is attributable to a change in elite circulation, not to elite alienation in the classical Western sense. Only the governing elite is changed, not the basic political mores and values. The political process is restricted to the conquest of the executive by a succession of elites, with the executive power usually ending up in the hands of the military praetorians.

To analyze the elaborate system of institutions and structural arrangements in the Arab East (except Egypt) and in North and sub-Saharan Africa might contribute to the fields of functional sociology and structural anthropology, but it would not help to explain political dynamics. A functionalist-universalist approach simplifies social structure, conflict, and, above all, political arrangements.[11] What separates developing from developed polities are not different political structures, institutions, or rules, but rather the *greater complexity* of political structures and the *self-awareness* of the complexity of political arrangement. According to Clifford Geertz, the developing political systems are not "systems" merely in the sense that they are composed of political coteries: "The social order is a field of small, pragmatical cliques gathering around one or another dominant figure as he comes, more or less transiently, into view and dispersing again, as largely traceless, he disappears." Geertz continues:

> North Africa does not even divide into institutions. The reason Maghrebi society is so hard to get into focus and keep there is that it is a vast collection of coteries. It is not blocked out into large, well-organized, permanent groupings—parties, classes, tribes, races—engaged in a long-term struggle for ascendency. It is not dominated by tightly knit bureaucracies concentrating and managing social power; not driven by great ideological movements seeking to transform the rules of the game; not immobilized by a hardened cake of custom locking men into fixed systems of rights and duties.[12]

The modernizing coteries (or elites) that form the basis for the short-term coalitions of political-military or bureaucratic-military alliances in the Middle East and sub-Saharan Africa are composed of three types of political functional groups—the politicians, the military, and the intellectuals. Within each type, age is an important source of political cleavage, for each generational group prefers certain institutional arrangements. Historical period, the geopolitical position of a polity, and the international political culture also help account for the different orientations and aspirations among the elites. Ultimately, the interaction among elites of different generations and orientations determines what type of political dynamics will operate.

The Politicians

In both the Arab states and Africa the founding fathers of the nationalist movements (1880–1919) were politicians trained abroad or at home in foreign schools. Their intellectual aspirations were modern and reformist. They were divided into two main political subgroups: liberal and progressive. The liberal group, the more traditionalist of the two, aspired to moderate politics and permitted considerable accommodation with the colonial authorities. Members of this group were primarily upper-middle-class writers, lawyers, engineers, and Islamic scholars. Imbued during the Wilsonian era with the ideals of the nation-state, they advocated self-determination for Arabs and Africans. They attributed the material success of the West to its superior political processes, and they believed that by grafting these processes onto their own societies they could eventually duplicate Western achievements. The progressive group, composed of teachers and particularly journalists, was also reformist but more secular and rationalist than the liberals. It also aspired to national accommodation with the colonial power, but it was pessimistic about the imperial state's good will.

In Egypt and Syria the politicians established political parties and formed interest-aggregating structures. In Egypt the liberals organized the Wafd and Sa'adist parties, while the progressives founded the Ummah party and various coteries favoring constitutional government. In Syria the liberal politicians coalesced into the Kutla al-Wataniyah (the Nationalist bloc) front, and the progressives founded the Sa'adist Parti Populaire Syrien (later fascist in orientation). In Algeria the liberals organized the UDMA party, while the progressives formed the MTLD party. In the Arab Middle East and Saharan Africa the liberals and progressives became bitterly divided over the future of Islam and its role in the modern society and state.[13] In Zaire (formerly Congo-Kinshasa), Uganda, Nigeria, and Kenya, religion did play a key role in political divisiveness. But the division between liberals and progressives in sub-Saharan Africa was nonetheless rudimentary. Progressive politicians in the Middle East also became very prominent in radical nationalist movements, and in Algeria they were responsible for founding both the radical party, the Ba'th, and the secular party, the FLN.

Between 1919 and 1939 a new generation of politicians appeared in the Middle East and North Africa. Unlike their predecessors, they were mostly university students, Ph.D.s, intellectuals, and former political organizers. This group provided the most prominent politicians of the Arab world in the early 1970s. These politicians, who subscribed to such doctrines as those of Marx, Lenin, Mao, and Castro, founded the left wing of the Arab Socialist party in Egypt, the Commune al-Arab in Beirut, and the left-wing Palestinian guerrilla groups. Having lost faith in parliamentarianism and traditional competitive party systems, they espoused proletarian dictatorships and the leftist authoritarianism of the mass mobilization parties. While some of the older politicians were radical fascists, the new generation included an assortment of radical Marxists and romantic revolutionaries.

A unique, protomodern stratum among the politicians, which predated the secular and nationalist generation, was made up of reformers. This religious stratum strongly influenced the earliest two political generations, particularly the first. Although traditionalist in social behavior, education, and orientation, the reformers were the first to try to cope with the modern world and the West. Proposing historical, nativist solutions, they were too optimistic about the capabilities of Islamic reform, and their political attempts to institutionalize Islamic thought failed utterly. Their successors, an urban elite—the Muslim Brotherhood, the Mahadist in Sudan, the Husaynis in Palestine, and the Iqbalist in Pakistan—became reactionary challengers to modernism.[14] Their impact upon the second generation was enormous. The ambiguity of this religious stratum left its mark on all the modernists.

In sub-Saharan Africa the types of politicians were similar to those in the Arab countries, Egypt, and Algeria, enjoying the peak of influence between 1920 and 1945. Some of the politicians were of the liberal type—lawyers, judges, and belletrists. In this region, however, the liberals also included a group of chiefs known as constitutional progressives who put pressure on colonial authorities to reform the administration and who sought greater political participation for Africans. The progressive politicians emerged a decade before the liberals although they were of the same generation. As in Egypt, the progressives developed in urban centers, which provided modern education, long association with the West, and nationalistic orientations. The progressives founded the first party of Ghana, the United Gold Coast Convention (UGCC). In Nigeria, especially in the west, the liberal politicians who emerged in 1923, led by lawyers and civil engineers, founded the National Council of Nigeria and Cameroons (NCNC), led by Nmandi Azikiwe, while the progressives founded the Action Group led by a journalist and radical national politician Chief Obafemi Awolowo.[15]

In Ghana there appeared a third stratum, which David Apter calls the "popular radical nationalists," made up of scribes, journalists, skilled workers, market women, and local "machine" politicians, as well as former servicemen. This coalition established the Convention People's party (1947–49). The messianic populist, Kwame Nkrumah, played a key role in bringing these groups together as Ghana's first ruling party. In Nigeria, the second generation had to contend with complicated ethnic differences among Hausa, Fulani, Yoruba, and Ibo cultural and tribal units as well as political and social complexities. The Nigerian People's Conference (NPC) in 1959 represented traditionalists, ruling emirs, and native government officials. Government and party representatives were indistinguishable. New entrepreneurial classes in the south—merchants, tradesmen, and lorry-owners—were represented in the NCNC party. The struggle was over the control of the center, over distribution of national profit, patronage, and offices. But it was this generation in Egypt, the Arab East, Algeria, and major sub-Saharan states like Ghana, Nigeria, and Kenya that first created a single party both to service an authoritarian regime and to control executive power and wealth.[16]

In Zaire, the lag in political development and the restructured educational policy of Belgium made all elites and generational groups (as well as the protonationalist stratum) compete for political offices and influence. The fact was that the Congo skipped the first generational group to a second generational type represented by the MNC party and its leader, Patrice Lumumba. The messianic radical, Lumumba, and his populists struggled unsuccessfully to control the center against a curious coalition of traditionalist chiefs, prophets, liberals, and ethnic secessionists (for example, in Katanga), led by local aristocrats like Moise Tshombe.[17]

The Military

Until 1919 the military orientation in the Arab East was satrapic, and the army served the colonial power (the Ottomans) and the liberal nationalists. It was the progressive nationalists who radicalized the military in the Middle East, and eventually turned the latter into radical nationalists. Thus sultanism was integrated with radical Arab nationalism, in uniform.

By the middle 1970s, with the exception of a few conservative oil sheikhdoms and states, the radical nationalists had control throughout the Middle East (Syria, Iraq, Libya, Moslem Lebanon, Southern Yemen, and the PLO). Whereas the politicians had accepted the

Wilsonian nation-state, the military radicals sought a united, pragmatic, Arab socialist, and pan-Arab world. The men of this generation sprang from a different subculture and class; they were more pragmatic, nationalist, and militant. The composition of this group was much more mixed and fluid than the earlier generation, and it was more representative, including journalists and scribes, religious fundamentalists, children of village notables and chiefs, political millenarians, and civil servants. Whereas the liberal politicians were intellectually precise and believed in the world of ideas as the framework for political action, the military group believed that it was necessary either to establish a political party as an instrument of mobilization or to use the military and bureaucracy as a springboard for the conquest of executive power. This group's most important political aspiration, in fact, has been the conquest of executive power.

Although willing to build on the ruins of the institutions and ideals of earlier generations, the military rejects their values and structures, as well as their aspirations and expectations. The military manipulates organization rather than depending upon letters or science. It does not face the dichotomy of the absolute division between ideology and organization, but the ideology has been transformed into a mesmeric mumbo-jumbo in defense of executive, bureaucratic, and military domination. This group may be divided into two subtypes: professionals and guerrilla-terrorists.[18]

The professionals are set off from the guerrillas by their background, education, and orientation. Corporate in orientation, they tend to protect a system based on order. Sons of village notables and of the rural and urban middle classes, their education is on the whole traditionalist-modern, with some Western secondary school training. Their modern education has mainly been secured in the military academy and through additional secular, professional training abroad.

Before World War II, the status of the professional military in the Middle East, with the exception of Egypt, was low.[19] Ignored by Islamic reformist ideologists and by the liberal and progressive politicians, the military also had a low status in the hierarchy of the nationalist movement. Only after the 1950s, when the radical nationalist parties took over, did its status rise. As a consequence of the low standing of the military and the deliberate policies of colonial recruitment systems, a great number of the officers had been recruited from the periphery. A large proportion of officers in the Middle East and Algeria

came from ethnic groups. In sub-Saharan Africa, many were members
of peripheral tribes. Thus they were late in developing a nationalist
ideological orientation (except in Egypt). Ultimately preferring to join
the radicals rather than the liberals, the military professionals became
the leaders of the radical politicians' group because of their organizational strength and proximity to political power.[20] Yet the radicals
eventually became their chief rivals for power and influence. Time and
orientation clearly separate the Egyptian, Syrian, and Iraqi officers of
the first and second generations. The Egyptian army between 1882 and
1936 was noninterventionist, as was the Syrian army between 1920
and 1948 and the Iraqi army from 1921 to 1936. But when the second
generation of officers emerged, the military orientation toward authority changed.

In sub-Saharan Africa the case was more complicated. There were
no African officers at all until 1950. The satraps, who were merely
colonial army NCOs, became commanding generals during the first
years of independence. The new officers of the next generation were
men who had been educated at Sandhurst and were antagonistic to
the NCO group. The NCOs rightly suspected that their Sandhurst
cohorts were more devoted to nationalist ideologies and self-aggran-
dizement than to the military organization and the political order
created by independence. The cleavage was not so much between
political generations as it was between newcomers and *anciens*, or
between two corporate orientations—satrapic and modern praetorian.
For example, due to rapid growth and more enlightened recruitment
policies, 60 percent of the combat officers in the Nigerian army in
January 1966 were under the age of twenty-five—a situation that contributed to a generation gap, if not necessarily to a political gap. Yet
as Ali Mazrui clearly demonstrates, the African cycle now is being
completed. The rural traditional NCOs have finally replaced the
Sandhurst boys with a vengeance.[21] The generation of Idi Amin
(Uganda), Mobuto Sese Seko (Zaire), and Jean Bedel Bokassa (Central African Republic) signify the victory of the ethnics and the traditionalists. Mazrui argues that the traditionalists are better representatives of decolonialization, that they are retraditionalizing Africa,
and that they are no longer cultural satraps. They represent a more
brutal rural ethnic culture than the urban Africa of the first-generation
politicians. But as soldiers, the Amins and Mobutos, in my view, are

reincarnations of the brutal Franco-British sergeants, even though they wear the shiny epaulets of African generals.

The members of the second military subtype, the guerrillas, are converted professionals, produced through radicalization by progressive politicians. The most remarkable fact about Arab guerrillas (except in Algeria) is that they did not emerge from a party of mobilization nor were they even connected with such a type. The guerrillas had not struggled with colonial powers (except in Palestine between 1936 and 1939). Instead they were the politically militant officers and adventurers among the Arab military professionals. Most, if not all, of the Arab guerrillas returned to the barracks as professional soldiers when authorities changed. (This was true of former Syrian-Iraqi officers defeated in 1936 and of Jordanians after 1971.)

Guerrillas first appeared in Palestine in the late 1920s and early 1930s and were mostly of Iraqi, Syrian, and Palestinian origin. Products of the progressive political group, they were all former professional soldiers trained in Ottoman, Arab, or European military schools. In the case of Algeria, however, the guerrillas came mostly from Berber ethnic groups, and they had low status and were the products of traditional schooling. In the course of the political-military struggle in Algeria, they succeeded in establishing in 1954 an autonomous political organization, the Organization Speciale. They were former NCOs and officers of the French army fighting with the Free French Army and joined by workers, clerks, and the unemployed.[22]

The guerrillas represented the most radical nationalist groups in the Arab world between 1930 and 1945, and their orientations ranged from reformist Islam to fascist. They worked closely with the radical progressive politicians of the PPS in Syria, and with the Muslim Brotherhood and Misr al-Fatat in Egypt. The Misr al-Fatat, like the Algerian FLN, was composed of both former and active radical nationalist officers. After 1948, the guerrillas were mainly Palestinians, although there were still some Syrian, Iraqi, and Jordanian officers among them. In fact, the contingent sent by the Muslim Brotherhood to the Palestine campaign before May 1948 (which included Egyptians) was composed of professional officers who volunteered to help the guerrillas.[23]

The most conspicuous characteristic of the Arab guerrillas between 1930 and 1945 was their adherence to conventional warfare. The guerrillas radicalized the language of warfare but not its structure. Although they were influenced by radical progressive ideology, the guerrillas radicalized warfare only by introducing terror, not by creating any new political-military doctrines. Their political experience was meager and their doctrines completely dependent on the radicals and the intellectuals. This was not true in the case of the Algerian OS and FLN, however. Both progressives and the military belonged to the Comité Coordination Edification, the FLN's executive committee. After the Soummam Conference of 1958, the military, which had gained considerable political experience since 1954, overthrew the progressive politicians.

In the end, the professionals rejected coalition with the radicals, ousting them from the Arab military regimes of Egypt, Algeria, Sudan, and Yemen. In 1976 only the military regimes of Southern Yemen, Syria, and Iraq were still based on a coalition of military professionals and radical politicians, and in both cases the politicians' influence was declining. In Algeria, the professionally oriented officers were the colonels who had taken over the local *willayas'* (administrative and military districts) military and political organization between 1962 and 1963, at the height of the revolt.[24] Thus the nature of the Algerian war and the structure of the FLN produced a more distinctive mixed type of guerrilla, a professional officer who was experienced in the practice of revolutionary politics. The FLN's rival was the ALN, a professional bureaucratic army influenced by the liberals and moderate politicians. After 1966, this group, led by the antiradical Boumedienne and his colleagues, took over the government and integrated the remnants of the OS and guerrillas.

Most of the Arab countries, including Egypt, failed to launch a guerrilla war against the British and French colonial powers. The authorities of the mandate established local military and constabulary units composed of lower class Sunis and ethnic minorities, thus creating a satrapic military organization whose nationalist commitment was low and whose ideological component meager or nonexistent. Only a decade after independence—1936 in Iraq, and in Egypt, and 1947 in Syria—did the military elite move into the political center. Before 1936 the Arab military establishments hardly participated in the struggle against colonialism of the radical politicians and intellectuals. The few Egyptian, Iraqi, and Syrian volunteers to go to Palestine during the 1936–39 and 1947–48 expeditions did not contribute to the rise of an autonomous guerrilla force, but returned to their respective services. Such a force did not appear in Algeria until 1954 nor in Palestine until 1965 during the war for national liberation. The Palestinian guerrillas were recruited after 1965 from the radical and military professionals, but the guerrillas' purpose and ideology were not compatible. Whereas the OS-FLN guerrillas established political and military organizations that were secular and modern, the Palestinian guerrillas derived their concepts of political strategy, military organization, and warfare (their methods were assassination and terror) from medieval Islam. Guerrillas like these have been labeled "primitive rebels" by Eric Hobsbawm.[25]

The group of politically autonomous Palestinian guerrillas that developed after 1965 was a mixture. The members of its mainstream, the Fatah, was reminiscent of the Husaynis, while the radical left fedayeen splinters had more in common with the Algerian guerrillas' modern, antitraditional, orientations. The radicals among the guerrillas were an alienated group whose leaders were mainly Christian Arabs. Although it espoused various "scientific socialisms," its mixture with the primitive rebel type produced a romantic guerrilla group whose military capabilities were essentially limited, but whose strategies were still more terrorist than guerrilla despite lip service to Mao Tse-tung, Ho Chi Minh, the FLN, and Che Guevara. Fatah's elite military core, as well as its radical splinters, was mainly composed of professional Palestinian and Arab officers who had been trained in various Arab military academies, and in China, Cuba, Eastern Europe, Syria, and Algeria. The socialization of the mainstream al-Fatah was traditionalist, and soldiers were recruited mainly from the nonskilled workers, the landless peasants, the unemployed, and the occupants of the refugee camps.[26]

The Intellectuals

Three types of intellectuals have existed in developing countries since 1919: the historical traditional belletrists, the ideologues, and the technocratic or strategic elite. The first was a member of the aristocracy or the upper middle class, Western-trained and socialized, possessing a university degree or its equivalent. The belletrists played a crucial role among the liberal politicians in influencing the second generation and inculcating modernism, secularism, and nationalist aspiration. In the Muslim world, these traditional intellectuals were the founding fathers of the nationalist movement, its conscience and guiding spirit.

The ideologues and the technocrats were allies of the progressive politicians and the military. Both were products of rapid urbanization and modernization: the former was a child of Islamic reform and colonial alienation; the latter was a product of industrial, technological, and managerial economic innovations.

There were two types of ideologues, the progressives and the Marxists. The progressive was a romantic, xenophobic, antisecular modernist, and was considerably influenced by fundamentalist national-socialist and fascist doctrines and ideologies. In many ways he resembled the guerrilla and the terrorist assassin. The ideologue of the 1930s and 1940s, for example, was a romantic revolutionary who resembled the Eastern European and Balkan ultranationalist militarists and ideologues. Engaged in clandestine organizations, paramilitary activities, political organizing, and terrorism, he was in many ways the forerunner of the Castro-Maoist ideologue common among the left Palestinian fedayeen, the left-wing Ba'thists in Iraq and Syria, and the left wing of the ASU in Egypt. The Marxist ideologue attained his greatest prominence in the OS-FLN in Algeria, where the nature of the war, the emergence of guerrilla warfare, and the influence of French Marxists combined with revolutionary messianism. In Algeria, however, both the intellectuals (ideologues) and the military (guerrillas and professionals) had had only meager experience in the politics either during the colonial era or later. Finally, the Marxist ideologues were also connected with student politics, and they played a prominent role in them in Algeria between 1957 and 1965 and in Egypt after the early 1960s.[27]

The technocrats, the strategic elites of industrially developing Egypt and Algeria and of oil-producing Saudi Arabia and Kuwait, were the major source of support, the structural pillar, of the military regimes. This stratum was modernization-oriented, professional, and pragmatic. What allied the technocrats to the military regimes was their shared pragmatism and bureaucratic organization, not any ideological inclination. Unlike the politicians, they did not threaten the ruling military dictatorship but instead became the backbone of the modernizing praetorian polity.

THE STRUCTURAL EVOLUTION OF MILITARY REGIMES

The characteristic features of the military in the developing countries of the Middle East and sub-Saharan Africa are its corporate orienta-

tion and its bureaucratic structure.[28] In Europe the military developed
in conjunction with the evolution of the historical nation-state and of
the modern bureaucratic organization, but in the African and Arab
nations modern bureaucracy and the modern military are derivative.
They are modeled on the European prototype, which was corporate in
orientation and shared political power and influence, but was totally
removed from the political and social experiences of the colonized
states.

The Administrative Grid

Because of the historical gap between tradition and modernity,
the asymmetry of political culture, and the low capability of cultural
vis-à-vis social and political mobilization, the military and the bureaucracy in developing polities since independence have gained an
influence far greater than that enjoyed by these institutions in nineteenth-century Western Europe. They have either become the political authority or they have propped up a faltering authority. The
political stability of the modern nation-state in the West was achieved
through the institutionalization of political cleavage—through interest
groups, political parties, social movements, and political control of
the military establishment—but in the developing countries (particularly those of sub-Saharan Africa, North or Moslem Africa, and the
Arab Middle East) the aspirations for political stability are restricted
to the instrumentalities of the executive, the rudimentary machinery of
the state, and therefore are subject to the influence of the bureaucracy
and to domination by the military. Modern Arab and African polities are distinguished by, first, the absence of highly institutionalized
social movements, interest groups, and political parties and by, second,
the extraordinary concern of the military to keep order.[29]

As the case of the Congo demonstrates, when independence was
achieved, African political party systems were utterly fragmented,
as were the other political structures of the societies. "With some
variation from country to country, the party was initially a loose movement which naturally incorporated the characteristics of the society in
which it grew; it was eventually transformed into a political machine
but continued to reflect the state of incomplete integration of the
territorial society." Even though Ghana's Convention People's party
(CPP) was well established by the middle 1950s and the Tanzanian
National Union (TANU) gained significant strength in the 1960s, an

institutional vacuum continued to exist in the modern African political systems.[30] In fact, very few contemporary African or Arab regimes were able to establish viable governments.

Arab regimes also underwent considerable change between 1950 and 1970. Parliamentary-party and monarchical-patrimonial regimes were replaced by military regimes in six Arab countries: Syria, Egypt, Iraq, Yemen, Sudan, and Libya. The old institutions were supplanted by bureaucratic systems run by a stratocracy that, in most cases, either created a single party (ostensibly in order to control the masses) or formed one from an existing radical party. With the advent of praetorianism in Arab "revolutionary" regimes, political development was restricted to the improvement and aggrandizement of executive and personal power at the expense of the army-dominated party. The centralization of authority in the hands of a small politicized military executive was particularly characteristic of the Arab military regimes. When a one-party system emerged in an exclusively executive political system, both the bureaucracy and the military took part in an untenable coalition of political groups that attempted to control the executive.

The one-party regimes in Africa in no way resemble the party movements or regimes found in Communist countries, or even in such socialist countries as Yugoslavia and Mexico, because in the communist and socialist states large-scale social and economic mobilization is directed by a process of political institutionalization. The one-party systems in Africa demonstrate not only the weakness or nonexistence of opposition, but also the instrumental nature of politics; that is, "whatever the particular arrangement laid down in West African constitutions, in all countries the President rules relatively unhampered either by separation of powers or by other limiting definitions of his authority."[31] Africans are ruled by the executive; regimes are administrative structures.

The major difference between single-party systems in sub-Saharan Africa and in the Arab Middle East is that the systems in the former were created before the military took power, whereas in the latter they were created by a military regime to legitimize its rule (as, for example, in Egypt). In Syria and Iraq, the military regimes conquered a radical nationalist party—the Ba'th—by force and purge and transformed it into a popular structure supporting the military regime. By eliminating all other political parties, the military in Egypt, Syria, and Iraq used a single military party to aid in the domination of the exective.

There is a clear distinction between African and Arab military attitudes toward the single party. The Arab revolutionary regimes of Syria and Iraq would not think of governing without the support of a single party, even though it is a pliable subordinate. (In Syria and Iraq the Ba'th is more powerful than the military-created Arab Socialist Union in Egypt.) The African military, in contrast, not only manages to rule without the support of a single party but on the whole rejects any suggestion that such a party should be reinstated or formed. The Arab military revolutionary would not seek the support of the old parties, whereas the African military in Ghana, Nigeria, Zaire, and Mali did seek such support.

Members of the new elites of the African countries and of some Arab countries emerged from different sectors, social strata, and economic and educational groups. These cleavages, however, are not the base for political elite recruitment or of executive power. Structurally weak institutions and a low degree of mobilization of men, resources, and values; limited political participation; and lack of economic differentiation have produced political and cultural cleavages in Africa. Functionally, there is class conflict in some sub-Saharan societies, but it is certainly not like that found in industrial societies. Instead, the conflict arises from the fact that stratification relationships are not relevant to political power and authority. The proper image here is not one of a social and political hierarchy in which everybody has his defined place.[32] The basis for political conflict is political power. There is rigid stratification is some African societies, but its impact on civil-military relations is negligible. Significantly, the stratification system in precolonial Africa, however loose, was also not particularly developed. Classes, in the Marxist sense of groups that relate to one another on the basis of production, were nonexistent. Thus, class conflict in Africa is conflict not over human but over authority resources, over positions in the system of hierarchy and over the state's distribution of ecomonic resoures or what Andreski prefers to call "Kleptocratic practices" or government by theft.[33] In the Arab East and Egypt political power is also derived from the administrative authority or the authority of the gun, not from the assembly line.

The administrative grid is the pre-eminent variable in any explanation of politics of the military in Africa. "Colonialism made Africa essentially a continent of bureaucratic rule and control." The military was used to police and control tribal outburst and violence. The French

excelled in military administration; the British were not their in-
feriors by much. According to Lord Lugard, the power of the tribal
chief "stemmed from his military training and mind, and the system of
one-man rule which he set up faithfully reflects military rather than
civil considerations." The colonial administrators were inbred, insular,
and "unreconstructed Victorian gentlemen." The first African generation after independence accepted the colonial model with little reserva-
tion. Calls for "Africanization" were ignored by subservient officials,
especially in the military establishment. Sub-Saharan African regimes
became semi-administrative states. "The power elite has even been
called 'the bureaucratic bourgeoisie.' " By the early 1970s the ad-
ministrations of independent regimes were still a major source of
employment in sub-Saharan Africa and to a lesser extent in Egypt
and the Arab East.[34] The military was eventually Africanized as well.

Military Regimes and Their Support

In the Arab and African countries both of the basic types of praetorian armies—the arbitrator and the ruler—have appeared.[35] (For a
more detailed illustration of regime types, see appendix to this chapter.)
While the arbitrator type imposes a time limit on army rule and
arranges to hand over the government to an acceptable civilian regime,
the ruler type believes in prolonging its own control. The arbitrator,
although it does not necessarily relinquish political influence, does
believe in returning to the barracks on the condition that the army
act as the guardian of civilian authority and of political stability. The
ruler army, on the other hand, plans to establish itself in power as the
only legitimate group. First it attempts to invent or adopt an ideology.
Then it creates a political party of the army, an executive committee
of "free officers." The most significant contribution of Arab officers to
establishing political control of the executive was the Revolutionary
Command Council (RCC), an ad hoc cabinet or executive instrument
of the military, which runs the government and guides or directs the
society. This body is also in charge of eliminating internal opposition
within the military and the society. The RCC has been adopted in all
praetorian Arab countries and is gaining wide recognition in military-
dominated polities in sub-Saharan Africa. When the Egyptian, Syrian,
and Iraqi officers first established the RCC, it served as a political
instrument to control politicized army officers. African officers, although
imitating the Arab institution, see the RCC as a purely administrative

instrument, not an executive base for a future military party. The whole arbitrator-ruler syndrome is closely linked with three factors in both Arab and African countries: the life span of political military coalitions, the type of regime and regime support, and the relationship of the professional to the bureaucrat.

Civil-military relations in developing countries are uneven. Politics involves short-term alliances and is based on expedience; limited and sometimes strange political coalitions rapidly appear and as quickly wither away. Coalitions of political elites of the same or different orientations are kaleidoscopic, rootless, and unstable. Today's group in power is tomorrow's group in limbo. Between World War II and the 1970s the life span of ruling praetorian groups has grown shorter. The first lasted approximately two and a half decades (1919–45); the second, less than twenty years and, in some cases, less than ten years. By the middle 1970s the life of the third was less than ten years. (See table 5.1.) The capabilities of the various strata to form coalitions within and between the generational groups also declined. Moreover, the transferral of power one generation to another was followed by the movement from the arbitrator to the ruler type of praetorianism.

Under the reign of the liberal politicians, there was little chance of military intervention. Not only was the military civilian-oriented, but the first political generation was still willing to collaborate with the imperial powers and its political demands were low. The military was loyal to the first generation, not because it subscribed to Mosca's rule that a civilized society is not governed by the military but because its expectations were not manifest. Its concept of politics, which was restrictive, did not involve radicalism. That change occurred with the next generation. The progressive politicians entered executive politics in two ways: either by encouraging the radical-nationalist officers to move into the political arena or by exploiting the terrorist and violent instruments of the fundamentalists and fascists (rovers, militias, and other paramilitary structures). Their entry was marked by a direct coup, by mob action instigated by the paramilitary organizations, or by the threat of military or terrorist power. The radical politicians and ideologues formed a coalition with the professional military, which was oriented toward an arbitrator type of praetorianism. This type of regime had a brief life: either the military returned to the barracks and the paramilitary organizations were outlawed, or a more distinctly military-dominated regime evolved.

Military intervention in the liberal-progressive era was generally undertaken by an arbitrator army. When the arbitrator officers attempted to transfer power to a ruler through a countercoup (as in Iraq in 1937 and 1941 or the first Syrian regimes in 1949), they were overthrown or assassinated by the civilian regime with help from the army. When the progressive-radical group took over, however, military interventionism reached its apex, ushering in the golden era of military praetorianism. Ruler-type praetorianism was contagious. The military coups in Syria in 1949 were followed by a coup in Iraq (1949) and one in Egypt (1952). In Syria successive coups and countercoups continued into the early 1970s. Since 1958 there have been successful coups in Iraq, the Sudan, Yemen, Libya, and several unsuccessful coups in Jordan and Lebanon.[36] Thus in the Middle East the radical regimes developed and improved upon the praetorian ruler type. In Africa, by the middle 1970s, the arbitrator-ruler syndrome had not yet been institutionalized. The modernizers—the Sandhurst group—were more distinguished interventionists than the satraps. This was true again until a decade after independence, when satraps became more influential in the army than the educated professionals. The satrap sergeants in Uganda, Zaire, the Central African Republic, and Sierra Leone also became interventionists; once the cycle of interventionism had begun, it was hard to stem the tide of military praetorianism. The ruler type gained power in country after country. The role of the radicals was growing in the Middle East and Egypt, and in Africa. But in 1976 the chances that they might take power in most Arab states and sub-Saharan Africa are indeed utopian. Nevertheless, the traditional African officer has become today's radical nationalist.

In addition to being related to the span of political-military coalitions, the arbitrator-ruler syndrome is linked with the type of regime, its source of support, and its longevity. The arbitrator type usually appears when the civilian regime has established a long tradition and has achieved enough resilience to successfully avert military intervention, or when the officer corps is small and inexperienced. The ruler type is likely to emerge when regimes are short-lived and the military establishment is large and secure. The ruler type can also arise when the military establishes and supports an authoritarian regime (Egypt, Syria, Iraq). In Africa, the fragility of the regime can provide a temptation for the military. Here the ruler type is established only because there is no civilian alternative and the regime is weak. When a civilian government has been established, the military returns to the barracks, as it did in Ghana between 1969 and 1972. A civilian regime supported by a nonmilitary coalition (labor, trade unions, or tribes loyal to the regime) could impose an arbitrator role on the army. On the other hand, a military regime dominated by an ethnic group tends to become a ruler type. On the whole, the odds are in favor of the development of a ruler type of praetorianism. For example, Nigeria, where the army elite abhorred politics and rejected military intervention in internal security, produced the ruler type.[37] Even Nigeria has specified a date for return to civilian rule and set out the ground rules for the transition. But the parentheses between civilian and military rule are still open— even the politicians were invited to join the government. It is in the nature of the secure ruler that he takes civilians into his cabinet. However, executive control is still in the hands of the military.

A coalition government of progressive politicians and the military may also lean toward the ruler syndrome. But the arbitrator officers who, having lost confidence in civilian rule, help set up a ruler type of regime may discover that its threat to military corporatism is as high as, or higher than, the threat existing when they dominated the regime from the barracks.

Most Middle Eastern and African military elites are not cohesive. Military intervention contributes in many cases to fratricide among the officer class, as in Syria, Iraq, Yemen, Nigeria, Uganda, and Dahomey. In attempting to confront the civilian challenge to military corporatism, the military dictatorship usually destroys the very thing it sought to protect. The persistence of coups and the decimation and permanent purge of the officer class—Syria, Iraq, Nigeria, Sierra Leone, Uganda, and Zaire are the most notorious cases—build up their own momentum, which contributes to the persistence of praetorianism. The military also becomes embroiled in alliances with a motley assortment of civilian politicians, which tends to increase internal conflict. The fragility of some ruler-praetorian regimes has only been equalled by their fratricidal conflicts. There are eras of intense praetorianism: for example, the years 1949 and 1963–66 in Syria and 1937–41, 1963, 1968, and 1973 in Iraq.

But caution must be exercised in generalizing on the type of regime (ruler or arbitrator) that results at the end of a series of coups and countercoups, as has already been demonstrated in the case of Syria's ruler regime since 1966. After 1941 Iraq enjoyed some seventeen years of autocratic parliamentary government. Yemen, after the end of the civil war (1965) and after a long military dictatorship, had an era of relative stability even without the support of an arbitrator army. In 1974 the ruler army appeared in Yemen. But these cases, of course, cannot be used to refute this book's major contention that ruler praetorianism is the radical generation's favorite regime. Only when confronted with its own fratricidal conflicts and challenged by other political forces do the military elites opt for an arbitrator role and return to the barracks. The eras of intense praetorianism harass, decimate, and exhaust the officer corps, leading it to accept a truce and reduced political influence when faced with serious opposition from the civilian groups. When this situation exists, as it did in Egypt after 1953, the officer corps seeks to preserve its corporate entity by consciously trying to abstain from politics. Only under duress, when the corporate orientation of the military is openly challenged by a civilian regime, or when the regime is unable to satisfy a discontented military, will the army try to return to politics, an attempt it made unsuccessfully in Egypt in 1971.

A cyclical pattern can be seen in the structural evolution of executive control in both the arbitrator and the ruler type of praetorianism. Beginning with executive arbitration, it develops into executive control and then returns to a type of arbitration. Each kind of praetorian regime has institutional and structural arrangements that reflect its orientation and role. The syndrome, however, is more complex. Only a schematic model of military executive control—arbitrator-ruler—will be considered here, along with a few case studies to explain it. Thus the types may be oversimplified.

There are two kinds of military regime structures and legitimization: political and administrative.[38] The military regime structure in Egypt and the Arab East is political. It tries to dominate the nation's social, economic, and political forces; structures; and groups, centralizing authority in the RCC. The sub-Saharan military regime structure is administrative. It has limited ability to dominate social, economic, or political forces, structures, and groups.

The Egyptian-Arab political type concentrates on occupying and dominating every political and economic structure of society. This orientation is derived from three sources: the radical nationalist attitudes of Arab praetorians, their sultanist legacy, and the political procedures and structures of the old regime. The desire of a military regime to dominate and establish a political model—as in the Arab countries—

is highly correlated with the praetorian commitment to modernization. The sub-Saharan African military regimes' preference for the administrative model derives from its satrapic legacy and its rather vague commitment to nationalism and modernization. However, should the level of sophistication, political and executive, of the African military rise, it might opt for another solution to the problem of executive control. Here again the time variable is important. The Arab RCC model prefers to rule, using civilians only for support (Egypt, Syria, Iraq, Sudan), but the African National Command Council (NCC), especially in West Africa, still depends on civilian and consultative bodies to aid in governing. In East and Central Africa, the ruler is the hero of the day. Whereas the Arab regime co-opts the civil service, the African heavily relies on the civilian bureaucracy for help in governing, as in Ghana, Dahomey, Zaire, Mali, Sierra Leone, and Nigeria, and even in the Central African Republic.

While the Egyptian-Arab type prefers an authoritarian structure (as in Egypt and Syria), the African type will opt for a mixed administration and a laissez-faire structure—an arrangement obviously lacking any ideological inspiration. In Egyptian-Arab civil-military relations, the military praetorians are dominant, whereas the African military in most cases still collaborates with the civilians. The concept of political "neutrality" is a military orientation that is more African than Egyptian-Arab. The Egyptian-Arab type prefers to break off relations with incumbents—including senior politicians, civil servants, and military from the old regime—but the African military junta protects the continuity of administration, the civil service, and the military. Even its foreign policy is more dependent and less volatile than the Egyptian-Arab type.

The Arbitrator Regime

The arbitrator regime type (Type A) is a structure designed by the military to further its arbitrator role. (See figure 5.2).[39] The general headquarters of the army has been taken over by a group of free officers whose major source of support is the military. They indirectly control the political and civilian institutions, but they do not dominate the executive, the government, or the bureaucracy. This type of regime divides power between the government executive and the executive (the general headquarters ruled by the free officers) that indirectly controls it. This kind of military rule may disintegrate when members of the general headquarters, as well as others within the army, join with the bureaucracy or with the government and turn against the military regime.

Type A was first introduced by the military regimes of Iraq between 1936 and 1941 and was used in three of the Syrian military regimes in 1949. In sub-Saharan Africa the control of the executive was more direct, even if it had an arbitrator orientation. Until the middle 1970s, most military regimes in sub-Saharan Africa "leaped" over Type A, for most independent regimes collapsed before or after the coups and little structural authority existed for the military to inherit. Nevertheless, the ruler type began to emerge after 1973 and new military dictatorships were established in Uganda, Zaire, and the Central African Republic.

In the Middle East, however, parliamentary regimes and party structures were entrenched and did not collapse when coups took place. The monarchy in Iraq and the parliamentary regime of Syria demonstrated a remarkable capacity for survival over a period of some thirty years although these countries were in a state of almost perpetual crisis. The military in Iraq did not even contemplate overthrowing the monarchy until the late 1950s, nor did the Syrian army consider doing away with parliamentary government until 1966. In fact, the Ba'th party, the sponsors of military interventionism, advocated the sustenance of parliamentary and party rule until 1966, when the radical and 'Alawi officers took over the party and the army.

In the Middle East the military has generally found the Type A model unsatisfactory for two reasons. First, indirect rule over the executive does not permit the military to be completely responsible for the government and the bureaucracy, nor can it control the rivalries between bureaucracy and military. Second, political parties, civilian institutions, and the bureaucracy have successfully circumvented the military by virtue of their semi-independent rule. The arbitrator regime in the Middle East, which was designed to strengthen political authority and create order, actually bolstered the radical, nationalist groups and parties and weakened military authority. It could be argued, of course, that during this period the military was not yet in a position to rule.

The Type A coalition of politicians and professional military usually evolves into a military dictatorship that ousts the civilians from executive power and establishes an army executive. The ALM (Arab Liberation Movement) took this course in Syria (1952–53), as did the RCC in

Egypt and in other Arab military regimes after 1953. In Algeria, the professional military ousted the progressive politicians along with the ex-guerrillas in 1965. Military dictatorships of the second generation are dominated solely by the professional stratum of the military. By 1976, there had been no case in the Middle East, North Africa, or sub-Saharan Africa in which military regimes were dominated by guerrillas in coalition with guerrillas, except for a brief uneasy period in Algeria between 1962 and 1965. Unlike the Type A regime, the ruler regime (Type B) seeks support from the professionals in the bureaucracy and

Figure 5.2   Type A: The Arbitrator Regime

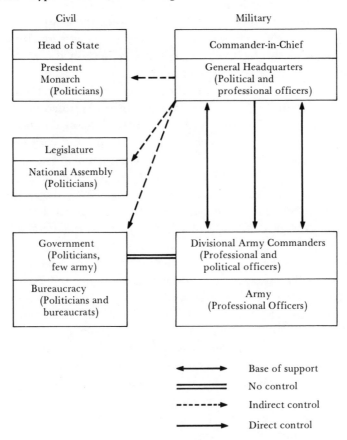

SOURCE: Amos Perlmutter, *Egypt, The Praetorian State* (New Brunswick, N.J.: Transaction, 1974), p. 133.

the technocrats in the economy in order to replace the progressive politicians, ex-guerrillas, intellectuals, and paramilitary groups.

The Ruler Regime

Type B is a modification of Type A, designed to overcome its failures.
(See figure 5.3.) It makes possible efficient domination of the executive
by the military. The Revolutionary Command Council is established as
the instrument to control the executive, and the officer who heads the
RCC is both president and prime minister of the country. The veterans
of the RCC still constitute the major source of support. In this type of
regime, however, the general headquarters is composed of nonpolitical
officers. Thus there is no chance of a coalition between the senior military and the bureaucracy. Relations between the head of the RCC and
the chief of staff are close, however, and the chief's loyalty is essential.
The head of the RCC can sometimes relinquish the presidency to a
civilian, but only under the condition that military rule over the bureaucracy will continue, usually in the form of a military dictatorship. There
is a good chance that the legislature will be abolished or at least completely dominated by the military. As this type of regime develops, it
begins to pack the legislature with loyal officers and with new members
of a political party of the military. The government executive becomes
a mixture of soldiers and bureaucrats, as does the bureaucracy. Both
structures, however, are controlled by the RCC. The prototype appeared in Syria under Colonel Adib Shishakly, who in 1952 transformed
a Type A military regime into a Type B by uniting general headquarters
and the government under the control of an RCC.[40]

The best example of a Type B regime was that of Nasser between 1953
and 1961. The struggle for power against Nagib, the Wafd party, and
the Muslim Brotherhood was conducted by an executive committee, the
conspirational Free Officers Club, designed by Nasser to consolidate
and activate the RCC. The club was established in 1949 and became a
political apparatus in 1953. The RCC functioned as the sole representative of the military coupmakers· Nasser himself participated in its
design and worked closely on organizational details. The major functions of the RCC were to eliminate opposition parties and personalities,
to organize the masses, and to establish a political organ to enhance
legitimacy and attract support.

In sub-Saharan Africa, Type B is the most representative type of
regime. A modified version of the Arab Type B regime, it rules in the

sense of dominating executive power. In contrast to the Arab-Egyptian RCC, the sub-Saharan National Liberation Council (NLC) is only the chief administrative instrument of the state. It is not a political instrument, a mini politiburo of politically minded officers like the one that dominated Egypt after Nasser's coup. The military-bureaucratic alliance is a political device "in which armies have the physical power to conserve the regime, while the civil service will hold effective executive power in the state." In Nigeria, the Second Republic (1966–67) passed control from the politicians to such an alliance, in which the military, both federal and Biafran, drew upon civil servants to strengthen the executive rule established by the First Republic (1961–65). In Ghana this partnership was established after the 1966 coup, shutting out Nkrumah's politicians. The NLC represented an alliance of middle-ranking officers, policemen, technocrats, and anti-Nkrumah liberal politicians.[41]

It can be argued that Type B African regimes are military autocracies; for example, Zaire, Dahomey, Uganda, and Sierra Leone. No African military ruler has yet tried to convert the executive administration into a protopolitburo like those in Egypt and the Arab East. He rules instead by dominating the military and the civil service. It can also be hypothesized, though there is little supporting evidence, that the satrapic officer prefers a military tyranny whereas the Sandhurst officer will opt for the Egyptian-Syrian-Iraqi type of political ruler who governs with the support of a military-dominated single party. Certainly the Ghanaian army rejected Nkrumah's Workers' Brigade, a people's militia invented by the dictator to control the military and probably to transform its organization. But the Syrian and Iraqi military also rejected and dissolved people's militias that they considered a threat to the corporate military establishment.

In Type B regime the military dictatorship evolves to the point where the executive is largely dominated by the professional military while the rest of the governmental machinery, except for the secret service and the structures for internal surveillance, is controlled by the strategic elites. If the military dictatorship moves to annihilate the intellectual stratum by purging it from the political party and installing governmental scribes and officially approved "ideologues" in its stead, the structure of the government-dominated party and the establishment will depend on an alliance with the ideologues and the technocrats. Thus Type B may evolve into Type C.

Figure 5.3   Type B: The Ruler Regime

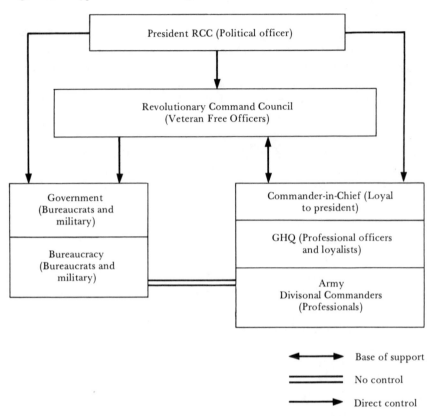

SOURCE: Perlmutter, *Egypt,* p. 136.

Back to the Arbitrator Regime

The party-army regime, or Type C, is the most recent of the three types. (See figure 5.4.) It held sway in Egypt in 1961 and 1971 and in Syria after 1966, and was in power in Iraq between 1958 and 1963 and again after 1968. No Type C regime has appeared in Ghana and Nigeria or anywhere in sub-Saharan Africa for that matter. The military dictator, the head of the RCC, still totally dominates the executive in Type C regimes. His major source of support remains the military high command. As head of the RCC, he appoints to general headquarters loyal and cooperative professional and patrimonially oriented officers. The military is then rewarded with a great measure of corporate autonomy. Thus the relationship between the military dictator and the high command is corporate and patrimonial. If the military dictator is successful in both establishing order and respecting the military corporate orientation, the neutralized military returns to the barracks and its orientations are transformed from ruler to arbitrator. If the military intervenes again, it may face the opposition of both the successful military dictator turned head of state and of the political organization at his disposal. Although allied with the bureaucracy (capitalist-oriented in Ghana, socialist-oriented in Nasser's Egypt, and capitalist-oriented in Sadat's Egypt since 1973), the military in the barracks is still divided.

Besides the military high command, the military party (the party dominated by the RCC) provides direct control and support for Type C. In the Arab Middle East the military either innovates such a movement or takes over an established radical nationalist political party to legitimize its rule. The party is then harnessed as the main source of support for the regime. The highest development of this form was Nasser's regime between 1961 and 1969.

Almost immediately after establishing the RCC, which acted as an executive committee for the Free Officers, Nasser established the Liberation Rally, the army-dominated party, whose purpose was to infuse the military's ideology into society and to gain its support. The Liberation Rally engaged in propaganda and recruited scribes and other writers to provide it with intellectual and ideological legitimacy. It failed utterly, and in 1958 Nasser founded another type of organization, the National Union (UN), which was to be a participatory party encompassing the UAR (Egypt and Syria). The National Union also failed to organize mass support, however, especially in Syria. The RCC, although it delegated fictional authority, failed to control the mammoth political organization it had established. When Syria broke with the UAR in 1961, the UN collapsed. Nasser's third attempt was the Arab Socialist Union (ASU). The new party was formed on the basis of two principles: (1) to strengthen the control of the RCC over the party, that is, to narrow the organizational scope of the top party structure; and (2) to form a permanent party base of party "activists" (leaders) thus transforming them into political influentials in the country's modernization programs, structures, and activities.[42]

The ASU between 1965 and 1971 represented a considerable modification of Nasser's original concept. He could no longer deny that the ASU activists were cadres and a political elite in the industrial-economic

Figure 5.4 Type C: Back to the Arbitrator Regime

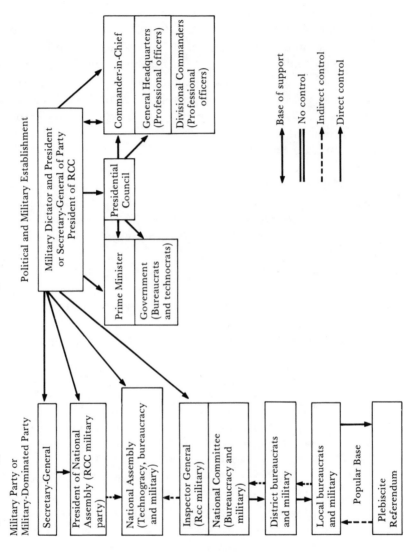

SOURCE: Perlmutter, *Egypt*, p. 137.

realm. Old-style bureaucrats were distinguished from the functional-modern bureaucrats attached to and influenced by the ASU. The most significant development during this period was that the governmental corporations and industrial centers controlled by ASU provided an alternative to the army as a source from which to recruit the power elite. This change naturally intensified the struggle between the senior military members of the RCC and the leaders of the ASU, which in the end led to the 1971 abortive coup against Sadat by the ASU activists political officers.

The relationship between the government and the ASU was complex. Each level of the ASU was dominated by a corresponding governmental structure. Indirect control was ruled out. Control was horizontal, but not total. For instance, between 1965 and 1967, Ali Sabri, vice-president of Egypt and head of the ASU, succeeded in mobilizing into ASU level B, the strategic elite (see figure 5.5), the factory managers and technocrats (whom he called activists), who were neither bureaucrats nor pawns of the government. Level A, the executive of the ASU, however, remained closed to the "masses" and was composed strictly of veteran RCC officers or new officer recruits. The activists were organized into steering committees independent from the RCC.[43] Yet the political function of the Liberation Rally and the National Union was extremely limited and the social impact of both was restricted. These political structures served to provide support for the government and to eliminate opposition, to spread Nasser's ideology and inculcate his teachings to Egypt's masses, and to act as ad hoc instruments for resolving some critical political issues of domestic (especially economic) policy. In foreign affairs and national security, the *Rais* and a few of his lieutenants dominated without interference. After the attempted coup against Sadat the military establishment became the chief arbiter of the regime.

The Type C regime was not successfully institutionalized in Egypt. Between 1971 and 1973 Egypt oscillated between Type B and Type C. The military, so jealous of its corporate identity, brought an end to the leftist domination of the ASU (in 1971), reduced the ASU's influence, and in July 1972 ousted the Soviet advisers who had intervened in the military's internal organization. Since the October 1973 war, the ruler regime has returned. Sadat is in total control supported by and of course dependent on the loyalty of the military.

In Syria (February 1966) and Iraq (at the end of 1968), the military

Figure 5.5   Authority Relations between ASU and Government in Egypt,
1965–71

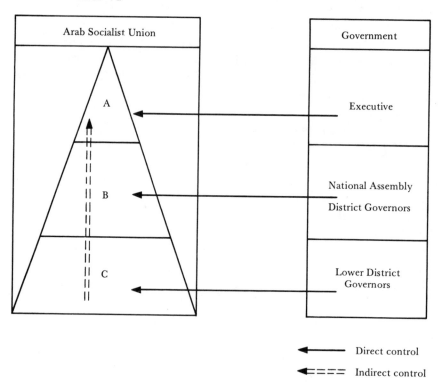

SOURCE: Perlmutter, *Egypt*, p. 165. Adapted from Sarah Lulko, "The Popular
Organization of the Nasserite Regime" (Mimeographed, Shiloah Institute, Tel Aviv University, 1970).

regimes opted to harness, transform, and control an established radical
political party, the Ba'th Arab Socialist party, which had welcomed the
military politically and intellectually and had espoused its role in
politics. At the end of 1970 the Syrian army finally moved to dominate
the party by ousting all the officers who still adhered to the idea that the
party should have a quasi-independent role. The Syrian regime after
1970 seemed to be shifting to a modified Type B. The takeover by the
'Alawi officers was paralleled by an 'Alawi takeover of the party. An
army-party symbiosis was established in which the army had primacy.[44]

The development of the African civil-military alliance was markedly
different from that of its Egyptian counterpart. The African military regimes were not oriented toward the formation of an alternative political

system, thus neither the satraps nor the "Sandhurst" military politicians were ideologically motivated nor were they radically nationalistic like the Egyptian and Arab military praetorians. Corporate orientations, British-French military schooling and command, and, above all, meager participation or nonparticipation in pre-independence nationalist politics made the African military conspicuously nonideological, perhaps even anti-ideological. The African officer was not radicalized as was the Egyptian-Arab officer (at least not until the rise of radicals in Uganda and Zaire in the 1970s). His politics were administrative, and he felt quite at ease in allying with the civil service and the old civilian politicians. In sub-Saharan Africa the military did ally with the old politicians—in Nigeria with the old NPC-Action Group; in Ghana with the anti-Nkrumah United party Ashanti politicians. Thus the military regime returned to power pre-Nkrumah communal and tribal politics. In Lagos and Biafra, the army toppled an "unproductive government" and replaced it with a war party government.[45]

In order to institutionalize the domination of the military praetorian over the bureaucracy and technocracy, the single party, and the military establishment, it was necessary to expand the executive office of the military dictator. Nasser's Egypt, the most mature praetorian regime of the Arab Middle East, is credited with originating a new type of executive appendage, which was called the Office for Presidential Affairs. Its function was to neutralize pressure on the military dictatorship, especially from the military establishment, and to coordinate the functioning of the praetorian system. The head of the office was usually a military praetorian chosen by the dictator for his unswerving loyalty and his long experience in internal espionage and counterespionage.

This executive appendage institutionalized praetorian political procedures and at the same time increased the government's efficiency. The office's powers were substantial. In fact, its former head, Sami Sharaf, a Nasser loyalist and alleged KGB agent, was the chief anti-Sadat leader during the abortive 1971 coup. Such machinery and procedures were reminiscent of those of the sultanist court, represented by the reign of Muhammed Ali in Egypt (1805–49), and they were not duplicated elsewhere in the Arab Middle East. Even in Egypt the office lost its influence after the death of Nasser.

Sustained praetorian rule in Syria or Iraq could produce a similar system, but it would not be essential to the survival of military power. In Syria, for example, the military could depend on the 'Alawi officers and the Ba'th party. Although it is doubtful that the African administrative praetorians would emulate a sultanist system, the Muslim-dominated African polities might choose to follow the Egyptian model even though they lack Egypt's extensive and well-established bureaucracy or they might select the Syrian Arab model. Both sub-Saharan Africa and the Arab Middle East lack the large entrenched bureaucracies that are almost a prerequisite for the development of sultanism. But the African militaries might need ethnic groups or tribes, as Syria does, for political support.

So far, Type C has been restricted to Egypt, and its expansion to other states is doubtful. Praetorian polities are hardly "systems" and cannot be explained in terms of permanent groupings engaged in a long-term political struggle. Political structures are in a constant state of flux. To repeat the major theme of this work, praetorianism is characterized by the absence of social mobilization, lack of political institutionalization, and deficiency in executive institutionalization and effectiveness. Therefore, Type C should not be taken out of context. It is not Lenin's or Mao's party or army. Nor is the RCC the British cabinet. At best, it is the court of the praetorians. It is sometimes legitimized, although it usually is not—it is a new political structure nevertheless. And in several cases, including Syria since 1966 and Egypt between 1952 and 1961, praetorianism contributed to executive domination and control even though it did not become a permanent fixture.

The major weakness of all military praetorian systems is that the military and the military dictator (except for a few like Atatürk) consider politics and institutionalized political processes to be little more than a conspiracy, an abnormal state of human affairs, to use Nasser's phrase. Therefore the army, made watchful by its insecurity and insularity, must permanently "patrol" society. Furthermore, the kaleidoscope of short-lived institutions and collective arrangements prevents the military praetorian from "trusting" civic society (and vice versa). Even the RCC is a short-lived project—an institution created to engineer a coup and sustain a military cabal in power that quickly loses its raison d'être and is dissolved. To speak of the RCC as if it were the British cabinet, Lenin's politburo, or the United States presidency is as futile as speaking of the Syrian parliament as if it were the British Parliament or of the Ba'th party as if it were the equivalent of the British Labour party. The point is not that the RCC must approximate the British cabinet, or the Syrian legislature the British Parliament, but that one of the newer institutions approximates an executive; the other, a legislative system.

The military in the Middle East has failed to improve on the political stability and political development created by the civilians they call corrupt. In fact, the pre-independence Arab political parties had far wider political support than any military regime in the Middle East (including Nasser's). Praetorian rule is a consequence of political and institutional decay, a process it accelerates.

Confrontation to Corporatism

The military entered politics under the pretext of saving the corporate military establishment and, of course, the nation; but once in politics it declared war on the civilian politicians. However, the military found the practice of politics similar to crossing a minefield. Its failure to stay aloof led it into a corporate debacle—the perpetual alternation of coup and countercoup. "Once an army enters government, the possession of power proceeds to divide it: army cohesion disappears as soon as the army stops performing the function for which it was drilled."[46]

Nigeria is a case in point. There the military increased in numbers from a few thousand in 1958 to 10,500 in 1966, and the budget grew accordingly. Control over the forces and their budget was transferred to the Nigerian government in 1958, and the command structure of the army was manned by Nigerians beginning in 1964–65. As the military emerged from its colonial yoke, its self-image and morale improved. The new officer, who aspired to be modern in appearance, dress, and language, emulated the Sandhurst style and strove for corporate integrity and material mobility. One-upmanship became his only motivation. Service to the army, the state, or the nation was not considered. The growth of organization and the rising level of aspiration created both stresses in organization and strains on individual personalities. The military self-image of "neutrality" in politics was called into question by the "corruption" of political life.[47]

The growth of the Nigerian military in manpower and resources and the rise of the Sandhurst "boys" alongside the satrapic generals (former NCOs) exacerbated organizational strains.[48] Although Sandhurst had indoctrinated the new African officers with their role as professional soldiers in external war, at home they were concerned exclusively with internal security. This triggered interventionism, because the new officer felt degraded when assigned as a policeman; acting as an internal security force challenged martial values and left unfulfilled corporate professional aspirations. The disparities between satrapism and the Sandhurst orientation grew deeper as the civilian regime was further fragmented by political infighting and the military's domestic task led it to intervene in internal political strife. The coup of the Nigerian majors in January 1966, followed by the July 1966 breakdown of military authority over its own officer corps, resulted in the decline of the military's chief professional element—discipline. "A poorly institutionalized authority structure, like that of the Nigerian army . . . was badly placed to absorb either the dislocation in discipline produced by the January coup or the new pressures for allocation made upon it when its leaders held political power." Again, in my view decline in discipline was not sufficient cause for intervention, but a corollary of the professional's attitude toward the state. Isolation and a view of politics as "ugly" had not helped the military to acquire political skills. The first coup was made along military lines by a cohesive Sandhurst elite (and its allies, mostly Ibos).[49] The second coup involved civilian politicians, who had been working to subvert the army since the January 1966 coup. Corporate integrity fell victim as the military's declined into a security force, a development that created organizational chaos and eventually forced it to take political action.

In the Arab Middle East, where military intervention accompanied the army's organizational growth and its assumption of a political role, Syria is the best example of the praetorian syndrome. Syria lacked a stable government after 1949, the year of her first army coup; that year also marked the demise of the satrapic Ottoman-trained officer. Syria's political arena gradually became a theater for ambitious army men.[50] In the three decades following independence from France, Syria had only eight years of parliamentary rule (1945–49 and 1954–58) and five years of semiparliamentary government (1961–66). Long periods of military intervention alternated with shorter episodes of parliamentary and semiparliamentary rule, during which the government stood in the shadow of the military. Between 1949 and 1972 Syria experienced some thirteen army coups—seven of them successful. Only three times did the officers who achieved successful coups pass the reins of power to civilians. After 1963 a pattern developed in which civilians and the army alternated in power, but the army never retreated to the barracks. For example, in the coup of March 1963, officers who were members of or sympathetic to the Arab Socialist Ba'th party overthrew the parliamentary system and handed the government over to the civilian faction of the Ba'th. The army Ba'th faction acted as kingmaker.

Since 1963 Syria has been governed by the Ba'th army coalition. The army increasingly became the leading group in the Ba'th-dominated government. When unity talks with Egypt failed in 1963, the Ba'th succumbed to the military dictatorship of General Amin al-Hafez, thus ending parliamentary rule in Syria. The army Ba'th faction, which staged the February 1966 'Alawi coup, seemed ready to hand the government over to the civilians, but the transfer of power did not take place and the Syrian army failed to return to the barracks or to yield full executive power and political control. The Syrian coups were not always engineered independently by the officers; several were supported, encouraged, and initiated by individual politicians and by political parties and groups.

One important cause of the fratricidal tendencies in the Syrian army was the extraordinary role played by ethnic groups in the military high command:

> Ethnic groups form consolidated political-ethnic entities, and the political support these ethnic groups derive from their group identity has since become Syria's most acute political problem. Ethnic identity in an age of Arab nationalism has produced a series of conflicts between a Suni-dominated central government (this before the military 'Alawi takeover in February 1966) and the politically isolated but consolidated ethnic groups, most notably the 'Alawi, Druze, and Isma'ilis. Since 1966, these groups have gone beyond their "traditional" role as protest groups. Under the guise of the military the 'Alawi today [1969] rule Syria.

Although the army emerged as the political guardian of the country, the "savior" of society from the "corrupt" politician, it did not achieve consolidation nor did its officer corps become cohesive. Politicization of the military only encouraged independent officers and cliques to adopt a variety of rival ideologies to further their own ambitions and aspirations toward political domination. Nevertheless, the corps kept its image as the new modernizing elite and succeeded in dominating Syrian society in spite of its fratricidal tendencies and the decline of the professional orientation of the military elite in power.[51]

PRAETORIANS, MILITARY REFORMISTS, AND THE MILITARY DICTATORSHIP

I have derived from Be'eri's[52] and Dann's[53] works on the Arab military a table (table 5.2) that gives a graphic profile and suggests new hypotheses and concepts as well as reaffirming a number of older ones concerning the relationships between class, rule, and stratification of the politically oriented praetorians. The table is based on an analysis of forty-one successful and unsuccessful military interventions in seven Middle Eastern Arab states over a period of three decades (1936–69). Military intervention includes all attempts, successful and unsuccessful, by Arab officers to capture the government by a coup or to impose upon the government a specific political scheme. This narrow definition of military intervention excludes all other forms of violence and revolution not connected with or initiated by the miltiary. It does not include civilian governments that are headed by the military as a result of unpressured civilian appointment or clandestine activities of officers not connected with the immediate takeover of the government.

The table is arranged by the variables felt to be most helpful in explaining the type of military intervention most prevalent in the Middle East.

    I. *The organization of the intervention*
      A. The number of interventions conceived, organized, and executed exclusively by the military.
      B. The number of interventions that, although conceived by the military, were supported by organized civilians and political groups.
      C. Mass support for the intervention.
    II. *The political orientation and ideology of the coupmakers*
    III. *A typology of intervention*
      The legitimization of the intervention: personal, structural, ideological.

      David Easton writes on legitimacy: "Support mobilized on behalf of the authorities and regimes may derive from several different sources: from underlying ideological principles, from attachment to the structure and norms of the regime as such, or from devotion to the actual authorities themselves because of their personal qualities . . ."[54]
    IV. *The military rank from which the intervention was initiated: senior or middle and junior officers*

The detailed studies of Be'eri; and Dann as well as those of several other theorists suggest that we can begin to examine the nature of

Table 5.2 Coups in the Middle East (7 Countries, 41 Coups), 1936–69

	Category	Subcategory	Count	Sum Total
I	Military Intervention	Initiated, Organized, Executed by Nonmilitary	1	
		Initiated, Organized, Executed by Military	40	41
II	Support of Organized Civilian and Political Groups	Opposition	27	
		Support	14	41
III	Mass Support	Opposition	6	
		No Opposition	31	41
		Support	4	
IV	Types of Coups by Orientation	Religious-Fundamentalist	0	
		Leftist	5	
		Fascist	3	41
		Nationalist	33	
V	Rank of Intervening Officers	Middle & Junior	12	
		Senior	29	41
VI	Types of Regime Legitimation	Ideological	7	
		Structural	9	41
		Personal	25	
VII	Outcome of Coup	Unsuccessful	18	
		Successful	23	41

SOURCE: Amos Perlmutter, "The Arab Military Elite," *World Politics* 22, no. 2 (January 1970): 241.

military-political intervention *in itself* and as an independent analytical unit. This approach should provide insights into some of its root causes and eventual consequences.[55]

A cross-tabular analysis of the different variables listed in the table in bivariate combinations yields several tentative conclusions and poses some interesting questions for further study. (1) Almost 80 percent of the "nationalist" coups resulted in a personal type of legitimization. (2) Over 50 percent of all coups were both nationalist and personal. (3) eighty percent of the civilian-supported coups were successful. However, 40 percent of the coups that were not supported by civilians were also successful, and none that had mass public support failed. (4) By controlling the variable of "successful coup" by the variables of "mass support" and "civilian support," it is evident that the first is not dependent on the second and third. (5) Fascist and leftist coups have tended to be more successful than nationalist coups. (6) Twenty-five percent more of the coups organized by middle and junior officers were successful than those organized by senior officers, but 70 percent of all coups were organized by the senior officers. The majority of the coups studied were not organized by junior officers, which contradicts a fairly common postulate. Moreover, there is no evident correlation between ideology, radical coups, and the rank of the intervening officers. (7) It should also be recognized that out of the forty-one coups, thirty occurred in Syria (thirteen) and Iraq (seventeen). Since these two nations are pluralist societies, we might wonder whether there exists a specific relationship between military intervention and the failure of political integration in such societies.

Analyses of the material lead to three preliminary conclusions. First, the military's rule in the Middle East is oriented toward one-man military dictatorship; challenges to military authority by mutinous, disgruntled, or rival officers have the same end in view. Second, military coups, countercoups, and interventions are planned, organized, and executed by the army and for the army, with little or no support from movements and classes, even if the officers were inspired by them. Third, the relationships between class and politics are of little or no value in explaining the type of authority, regime, and ideology espoused by the military praetorians.

To elaborate on the first conclusion, the orientation of the military toward clandestine operations and military dictatorship: like most Middle Eastern coups since 1936, Qassem's in Iraq was secretly contrived within the military barracks with some "awareness" by outside groups (sympathetic civilians and generally radical nationalists who lacked parliamentary support). The most important fact is that civilian support was *not* crucial to the military; Qassem even rejected it, as did Nasser in 1952.[56]

After the coup, the military establishes an autonomous executive arm, the Revolutionary Command Council, as an instrument of authority in the quest of legitimacy (Nasser did this in 1952, Shishakly in 1952, Qassem in 1958, and the Syrian 'Alawi in 1966).

The RCC eventually takes over all sources of power and, in the end, becomes an instrument dedicated more to suppressing the opposition and expropriating the "old" regime than to progress. The issue of legitimacy is crucial, but the military dictatorship has rarely been made legitimate without the use of force, or the secret police, or the powers of patrimonialism (the extended family or ethnic group). Qassem failed, chiefly because he was unusually merciful (sparing the life of his future assassin 'Abd al-Salim 'Arif), tolerant, and forgiving.[57] Furthermore, unlike his rival on the Nile, he did not devote much time to intrigues. Nasser's resilience, for instance, stemmed from his capacity to manipulate palace coups, the military, and the masses (an example was the "suicide" of Marshal 'Amer in 1967).[58] This finesse is certainly also a trademark of the master of Middle Eastern coups, Anwar al-Sadat.[59]

Nasser, and particularly Qassem, could not survive without the support of the military and the threat of force or the manipulation of the mob.[60] This does not mean that civilian groups or organizations played no significant role under Nasser and Qassem. Civilians were prominent among the Iraqi Communists in 1959–60—and the Arab Socialist Union in the early 1960s in Egypt. But these "civilian" interregna are short and involve more violence and brutality when the officers reestablish military dictatorship. Military dictatorship or domination prevails mainly because the leader conceives of no alternative to his *personal* rule or military rule, and to legitimize his rule he turns to secure structural and ideological resources—by force and by the suppression of opposition both within and outside of the military.

It is equally true that in the era of military-civilian cooperation in Iraq, the Iraqi Communist party (ICP) supported the militia that it infiltrated and dominated (1959–61). But its power did not last long— the party soon collapsed, leaving the military dictator to the mercy of his own failures and the ICP's. Why did the party collapse? In its heyday it was supported by Qassem; its membership swelled; and its organization prospered. It dominated the militia (PRF) and took advantage of the army's fratricidal tendencies. During the Shawaaf army mutiny (1959), helped by the powerful and well-organized Kurdish minority, it restored Qassem's rule. The ICP also brought about Iraq's withdrawal from the Baghdad Pact and presented the most powerful political front at home with the exception of Qassem's.[61] Yet "it was caught in a situation [the Kirkuk massacre, 1959] which it could not master by assault. . . ." The same was true of the Egyptian Muslim Brotherhood, which captured the imagination of Egyptian nationalists for three decades, and which, if Mitchell is correct,[62] claimed over half a million members. To all intents and purposes the Muslim Brotherhood ran a parawelfare state, infiltrating unions, universities, and the intelligentsia, and maintaining close contact with and even dominating various Free Officers. Providing a doctrine and an explanation of the plight of Egypt under colonial rule, the Muslim Brotherhood sought personal, psychological, and political redemption for Egypt. In short, it was the mass movement par excellence of the modern Middle East, and yet, like the Iraqi Communist party (or the Syrian PPS and Ba'th parties, for that matter), it disintegrated and was finally destroyed by a simple, little known, politically inarticulate, ruthless military dictator.

An explanation of the failure of the Muslim Brotherhood, the PPS, Ba'th, Iraqi Communist party, Wafd, and others must be sought not only in the nature of the "praetorian society" but in the relationship that exists between ideology and organization in nationalist movements, when organization is not buttressed by ideology and ideology disintegrates.[63] The organizational and political ideology of the praetorian supports the military dictatorship. Organization creates a relatively stable order that approaches a state of political mobilization while remaining unresponsive to political change. The military dictatorship does not evolve beyond a clandestine coterie, for it has barricaded itself of its own volition. While the nonmilitary political groups are in permanent quest of a constituency, an all-encompassing ideology, and some type of electoral machinery, the military is self-contained and derives the capacity to govern from the barracks. The military dictatorship is sustained by the power of a single manipulator or, as in Syria, by a coalition of manipulators. Thus the most "effective" governments in the Middle East were and still are those of military dictators; their "effectiveness" is related not to organizational infrastructure or ideology, but to the dictator's personal capacity for governing.

Out of 229 coups (1946–70), William Thompson demonstrated that only 19 were strikingly reformist in nature, i.e., that their motivations were reformist. Six out of those 19 involved organizational or corporate factors and 6 out of the 19 were unsuccessful.[64] (See table 5.3.) Eight out of the 41 Arab coups (1936–69) were reformist, either leftist or fascist.

Table 5.3 Strikingly Reformist Coups

	1946–50		1951–55		1956–60		1961–65		1966–70		1946–70	
	No.	%	No.	%	No.	%	No.	%	No.	%	No.	%
Coup Zone	1	3	2	8	5	9	5	8	6	11	19	8
Latin American	0	—	0	—	2	7	1	5	0	—	3	3
Arab	1	25	2	40	1	14	1	6	3	21	8	17
Southeast & East Asia	0	—	0	—	0	—	1	8	0	—	1	3
Sub-Saharan Africa					1	50	0	—	2	9	3	9

SOURCE: Thompson, "Explanations," p. 111.

A study of 320 Egyptian officers held by the Israelis after the 1967 war, as well as a comparable 1956 study of prisoners of war, to which Be'eri and I have had access, illustrates a similar phenomenon in Egypt. Under Nasser, the Egyptian officer class clearly exhibited traditional bureaucratic attitudes toward the "lower" classes—the troops, the peasants, the unskilled workers, and the undereducated. Furthermore, the Egyptian army, on the whole, has failed to institute successfully the land and tax reforms that it has promised to carry out. Yet, incongruous as it may seem, the Egyptian military establishment and its Syrian counterpart (to a lesser extent) are probably the most modern military establishments in the Arab Middle East.

The second hypothesis derived from analysis of the material, that military coups are militarily organized, inspired, and executed, is corroborated by Be'eri's careful study of the rise of the Free Officers and their consolidation of power from the "prehistoric" 1930s through 1956.[65] In view of the comprehensiveness of Be'eri's survey of the rise of the Free Officers and Nasser's consolidation of the military dictatorship, it seems accurate to state that the case is analytically analogous to that of Qassem.

The third and most controversial hypothesis, that the military does not represent a class, even functionally, is supported by Dann's study, but the issue is not yet decided. Class consciousness has always provided only a slight portion of a Middle Eastern officer's identity. The military conceive of themselves not as an economic group but as a corporate group. Since the collapse of Ottoman rule (in which the army played a large part), the military has awaited the formation of a new, powerful "state" on the European model that would sustain the military establishment. The military in the Middle East do not represent or dominate classes, nor are they dominated by them. The middle-class sector is sharply divided in outlook. The interventionist tradition is nurtured by splits and schisms in Arab nationalist and progressive camps: neither progressives nor moderates could, by political victory, impose their conception of reform. Thus the military organization imposes on society the morality of order, not the ideology of class. This morality, of course, is buttressed by the organizational weapons at the military's disposal. A modern military establishment can sometimes work against the success of large-scale socioeconomic reform. In the Middle East the sum of the military establishment's professional, corporate, and personal experiences is, on the whole, modern, but not necessarily reformist.

The first Syrian coups of 1949, in the wake of the Palestinian debacle, were not ideological or class-oriented. The concern of the reformers was to strengthen the machinery of the Syrian state so that a similar disaster would not recur. The armed forces were quadrupled. The military had little sustaining interest in economic change. They had not considered the problem of reform in any other context than that of ending the general "corruption" of "order." Nasser's rise to power stemmed from the concern of the Free Officers about the Egyptian military defeat in Palestine, which to them illustrated the corruption of the regime. Nasser opposed the regime in general terms. No label except "corrupt" was attached to the regime until 1956, when the Wafd and the Faruq regimes became "bourgeois-capitalist" and "feudalist monsters." The greatest trauma to the officers was the corruption of their own military establishment while fighting in Palestine in 1948. Sadat's concern between 1967 and 1973 was to prepare for war, not to further reform.

In the name of strengthening the state and ridding it and the army of corruption, one praetorian regime was replaced by another in the

Middle East. The military reforms do not reflect the class origin or interests of the military establishment. Military reforms succeed or fail in the Middle East not because they are middle-class or revolutionary, but because of praetorian conditions of low institutionalization, fratricidal tendencies, and the decay of the polity and of economic reforms. The concepts of politics, society, and authority among Middle Eastern officers are couched in terms of simplistic, xenophobic, radical nationalist slogans and doctrines.

At present, there is obviously no contradiction between a commitment to nationalism and a commitment to reform. But commitments to either or both are not sufficient indicators that the motivations of the nationalist are reformist. What seems conclusive, at least in the Middle Eastern case, is that the correlations between the existence of a middle class (however "new") and reform are negative. Nor can a positive correlation between peasant origins, mobility, and reform (say, in the case of Syria) be established. Military interventionism is better explained as a result of the caprice of the praetorian, of his taste for political intrigue and manipulation, of his concern for the army, and of the effect of war with Israel in the Arab case than of his social origins and class commitments. The army acts as a ruling class, not as an economic group or a surrogate for one.

Atatürk conceived of the military as the Romans did, in its historical praetorian cohort role: as the protector of the republic against the legions. Thus he advocated the separation of the military from politics with the proviso that the army, while residing in the barracks, should nevertheless protect the constitution. Nasser assigned to the army the role of patrolling Egypt and believed that only the military could successfully reform, govern, and strengthen the country.[66] Atatürk believed that republicanism and civilian control over the military were the secret of European strength, and he did his utmost to emulate the European model. Nasser, mistrustful of foreign (especially European) imperialists and convinced of the futility of parliamentary rule in Egypt, opted first for state capitalism and then, after 1960, for Arab socialism, hoping that this new course would restore the Egyptian state. The Ba'th officers in Syria believe in a variety of leftist and neo-Bolshevik remedies, but none of them have helped institutionalize the military regime in Syria. Ba'th military rule became entrenched as a result of the 1973 war, not as a consequence of reform. The reforms of the military in Arab societies have not been institutionalized, but officers come and go, claiming they can do better. When rivals emerge, rulers ignore persuasion as a tactic and favor suppression and physical elimination. The officers want to reform their "government" and protect their corporate entity and profession; they have conspired to do this by coups and force.

The officers' convictions are not the result of a particular class origin or class consciousness. Their major aim is to make the state strong and effective. The pre-1939 generation in the Arab world believed in parliamentarianism and republicanism as sources of political strength and mastery. The post-1939 fundamentalists, radicals, and xeno-phobes put their eggs in several baskets: fascism, state capitalism, Arab socialism, leftist nationalism, and even communism, and clothed their personal ambitions with colorful if incoherent "ideologies." As a ruling class, they advocate the restoration of power, especially of mili-tary power, not the fulfillment of class ideologies and group interests. In the Middle East military rule means that the modern regime of the military lacks executive responsiveness to electorate, that the social structure is chaotic, that political life is decadent, and that military praetorianism is the most usual form of government.

Appendix

The three types of regimes (A, B, C) are highly correlated with three types of military coups. The first type of coup, the organizational coup, is linked with the arbitrator regime (Type A), that is, the army stays in the barracks but indirectly controls the regime.

The ruler type of regime (Type B) is linked with the army-party coups, that is, both the army and the civilian politicians participate in the coups. The army acts autonomously, however, and directly intervenes in politics, while the politicians provide support.

The Type C military regime is linked with the military-party coup, that is, either the army creates an independent party organization or it takes over an established party.

Out of 56 coups in the Middle East between 1936 and 1973, I have found a strong correlation between the type of military regime and the types of military coups. Most significant is the fact that the second and third types, the army-party and the military-party coups, are more durable and sustaining than the organizational coups. (See table 5.4.)

Table 5.4 Types of Military Coups Correlated with Types of Regime Support: Middle East, North Africa, Pakistan, 1936–73

	Organizational			Army-Party			Military-Party			
	S*	F†	Total	S	F	Total	S	F	Total	Total coups
Egypt	2	–	2	1	2	3	–	–	–	5
Jordan-Lebanon	–	1	1	–	1	1	–	–	–	2
Libya	–	1	1	–	–	–	–	–	–	1
Iraq	3	4	7	2	1	3	2	1	3	13
Syria	3	4	7	4	–	4	3	–	3	14
Sudan	1	1	2	2	–	2	1	–	1	5
Yemen	3	1	4	–	–	–	–	–		4
Algeria	–	1	1	1	–	1	–	–	–	2
Morocco	–	2	2	–	–	–	–	–	–	2
Turkey	2	1	3	1	–	1	–	–	–	4
Iran	2	–	2	–	–	–	–	–	–	2
Pakistan	1	1	2	–	–	–	–	–	–	2

*Success
†Failure

NOTE: I am grateful to my colleague Reinhard Selten for helping me conceive this table.

6

The Latin American Army:
From Libertadores to Role Expansion

By the end of the nineteenth century, the Latin American military had developed a high level of professionalism and conscious, in fact zealous, corporatist orientations. Today's militaries in Latin America have their origins in the postindependence (1805–11) era, when they began as nation-in-arms armies, having rejected the Spanish-Portuguese colonial models. In general, this type of army disintegrated (as the Spanish army did in the same era) a decade after independence and was transformed into caudillismo-personalist and bandit type.

The professional revolution in Latin America lagged close to a century behind that in Europe. Only at the end of the era of the caudillos, when modern-bureaucratic national states emerged on the Latin American continent, did the professional revolution create militaries imbued with liberal and nationalist orientations (Brazil and Chile were first, followed by Argentina, Venezuela, and Peru, among others).

The Latin American military was professionalized under the guidance of Prussian, French, Italian, and British officers. These foreign advisers did not produce satraps, but trained the Latin Americans in the best traditions of European professionalism. In addition, unlike the Arab and the African militaries, the Latin American militaries, at the beginning of the nineteenth century and especially during the rise of professionalism, became the clients par excellence of their states. The African and Arab militaries (particularly the latter) rejected the regimes of independence and the parties, procedures, and political structures associated with them. Instead, they established their own ruler-type surrogate executives, to preserve military autonomy and support the military's independent political actions. Between 1890 and 1930 the military in Latin America did not reject the state or the regime. When they finally did, in the 1930s to 1950s, it was because they were apprehensive about its political effectiveness. During that period, the army acted as the ultimate arbitrator, supporting presidential, that is, executive power. This era represented the first phase of arbitrator praetorianism, in other words, support of established regime and executives.

Since the 1960s, ruler-type praetorianism has emerged in Latin America (Brazil, Argentina, Peru, and Chile). During this period the military created executive structures to both assert its autonomy and to *direct* modernization.

The professionalism, which was directed toward external defense and the use of the military as an instrument of foreign policy, was abandoned in favor of the new professionalism, which was concerned with internal security and national development.[1]

The second generation in the Latin American military internalized the nationalist weltanschauung, and its corporate ideology is one of the most sophisticated among modern militaries anywhere. The influence of positivism and Comtism, the most sophisticated corporatist philosophy of modern times, on the militaries of Brazil, Argentina, Peru, and even Chile is enormous. Thus, in addition to a professional orientation, the Latin American military has a St. Simonian and Comtist corporate ideology, which is distinctly absent in African and Arab military corporate orientations. Therefore ideology and organization are probably the dependent variables that explain civil-military relations in Latin America, while the regime orientation and support more appropriately explain civil-military relations in the Middle East and North and sub-Saharan Africa.

The contributions of the Latin American military to politics for close to a century have been organization, ideology, and managerialism, which is certainly not true of African military. The Arab military's contributions were the radicalization of Arab nationalism and the development of anti-imperialist and anti-Zionist ideologies. The Latin American military's contributions to the modern state are considerable. The military in Latin America played, and still plays, a much greater and more durable role than its counterpart in the Arab states and Africa, even if they are all imbued with praetorian interventionist orientations.

During the last decade of the nineteenth century, the arbitrator type of praetorian army began to be institutionalized in Latin America. Since then the major Latin American states have been either dominated or strongly influenced by the military, and the Latin American soldier, the heir of nineteenth-century Spain, has approximated the ideal model of the corporate professional more than the praetorians of any other country.[2]

A Modern Praetorian Regime: The Spanish Model and Legacy

Restoration of order in Spain after 1815 coincided with the rise of the first modern praetorian military, who were recruited by liberal republicans; ironically, absolutism, not liberalism, accompanied the restoration of the monarchy and the military. The pronunciamientos (the "Spanish method of making revolutions") expressed the officers' revolt against the patrimonial system in Spain, and the revolution of 1820 introduced the political procedures for the liberal revolution and modern military praetorianism.[3] Thus Spain became the model for the praetorian state in the nineteenth century.

"Military rule was a symbiotic growth where politicians leaned on soldiers and soldiers appeared as working politicians."[4] The army in Spain became powerful with the growth of the republic, particularly as the result of the Carlist Wars of 1834–39. While generals demanded political support for particular (and local) interests, military intervention was the handiwork of liberal and republican civilian politicians who, in the absence of effective political power, needed military support against Carlist forces. The army thus became a haven for liberals. What is most interesting is the reluctance of the officers to become involved in factional politics. Strongly nationalistic, they saw themselves as unifiers of the nation.

The common soldiers preferred guerrilla warfare, rural brigandage carried on by small units, which had begun as a peasant rebellion against Napoleonic forces and grew into a lengthy and violent conflict for the sake of conflict. The legacy of guerrilla warfare left its mark on Spain in the nineteenth century: it became the central feature of Spanish praetorianism. So did the ethic of partisan warfare. "Patriotic contempt for the law of the foreigner and his collaborators introduced a new element of instability into society . . . It romanticized revolution and regularized insubordination, sanctifying that preference for violent individual action that was to bedevil the politics of nineteenth-century Spain . . . Both the Carlist right and the extremist left could later appeal to this primitive rebellion."[5]

The major reason for military political interventionism in republican Spain was the emergence of the periphery, which grew in population, political activity, and economic production. (Stated another way, this was the failure of the central authority to deal with a new force.) The rivalry between the center and periphery frightened the generals and encouraged them to enter politics. Furthermore, civilian cabinets failed to fill their requests for men and arms. Although the social divisions betweens soldiers and civilians were indistinct, political rivalry between them increased as republican authority deteriorated. The rise of the rural bourgeoisie in coalition with the urban center forced the rural notables to challenge the center in alliance with the local military commanders. All this produced the familiar pattern of praetorianism: mutinies (cuartelazos), coups, fratricide, personal and ideological separatism, and lack of cohesion.

A cardinal fact about praetorian-oriented polities is that military intervention (at least in its early stages) is instigated by disgruntled civilians and power-seeking politicians. In Spain political cleavages were so closely tied to personal rivalries that in the end it was hard to disentangle them.[6] Lacking political support (electoral, economic, or traditional), liberal and progressive politicians sought military backing. The army seemed the repository of hope and liberation, and it became the arbiter of political affairs.

The Spanish case suggests additional generalizations on the evolution of praetorian states. In seeking the support of the military, politicians threaten the constitutional and political practices to which they are dedicated and on whose behalf they have recruited military support. Furthermore, once the officer politicians have assumed civilian characteristics and expectations, they lose their hold over the army and are then challenged by rivals within the military. This challenge may come from any of several sources: from professional officers dedicated to the separation of the military from the political life; from branch, section, or service dissatisfied with its position within the military; or from peripheral and fratricidal elements. The immediate cause may be the civilian government's failure to supply generals with armies, a soldiers' revolt, or defeat in war.

Conditions in Spain in the second half of the nineteenth century were ideal for classic praetorianism. Population was increasing on the periphery while the dominant center was experiencing population and economic decline—a situation that aggravated the center's unsuccessful attempts at reform and liberalism. The middle classes lacked cohesion: retrograde conservatives and rebellious students confronted each other, as did the bourgeoisie and urban cafe society. At a time when there was no liberal challenge to the Church and the government held a monopoly over the Enlightenment and its instruments, the social structure was unable to cope with its own internal conflicts.

In both Spain and Latin America modern praetorianism was preceded by a long period of rural populism (known as guerrillaism in Spain and the caudillo system in Latin America), which grew out of the Spanish war of independence and the Latin American revolutionary wars. The war against Napoleon

> moulded the subsequent history of Spain itself. It gave liberalism its programme and its technique of revolution. It defined Spanish patriotism endowing it with an enduring myth. It saddled liberalism with the problem of generals in politics and the mystique of the guerrilla.

Guerrilla warfare, which "accustomed the Spaniard to live outside the law, to reject the norms of social life and take as his great achievement the maintenance of his own personality," actually brought about the collapse of the military establishment. In Latin America, the revolutionary wars against Spain created a nation-in-arms military organization that espoused strong antimilitary attitudes. The lawlessness, amorality, and capriciousness of the popular army of the Libertadores (liberators) undermined the professional, corporate orientations characteristic of a military establishment of the late eighteenth century—the "Age of Democratic Revolution." Both the pronunciamientos in Spain and the republican regimes in New Spain were products of this age.[7]

The postrevolutionary liberating armies of Spain and Latin America decayed into small groups of violence-prone bandits. In Latin America the *criollos* (creoles) joined with the *mestizos* (mixed Spanish and Indian) to produce the political system of *caudillaje* (the power of the chief). This alliance between the privileged and unprivileged had been forged during the wars of liberation. The caudillo system took hold because there was no socioeconomic class with sufficient power and wealth to create a centralized political organization. Like the heads of other revolutionary armies, the caudillos came from all sectors and social groups in society. During the revolution their system was nonpraetorian in the sense that it was characterized by personalism, amateurism, and loose discipline, but the conditions that prevailed in postrevolutionary Latin America had a tendency to create praetorianism. Above all, the caudillo lacked the high level of skill and competence expected of the corporate soldier.[8]

The caudillo system was a traditional, patrimonial political system, lacking continuity, political sustenance, and hierarchical social organization. It perpetuated the Spanish imperial legacy of patron-client relationships and undermined the political authority of the center, the republican power that had replaced the old patrimonial state. Caudillo-guerrilla leaders exercised considerable local control and allied themselves with either royalists or republicans as the situation demanded. Unable to renounce personalism, patrimonialism, and tradition for corporatism, rationality, and modernity, the caudillos, acting as "presidents" and "national leaders," worked against the institution of the modern state. Their policy of inflating ranks and commissions on the basis of personality and patrimonial relationships rather than promotion on the basis of expertise and rationality had a particularly severe effect on professionalism. Thus throughout the nineteenth century the Libertadores not only freed the Latin Americans from Spanish rule but also "liberated" the Spanish military tradition in Latin America from its corporate orientation, replacing it with personalism and greed.[9]

The caudillos went even further in destroying the municipal corporations and the Spanish *fuero* system. In Spain, the law known as *fuero de guerra* defined the military as an autonomous and privileged group. Before the revolution, the military had held this position in New Spain as well, but the Libertadores and caudillos had destroyed it. The *fuero* system, a legacy of the viceroyalty system, was abused by the new rulers, who used it to stimulate civil-military disputes and extend military privileges. It thus "became a powerful element in promoting praetorian government in Mexico."[10]

It was the professionalization of the Latin American military and their adoption of corporate orientations at the end of the nineteenth century that finally restored order and created a national political system. To overcome anarchy and eliminate the caudillos, the military establishment undertook a program of professionalization: (1) Foreign military instructors and traditions were imported from France and Prussia, the two leading corporate-professional military establishments of the late nineteenth century. (2) Native military schools and academies were established. (3) Authority was centralized in the government and the bureaucracy. This program was achieved successfully in Argentina, Brazil, Venezuela, and Chile. At the same time, it paved the way for praetorianism and the emergence of the arbitrator army.

THE CORPORATE PRAETORIAN: A LATIN AMERICAN PHENOMENON

Between 1890 and 1920 the military in Latin America played a key role, establishing order and encouraging the rise of constitutional government out of the chaos created by the caudillos. The professionalization of the military was the result of a conscious effort on the part of the liberal constitutionalists in the military and in society, specifically to maximize order. Thus from its outset the Latin American military, unlike its European model, was conscious that it was *designed* to achieve and maintain political order. Whereas in Western Europe a "natural" course toward the civilianization of the military had been followed (the military adopted an innovative role in the realm of bureaucracy and order) and civilians had successfully set up regimes whose dynamics excluded the military, in Latin America the subjective control model, in which the military was integrated into society and supported the dominant political ideology, was preferred by both the military and the liberal civilian politicians.

The political groups and structures and the institutions formed in Latin America after 1890 were established to "protect" the corporate integrity of the professional soldier. The military establishment of the late nineteenth century was counterrevolutionary compared with the armies of the Libertadores. Unlike the European military, which clearly had distinguished itself in external control functions (although military force in Prussia, France, and Russia was frequently also used to suppress internal strife), the function of the Latin American armies was internal order. Yet this was not their sole function, for in a sense both the fight for independence and the struggle against the native Indian population were external control functions; and the military had played a key role in the settlement of the continent's interior.

One of the first major institutional reforms in patrimonial and caudillo-oriented Latin America took place in the military establishment. The emergence of military professionalism in Argentina, Chile, Peru, Venezuela, and Brazil clearly signified a structural change to rational-normative statism. The emergence of professionalism and of the functional role of the army as a "liberator from the caudillo chaos" also constituted the emergence of corporatism.

> The last half of the century [nineteenth] saw the establishment
> of the military academy and the formation of the professionally-
> trained career officer. *Socially the change was marked by a growing
> disengagement between the officer corps and other social groups.*

To establish a rational military organization it was necessary to raise
the prestige of the profession "based on the training of men who enter
it, their dedication to established ideals and observance of standards,
the social importance of the service performed, and the exclusive pro-
prietary right of its members of fulfill their professional functions."[11]

The new military establishments in Argentina, Brazil, Venezuela,
and Peru were influenced by their foreign instructors, the Germans and
the French, the most noted European corporate professional types.[12]
Its aspirations were positivist-Comtist, but at the same time anti-
Jacobin.* As the defender of order, the military followed the European
model. Like the Prussian army, the Latin American military establishments became the allies of the ruling classes, conforming to Mosca's
dictum that recruitment of the military from the aristocratic classes
ensures the stability of both regime and class.

According to some authors, military praetorianism in Latin America
had three stages. Huntington distinguishes the stage following Aristo-
telian regime classifications: (1) oligarchic praetorianism, in which
"the dominant social forces are the great landowners, the landed clergy,
and the wielders of the sword" (1890–1920); (2) radical praetorianism,
in which "the revolt by more progressive, Western, or radical military
officers, which overthrows the traditional political institutions or
oligarchical rule, clears the way for the entry of other middle-class
elements into politics" (1920–50); and (3) mass praetorianism in which
"the military can retain power and permit or, indeed, capitalize on
the expansion of political participation" (beginning in the 1950s).

---

*Comtism is a system based on the view "that in the natural as well as in the social sciences
experiences and their logical and mathematical treatment are the exclusive source of all
worthwhile information" (Franz Adler, in *A Dictionary of the Social Sciences*, ed. Julius Gould
and W. J. Kolb [New York: Free Press, 1964], p. 520). The founder of modern sociology,
Auguste Comte, used the term *positif* to apply to a philosophy based on facts and experience,
which was mainly a technocratic rejection of theology and metaphysics. The impact of the
Comtist phenomenological school on Latin America was considerable, especially in the
military colleges. (The Comtist symbol is emblazoned on the flag of the Brazilian army.)
Jacobinism was considered by Comtists to be a metaphysical, moral philosophy without
"factual" or phenomenological foundation.

Huntington's model is developmental and rests on his praetorian theory of prolonged political institutionalization. The strength of a political organization depends on the scope of support for the organization and the level of its institutionalization, which Huntington defines as "the process by which organizations and procedures acquire value and stability." The scope of support refers to "the extent to which the political organizations and procedures encompass activity in society," while "the level of institutionalization of any political system can be defined by the adaptability, complexity, autonomy, and coherence of its organization and procedures." Huntington's model evolves in the context of a long period of political development and the orientation of the political order toward rational institutionalization.[13]

Liisa North offers an identical chronological and evolutionary model that is, however, based on the interaction between social class forces and ideology and on a political-institutional interpretation. Thus during the 1890–1920 era the military was "identified with a Ruling Group"; between 1920 and 1950 it was "politicized by Middle Class Parties," and after 1950 it was politicized "but with an Independent Ideological Orientation."[14]

My model differs from both of these in several respects. First, the so-called era of oligarchic praetorianism was oligarchic but it was not praetorian. The era of the caudillo (1800–90) should actually, in my view, be Huntington's oligarchic and historical praetorianism. Since the caudillo system was not modern or corporate, it represents the opposite of the professional. Furthermore, the professional becomes praetorian only if military corporatism is threatened, and this occurs when soldiers with political leanings actually become working politicians. During the second era, the distinction between *manifest* and *latent* praetorianism is crucial in any explanation of civil-military relations in Latin America. The period between 1890 and 1920 was one of latent or potential praetorianism (not oligarchic praetorianism, as Huntington argues); manifest praetorianism appeared only after 1920. On the whole, the 1890–1920 era was not characterized by military intervention although the role of the *Logias* in Argentina represented latent praetorianism. It should also be stressed that there was considerable variation in the time countries reached the era of "mass praetorianism": for instance, Venezuela and Brazil did not reach this stage until the late 1950s and early 1960s. Third, in Latin America, unlike the United States and Western Europe (with the exception of Prussia, Russia, and England), the military was identified with the ruling class; the military was politicized by the middle class once they had replaced the ruling landed aristocracy; and the military developed independent orientations.

My model of civil-military relations in Latin America since 1890, which will be used here to examine the patterns of evolution of Latin American military praetorian regimes, attempts to integrate Huntington's and North's political-institutional explanations. It rests on two independent variables: organization and ideology. The interaction between these two variables produced the various types and combinations of civil-military dictatorships in modern Latin America.

The growth of an independent and politically influential military class is linked to the bureaucratic-corporate structure and ideology that evolved in a period of over a century in Latin America. Unlike the Arab and African military the Latin Americans are not latecomers to professionalization and modernization. In fact, in glaring contrast to their Arab and African counterparts, the Latin American military of the end of the nineteenth century were innovators (not unlike the military in Europe at the beginning of the nineteenth century) in matters of organization and corporate ideology. The Arabs and Africans possess a political weltanschauung that arises not from national security concerns but from alienation or deprivation of political power; the Latin Americans represent an independent, self-contained technocratic corporate elite that now more than ever wields political influence and enhances authoritarian practices and orientations. The Arab military academies produce xenophobic and radical nationalist officers. The Latin American military academies are technocratic institutions that favor Comtist ideology. Furthermore, the Latin American officer class is oriented toward technocracy and managerialism. The Arab-African military is definitely not similarly inclined.

Organization

The most conspicuous characteristic of the modern praetorian is his corporate orientation, a function of the professional revolution. Each era in the evolution of military intervention in Latin America was marked by distinctive attitudes on the part of the military and society toward the military and toward its corporate, exclusivist orientation. The era of caudillismo and chaos led to the rise of professionalism, institutionalization, and order. Thus the 1890–1920 period saw the rise and consolidation of corporate professionalism. The era between 1920 and 1950 was characterized by an ideological challenge to corporate professionalism both from within and from without the military organization. The period following 1950 was characterized by the decline of the corporate reputation, the rise of mass praetorianism, and the emergence of military-political and technocratic autonomy and role expansion. Again, there was much variation in the timing of these stages among the countries involved.

Ideology

The era between 1890 and 1920 could be called a Comtist-positivist era. During this period the ideology of military praetorianism was launched. Support was found for the belief that intervention was the duty of the military as the guardian of liberal, nationalist regimes. The ideological raison d'être for interventionism was buttressed by a professional and nationalist stand. During this period, the ideology of the officer class had been incubated. The military's ideological concerns were restricted to its professional evolution out of the caudillo system. Not until professionalism was challenged after 1920 did the nationalist-fascist ideology affect the military and its relationships with civilian authorities. The rise of modern military professionalism and of patrician liberalism as well as the alliance of class, ideology, and the military helped consolidate the professional stance of the military and its latent praetorian ideology. Yet the fragility of society and the fratricidal tendencies of the military under praetorian conditions prevented the emergence of the objective civilian control type except in Chile. Thus the 1890–1920 period can be called the era of subjective domination of the civilian over the military.

The period between 1920 and 1950 was characterized by the rise of radical, nationalist ideologies. It was the time of the second generation and of the emergence of progressive politicians. Latin America differed sharply from the Middle East during this era: Latin American coalitions were broader and more enduring and included the military, the progressive middle class, and organized labor, whereas in the Middle East and sub-Saharan Africa labor was not a serious partner. During this time, nationalist, fascist, and social corporate ideologies were embraced by some members of the military establishment, which had allied itself with some strata of the middle class. The challenge to corporate professionalism was beginning to take form.

During the era beginning in 1958, the neo-Marxist, romantic revolution of Che Guevara and the Communist statism of Castro had its impact. Thus, while corporate professionalism declined, weakened by the ideological and structural cleavages in the rapidly developing polities (Argentina, Chile, Brazil, Venezuela, Colombia), the political autonomy of the military grew and was oriented toward buttressing the society and the regime against radical neo-Marxist tendencies. Military role expansion, modernization, and political participation in reform were reactions to the rise of the third-generation ideologues and guerrillas. But a military imbued with Comtist corporate ideology and authoritarianism can play a significant role in economic modernization. Here the Latin American praetorians proved superior to their Arab and African counterparts whose managerial skills, commitment, and proficiency are poor.

THE PRIMACY OF CORPORATE PROFESSIONALISM

Two fundamental and related orientations guided the military establishment in Latin America: (1) their subjective control role and (2) their orientation toward corporate professionalism. Huntington argues that the function of civilian domination is "the maximizing of the power of civilian groups in relation to the military." There are at least two ways, however, to maximize civilian domination: one is the subjective model; the other is North's adaptation of Huntington's objective civilian control model, which states that "the power of civilian groups is maximized by making military officers identify with those specific groups which are in control of the state." Huntington also states: "Subjective civilian control achieves its end by civilianizing the military, making them the mirror of the state."[15]

The new social type, which was to influence Latin American politics both directly and indirectly, was the corporate officer, jealous of his professional standing and proud of his new role. In fact, it was in Latin America after the War of the Pacific (1879–83) that military functions first became exclusively internal and reformist and were supported by institutional and corporate dogma. True, the army's participation in colonization and nation-building in southern Argentina and Chile, in western Brazil, northern Mexico, and Yucatán were examples of an external function. So was the army's involvement in the Chaco War and in the wars between Chile and Peru (1879–83), Chile and Argentina (1879), and Argentina and Brazil (1866). Yet the army also functioned, as it did in Europe and the United States, to suppress native labor protesters and socialists, clearly an internal control function but a "legitimate" historical function of the European professional military. The Latin American military establishment, designed to establish order and to protect the constitutional process, could also be plagued with internal conflict, which in the end drew it away from the barracks and into the presidential palace. From that point on, the presidency served as the "barracks" for the potential arbitrator praetorian. A professional military subculture (Huntington's "military mind") blossomed and was highly correlated with corporatism. This subculture, which had internalized the lessons of the caudillo past, instilled in the officer class the attitude that the role of the "superpolitical" corporatist was to function from the barracks as the defender of the constitution. The role of the military was conceived in terms of an arbitrator corporate tradition, which was at variance with civilian domination. Thus the subculture demonstrated in Latin America, as elsewhere, that the military's view of itself could conflict with society's view that civilian control was best achieved via the objective control model.[16] In the absence of a strong conviction that a precarious military tradition could coexist with fragile political institutions, military praetorianism arose.

Military praetorianism resulted from both the corporate and the nationalist commitments of the military establishment. The historical model of classic corporatism in nineteenth-century Europe was founded when patriotism and statism converged. The sword of the state was thereafter to be drawn only when corporate or nationalist aspirations (or both) were threatened. The subjective control model became "the army in the barracks protecting the constitution," which was the ideal arrangement for military praetorianism. These orientations gained a considerable reputation in the 1920s and 1930s when constitutional arrangements and structures in Latin America were threatened. The military, imbued with a zeal for the nation-state, intervened in Argentina, Chile, Peru, and Brazil. An examination of these countries indicates that each intervention was of the arbitrator type, a military role that persisted into the 1950s.

In Argentina, the Logia militar, a secret society, was the first political body to be formed in the army, but it had no autonomous political designs. "Its primary aim was rather to eliminate from the Army all partisan political activity, which its founders regarded as the chief threat to discipline [professionalism] and consequently the root cause of most of the Army's ills. Unfortunately, in the effort to eliminate partisan politics, the Logia members surrendered themselves to politics of another sort." Thus, "the tradition of military abstention from political ventures that had lasted for twenty-five years was cast aside." The military challenge began with anxiety over its corporate role, not, as expected, with its desire to support the constitution. The appointment of civilians to the war ministry upset the Argentine military establishment, which was more concerned with corporate integrity than with public order.[17]

Much of the subsequent struggle for power between President Yrigoyen and General Justo, the new war minister, was over jurisdictional boundaries between the military establishment and the state. "Argentine officers then as now regarded the laws and regulations governing military status (*estado militar*) as a contract defining both their own obligations to the state and those of the government toward them." Yrigoyen defied the military corporate establishment. He increased government outlays for pensions and salaries, thus benefiting the individual officer rather than the corporate entity, and he meddled with promotions, retirement, and differential pay. His denial of the military's exclusive principle and its organizational integrity created a malaise.[18] In 1930, alienation, deprivation of autonomy, and uncertainty concerning its role catapulted the Argentine military into the dominant role that it was still playing in 1976.

Until 1973, Chile was unlike Argentina in its political stability and the aristocratic complexion of the military establishment. The Chilean victory in the War of the Pacific (1879–83) bolstered professional pride without injecting the middle-class Comtist corporate ideology that was incorporated into the militaries of Argentina, Peru, Venezuela, and Colombia. The rule of oligarchy in government and in the military resulted in one of only three civilian objective control models in Latin America (the others were Uruguay and Costa Rica)[19] The military in Uruguay and Costa Rica, however, can hardly be compared to the Chilean military, which consisted of a large, highly institutionalized professional group with a distinguished record in foreign and Indian wars. Sixty years of objective civilian domination left its legacy in the noninterventionist subculture of the Chilean military. Although the state was threatened by military intervention in 1912, 1919, 1924–25, and 1931–32, the politicization of the military was not complete and their corporate orientation, although high, was strictly noninterventionist until 1973. Chile's nonpraetorian tradition persisted because of the stability of the military establishment's aristocratic base, the cohesiveness of the military elites, and above all, the lack of any clash between military Comtism and the civilian authorities. The first intervention in 1912 was actually prompted by the professional demands of the staff officers. Nevertheless, praetorianism has a momentum of its own; it is contagious. Repeated challenges to civilian rule led to a short era of military praetorianism in Chile, with the rise to power of Lieutenant Colonel (later General) Cárlos Ibáñez in the late 1920s. Even in Chile, parliamentary rule was overthrown by presidential government, which relied heavily upon the "barracks" for support. After a long absence, praetorianism reappeared in 1973.

In Peru, a military force was established in the middle of the nineteenth century, in what North calls an "unlegitimized patrimonial order." Politics in Peru consisted then of the struggle for control among officers in a patrimonial system—a system in which the dependency relationship was based on loyalty and fidelity and in which military and judicial authority was exercised without restraint by the patrimonial prince. The rulers of Peru were dependent on persons who had been granted land and who in return provided the patrimon with military service. As late as the 1870s the efforts to build a military institution in Peru destabilized patrimonial rule, causing the ruler to establish a national guard as a counterbalance to the army. Through its struggle with the caudillo and its failures in institutionalization, the Peruvian military was "politicized" rather than "militarized" or "professionalized" by its association with the ruling class. Professionalization was restricted to the upper classes. The military "wanted to join the upper class and share its privileges, not to destroy it." In the 1890s the alliance between the coastal plutocracy and the landlords of the Sierra produced a praetorian and patrimonial presidency which lasted until 1930. In the absence of stable patrimonial rule, the military became the major recruiting ground for the presidency. The presidency's effectiveness declined with the rise of the Alianza Popular Revolucionaria Americana (APRA), a progressive party that had called for land reform and extensive social legislation during the mid-1920s. APRA had infiltrated the military and gained considerable influence within it. However, during the 1930s its influence on the army was negative, similar to the effect of the PPS on the Syrian army in the mid-1950s. APRA's militant policies and its call for revolution challenged the essentially patrimonial, praetorian orientation of the military. When, in July 1932, militant members of APRA captured the provincial town of Trujillo and massacred an army garrison, a split occurred between the army and party that was still evident in the 1970s.[20]

Brazil had a decade of military rule (1889–98), and, like Argentina, it developed in this brief period a distinctive type of modern military praetorianism which it was to return to in 1930. The Paraguayan war in the 1860s led to the creation of a large professional army in Brazil, following the pattern set by Argentina, Peru, Venezuela, and Chile. The war, however, weakened the Brazilian monarchy, which had ruled since 1810. "By the late 1880s the once firm foundations of the monarchy had been gradually weakened—it had lost the support of vital groups like the landowners, who had been alienated by the abolition of slavery without compensation, and republican sentiment had grown in Brazil. The structure was tottering, and only a strong, decisive blow was needed to make it crumble, a blow which the army provided. The Brazilian armed forces have tended to view themselves as the guardians of the republic they helped establish in 1889."[21]

The praetorian conditions of the monarchy prepared the ground for a short era of modern military praetorianism in Brazil. The decay of the monarchy and the rise of extreme republicanism (embracing Comtist positivism), which divided the civilian groups, catapulted the army into power. Its modern, professional stance and positivist education became the mainstay of the provisional republican regime. The attitudes of the military, though latent, were markedly praetorian, in keeping with the army's destiny as the defender of republican virtue, the nation, and the liberal constitution. Strangely enough, the praetorian conditions of Brazilian society and politics had pushed the military out of the saddle by 1898. Two contradictory but converging political forces put a stop to praetorianism for the next forty years: (1) the fratricidal tendencies of the military establishment and (2) the rise of a cohesive political group, the Paulistas—large landowners from São Paulo who were profiting from the coffee trade. As president, Marshal Deodoro da Fonesca proved politically inept. An abortive naval revolt divided the military and exacerbated army-navy rivalry. With the monarchists weak and other civilian liberals divided, the cohesive Paulistas took advantage of the division between army and navy to install a stable civilian government led by President Prudente de Morais, which restored political order. Thus, as in Spain, the era of pronunciamientos in Brazil began when both the military and the civilians were divided. But praetorian rule came to a sudden end when one cohesive political group established its own local militia as an alternative to the national army and took advantage of the division in the military to restore order.[22]

The Brazilian case suggests an approach to praetorian evolution based on the political attitudes of the officers. It seeks to "analyze the substance of the military mind—the attitudes, values, views of the military man." The Brazilian military between the Paraguayan war and the end of the praetorian period (1879–89) was composed of three types: (1) the aristocratic officer; (2) the corporate arbitrator professional; and (3) the modern praetorian interventionist. The attitude of the aristocratic officer was antitheoretical (and in many ways antiprofessional), martial, and conservative. One such officer wrote: "[Military schools had been transformed from] establishments making good soldiers into factories producing cliques of degree holders, more apt at their unwholesome altruistic mysticism, constructing abstract conceptions of Platonic republics, than for the rude task of commanding battalions." The corporate professional's attitude, on the other hand, was classically praetorian: the military is an arbitrator, with a "role somewhat similar to that once exercised by the emperor with his moderating power." Although the attitude of this type was clearly noninterventionist and generally nonpolitical, his republican inclinations compelled him to intervene as an arbitrator. Marshal Deodoro was a representative of this type. The third category, the praetorian officer, was oriented toward the new doctrine of positivism, as championed by Benjamin Constant, professor of mathematics in the Military School. Only a small group among the cadets at the school advocated Constant's doctrines; yet it was this group that attacked the government for trying to humiliate them and to "humble the pride of the army, under the pretext of military discipline."[23]

Besides Constant's group of Comtist positivists, there was another group led by Emile Littre. But many of the young officers did not follow either. Instead they selected "the authoritarian connotations of this doctrine and interpreted to their liking the positivist concept of a republican dictatorship . . . the ideas of the French positivists were often poorly assimilated, and the result was sometimes a half-baked positivism, full of undigested lumps of thought."[24] In this, the Brazilian officers resembled the Syrian Ba'th officers of the twentieth century, who assimilated the authoritarianism of Leninism-Stalinism—though not the rigorous postulates of Marxism—along with the messianic aspirations of romantic revolutionaries. The Brazilians, however, were markedly different from the Syrians in that their orientation was of the arbitrator rather than the ruler type and they took their Comtism seriously.

The argument that the military coup in Latin America was a middle-class phenomenon does not hold for the republican interventionist officers of Brazil. Strong middle-class consciousness was missing both in the society and in the army. "The middle class lacked decisive political strength as well as social and ideological cohesion. Certainly the army officer corps as a whole could not have represented the middle class or taken any position reflecting coherent middle-class views since neither the army nor the middle class was unified." Their corporate orientation, not their class origin, was responsible for the officers' political attitudes, their determination to participate in government, and their desire to increase the size and importance of the army. In the era of republican military rule the army did increase in size, and the officers succeeded in taking over many government jobs that had previously been occupied by civilians.[25]

The corporate professionals, an active and influential minority at the end of the nineteenth century, established a temporary praetorian rule in Brazil, but their influence declined. In 1930, however, they again returned to power. Although again a minority, they re-established praetorian rule in Brazil. The legacy of this praetorian type was resurrected throughout Latin America after the 1920s, its fires kindled this time by radical nationalism and fascist authoritarianism instead of by Comtist positivism.

THE CHALLENGE TO CORPORATE PROFESSIONALISM

The emergence of corporate professionalism was contemporary with the rise of the liberal politicians and the first-generation nationalists in Latin America. The challenge to corporate professionalism was raised by the second-generation politicians—the radical nationalists and progressives. The challenge began when the radical nationalists actively intervened in internal military matters and inculcated radical nationalist and fascist ideologies. Subjective domination was extended slightly, and the military edged closer to the presidential palace.

The Civilian Coup

The change started in 1929 with the Great Depression, which racked the precarious regimes of most if not all Latin American polities. The depression was a most significant factor in the emergence of manifest praetorianism in Latin America and of some type of praetorianism in many European countries. Republican and civilian structures failed to withstand the economic avalanche, but the military were ready to re-establish order and to perform the daily routine of administration. In most Latin American countries the civilian regime was replaced by a military regime of the manifest praetorian type. Because the military of Western Europe was not composed of praetorians, a crisis in civilian order did not trigger manifest praetorianism there. With the exception of Germany and Italy, the liberal regimes were replaced by other civilian regimes (from conservative to socialist). In Germany latent praetorianism was tapped by Hitler, but in Germany and Italy the civilian regimes were replaced by mass ideological totalitarianism rather than military praetorianism. As for the Balkan states, the economic depression did bring on manifest praetorianism in Greece, Bulgaria, Hungary, Roumania, and Yugoslavia (the last two developed mixed monarchical and praetorian regimes). Several of these praetorian states embraced fascism, the most fashionable nationalist ideology in the 1930s in both the Balkans and Latin America. Civilian fascist ideologues and intellectuals played a key role in providing the praetorians of Latin America and the Balkans with a problem-solving, chauvinistic pragmatism. Fascism stood for modernism and revolution against the old aristocratic or liberal regimes.

The depression increased the social strains in these societies; coups, in one form or another, took place in almost every country. Some of the alliances that produced the coups had little to do with the middle class. In Argentina, it is true, generals and conservative cattle men of the upper class engineered a coup, and Brazilian coffee growers, labor groups, and officers made a predominantly middle-class alliance for the same purpose. But in Cuba, sergeants and corporals combined with students and professionals to bring about an essentially class coup. Alliances were forged among middle-class factions, progressive politicians, parts of the labor movement, and junior officers of the army.[26] It was a struggle of all against all, with alliances and alignments changing as rapidly as they could fade away and be recombined. In the military, a struggle took place over the rectitude of civilian intervention, a process that gradually destroyed senior corporate professionals. The junior officers accepted the glove, while the seniors battled vigorously to maintain the corporate integrity and apolitical stance of the military. The civilians and junior officers triumphed as a result of the coup; a new ruling class was established—an alliance of the military and the progressives.

Social Stratification and the Military Establishment

In Argentina there was considerable mobility in the army officer corps during the 1920s. Reflecting the composition of Argentine society in general, about a third of the officers were immigrants. Those second-generation Argentines who were willing to give attention to public policy that did not affect their class and family origin gained political power. The military became champions of urbanization and industrialization; they even formulated their own attitude toward change; expressed as "everything is transformed, everything evolves."[27]

During the 1920s the military assumed an arbitrator praetorian role in Argentina. They conducted exploratory talks with civilian parties, particularly those that opposed Yrigoyen's regime, including the radical party. They then began to manipulate public psychology to paralyze Yrigoyen and his civilian supporters. The praetorian candidate was General José Uriburu, the most senior and best known officer, a German-trained advocate of neutrality in World War I and inspector general of the army in 1923. "Supported and encouraged by nationalist intellectuals and certain conservative elements, he proposed to replace the existing system of representative government with one based on the corporativist idea."[28] His stated purpose—"to eliminate the 'reign of demagoguery' "—was an age-old praetorian cry. Uriburu's presidency (1930–32), one of the earliest praetorian regimes in Latin America, relied heavily on civilian paramilitary and ultranationalist organizations, on the army's general headquarters, on assorted political parties, and on the radical politicians. His regime was hardly a middle-class government or the result of a middle-class military coup, although some of the middle-class strata were influential in it. The senior military intervened to protect their corporate autonomy; the progressive politicians, to enhance their organization and ideology. Both were dependent on the support of the junior officers, particularly those who had enjoyed upward mobility since the 1920s.

The armed forces were not directly represented in Uriburu's government, which was an excellent model of an arbitrator praetorian regime. Support for the government was polyglot, haphazard, and unstable.

The regime had to act cautiously because it was dependent on several groups that were antagonistic toward each other. The lessons of the Yrigoyen period had been learned, especially with regard to the military: there was no further intervention, and military corporatism was protected. Yet the political nature of the intervention that had sought to bring order resulted in the further attrition of all institutions, including the military establishment itself. This development seriously challenged corporatism: "Professional values tended to be subordinated to political issues, and what had once been regarded as beyond their [military] competence became matters of daily discussion. The harmful effects on professional standards were evident even to the officers who had supported the revolution."[29]

In Chile the army entered politics in much the same way as they did in Argentina. A coalition of junior officers and progressive politicians known as the Liberal Alliance sought intervention. Their coup placed political power in the hands of the most influential strata of the middle class—the urbanites and the junior officers. Unlike Argentina, however, a powerful executive was provided by the constitution promulgated by Major (later general) Cárlos Ibáñez in 1925. Public support for Ibáñez strengthened the executive, and Ibáñez successfully turned the military into an instrument of government, plunging it into modernization programs that fostered the growth of labor and urban groups. He succeeded in keeping the army in its place and also in satisfying the younger officers, who were suffused with reforming zeal. Nevertheless, general discontent with his economic measures forced Ibáñez to resign, and in 1932 civilian government was re-established in Chile. By then, "political stability and an increasingly effective national police force [had] reduced the importance of the military role in maintaining internal order." The exercise of power planted the seeds of organizational decline in the military by 1932.[30]

In Peru upper class domination and the conflict between the radical middle-class party (APRA) and the military, between 1930 and 1950, along with the community of interests that existed between the military and the upper class regime, prevented for many years the type of civilian coup that occurred in Argentina, Chile, and Brazil. Only in the middle 1950s did the community of interests between regime and army begin to weaken. A rapprochement between APRA and the upper class caused "unfavorable reactions within the military establishment." The rise of the Center of High Military Studies and of a military poli-

tical ideology also worked toward ending the alliance. Professionalization of the military was accompanied by an interest in civic action as
the Peruvian military attempted to find alternatives to APRA, Castroism, and communism. The military establishment set itself up as a
modernizer. It directed itself toward new alliances with middle-class
groups and toward changing its role in society.[31]

The Decline of Corporate Professionalism

At the end of the 1950s, functional and structural changes occurred
in the role of the military establishment and in its corporate professional
stance. Corporate professionalism was weakened in different ways in
different polities. Both the extraordinary growth of the military establishment (in Brazil, Argentina, Peru, and Cuba) and its shrinkage (in
Chile) eroded corporate professionalism and prompted the military to
intervene in civilian affairs.[32] There were at least three major causes of
military structural and functional change: (1) the rise of the ruler type
of praetorianism; (2) expansion of the military's role to include civic
action; and (3) the rise of labor and labor unions.

The Rise of the Ruler Type of Praetorianism

In reference to the rise of the army to power in Argentina under
Uriburu, Juan Perón, who was to become the first articulator of the
ruler praetorian ideology and the inventor of its structural and executive instruments, wrote:

> I think this revolution has done great harm to the officer cadre.
> It will be necessary for the men who govern in the future to return
> things to their place. There is no other solution than to multiply
> the tasks. The year 1932 at the least ought to be for officers in
> general a year of extraordinary work of every sort; only in this
> way can we avoid the harm produced in the Army by idleness,
> backbiting, and politics. Every officer will have to be kept busy in
> professional tasks from reveille to retreat. Otherwise this will go
> from bad to worse.[33]

Military intervention in the arbitrator style of Uriburu failed to
re-establish order and thus did not eradicate the institutional and
political ills of Argentina. The military of the 1930s hoped that if they
intervened behind the scenes—from the barracks—they could achieve
political stability and corporate, professional integrity and also re-

establish the conservative order. Failure on the national and institutional planes was not so devastating as the challenge of military praetorianism to corporate professionalism. Once the military establishment was infected with praetorianism, the professionals opted for still more intervention and a tighter hold on the executive and the nation, hoping that a ruler model (total military intervention and "patrolling" of society) would cure the state of "politics," "demogoguery," "venality," and all the other evils in the praetorian vocabulary.

In the early 1940s Perón realized not only that the Uriburu and Justo regimes of the previous decade had failed to attain stability but that, since 1940, the poison of anarchy had been threatening the military establishment. In the tradition of the corporate professionals of the past, the military had become the chief "nonpolitical" establishment to intervene and guide the ship of state. But its capacity to bring order had been reduced to such a low level that one civilian critic wrote: "The Army will have difficulty, henceforth, in convincing anyone that it is the patrimony of the entire country, that alien passions are not playing in it nor self-centered or irresponsible elements meddling in it. It will have to work to recover its prestige and good name."[34]

To prepare for the revolution, junior regimental officers and nationalist radical officers in the Argentinian army had already organized an army "political club," an executive instrument of conspirators that began to operate sometime in 1942. Working in the ministry of war, Perón occupied one key position after another, with his climb culminating in his appointment as interim war minister in February 1943. On March 10, 1943, he founded the first organization oriented toward ruler praetorianism, the Grupo de Oficiales Unidos (GOU), made up of anti-Communist officers who stood for stability, nationalism, modernization, and order.[35] The establishment of the GOU marked the decline of the arbitrator praetorian orientation. Although arbitrators and rulers alternated between 1940 and 1970, the monopoly of the arbitrator was challenged by a new political-military type—the permanent patrolling squad.

The GOU, though it established a new military interventionist type, was still bound to old patterns: it insisted on "absolute lack of personal ambitions" and on becoming an "executive body working anonymously." It was dedicated to the welfare of the army and the fatherland.[36] Not all GOU members were Peronístas. In fact, Perón himself was jailed by the GOU-dominated government between 1943 and 1944. When Perón finally took power, the GOU members were divided on policy toward labor although they generally agreed on concepts of nationalism, order, and economic growth. Perón, however, believed a prolabor policy was compatible with these goals.[37] The GOU allied with various civilian radical politicians to stage the June 4, 1943, coup. But Perón's GOU faction was consolidated only when he succeeded in becoming second in command in the war ministry.

These were the modest beginnings of the most common modern praetorian army—the ruler, mass mobilization type. The pattern included structural consolidation of the officers' coterie and the careful selection of candidates; contact with civilian figures and patrons and the cultivation of sympathetic senior officers, especially the minister of war and the president; infiltration into the intelligence services, army communications, and cultural headquarters. Here staff officers played a crucial part. Perón and his fourteen military allies dedicated themselves to intensive staff and administrative work in preparation for their coup of June 4, 1943. The mark of the new professional officer was stamped on that coup. It was an independent political effort by an autonomous and well-defined military cabal that afterwards asserted leadership over the masses.[38]

Nasser's 1952 coup, which was conducted by eleven staff officers, resembled the GOU-Perónist coup. Both had preparatory staff work, their own communication networks, and the screening of candidates. In both cases radical nationalism was the primary cause of the cabal's consolidation and mobilization. One of the reasons the military revolted was to achieve status and respectability. Thus among Perón's first actions was the task of "achieving personal ascendancy over the officer corps," a task he accomplished from his station in the war ministry. From this point on, however, Argentina and Egypt took sharply different paths. In Egypt, Nasser was not forced to make political alliances to sustain his military dictatorship. All he needed were loyal and subservient bureaucrats and an efficient secret service to control the military. But Argentina, a more developed polity with a much higher per capita income, could not simultaneously be governed by a military dictator and undergo political mobilization. To push his program of modernization, to mobilize men and resources, and to maintain order, Perón allied with labor. In Latin America the ruler mobilizing type was obliged to seek such an alliance—but this combination aroused the opposition of the middle classes and the liberal politicians who earlier had espoused arbitrator-type intervention.[39]

The case of Argentina during and after Perón's regime demonstrates that the political assertiveness of the military "affected the values and attitudes of the officer corps."[40] Role expansion, military management of modernization, and the propagation of cold war and anti-Castro doctrines through the war colleges all challenged the professionalism that had placed restrictions on the military as an instrument of violence. Nevertheless such innovations were in keeping with corporate postivist ideology and technocratic orientations and practices.

Military Role Expansion

The Argentine (and Brazilian) army's role in civic action and industrial modernization since the 1940s was actually an effort to redefine military professionalism. No longer was the military establishment restricted to the defense of the realm or to constabulary duties. It adapted the skills of violence to nation-building. The transformation of aspiration and expertise from violence to civic action presented the greatest challenge to corporate professionalism. In Argentina and Brazil the aggrandizement of the military establishment and its role expansion began to eat away at historical noninterventionist corporate professionalism; at the same time it prompted the military to defend its autonomy, both as an instrument and as an orientation.

In Chile the decline of the military organization rather than its aggrandizement speeded the attrition of professionalism and challenged the military's corporate integrity. The military's apolitical stance, its distaste for even arbitrator praetorianism, and its loss of influence compelled the army to search for a new role in order to arrest or reverse its gradual decline in size, budget, technological capability, political influence, and prestige. Role expansion was sought to sustain the military establishment, and the military became an instrument of economic modernization.[41]

Noninterventionism and the tradition of nineteenth-century professionalism among the military reflected the political culture of the Chilean middle classes, which were oriented toward the objective control model and had a low opinion of military culture. The military elite was recruited from lower-class workers with little education; there were no members from working-class backgrounds among the civilian elite.[42]

The organizational decline of the Chilean army could have led to three forms of adaptation: political intervention, redefinition of military goals, or professional isolation. The Chilean military opted at first for accommodation and redefinition of goals, moving toward new goals relating to socioeconomic development and retreating from professional isolation. Still, the organizational adaptation created an interesting cleavage within the military establishment. There were three responses to organizational decline: traditionalist-professional, corporate, and adaptive. The traditionalist officer's orientations were martial and professional. He saw the military as an instrument of violence. Because he came from either the lower class or the periphery, the traditionalist's concept of professionalism was isolation from society and subordination of the military to the state, and he opposed civic action and role expansion. The corporate officer was the best-known type of modern praetorian: he was a professional, a jealous guardian of military exclusivity, an adherent of the military life-style, and an anti-Communist, anti-Castro patriot with right-wing tendencies. This officer saw civic action as a threat to professional values. However, because he perceived professional isolation, loss of prestige, and affinity with civilian bureaucracy as greater threats, he reluctantly acquiesced to the military's new role. The adaptive officer had the most civilian contacts, favored civic action, and promoted military involvement in it. Such officers were well-educated, pragmatic, and highly conscious of the need for adaptation. They were also more leftist, but, like the corporate offices, they were conscious of the status, prestige, and autonomy of the military. The adaptive officers demonstrated resiliency, for they sought new roles for the military organization to arrest its decline. Nevertheless, as a group "the officer corps was significantly less favorable to civic action than were [sic] the population at large."[43]

Officers who favored traditional-professional and corporate responses to decline tended toward the right and reluctantly favored professional adaptability. They were clearly the defenders of corporate military autonomy. Officers who supported an adaptive response were flexible only in order to arrest organizational decline and prestige. In accommodating, this group was in fact enhancing the "nonprofessional" functions of the military. By the middle 1970s, however, this group was on the decline, and the first two outnumbered it in the military schools. Thus the recruitment, appointment, and education of the military were in the hands of the corporate professionals,[44] even though the Allende regime sought to make the adaptive officer a tacit ally.

Although the Chilean army's importance as a protector of the social order had diminished, it generally avoided a return to professional isolation, which would have furthered organizational decline. (The French army made a similar choice between 1789 and 1870.) To compete with the new regime of socialist modernizers and revolutionaries would mean either that the military's new role would be enhanced or eliminated. If the military's readjustment and transfer of orientation failed to sustain its organization, the threat to civilian rule would become more serious. Thus "'the decline of the military could pose a distinct threat to the future development of Chilean political institutions."[45] Hansen, in 1967, predicted that a progressive government needed ability and vision in supporting the new organization aspirations of the military, because otherwise it might single out the Marxist government as the scapegoat for its organizational decline, as it eventually did in 1973. In the middle of that year, the Chilean military opted for a praetorian solution, and the brutal struggle for power with Allende's coalition turned the military toward a praetorian regime.

The Army and Labor

Labor in Latin America has been notorious for its poor organization. Because it was a supportive political force, not an independent and autonomous political group, its freedom of action was restricted by praetorian conditions. Labor organizations and leaders were created by the government, the military, or, in earlier days, by the plutocrats. Mass leadership and support were minimal. The mobility of the workers was restricted, and leadership was dependent on support from public or private structures, institutions, and resources. In the late 1940s, however, labor became an important (and, in the case of Perón, a significant) source of support, and was an essential partner in various civil-military coalitions. Whether or not labor gave its support depended on its internal evolution, the classes it represented, and especially on the nature of the relations it developed with the military.

FROM ARBITRATOR TO RULER: TOWARD MASS PRAETORIANISM

The transformation from arbitrator to ruler in Latin America signified the change from liberal and fascist to mass praetorianism. The argument that the military either defends or represents classes in society (as seemed to be the case with the oligarchic liberal and fascist types) can no longer be accepted. In the mass praetorian phase the military had three motivations: first, to head the modernization revolution; second, to institutionalize mass mobilization; and third, to prevent a Marxist or Castroite revolution, especially one within the military. The military also changed its role and, instead of supporting the executive during crises, it sought to dominate it.

Brazil

Until 1964 the Brazilian army represented a Latin American phenomenon, the arbitrator moderator type, O Povo fardaclo (the people in uniform). The military had been a legitimate political actor, a participant in national and governmental coalitions, since its resurgence in 1930. It served to check and protect executive power: "The relevant political actors grant legitimacy to the military under certain circumstances to act as moderators of the political process and to check or overthrow the executive to avoid a system breakdown."[46]

Thus the military establishment was legitimized as a temporary organizer of political arrangements. Civilians perceived it in this short-term arbitrator role as a coalition maker, a political broker, but not as the leader of a sustained rule or regime.[47] Civilian co-optation of the military had been institutionalized into coalition politics. The propensity toward military intervention was restricted to the office of the executive, the president. When the three-cornered political model of president, proregime politicians, and opposition failed to resolve legitimacy crises, an arbitrator military rule resulted. Because the purpose of the arbitrator army was to resolve a constitutional conflict, the society responded positively to it.

An analysis of editorials in the Brazilian press during 1945, 1954, 1955, 1961, and 1964 demonstrates that the success of a coup could have been predicted by correlating the degree of legitimized intervention with the level of executive legitimacy.[48] Unsuccessful coups occurred when the legitimacy of the executive was high and that of military intervention was low, for example, in the coups of 1955 and 1961. A favorable orientation toward military arbitration produced the successful coups of 1945, 1954, 1964. A successful coup led to successful coalition arrangements. An unsuccessful coup demonstrated that the failure of civilians to organize a coalition with the military was equivalent to a failure to legitimize the military arbitrator role.

Up to 1964 Brazil was the model for civilian praetorian coups in Latin America. The military as a powerful political group was not monolithic; in fact, it reflected most of the orientations and cleavages in society and politics. The heterogeneity of the military and the historical role of autonomous provinces, militias, and independent and ambitious governors led to the institutionalization of the arbitrator type of civil-military relations in Brazil.

The years preceding the 1960s were years of growing mobilization in Brazil, marked by population growth, urbanization (among the highest rates in the world), an increase of 140 percent in the voting population between 1945 and 1962 (from 6 million to 14 million), a dissimilarity between political support and demand (a high rate of governmental output and a low rate of demand for public services), inflation, and the rise of the labor movement and the left.[49] The relationships among socioeconomic change, social mobilization, and political institutionalization conformed to Huntington's praetorian model. Social and political institutionalization were paralleled by institutional growth, and the level of military corporatism rose.

The emergence of the Escola Superior de Guerra (ESG), the war college, and the rising level of military professionalism and autonomy were accompanied by the emergence of a cohesive military group, the veterans of World War II. The Brazilian Expeditionary Force (FEB), now, integrated with the staff and graduates of the ESG, was further strengthened by the rise of a corporate senior military elite, which was oriented toward civic action, was opposed to communism and Castroism, and was committed to the cold war, counterinsurgency, United States training, and the United States military doctrine of the 1960s. The Brazilian military establishment was reformed and modernized, and it was politicized in terms of the United States military world view. The combination of corporate professionalism with anti-Castroism strengthened the FEB-ESG elite. In the early 1960s, the ESG produced a hard core of corporate professionals and anti-Communists, the Frente Patriotica Civil-Militar (Civil-Military Patriotic Front), a group of committed civil and military nationalists who were authoritarian and reformist in military affairs. The most active members of this group were the air force officers, whose anti-Communist doctrines became the front's political program. The leading military figure in Brazil was General Castello Branco. He was at the center of a group of powerful generals, 90 percent of whom had attended the ESG and 70 percent of whom were on its permanent staff. All of them had graduated first in their respective classes and had attended military colleges abroad; 80

percent of the generals had attended colleges in the United States.[50] This group also represented the most technically advanced professional soldiers from the most sophisticated branches of the military.

The socioeconomic expansion of Brazil and the modernization of the military were not perceived as compatible. The generals around Castello Branco were apprehensive that the military might be divided by the Communists and other leftist parties and then replaced by a militia, like Castro's Peoples' Revolutionary Army.[51] The leftists' rhetoric of mobilization and radicalization, coming in the wake of the Cuban revolution, was feared by many officers as the prelude to the destruction of the traditional army.

The presidency of João Goulart (1961–64), marked by antagonism between military and civilian groups, triggered a military counterrevolution in Brazil. Goulart, a progressive politician, was unhappy with the politicization of the executive, a process that had begun in the late 1950s. He resolved to change the balance between civilians and military in the governing coalition by seeking support from liberal, progressive, and leftist groups and political clubs. His support in the army was diffuse, and his premature call for social mobilization, along with his leftist rhetoric, put the military on guard.[52]

Another significant challenge to the officer corps was institutional. The years from 1961 to 1964 were characterized by a series of serious threats to military corporatism. The impact of events in Cuba cast a long shadow, especially because in the late 1950s a tacit alliance had been forged between the sergeants and the trade unions. The sergeants' professionalization and their efforts to unionize were a direct affront to the officers. On September 12, 1963, the sergeants revolted; they "occupied strategic centers in the capital, captured a Supreme Court judge, the acting president of Congress, and a number of military officers." When Goulart took a pusillanimous attitude toward the revolt, the corporate group went into action. The high command and the ESG created shadow national security councils to support the military institution.[53] The military in Brazil (like its counterpart in Argentina) could tolerate as politically legitimate a liberal democratic or a national fascist regime, but it abhorred a leftist, Castroite, Communist arrangement.

Goulart reached an impasse early in 1964 when he was mobilizing political power and calling for reforms and a plebiscite. The crisis was "over the appropriateness, effectiveness, and legitimacy of the political system in meeting the challenge of development." Goulart's meddling in the politics of mobilization threatened the army-civilian centrist coalition, which had historically espoused either an objective military attitude or, more frequently, arbitrator, short-run intervention. Except for a few governors who had militias, there were no authoritative political groups to support a civilian arbitrator coup. The center and liberals had been overwhelmed by the rhetoricians and by mobilization politics. The small, divided new groups (composed of union members, intellectuals, students) viewed military corporatism as anathema to the type of regime they espoused. Goulartism, reminiscent of Perónism, contributed to the officers' rejection of their role as moderators. When Goulart granted amnesty to the enlisted men involved in the navy mutiny of March 1964, the military split into three groups: loyal Goulartists, active plotters, and uncommitted arbitrators. The activists won out: a ruler military regime was established, headed by General Castello Branco. He made significant changes in the Brazilian government by recruiting ESG, FEB, and Frente officers to his cabinet, and creating a cohesive group of hard-liners.[54] The 1964 revolution brought a new era to Brazilian military-civilian politics.

The ruler army soon turned its attention to the problems of modernization and mobilization. But the national crisis was not resolved by Castello Branco and his supporters, whose civic action programs failed. In 1965 General Costa e Silva led a revolt of the middle and lower ranking officers against the military government—a revolt prompted by the officers' apprehension concerning their image and the threat to military corporatism. Three years later, fear of isolation and growing resentment and frustration on the part of the same group of officers brought Costa e Silva to power. This time the military moved without civilian mediation or legitimacy and without a program or direction.

By the middle 1970s the challenge to the Brazilian regime had become serious. Several civil-military scenarios for the future of Brazil could be written, but certainly none would portray a return of the military or the regime to the pre-1964 arrangements.[55]

Peru

After 1968 Peru resembled Brazil in that its military establishment was also professionalized, modernized, and expanded. Although Peru's socioeconomic development lagged behind Brazil's and Peru was not faced with such serious consequences of social mobilization, the

Peruvian military had to meet both challenges nonetheless. They became "rulers," intervening in areas that were not within the military purview. The Peruvian military became preoccupied with rural development, national planning, educational policy and, above all, foreign affairs. They also showed their concern for corporate autonomy, and they raised the professional standards of officers and their political skills, updating their education in both types of modern warfare, guerrilla and strategic. The Center for Higher Military Service (CAEM), the national war college, and the Center for Military Instruction (CIMP) played the same role that ESG did in Brazil in expanding the functions of the military. As in Brazil, the threat of guerrilla warfare and the influence of American counterinsurgency doctrines and practices promoted the formation of interventionist military groups. The curriculum of the national war college, which reflected the motivations, perceptions, and concerns of the new ruler praetorians, included courses in insurgency, land reform, tax structures, and foreign policy studies.[56]

Brazil and Peru demonstrate the reaction of the military to social mobilization and change, but by the middle 1970s there were still many unanswered questions concerning the future of the ruler type of praetorian army in Latin America. Did the military act as a rear guard, controlling rather than promoting political mobilization? Were the military action groups working to thwart the mobilization revolution because they did not trust civilian politicians to deal with it? Did the military genuinely believe in the need to establish an equilibrium between modernization and the mobilization movements? Did they react because they were institutional conservatives and identified corporate autonomy with national fulfillment, equating "honor" and "duty" with "country"? Or had they moved into counterinsurgency action to "save" the nation from populism and to save modernization from romantic revolutionists who wished to thwart it? All these questions were fundamental for evaluating the Latin American ruler type.

Although there is no doubt that the corporate orientations of the Argentine, Peruvian, and Brazilian armies were paramount, their alliances with other groups represented a "class" interest, for military support of a certain group enhanced that group's interest and power.[57] But the military were not moved primarily by economic or group interest even if politically they tended to ally with particular groups, progressive or otherwise. The social class implications of the rise and fall of Juan Perón were quite clear. The Brazilian middle class was clearly overjoyed at the 1964 coup and gave it considerable support.

In countries where labor and the middle class were both powerful and hostile to each other, the military was not usually prolabor. In Argentina, Brazil, and Peru a significant middle class opposed labor; there the military opposed Perón, Goulart, and APRA. There were middle-class coalitions in Venezuela, Mexico, Uruguay, and Costa Rica, and the military did not intervene. Chile had the characteristics of the first group, but, at least until 1973, it also had the second group's tradition of civilian control. In Colombia, labor was weaker than in other countries, but the military backed the establishment in every case.

In Latin America the military are a ruling class. They are not a working class either conceptually or ideologically, and they are not an ideologically oriented middle class. The defense of corporate professionalism and the expansion of civilian and military bureaucracies are the military's chief priorities.[58] A desire for role expansion, an antirevolutionary orientation blended with military professional conservatism, and a concern for social exclusivity and the protection of the organization are its major expectations and aspirations. Development, modernization, and political stability were consequences of those causal factors and are therefore limited by the military perception of the contribution that participation could make to the resiliency of the military organization. The primary commitment to the security of corporate professionalism continues, although it has been adapted to increase organizational resiliency (for example, in Chile). In the middle 1970s the modern military organizations in some Latin American countries, such as Chile, were still committed to the type of liberal regime that had existed in nineteenth-century and twentieth-century Europe. In others—Brazil, Argentina, Peru, and possibly Chile since 1973—this model has been abandoned in favor of a ruler type praetorian regime, even if in Peru the transformation was disguised as reform.

In summary, when corporate autonomy was successfully welded to national security (internal and external), it produced a ruler type of praetorian army that was socially conservative even when it was engaged in social action. The ruler officer was inspired by his corporate training and orientation; except for the political opportunist (styled after Perón), he was an antirevolutionary force. By 1976, the classical liberal arbitrator army was no longer operational in the high mobilization polities of Latin America. In these countries the choice lay between the ruler type of praetorian army, with a military dictatorship, and the quite different military force associated with a revolutionary regime.

In contrast to Arab and African regimes, Latin American regimes demonstrated an impressive institutional and authoritarian continuity,[59] and the military had a long tradition of autonomy and considerable political power. The ruler-type military, Latin American corporate ideology, and regime authoritarianism were now linked to the modernization revolution and the increase in the importance of technology in political and military affairs in Brazil, Peru, and Argentina.[60] The same may possibly apply to Chile although that country experienced a long period of liberal democracy and military noninterventionism between 1925 and 1973.

The regimes in Latin America in the 1970s are products of military coups of the 1960s. They are ruler-praetorians in spirit and in structure. In the case of Brazil, an authoritarian tradition converged with military managerialism and internal security doctrines to avert Castroism and communism to produce mass praetorianism. The ideology and organization of the states that were produced by military fiats possibly will follow the Brazilian ruler-type of managerial praetorianism.

There have been new attempts to identify the military ruler-type in Brazil as another authoritarian situation, *an instance* rather than an institutionalized authoritarian regime,[61] because the military regime has also failed to institutionalize itself. "It is also evident [in the Brazilian case] that consolidation of power and even considerable success in specific policies do not in themselves ensure institutionalization and that the weaknesses of regimes is not determined only by the strength of the opposition."[62] I must concur with this argument, because it has been the major thesis of my praetorian state and army theory that neither has succeeded in institutionalizing or, for that matter, legitimizing regimes. However, as I have clearly demonstrated in the last three chapters, the military has succeeded in staying in power longer than any other authority in a praetorian state, and in the case of Brazil and Argentina, longer than any other authoritarian regime in Latin America. Thus the ruler-type praetorian "situation" has demonstrated a more remarkable longevity and support than other regimes. Schmitter prefers to call the military regimes of Brazil regimes of "defensive modernization,"[63] in conformity with ruler-type praetorianism—the government without

Table 6.1 Types of Praetorian Orientation over Time, 1930–76

	Arbitrator (A)	Ruler (B)	Army-Party (C)	Administrator (A)
Argentina	1931–43 1958–66 1974–76	1930–31 1943–45 1955–58 1966–74 1976–	1946–55 1974–76	
Brazil	1930–45 1946–64 1968–76	1964–68 1976–		
Chile	1924–25 1970–72	1973–76	1932	
Peru	1914–25 1968–71	1930 1971–76	1931	
Egypt	1952–54	1954–61 1973–76	1961–73	
Syria	1949–51 1958–59 1961–62	1952–54 1960–61 1963–66	1901–63 1966–76	
Iraq	1936–37 1939–41	1938 1958–63 1963–68	1941–42 1968–76	
Libya		1970–76		
Algeria	1962–65	1965	1966–76	
Sudan	1958–64 1964–69	1969–71 1971–76	1971	
Pakistan	1966–68 1971–76	1969–71		
Congo(K) (Zaire)		1969–76		1965–69
Congo(B) (Congo)		1966		1966–76
Nigeria	1966	1966–68	1968–74	1974–76
Ghana	1965–66 1970–76			1966–69
Dahomey	1963–65			1965–76
Togo	1963–67			1967–76
Central African Republic		1966–76		
Uganda		1971–76		

consensus. Even Linz, a sociologist, entertains a theoretical position that emphasizes the more strictly political factors of praetorianism: the relative autonomy of the military in making their choices. Furthermore, he states that the long-run implications of decisions they have made "could not be explained in traditional sociological categories."[64] Linz's essay on the future of authoritarianism in Brazil is concerned with institution building and alternatives open to rulers. The alternative regimes in a praetorian state, authoritarian or otherwise, are either the arbitrator or the ruler type, and neither type has been institutionalized. The tradition of authoritarianism in military regimes is certainly linked with the type of corporate praetorianism developed in Latin America over a century.

Part III

The Professional Revolutionary Soldier

. . . every republic and every kingdom must draw its soldiers from its own countries . . . in every country training could produce good soldiers, because where nature fails, the lack can be supplied by ingenuity, which in this case is more important than nature.

Machiavelli, *The Art of War*, translated by Allan Gilbert

The purpose of the army is to win. Professionals obstruct that goal.

Attributed to General Moshe Dayan, 1954

7

The Professional Revolutionary Soldier: Definitions and Types

The orientation, organization, and inclination of the revolutionary soldier are anticorporate or noncorporate.* Thus he stands in sharp contrast to his historical predecessors, the praetorian soldier and the classical professional.

Contrasts: Revolutionaries, Praetorians, and Classical Professionals

Both the historical professional soldier and the praetorian soldier are committed to the principle of exclusivity. The revolutionary soldier, however, will not defend this principle. His refusal to do so may vary from a passive and informal failure to accept it to formal opposition, but in all cases his first concern is professionalism, not exclusivity.

The revolutionary soldier is dedicated to the defense of professionalism as the independent and exclusive property of the military, and he is certainly one of the finest, best-disciplined professionals. Nevertheless, his definition of the military organization and of corporatism is broader and less restrictive than that of the historical professional soldier in the West. For the revolutionary soldier, the organizational autonomy required to enhance and preserve high professional standards relies on something other than the pursuit or defense of corporatism or social status. The revolutionary soldier's orientation toward efficiency and his relatively high standards do, however, require some organizational controls, some form of corporate exclusivity, especially to maintain the level of expertise. To manipulate the environment and to restrict the degree of military mobilization is a protective device for successful

---

*I must stress again that like the classical soldier and the praetorian, the revolutionary soldier is an ideal type—ideal in the Weberian sense that the type does not exhaust all empirical reality. The definition is a mode of accentuating a type to make it objectively possible and subjectively meaningful. It is not categorical.

institutionalization and it requires some form of corporatism. However, the type of corporate organization and the soldier's attitude toward it are unique to the revolutionary.

The revolutionary soldier has transformed the thinking, the organization, and the internal structure of the military, causing it to abandon archaic ceremonialism and other traditional practices. What distinguishes the revolutionary from the historical professional is the absence of a socially conscious political effort to defend the principle of exclusivity in such activities as recruitment and promotion of the officer class. In this respect the revolutionary soldier is also distinguished from the praetorian soldier, who dominates the political structures that grant recognition, patronage, and titles to officers.

The revolutionary soldier is part of a professional group that aspires to maximize the requisites of professionalism, such as expertise, military education, and training, but it does not consider itself an exclusive association of experts defending the level of technical competence per se. Nor does this group defend or perpetuate class interest. Furthermore, the revolutionary soldier does not seek a homogeneity that is solely defined by skill and occupation, although to preserve professionalism he may restrict his group contacts. The revolutionary soldier is engaged in acts of violence but he does not seek to institutionalize violence as the autonomous and exclusive occupation of the military. Though it is the function of the revolutionary soldier to develop the art of war, he has not produced an exclusive military science.

The revolutionary soldier does not regard his specialized craft as a means of achieving social mobility; instead, he sees himself as a partner in the revolutionary movement. He does not separate his function as soldier from his role as the servant of the people, but failure to discriminate does not damage his professional integrity. On the contrary, his revolutionary commitment enhances professional skills and training and gives them a high value because they do not exclusively "belong" to a specialized functional group. Professionalism is not regarded as an end in itself. For the revolutionary soldier, the military was not necessarily the first or highest occupational aspiration, and he certainly rejects the boundaries the professional soldier establishes around the military, society, and regime. He requires no such line of demarcation to distinguish himself from the rest of the political system. As a defender of revolutionary order he is an instrument of society. In this sense he becomes political and thus potentially interventionist; but it is in the realm of policy rather than politics that he considers himself a senior partner. Unlike the corporate professional, the revolutionary solider is not on the defensive, because he is integrated with the revolutionary movement. He does not clamor for recognition because he is already a hero. Although the revolutionary soldier is objectively anticorporate, he is subjectively corporate in the sense that he is an integral part of the regime. He may even *be* the regime, as he is in China and, to some extent, in Israel. The classical professional soldier is a most significant bureaucratic agent of the state who derives his corporate identity from playing the double role of professional and bureaucrat. The revolutionary soldier derives his corporate orientation, not from his professional function, but from the symbiotic relationship between the soldier and the regime. He is not a bureaucratic agent of the state, nor the privileged son of the dynasty, nor the praetorian guard of the regime. He is as much a part of the regime as are his equals and rivals in politics who are not military professionals.

The guerrilla warfare that is so strongly associated with the revolutionary soldier is not a soldier's innovation. As a type of warfare and a a type of politics the guerrilla form was invented by nonmilitary professionals. Certainly the revolutionary soldier has distinguished himself in this type of warfare, but in some cases, as in China and Israel, he has distinguished himself even more in classical warfare.

The caudillo was a guerrilla. So were Robin Hood and various bandits. However, only Hobsbawm finds them revolutionary and they certainly made no contribution to professionalism, modern warfare, or politics.

Revolutionary and praetorian patterns of political intervention also differ. The common type of praetorian intervention is the military coup, the clandestine work of a small, illegitimate coterie of officers who do not usually cooperate with other groups before and during the process of intervention. Revolutionary intervention is also the work of an illegitimate military group operating under cover, but its efforts are on behalf of an established revolutionary group that openly strives to come to power with the help of large-scale institutional support. Praetorian interventionism seldom supports a revolutionary movement; revolutionary interventionism occurs only in support of the revolution.

The hallmark of military praetorianism is that a small group of political officers engineers a military coup d'etat and then strives to become the prime and exclusive source of authority, either as arbitrator or as ruler. The military revolutionary, on the other hand, is neither the exclusive author of the revolutionary coup nor the primary or exclusive source of authority once the transfer of power has occurred. A military coup d'etat is simply one technique for the transfer of authority—the most characteristic technique of praetorian systems. It is not a movement or an ideology or a political structure. Like guerrilla warfare, it is a transitional ad hoc method often employed by a revolutionary party. Other ways of transferring power include domination of the executive, plebiscites, elections, strikes, terrorism, and the encouragement of generalized violence in the society. These options are not so readily available to military praetorians. Although some of the most significant changes in history took place without violence, recent history has shown that revolutionary soldiers are often the practitioners of violence, as were, for example, the soldiers of the Red Army, the People's Liberation Army, and the North Vietnamese army. The case of the Israel Defense Force (the IDF or Zahal) demonstrates the role of the military as the mailed fist in an anticolonial war and a war against Arab aggression.*

The revolutionary soldier is the demiurge of the modern professional soldier. His expectations are higher than the corporate professional's, for he sees himself as a builder and innovator of structures beyond a "narrow" military professionalism and corporate orientation. (This was as true of Gerhard von Scharnhorst and August von Gneisenau as it has been of P'eng Te-huai and Generals Giap and Moshe Dayan.) The revolutionary soldier may see himself, perhaps, as an instrument for the successful consolidation of society and the regime. Few modern political and ideological or revolutionary movements (nationalism, socialism, fascism, and communism) have succeeded without some form of violence. Political violence may indeed be necessary for total (that is, paradigmatic) change. Whether violence occurs before, during, or after revolutionary change, the military is always its instrument and may be used by the new order as a tool in tacit bargaining with the remaining elements of the old order.

Since 1789 there have been several new military organizations of an exclusively revolutionary type. These include forces in early nineteenth-

---

*It is interesting to observe the minuscule role that African professional armies played in anticolonial struggle compared to the Arab armies of Iraq, Syria, and Algeria. In fact, with the exception of the Latin American military during the wars of independence, few praetorian armies have participated or distinguished themselves in wars of national liberation.

century Prussia, France, and Spain, the Red Army from 1918 to 1920, and the military in Latin America during the wars of liberation (all these eventually turned corporate). The praetorian soldier, the model of corporate professionalism, is the epitome of the modern antirevolutionary movement and demonstrates the failure of political institutionalization. Claiming that great revolutions are rare, Isaac Kramnick argues the "existence of non-revolutionary violence" and of "nonviolent revolution."[1] Nevertheless, many successful revolutions were achieved at the cost of considerable bloodshed and political violence: the English Civil War and the French, Bolshevik, Chinese, and Cuban revolutions. If one accepts Kramnick's idea that there is no distinction between "internal war" and "external war," it is difficult to recall a political revolution that lacked foreign intervention and violence. Violence, whether it is internal or external, accompanies the transfer of style and political position of peoples in a revolutionary situation.

The revolutionary soldier is not a permanent type. As the instrument of a large-scale political movement, his impact is greatest during the period of transition to the revolutionary regime. Once institutionalized, order and a more normal regime are needed. While the classical professional soldier becomes either a corporate professional or a corporate praetorian, the noncorporate revolutionary soldier may assume practically any form of social and organizational formation and orientation. In the realm of skill, training, and organizational performance, however, the revolutionary soldier does not compromise. He demands training and discipline, even though it may differ from that of the nineteenth-century professional. A revolution expects total political self-mastery from its army. And the army's professional training needs conditioning that is not necessarily restricted to modern practices but that may incorporate "archaic" military skills, such as the stratagems of the warlord in Communist China and the Maccabean in Israel. In Israel and Communist China, deception, stratagem, and the "indirect approach" of Liddell Hart constitute, along with other methods, the unwritten manual of military professionalism. The debate over deception and its role in military strategy was crucial in the military successes of both Israel and China. Many military professionals disdained and even disapproved of nonconventional or standardized warfare. But the revolutionary officer does not just prepare for drill; he also prepares for a purpose.

The key difference between historical corporate and revolutionary soldiers is their attitude toward size and type of military structures. As Huntington demonstrates, the corporate type prefers the formation of a small military elite through a screened recruitment and promotion system based primarily on principles of social exclusivity. The revolutionary soldier, on the other hand, is dedicated to mass military mobilization, the professionalization and standardization of large-scale armies whose elite is not recruited primarily on the basis of "heart and character" but on merit and political loyalty. The revolutionary soldier is a strategic elite in the sense of Suzanne Keller's "specialists in excellence." They are recruited on the basis of "merit regardless of other attributes—sex, race, class, religion, or even age." Group cohesion, loyalty, and morale are interdependent at the top. The military elite in the case of extreme corporate professionalism (Prussia-Germany and Japan) is a social core group (Keller's kinship, lineage, and hereditary types). The revolutionary soldier, in contrast, represents no social class. Stratification and status gratification lie in the social division of labor and of political power, not in a natural aristocracy. Corporate and professional standards are neither anchored in nor derived from a social class. Instead, they are a matter of training, discipline, and orientation toward authority.[2]

Social stratification is a poor indicator of the orientation of professionals, and the revolutionary soldier is no exception. As we shall see in the cases of China and Israel, the political role of the military is linked to its role in the nationalist and socialist revolutions and social ambitions, not to its class origins.

Clientship also separates the professional from the praetorian and the revolutionary. In contrast to the historical professional soldier, the praetorian and the revolutionary are more dependent on socioeconomic and political groups and structures, or they may even emanate from them. Revolutionary structures are defined by political forces. Revolutionary organization and tactics are also determined by the type of war fought and the type of enemy opposed. The modern revolutionary soldier's most conspicuous contribution to the military and to society is the mobilization, orientation, and radicalization of war.

Nevertheless, the "revolutionary" nature of these soldiers needs qualification. If the terms "revolutionary" and "soldier" are contradictory, indicating a craving for both change and order, the dialectics introduced by "revolutionary" could explain the re-emergence of the professional soldier. If "the modern officer corps is a professional body and the modern military officer a professional soldier," the modern revolutionary soldier is professional in the following sense: he functions as the instrument of the revolution, not as an independent agent, and in a revolutionary situation he has the monopoly over acts of war, violence, and insurrection. There is no necessary contradiction between a revolutionary regime and a professional soldier; in fact, they often coexist. What makes a soldier "revolutionary" is his orientation toward the new order and toward the radical and nonconventional in military organization and structures. The most impressive change is the mobilizing orientation. The clash between a nonrevolutionary regime and a revolutionary army will produce a civil war because the function of a revolutionary soldier is to replace such a regime with a revolutionary one. Without violence, the revolution would be doomed. Therefore, the revolutionary soldier's first act is to eliminate the professional army of the "old" regime or to integrate it into a new army, thereby helping to replace one regime with another through the reform and change (violent if necessary) of both the regime and the military organization. It is impossible to conceive of a revolutionary soldier not dedicated to revolutionizing the military establishment.

Four main types of soldiers may be distinguished along the revolutionary continuum, from the dedicated anticorporate fighter at one end to the noncorporate, professionally oriented soldier at the other: the romantic revolutionaries (Storm Troopers), the Marxist national liberation army, the Maoist Chinese People's Liberation Army, and the Zionist Israel Defense Force. The first two will be discussed in this chapter; the other two in succeeding chapters. The romantic revolutionaries, antimodern and antifuturist, are dedicated to violence and terror; they use a military or paramilitary organization as their vehicle for political takeover. The Storm Troopers and the Waffen SS are the most prominent examples of this type.

THE ROMANTIC REVOLUTIONARY: THE STORM TROOPERS AND THE WAFFEN SS

Between 1918 and 1945 Germany spawned the most remarkable paramilitary movements in modern history. These organizations, which combined worship of youth, idealism, nationalism, and violence, were motivated by zealotry and buttressed by elitist practices. Marching, plundering, and killing were widespread. Between the Free Corps (1918) and the Waffen SS (1941) the paramilitary organizations in

Germany were so numerous that they cannot be listed here.[3] The SA, the Waffen SS, the Allegemeine SS, the Steinwerke, Himmler's system RSHA, the Gestapo, the Schutzpolitzei, and others shared a common dedication to rightist revolutionary activities, political violence, political assassination, and paramilitary action undertaken to police and silence liberalism, socialism, and democracy. Even before the Nazis rose to power, several paramilitary groups had become autonomous. They represented a movement as well as an instrument of violence, and the instrument of violence served also as a political movement. Hitler's most remarkable achievement was to harness and subjugate paramilitary organizations to the Nazi state and military apparatus by professionalizing the nationalist romantic revolutionaries.

A movement involving this type of revolutionary soldier exhibits definite ideological and organizational characteristics. Ideologically, it resembles a *jugendtkultur* (youth culture). It is antibourgeois, antidemocratic-liberal, and fascist; it is chauvinist and extremist, nostalgic, romantic, and past-oriented. Dedication to war is a personal and group aspiration. "War," writes Ernst Junger, "the Father of all things, is also our father." "What we wanted . . . was war and adventure, excitement and destruction." Violence is considered an act of personal and national liberation. To crush the left, especially leftist revolts, is an overwhelming need. Activism and nihilism are the proper attitudes toward established order. As Junger expressed it: "What do we believe in? you ask. Nothing besides the possibility of action." Organizationally, there is a well-trained and cohesive elite. Superlative fighting abilities are developed and maintained, including cloak and dagger skills. There is strict discipline, or "discipline to the death" (*Kadaver* discipline). Though it is hierarchical, the society is egalitarian and classless. It is an organization of captains and lieutenants. (The familiar "du" is used, and there are a large number of noncommissioned officers, who may even serve as battalion commanders.) The society is celibate and Spartan, and emphasizes excellent physical condition for its members. Its membership is secret and its operations clandestine. Recruitment is strictly voluntary.[4]

Roehm's Storm Troopers were the ultimate political soldiers and revolutionaries. They were an anticorporate and antiprofessional (that is, not classical professional) elite of fanatics composed mainly of noncommissioned junior officers contemptuous of both the political and military orders of the "bourgeois state." They were antiprofessional in the sense that they never accepted subservience to the capitalist nation-state. (They even staged an unsuccessful revolt against Hitler in 1934.) They denied classical military discipline and organization. Impressive warriors and believers in action, they were no ordinary professional soldiers. They did not make the military a lifetime career, but were dedicated to violence as a political way of life and an instrument of the revolution against the bourgeois and liberal political orders. They rejected the professional soldier's code and coat of arms as well as his historical responsibility to the established order.

The emergence of the Waffen SS signaled the change from anarchy to Nazi order. The SS, the private army of Hitler and the Nazi party, was distinguished from the pre-Nazi Storm Troopers in that it was subservient to Hitler. It eventually became a highly disciplined army of romantic revolutionaries, a professional, elitist, military group. It was Hitler's praetorian guard and military pride in wartime. By 1936 the armed SS had been divided into two clearly defined services: the SS Verfugungstruppe, Hitler's bodyguard, which eventually became a military SS or Waffen SS; and the SS Totenkopfverbande, heir to the Storm Troopers, an organization of bullies and sadists in charge of concentration camps and the "final solution" for the Jews and others. The SS Verfugungstruppe became Hitler's own military organization; the second performed police and extermination functions. Both SS revolutionary armies were legitimized as "organizations in the service of the state" only because they served the dictator himself. But their functions, roles, and behavior were clearly differentiated.[5]

If the Nazi party aspired to the role of vanguard of the "German race," the armed professional SS sought the revolutionary role in leading the German military establishment. Although the Waffen SS fought valiantly and won a considerable military reputation on the eastern front, it was never accepted by the Wehrmacht as a legitimate military organization. Beginning as an instrument of terror, the revolutionary soldier organization became an appendage of the state war machine. However, failing to achieve legitimacy through its professional merits, it never became institutionalized as a regular bureaucratic-military establishment. Its function was revolutionary action, and, being imbued with the Nazi *geist*, it served as the vanguard of the revolutionary party. It was never an instrument of the state as much as it was an instrument of the dictator. Nor could it become part of military corporatism since its functions were not strictly military even when it acted as a military combat group, as it did after 1941.

> The more important provisions separating the armed SS from the Wehrmacht stated that the SS Verfugungstruppe was a special formation unconditionally at Hitler's personal disposal; that it was part neither of the Wehrmacht nor of the Police; that during peacetime its command was vested in the Reichsführer SS and Chief of the German Police; that regardless of its employment it remained "politically" (but not juridically) a formation of the NSDAP; and that its financial support was to continue to come from the police budget of the Ministry of the Interior.
>
> Included among the provisions linking the armed SS to the Wehrmacht were those which decreed that duty in the SS Verfugungstruppe counted as military service (*Wehrdienst*); that its weapons and equipment were to be provided by the Army; that its officers were to attend Army training courses; that its personnel were to receive their pay and allotments according to Wehrmacht regulations; and that in the event of mobilization it might (with Hitler's approval) serve within the framework of the Wehrmacht and under the tactical command of the Army.[6]

"Indeed," writes Stein, "it was the SS, not the National Socialist Party, that proved to be the dynamic core of the Nazi system." The Waffen SS took the following oath to Hitler: "I swear to you, Adolf Hitler, as Führer and Reichschancellor, loyalty and bravery. I vow to you, and those you have named to command me, obedience unto death, so help me God." Like all revolutionary armies it was task- or project-oriented. It was to serve as Hitler's elite guard in the period of transition, probably until the great war ended. It was designed to protect the führer and his regime by acting as a militarized police force. Hitler (unlike Himmler) never intended it to become the established military institution.

> Hitler's decision to allow the armed SS to take an active part in the war was based on his conviction that it would not be able to retain the respect of Germans unless it did its share at the front. Hitler regarded the Waffen SS in its military role as a Guard formation, in the eighteenth- and nineteenth-century meaning of

the term. As the military apotheosis of National Socialism, its task was to set an example for the Army. But Hitler assured the generals in 1940 that after the war the Waffen SS would become the "militarized state police" of the Third Reich and would not exceed 5 to 10 percent of the Army's peacetime strength.[7]

Hitler clearly distinguished between the functions of the revolutionary and the professional soldier. "He had no intention of creating a fourth branch of the Wehrmacht," which was the prime instrument of Nazi militarism, "the spearhead of Nazi aggression." The Waffen SS was an heir to the Free Corps. "Few of the men in the Waffen SS were old enough to have had any personal contact with the post-World War I Freikorps movement; yet it was the spirit of their movement, its nihilism and elitism, which perhaps comes closest to that of the Waffen SS." The Waffen SS, like the Freikorps before it, was distinguished from the established military by its emphasis on toughness, recklessness, and savagery instead of skill, training, order, and military education. The heroes of the SS troops were not the brutal police, the *alte Kampfer* type of Hitler's early days, but regular army officers who had commanded the SS Verfugungstruppen.[8] From these officers they acquired their ruthlessness. The early officers' group egalitarianism and cohesion were emulated, even down to the military uniform. The Waffen SS shared the egalitarianism, as well as the high political commitment, of the modern revolutionary soldier. Nostalgic for the strict feudal values of the medieval northern German forests, the Storm Troops and the Waffen SS were two of the most notorious groups of anticorporate revolutionary professionals of modern times.

The Marxist National Liberation Army

The most prominent modern revolutionary soldiers are those in the Marxist national liberation movement (NLM). Although there are non-Marxist national liberation movements and armies, the generic Marxist type approximates most nearly the ideal type of the revolutionary soldier.

The outstanding contribution of modern revolutionary movements is the political revolution, which appeared in 1789. Unlike the earlier revolution, which was the product of a narrow elite, a group of elites, an alliance between peasants and priests, or an ideology, the modern revolution mobilizes the masses for political action. When the regime changes not only are the authority and structural arrangements altered, but a new type of political mobilization is set in motion. Modern revolutions are characterized by total orientation for action, a high degree of brutality, a high level of violence, a wide network of politically oriented elites, a tightly controlled mass mobilization organization in the form of a party and a large-scale permanent military establishment, and ideological cohesion buttressed by a system of revolutionary rules that are upheld if necessary by internal police.

The national liberation movement does not represent an individual, a group of individuals, a family clan, a tribe, or a province, although it could represent the class system, the nation, the movement, or "the idea." No national liberation movement exists without an ideology, an elaborate sustaining organization, and a complex scheme for agitation, professionalization, and propaganda. The NLM is modern in the sense that it is not anomic, capricious, or self-propelling.

NLM-NLA Relations

The national liberation army (NLA) is the revolutionary instrument of violence. No national liberation movement (NLM) conceives of its army as an independent, autonomous organization or as an end in itself. The dynamics of the NLM-NLA relationship vary with the nature, structure, and length of the revolutionary war. The relationship between party-movement and army produces different NLA types and dictates the nature of civil-military relations, the longevity of the revolutionary war, and the duration of mass mobilization. On the whole, both the movement and the army are engaged in the mobilization of the masses, but they differ in their underlying structural and ideological roles. The NLM's function is to control the mobilization process. Absorption of peasants into the "nation" is carried on by a complex civilian-bureaucratic organization and by propagandists, led by professional revolutionaries recruited on the basis of their political and propaganda skills. Organizational mobility is often restricted according to stringent rules. The NLA, with the exception of the Soviet army and its commissar system, is not engaged in much political and propaganda work. It is an elite or merit organization. Mobility in the NLA depends more on the objective criteria of military professionalism than on skillful political agitation. Much of the dynamics of civil-military relations in China and North Vietnam can be explained in terms of this difference.

Relations between the NLM and the NLA follow the professional soldier's cardinal rule: the instruments of violence are subordinated to the civilian-oriented party regime. This relationship is achieved through a permanent struggle against potential and real praetorianism. Continued agitation and propaganda in the military is balanced by an intensive program of professionalization and institutionalization. The party dominates the machinery for political mobilization (conscription, mobility, and so forth). The military is encouraged to harbor egalitarian rather than corporate aspirations at the expense of professional requirements, organizational demands, and the party (the revolution's chief structure of mobilization). The military undergoes political institutionalization, not at the expense of the party but by making the political boundaries between the two ambiguous. The struggle, which is not limited to ideology, extends to political influence and power, and it is not a matter of simple competition between civilian and military bureaucracies. Instead, there is conflict among persons, structures, and ideas over the nature and the direction of the revolution.

Marxism-Leninism and the Professional Soldier

It is unrealistic to associate most modern revolutionary and guerrilla movements and ideologies with Marxism-Leninism. Those who have internalized Marxism-Leninism as their *weltschmerz* probably have not read more than a hundred pages of Marxist-Leninist literature, and some have not even seen one printed sentence. Few, if any, have read the "basic" writings of Marx or Engels, Lenin or Trotsky. From Quebec to Azania in South Africa, from Malaya to Guinea, there are some fifty-odd revolutionary movements, with guerrilla armies and urban guerrilla coteries. Few of these "Leninist revolutionaries" are aware that the USSR never has experienced a prolonged revolutionary war or that Trotsky organized the Soviet military along professional lines, paying only lip service to such revolutionary ideas as levée en masse and Babeuvism. In theory and practice, the only Marxist-Leninist revolutionary militaries were Mao's and Tito's, and they were primarily the outgrowth of nationalist revolutions that incorporated Marxist-Leninist stratagems.

The Indo-Chinese national liberation movement in North and South Vietnam, Laos, and Cambodia, the Huks of the Philippines (in their early years), and the Burmese and Malaysian Marxist guerrillas have only approximated a Marxist-Leninist model. Algerian, Cuban, and Palestinian guerrillas, as well as Che-Debrais groups and ideologies have never experienced a Marxist revolutionary war; at best they only apply Leninist military ideas *ex cathedra*. If the military structure of the Cuban army is Marxist-Leninist, it became so only after Castro defeated the Batista regime. Che never succeeded in forming a Marxist-Leninist military organization or in fomenting such a revolution in Cuba, not even after the Gramma group assumed power. Except for Mao, Chinese military professionals abandoned some of their Marxist-Leninist élan after they took over the mainland in 1949. In fact, the Cultural Revolution signified the desire to abandon all that was not Maoist about Chinese communism. After the defeat of Hitler's Germany, Tito's army became as professional as the Soviet army. No military establishment in Eastern Europe has been Marxist-Leninist or revolutionary either in structure or in spirit. All are professional in the classical sense.

The professional soldier passed from the scene in Europe after World War II; in the United States he began to decline in the early 1970s with the gradual disengagement from the Vietnam war and the rise of a volunteer army; in Latin America, sub-Saharan Africa, and the Middle East he became corporate. As the professional soldier declined in the West, sub-Saharan Africa, and the Middle East, he gained new life in the national liberation movements of communist countries. The protracted wars of national liberation going on in the Balkans and in the Middle East since the 1930s have enhanced the growth and influence of the military.[9] But such a movement could only happen after a successful Marxist-Leninist revolutionary takeover that subordinated the military instrument to the supreme political structure—the political party. Revolutions are successful only if they achieve an equilibrium of sorts in the relationship between the military establishment and the political structures.

Why has Marxism-Leninism, a Western political theory of society and organization, given new life to the nineteenth-century idea of military professionalism in a twentieth-century world of revolution and change? Marxism, probably the most rigid political doctrine of the age of capital that began in 1848, thrives in the modern nation-state and the modern corporate organization. It manipulates human resources and orientations by using the military as an organizational weapon to fulfill the practical premise of a particular social theory. Lenin paid considerable attention to military theorists and writings, carefully reading and annotating Clausewitz's *On War*. Engels's studies on the military demonstrate his deep interest in analyzing the German, British, and French armies. Trotsky too devoted considerable time and effort to the study of the military. To the pragmatic Marxist, the immediate and manifest foe was the professional army, a nationalist instrument of the capitalist state. Yet at the same time this army fascinated the Marxists, and they patterned the Soviet army after it, even if Trotsky and others nostalgically preferred the Paris Commune. Fundamentally, Karl Marx was a high priest of philosophical utilitarianism, although he rejected its moral commitments to the capitalist social system. Dedicated to change and to analyzing the relationship between capital and labor, Marx was a theorist of the rational organization. In his practical politics (so well illustrated by the organization of the First International) and in his trade union and socialist activities, Marx was an institutionalist. As a Hegelian, he believed that the dynamics of history were to be harnessed and manipulated by the political and social organization of society and the marketplace. According to Engels, the political included the military organization.

The Organizational Weapon

Marx identified the bureaucracy and the military as the most potent instruments of capitalism. Engel's "administration of things" (the socialist state), run by the dictatorship of the proletariat, was to reverse the relationships between capital and labor, but not the development of capitalism and industrialism or the centralized, bureaucratic state. These orientations, transformed by Lenin and Trotsky, formed a commitment to the rational economic man. After all, what could be more rational in the Hegelian sense than the socialist state? In theory it did not exclude corporatism, hierarchy, organization, or legitimacy. What Marx and Engels aspired to do was to change the authority relationships of the state, and they hoped the revolution would cause the state to wither away. Lenin, however, accepted the state, and his successors accepted its instruments.

Marx opposed anarchy, disorder, and irrational romanticism. He rejected any historical role for the peasant, referring to the "idiocy of rural life." He also rejected student elites and peasant masses, which have turned out to be the founders of most if not all modern revolutionary and NLM movements and ideologies. Marx was vigorously opposed to spontaneous revolution, which he identified with philosophical and political anarchy. He ridiculed the peasant insurrection as "an historic piece of buffoonery."[10] He opposed guerrilla warfare, Jacobinism associated with anarchism, and mob insurrection. Above all, Marx demonstrated little or no perception of modern nationalism, showing tacit disapproval of the parochial exclusiveness of narrow-minded nationalist braggarts like Mazzini. For Marx, terrorism was anathema. In short, no political philosophy could have been a less logical fountainhead of the modern guerrilla and revolutionary movements than Marxism.

Although the state and its oppressive capitalist machinery were to be relegated to "the Museum of Antiquities by the side of the spinning wheel and the Bronze Age,"[11] the Soviet state, and, for that matter, the Communist Chinese and North Vietnamese regimes, have become the most bureaucratic, rigid, hierarchical, and authoritarian of modern states. The Chinese and North Vietnamese regimes could not have been established without the help of the military professional. In the USSR and in its satellites the regime has been sustained with the support of a highly developed military organization. There corporate and professional orientations commingle with those of party apparatchiks and ideologues. Before and during the takeover of the state, the Marxist-Leninist has been known to engage in guerrilla and irregular warfare, though not at the expense of the professional soldier's orientation and strategy. As soon as the socialist regime is installed, the military becomes one of the most prominent instruments of the authoritarian state. The continuance of military anticorporatism depends upon the type of revolutionary war. The longer the revolutionary war lasts, the more prestigious, influential, and political (and less exclusive) the military professional becomes. In China and in North Vietnam, the military has been the very cradle of the revolution. The prolonged military campaigns waged by Mao from 1927 to 1949 and by North Vietnam between 1945 and 1975 have increasingly elevated the prestige and political power of the military elite—Mao Tse-tung, P'eng Te-huai, Lin Piao, Liu Po-ch'eng, Chu Teh, Giap, and other North Vietnamese and Vietcong officers. In the USSR and Yugoslavia, the revolutionary wars were short (lasting from 1918 to 1920 and from 1941 to 1945, respectively), "depriving" the military of its historic opportunity to rise to political influence and social power. The army remains a source of power in the USSR nevertheless. There are, therefore, few sanctions against military power in the Marxist-Leninist ethic, and there is no pragmatic aversion to the rise of military power, military professional-ism, and military-bureaucratic practices, for as Lenin wrote, "the unity of theory and practice is based on the primacy of the latter." Marxist moral commitment to a just industrial system actually implies support of organization, bureaucracy, and hierarchy. The struggle for power in Bolshevism is conspiratorial. Here the dictatorship of the proletariat and the administration of things merge.

> Leninism, with its strong emphasis on the power of disciplined minorities, affords a most useful case history for the study of organi-zational weapons. At the same time, it is important to learn about organizational manipulation if we are fully to comprehend the bolshevik experience.
>
> Using the special role of organization as a key, we may expect to learn something about the inner dynamics of bolshevism—that pattern of motivation and action which impels it onward to ever-renewed power struggles. . . .
>
> The bolshevik type of party was an effective organization weapon because it solved many of the problems associated with transforming a voluntary association into a managerial structure. But once a strong managerial structure had been established and ideology made a mere adjunct of organization, the party became obsessive in exploiting opportunities to conquer social institu-tions.[12]

What, then, is the relationship between the Bolshevik organizational weapon and the revolutionary soldier? The Bolshevik revolutionary is motivated by the ethics and morality of Marxism-Leninism, a disci-pline that also provides him with the strategy and tactics for the con-quest of political power. "The Bolshevik pursuit of power is carried on everywhere in the social structure, wherever an *increment of power* can be squeezed from control of an institution or a portion of it." Tools of inter-vention—infiltration, propaganda—are used to weaken vulnerable institutions. The usefulness of Leninism for the military lies in the strategy of psychological warfare. Lenin, the master strategist of Bolshe-vism, successfully devised a dual-power concept, creating conditions for insurrection so that the "advanced class," the party dictatorship, might take advantage of the crucial moment. As he states:

> To be successful, insurrection must rely not upon conspiracy and

not upon a party, but upon the advanced class. . . . Insurrection must rely upon the rising revolutionary spirit of the people. . . . Insurrection must rely upon the *crucial moment* in the history of the growing revolution, when the activity of the advanced ranks of the people is at its height, and when the *vacillations* in the ranks of the enemies and *in the ranks of the weak, half-hearted and irresolute friends of the revolution* are strongest. . . . And these three conditions in the attitude toward insurrection distinguish Marxism from Blanquism.[13]

Here lies the difference between the ethics of the romantic revolutionaries (Storm Troopers and Waffen SS) and the Bolsheviks. Taking advantage of mass action, the Bolsheviks built an organization, the cadre, to disconnect the mass from party dictatorship and to institutionalize the dictatorship of mobilization. Military organization is subordinated to political action, which is in turn organized along military lines. The Bolsheviks militarized politics in the sense that they modeled political structures after military and corporate organizations. The concept of domination over the military was derived from Western rational and bureaucratic practices, but Clausewitz's dictum on the subordination of the military organization to strategy gave Lenin an alternative to romantic and Jacobin revolution. Lenin harnessed the conspiratorial elites to revolutionary strategy by setting up a professional revolutionary cadre to mobilize the masses.

The cadre is essentially an exclusive professional group whose expertise is restricted to the technology of penetration, propaganda, and mobilization. It forms the general staff of the dictatorship of mobilization and functionally resembles a military general staff in designing and organizing the mobilizing strategy and campaigns. Insurrection is a tactic of mass action; so is guerrilla warfare. The scope of Marxist warfare is so wide that the military constitutes only one practitioner of revolutionary conflict. Thus the revolutionary soldier has a set of orientations different from those of the historical professional soldier. The apparatchik is the commander-in-chief of political subversion and organization; the revolutionary soldier is his chief aide.

Marx, unlike Lenin, considered that insurrection was doomed to fail. In the words of Shlomo Avineri, though Marx "naturally sympathizes with the Jacobins, he regards them as utterly misguided and muddle-headed and considers their recourse to terrorism imminent in their basic fallacy. Marx denounces Jacobin terror unequivocally, and the Jacobin dictatorship does not and cannot serve him in any way as a model for a future communist revolution." This kind of terror is a primitive military state in the sense that it is "still lacking its socio-economic preconditions." Marx's attitude toward terror and insurrection was grounded in his rationalist and utilitarian orientation. He rejected "political drama," which, he perceptively argued, would "end necessarily with the restoration of religion, of private property, of all elements of civil society, just as war ends with the conclusion of peace." Furthermore, "the classic *polis* is the model of Jacobin republicanism, as it implies the subsumption of the economic under the political sphere. But the anachronism of this model makes the Jacobin attempt utterly helpless. Since the Jacobins, according to Marx, lack any understanding of history, they overlook the significance of economic processes."[14]

Yet, in spite of Marx's views, armed insurrection became Lenin's favorite political-military doctrine, which he formulated in detail:

> In order to treat insurrection in a Marxist way, i.e., as an art, we must at the same time, without losing a single moment, organize a *headquarters* of the insurgent detachments, distribute our forces, move the reliable regiments to the most important points, surround the Alexandrinsky Theatre, occupy the Peter and Paul Fortress, arrest the General Staff and the government, and move against the officer cadets and the Savage Division those detachments which would rather die than allow the enemy to approach the strategic points of the city. We must mobilize the armed workers and call them to fight the last desperate fight, occupy the telegraph and the telephone exchange at once, move *our* insurrection headquarters to the central telephone exchange and connect it by telephone with all the factories, all the regiments, all the points of armed fighting, etc.[15]

The Bolsheviks came to power through political and military insurrection. The German Bolsheviks made an abortive attempt at military insurrection in Hamburg in 1923 and in Reval, Estonia, in 1924. There were several attempts at insurrection in China: in Canton, Shanghai, and Kwantung in 1927 and in Chang'sha between 1930 and 1932. By 1938, after Stalin had consolidated his power and the last series of purges had ended, the Bolsheviks officially "gave up" armed insurrection. (The countries of Eastern Europe were "liberated" by Soviet swords and plebiscites run by the secret service and the police.) In 1928

Piatnitsky, the organizing secretary of the Comintern, had created a Bolshevik "think tank," a staff composed of Soviet generals, apparatchiks, and Asian and European professional revolutionaries, including Ho Chi Minh, to formulate in detail the strategy and tactics of armed insurrection. But although insurrection was used by the early Bolsheviks and became a doctrine for international communism, it was not integrated into Soviet military doctrines. Lenin did not recommend that it be included in the Red Army manual, nor did the heads of the Red Army, including Trotsky and Tukhachevsky. Insurrection, Leninist and Maoist style, was a doctrine that linked party to army, and Lenin made it clear that "the Party supports every mass insurrection. However, if the insurrection does not break out spontaneously, but is organized by the Party, if the masses embark on armed struggle in response to the Party's call, then the latter bears the responsibility for both the timing and for the conduct of the struggle." Engels had already written that insurrection "is an art quite as much as war or any other art, and is subject to certain procedural rules which, when neglected, will bring about the downfall of the party neglecting them."[16]

Revolution and the Professional Soldier

The mystique of revolution did not awe the hard-headed team of Marx and Engels. Understanding the rational manipulation of organizational structures, they predicted that the revolutionary soldier would become a bureaucratic professional. Terror was at best a tactic and war a strategy. Wars could be won only by professional soldiers imbued with revolutionary doctrines.

The revolutionary army is in fact a professional army imbued with such extras as "commitment," "dedication," "purpose." Its organization and structure follow the professional type.[17] If the military is to sustain its élan and protect its integrity, to fulfill its revolutionary expectations and yet function professionally, it must follow the following principles:

    1. A revolution can be won only by capturing political power. This cannot be achieved without a well-trained military organization.

    2. The consolidation of political power and political institutionalization require a subjective control type of civil-military relations. This relationship continues into the post-

revolutionary era when the military is gradually harnessed to the regime.

3. The military should not be "Jacobinized," or "ideologized." It should not become isolated. To function properly it must both be imbued with commitment and possess good training.

4. Appointments to the middle and lower ranks must remain objective and be based on skill and performance.

5. The high command should be considered an ally of the revolutionary regime and an active partner in matters of defense and related foreign policy.

6. Procedure, practice, and professional behavior must be institutionalized, even at the expense of some rigidity in later years.

7. The criteria for recruitment, promotion, and advancement must remain universal.

8. A large-scale army should never be a mass movement, but a highly disciplined machine.

9. The rapid turnover of higher ranks and the reasonable rotation of middle ranks (major to colonel) should become a matter of policy.

10. The military should become a source of social prestige, political influence, and professional pride for its members.

According to Katharine Chorley, "a loose type of military organization, without responsibility to central authority, may be adequate and invaluable for the opening phases of insurrection or for guerrilla warfare; but for a serious war of siege and manoeuvre against trained troops, it is useless." Such features as skill, discipline, authority, communication, lines of command, and the use of manuals are essential for the revolutionary army. Successful revolutions do not emerge spontaneously. Rational organization and the qualities of the modern professional soldier are required. The blending of rational organization, Leninist doctrines, and ideological commitments (which are not necessarily a Marxist-Bolshevist monopoly but may also be found among religious fundamentalists, nationalists, and other zealots), produces a highly motivated and skilled professional soldier. To quote Katharine Chorley again, "the ultimate sanction of a revolutionary, as of any other political system, is the armed force."[18]

Revolutionary wars have given the most talented officers the opportunity to emerge. While corporate professionalism has a tendency
to produce officers who are political and military simpletons, revolutionary conditions and civil wars have often produced legendary
generals. Napoleon is neither the first nor the last great name on the list.
Cromwell, Dubois Crance, Washington, Lafayette, Bolivar, Garibaldi,
Lee, Forrest, Stonewall Jackson, Grant and Sherman, Trotsky, Blycher,
Tukhachevsky, Lin Piao, Chen Yi, Chu Teh, Mao Tse-tung, Giap,
Orde Wingate, Moshe Dayan, Yigal Allon, Yigael Yadin, Yitzchak
Sadeh, Durrutu Buenaventura, Castro, Che, Sy Azzaddine, and Ami-
rouche—all have been professional but dedicated soldiers whose skills
and interests were not restricted to the military. One could argue that
the most competent and talented professional soldiers do not emerge
under conditions of stability and order but in times of revolution and
drastic change; and they are not necessarily graduates of professional
academies. Although corporate professionals are required to adhere to
order and to maintain an apolitical stance, the best professionals in
times of crisis, revolution, civil war, and anticolonial struggle have been
those with a social and political orientation. Their political motivation
helps makes them excellent soldiers.

The professionalism of the revolutionary soldier may take many
forms. Its does not have to be the professionalism of the historical
military organization. Cromwell the parliamentarian, Carnot the
scientist, Von Roon the geographer, Mao Tse-tung the classical scholar
and librarian, Dayan the farmer, and Yadin the archeologist did not
aspire to be soldiers. Revolutionary commitment caused them to give
up their intended professions for soldiering. Lateral integration of other
professionals skills into the military brought many innovations to military
organization and practices; for example, in the revolutionary American colonies, Napoleonic France, and Prussia of the 1800s, as well as
in contemporary China and Israel. The revolutionary condition has
also added to the knowledge of other professions, but the military has
had particular benefit. The revolutionary soldier is public-oriented.
He performs the function that David Rapoport called virtu (public spirit)
which is functionally analogous to the economic term "surplus value"
for the entrepreneur. The marginal utility of the professional soldier is
his orientation toward virtu. The revolutionary soldier is a mission-
oriented professional who breaks most "professional" rules once war
begins. Rapid rotation of ranks and strategic flexibility in application of

the rules of war, deception, stratagem, and manipulation of human behavior and of cultural reservoirs of the armed forces—all are employed in times of revolution.

Yet there are severe contradictions between the professional and the revolutionary orientation. The revolutionary's professional behavior usually stems from the collegial group characteristics that appear even among revolutionary officers. And the tension between the routinization of professional orientations and revolutionary élan is critical for the formation and evolution of the revolutionary soldier, which will be illustrated by two case studies: China after 1927 and Israel after 1920.

Unlike the historical professional armies, the revolutionary armies of China and Israel embody the nation-in-arms concept; they are composed of citizens led by a small core of military professionals. Another difference is the successful integration of the professional officer group and the citizens' army that exists in both countries. But there the analogy between China and Israel ceases. In five crucial areas the two revolutionary armies stand in sharp contrast. (1) The officer class of the Israel Defense Force (IDF) is cohesive and apolitical; the Chinese officer class is divided and highly political. (2) The professional gap between officers and peasants is wider in China, which is essentially a developing country, than in Israel, a developed country. The primary group in Israel, the citizens, is more skilled than the primary group in China, and the IDF officer corps is more technocratic than its Chinese counterpart. (3) The nature of war is different in the two states. Israel is the last country in modern times to fight a classical war, though it did so with a great deal of skill, a high level of technology, and substantial flexibility. The Chinese, though moving toward professionalization and technocracy, have been fighting *extended* guerrilla warfare (with the possible exception of the Korean war). The Chinese are now preparing for a new type of warfare with the USSR, possibly nuclear, but they have yet to demonstrate their prowess in a major war. The large-scale guerrilla warfare of the last decade is out of fashion with the PLA but modern warfare has not yet made its debut. When it does, it will probably resemble that of the USSR, because the Chinese have mastered new skills and technology. (4) In Israel an officer's career is short and turnover is rapid, while in China the officer's career is for a lifetime and turnover is slow. In 1975, the average age of Israeli senior officers was between thirty-five and forty-five (the "oldest" group since 1948). The average was sixty to seventy-five in China. (5) The most fundamental difference between China and Israel lay in the nature of their civil-military relations. Above all, the authoritarian nature of the Chinese Communist party and of the single-party system requires an equilibrium between competing civil and military elites. In Israel, on the other hand, the political system depends on electoral support and party competitiveness, and in these activities the officers play an insignificant role. As the elite with the greatest military expertise, however, the Israeli high command does exert considerable influence on Israel's defense and foreign policies.

8

China: Professionalism versus Guerrillaism

A national liberation movement (NLM) is a revolutionary movement, bent on effecting radical social change. Its goals are to destroy the old regime, which is burdened by allegiance to outmoded traditions, and to overthrow the authority and prestige of dysfunctional leadership and of traditional social classes, symbols, and institutions. The movement introduces a new revolutionary personality, one that operates among movement activists to create party cadres and a political-ideological elite. Above all, the party, as the revolutionary organization, must be imbued with ideology, for its most important function is to get that ideology into the minds of the masses and the members of the revolutionary movement. It is through ideology that revolutionary movements mobilize the social energies of a people.

The most influential model of a revolutionary social movement has been Lenin's Bolshevik party movement, in which the party became the supreme and only vehicle of the revolution. The insurgent leaders became professional and fulfilled the double function of a revolutionary movement: to agitate (to propagandize) and to mobilize (to organize the people).

Lenin's ironclad rule was based on the concept that unity of theory and practice rests on the primacy of practice and that ideology and organization must merge into one combative structure—the party, the communist command post of revolution. The Leninist-Bolshevik model was emulated by China, Yugoslavia, and North Vietnam. It was, of course, amended, reformed, and "corrected" according to circumstances, environment, and historical-political conditions in each of these countries.

TASKS OF THE NLM

Mao reshaped Lenin's party rules to fit Chinese conditions. Mao's thought fused ideology and organization, with ideology remaining paramount. His ideology has been described as "a systematic set of ideas with action consequences serving the purpose of creating and using an organization."[1] Asia's NLMs have followed, with modifications, the Maoist version of Lenin's dictum that ideology is paramount. Thus the party movement is an all-inclusive and complex ad hoc regime, a government in exile, a transitional political system of a revolutionary social movement. In order to agitate, mobilize, and organize successfully, a revolutionary movement must be anchored among the people or within a territory. A territorial base is not absolutely indispensable in the early stages, however. Lenin's party operated mainly outside Russia until 1917, when the political Zionist movement crystallized in eastern Europe. But once the movement begins to mobilize, it must be rooted within a people and conquer for itself part of the territory that it intends to liberate and dominate eventually. The general aim of an NLM is to politicize the masses in order to mobilize a whole people and thus effect a radical change in ideas, orientations, and social, economic, and political structures.

With the exception of Israel, only nationalist movements linked with Communist parties have been successful in social and political mobilization in modern developing states. Again with the exception of Israel, the nationalist movement has allied with the Communist party only when a foreign aggressor has invaded peasant territory and refused to accommodate the peasants. Noncommunist nationalist movements of Yugoslavia and China allied with the Nazi and Japanese invaders and eventually failed. The peasantry, squeezed between the invaders and the collaborating nationalists, joined the Communist party, because it was the only party that opted for total and uncompromising war against an aggressor. The success of the Communist party was due to its extraordinary innovation in the areas of human manipulation and social organization. The bringing together of the ideology of Marxism and the Leninist-Maoist organizations is the most remarkable achievement of modern NLMs. Broadly, China, Vietnam, and Yugoslavia followed this pattern: following brutal foreign invasion, local peasants respond through self-defense groups, and peasant nationalism emerges. A Communist party organization uses education and agitation to inculcate a Bolshevik theory of society into a peasant nationalist movement. The Leninist leadership's ideological indoctrination of the peasants and the collaboration of an urban nationalist movement, coupled with the presence of foreign invaders, creates an alliance between a pre-existing

Communist movement and an uprooted peasantry. As Chalmers Johnson succinctly puts it, "Acting on the *side* of the peasantry has become more important than acting for the *sake* of the peasantry."[2]

The next task of the NLM is to begin the process of fundamental democratization of the peasants or the population under its jurisdiction. To make good its promise of social and economic justice, it must put into action large-scale programs like land reform, crop diversification, and elimination of social parasites and local bandits. Programs designed to help the middle-level peasant to overthrow his economic and social oppressors are particularly important since the organization and infrastructure of the NLM must live and operate among peasants; the organizers must dominate the peasant and make his enemies theirs.

Not all NLMs are Communist-nationalist alliances, however. The Socialist-Zionist movement of Israel, a democratic socialist party, succeeded in turning a colonizing population into a national liberation force, and it has established a regime of social justice, economic egalitarianism, and human freedom that the USSR, China, and North Vietnam are hardly likely to ever attain.

In China, Yugoslavia, and North Vietnam, the national liberation army has been an arm of the NLM, an instrument of the political-ideological structure whose function is to transform an uprooted population (the peasants) into a socialist and egalitarian nation-state. The army has no independent role or raison d'être of its own. It is an instrument of social mobilization as well as a military force. The experiences of both China and Yugoslavia demonstrate that, although the Communist party was a powerful political organization, only the bitter struggle against the enemy consolidated the NLA into a successful military force. This is also true in the case of the North Vietnamese army and the Vietcong, although the latter, left alone, could have been defeated by the Americans in the same way that the Algerian NLA lost the military campaign to the French.[3] The major theme of Mao, Ho, and Tito was political agitation through the education of an army elite in Marxist-Leninist ideology; the army, in other words, always remained the instrument of the ideological movement.

The Maoist NLM and PLA

How did the Chinese Communist NLM become operational? The answer lies in an analysis of the relationships between the two major sources of political power in China, the Chinese Communist party

(CCP) and the People's Liberation Army (PLA), and of Mao's struggle against the official CCP-PLA stance.

The history of Chinese communism and particularly of civil-military and party-military relationships in Communist China would be over-simplified if it were to be cast solely in Maoist terms. The struggle over ideas, men, and organization between Mao and the generals reveals a web of antagonistic relationships between the Maoist guerrillas and the military professionals. The debate over what type of war the country should prepare for began in 1927, and continued into the 1970s. It disclosed an ongoing battle over the political and constitutional role of the military in the revolution. The debate concerned one of the funda-mentals of Chinese communism, the role of the military in the social mobilization of the Chinese peasant. In other words, it was a contro-versy over *how* the Chinese revolution would reach its goals, not over the goals themselves. Controversy over goals did not arise until the Cultural Revolution.

The struggle was never over the subordination of the PLA to the CCP. It is not idly that the Chinese call the PLA a "party-army," for in China the army has long been the repository of the revolution. The tragic history of the CCP and the long revolutionary war from 1927 to 1949 left their marks on Chinese communism, and the army came to be the praetorian guard of the revolution, the defender of the ideology, and, above all, the protector of the CCP's legacy.

The deeper roots of the controversy between Mao and the generals lay in Mao's somewhat archaic weltanschauung of "learning from the PLA" and his peasant orientation, which he pitted against the modern, rational, professional orientation of the generals. The battle over the loyalty and authority of the PLA was still unresolved in the middle 1970s. In the field of warfare it was a controversy between the strategy of military professionalism and its implications—order, stability, ra-tionality, hierarchy, large-scale campaigns, the direct approach, and other modern bureaucratic methods—and Mao's guerrillaism, a modi-fied version of peasant warfare, involving deception, surprise, cohesive-ness, small units, and "human" action. These differences were much more than scholastic exercises. The vision of Mao and his generals was derived from the very history of China and from some fifty years of the trial and error of revolutionary political and military activities. The evolution of the CCP and the PLA and their relationships is not alto-gether clear. Both revolutionary action and military professionalism stemmed from the accumulated experience and response of Chinese communism to political reality and military necessities after 1927. The doctrinal debate between Mao and his generals over military tactics and policy was certainly motivated by the different orientations of the two sides, but the purpose of the debate was to meet the revolutionary needs of Chinese communism. By the middle 1970s neither Mao nor his generals had proven their claim to the universal truth of Chinese communism, although Mao relentlessly and often dogmatically pursued his own weltanschauung as the only truth. Historians of modern China and certainly military historians are no longer in doubt that the generals and the professionals, not the guerrillas, determined the strategy that eventually brought military victory. The history of Chinese communist military campaigns between 1927 and the 1970s demonstrates that the military structure of the field armies, the education of their elites, and their organizational behavior were professional.[4]

The Chinese communist military environment and experience do not lend themselves to a simple dichotomy of "guerrillaism" versus "professionalism" although the agenda for debate over military strategy between Mao and his generals was couched in those terms. The debate focused on the strategy and tactics of Chinese communism and the role the army should play in the Chinese revolution; it was not concerned with corporate professionalism. Here the revolutionary professional soldier must be distinguished from the historical corporate soldier. The corporate soldier is exclusively oriented toward the protection of the military establishment, whereas the revolutionary soldier tries to define through trial and error his organizational role in the revolutionary and national movement.

In the Brazilian or Egyptian military a controversy over professionalism would threaten the survival of the military establishment. The armies in these countries are so strongly corporate-oriented that for either to become guerrillaist would be to sign its own death warrant. Controversies within the Latin and Arab militaries are over the social integrity of the military establishment.

It is true of the PLA, as of every military organization, that the nature of warfare modifies the military. Thus the campaigns between 1927 and 1951 modified considerably the original orientations and the institutionalization of the military organization. But the purpose of the war was revolutionary, whatever the strategy—direct or indirect, open or deceptive. The nature and purpose of the war and the mobilization of the peasant dictated the type of military organization and the type of soldier in China.

The genius of Chinese communist insurrection lies in the fulfillment of two conditions for military success: effective military strategy and effective military leadership. An insurrection, however, does not operate in a vacuum, and not all insurrections have been successful. The explanation for the success of Chinese communism lies beyond its complex military infrastructure, brilliant command, and successful deceptive strategy. Four decades of insurgency, revolutionary warfare, and protracted political and military campaigns produced a special relationship between the CCP and the PLA.[5]

> For practical reasons the military has always played a far more important role in the history of the Chinese Communist movement than was true in the Communist states of Europe. The Communist Party of China came to power through more than 20 years of almost constant warfare. There is no national leadership in the world whose senior members have had as much military service, or certainly as much combat experience, as the present rulers of Communist China. Almost all of the aging Chinese leaders once served as senior commanders or combat-experienced commissars of the Red Army. Mao Tse-tung aptly described the military heritage of his Party when he stated in 1938 that "In China the main form of struggle is war and the main form of organization is the army." He also expressed the importance to the Party of the armed forces when he proclaimed that "Political power grows out of the barrel of a gun."[6]

Once Mao had established the People's Republic of China in 1949, the PLA, the armed instrument not only of the CCP but also of the regime, was faced with the problem of professionalism.

> When the Chinese Communists established their regime in 1949, they were confronted with the urgent and monumental task of converting the sprawling semi-guerrilla force that had brought them to power into a modern army capable of maintaining that power in the contemporary era. While highly skilled in the conduct of irregular warfare and thoroughly pervaded with the Communist party's ideology and organizational techniques, this gigantic army of some five million men, from a strictly military

viewpoint, was an anachronism: it lacked naval or air arms; its soldiers were irregulars; its command structure was decentralized and rudimentary; its equipment was heterogeneous and largely obsolete.[7]

In the West the military professional was a "new social type." During the Bolshevik revolution, the military had not become an ideological partner of the party. The initial harmony between army and party was short-lived, and it was not restored until after the Cuban Missile Crisis of 1962. The party of Stalin harassed, purged, and oppressed the officer class and the military establishment. Only with the death of Stalin, the ouster of Khrushchev, the Cuban fiasco, the modernization of the military, and the pursuit of militaristic policies did the army gradually achieve recognition and form a senior partenership with the top party elite.[8]

In contrast, the successful Chinese and Israeli revolutionary armies did not become forlorn orphans. But the symbiosis of ideology and organization, of commitment and modernization, of human and scientific organization could not be achieved without a struggle. In the case of China and Israel, and possibly North Vietnam, the emergence of expertise and scientific military management did not precipitate corporate professionalism; the military establishment did not need to seek the protection of corporatism against the anarchy of a nonskilled, highly mobilized citizenry. Expertise and professionalism can thrive under a social umbrella different from that of the corporate status system. The absence of corporate aspirations as a social shield for experts may even maximize professional aspirations and performance.

The New Skill of the Revolutionary Soldier: Stratagem, Deception, and Strategy

What is "revolutionary" about stratagem and deception if these ideas were practiced by the Greeks, the Romans (Frontinus), the Chinese (Sun Tzu), and the ancient Hebrews (Judas Maccabeus)? Surprise and deception in war constitute a well-established subdiscipline of strategy.[9]

The Chinese and Israelis, however, have developed stratagem and deception as two of the most significant skills of their modern military establishments. Stratagem and deception are part of the unwritten manual of the revolutionary soldier in both China and Israel, and the teaching of these skills as part of military education has helped to produce revolutionary soldiers. Their inclusion in the modern curriculum is certainly revolutionary, for since Napoleon, deception and stratagem have not been considered professional or scientific. With the rationalization of military science and organization and the rise of the modern Kriegsakademie, the ancient craft of deception was neglected, for good rationalist reasons. Thus the skill of deception used by the Chinese professional not only represents the restoration of an old art to its ancient dignity but also its legitimation as a respectable skill of the modern revolutionary soldier. Furthermore, the successes of the Chinese and Israeli armies have demonstrated its effectiveness. In terms of game theory, deception, "by shaping utility orderings, contributes to definition of the particular region of strategy-space from which a given player may reasonably select his response to a given strategic option."[10]

Despite the Maoist vision of the military and society, professionalism eventually did prevail over guerrillaism. The use of historical Chinese strategy was not unknown to either Mao or his generals. The division arose when Mao became obsessed with the invincibility of historical Chinese military skills. His efforts to manipulate and orient the PLA toward a unilateral strategic concept and military ethic displeased his generals, who contended that guerrillaism was only one of many military tactics. Certainly the strategy of regional defense was dictated by China's geographical circumstances.[11] Localism, provincialism, and warlordism, and the military skills and tactics they inspired, were determined by size and space as much as by face and double face.

The Maoist vision, which aspired to reverse the course of history, did not overwhelm the professionals, but it played a significant role in the "orchestration of specific techniques whereby peasant energy might be mobilized." Eventually a degree of equilibrium was reached, as well as a working division of labor between commanders and commissars. The commissars were responsible for crucial service support (supply, intelligence, civil-military liaison), which reflected the commissar's greater familiarity with the peasant base from which such services could be drawn. The fact that even professional commanders perceive strategy through lenses colored by their consciousness and expectations of peasant mood and capabilities was demonstrated in the Cultural Revolution between 1965 and 1969. Regional defense, mobilization of peasants, peasant warfare, and skills of "face" (deception) made the PLA fighter a new type of modern professional soldier. Stratagem, "the tradition of victory through non-violence," represented the difference between Chinese and Soviet strategic thinking and practices in all areas of military science and strategy.[12] A soldiery that knew nothing of professionalism functioned as well as, and may have surpassed, the rational nineteenth-century Kriegsakademie style.

GENERATIONAL CONTINUITY: PROFESSIONALISM VERSUS REVOLUTION

"The professionally oriented officers have developed views and values which in some basic respects differ drastically from those of the politically oriented party leaders and the officers who support the leadership's point of view. This divergence of views has brought part of the army into conflict with the party on a number of issues."[13]

Under Mao, generational continuity has become the theme of the Chinese political and military systems. Mao's China, a developmental political system, presents a generational syndrome different from that found in Arab and sub-Saharan African countries. The camaraderie of generational groups has been buttressed by intellectual, institutional, and ideological continuity. The evolution of the PLA from 1927 to the early 1970s demonstrates that such processes as specialization and professionalization have not affected its essential character. The powerful party organ that dominates military policy and strategy, the Military Affairs Committee (MAC), has been controlled by veterans of the CCP and the Long March.[14] Through an analysis of generational development some of the critical issues of professionalism versus revolution can be clarified.

The leaders of the Chinese Communist party in April 1927 were young: their average age was thirty-one, and more than half were between twenty-six and thirty. Hunanese and Kwantungese were predominant. Most of them were educated (a dozen were professors), but only eight out of twenty-seven had had formal military training. By the spring of 1928, twenty out of eighty-three had received formal military training, fifteen of them at the Whampoa Military Academy. Therefore, although they were experienced trade unionists and party propagandists, they had little actual military expertise. As a result of guerrilla warfare between 1927 and 1936, this inexperienced group of senior party leaders had produced four very talented officers: Chu Teh, Liu Po-ch'eng, Yeh Ting-yeh, and Chien Ming. The decade ending in 1938 transformed genteel professors, intellectuals, and students into tough organizers and warriors.[15] At that time it seemed that once the conditions were right for a successful insurgency, Mao Tse-tung would have but to wait for the opportune time to turn China into a Maoist system. But instead the professionals won.

In explaining the nature and evolution of the PLA and the success of Mao's antagonists, it is useful to refer to William Whitson's three types of Chinese military organizations: the warlord (traditional professional); the Soviet (modern professional); and the modified peasant (guerrilla).[16]

The Warlord Model

In Chinese history the term "warlord" has been used to describe a man "who was lord of a particular area by virtue of his capacity to wage war." Between 1916 and 1928 virtually all of China was divided among such military regionalists—the culmination of a process that had begun after the Taiping rebellion of the mid-nineteenth century. It was in the 1916–28 era of "pure warlordism" that Chinese Communist warlordism began.[17] But the early warlords were not necessarily warriors; they were civilian bureaucrats and shrewd political men. Not until the latter part of the nineteenth century were the warlords identified with prominent regional military commanders. Thereafter warlords, like the powerful Yuan Shih-kai, were military professionals, and, at the turn of the century, Chinese nationalists. After the 1911 revolution, Yuan Shih-kai's Peiyang army was "the most formidable military organization in China." The hallmark of military warlordism was its personal authority structure. Soldiers were identified by their warlords (and sometimes by their unit commander) rather than their place of origin.[18] Outstanding warlords were former professional soldiers of Manchu armies, and several had been trained in military academies in Japan, Russia, and Germany. The warlord was distinguished from the classical professional soldier by his organizational orientation, clientship, and purpose. He was a power-hungry and mercenary bandit whose power was derived from his own wealth. The classic professionals, in contrast, drew power from the legitimacy of the state. As technicians of violence, however, several warlord armies were model professional groups, well trained, educated in military science, and rationally organized.

In contrast to the classical professional, whose purpose was political unification and the formation of the modern nation-state, warlords opposed national unity and imperial rule. Their devotion to tradition and their economic exploitation of China were major barriers to national unity, although some prominent warlords were fervent Chinese nationalists. Ching Pai-li, the Chinese "Clausewitz" and commandant of Paoting Academy in 1922, played a key role in training the next generation of Chinese military professionals, who soon influenced the Kuomintang (KMT—led by Chiang Kai-shek), the Communists (Chu Teh, P'eng Te-huai), and the warlords. Though they had been taught about the virtues of national unity, they opted nevertheless for personal political power. The legacy of warlordism was that the soldiers' loyalty stopped at the next highest authority, and emphasis on the small unit thus became the basis for Mao's guerrilla doctrines. Mao made use of the economic stability of the small unit as a basis for the party-army organization.[19] After 1924 the KMT and the warlords found a way to coexist, with each having a "sphere of influence." This veritable balance of power was later to be used by the CCP in negotiating with and fighting against the KMT and the warlords. Neither the warlords' concept of warfare nor their preferred type of battle was oriented toward central authority. In the beginning most fighting took place in the countryside, for the soldiers of the warlord army were peasants whose culture and aspirations were deeply rooted in rural China. But warlords soon seized urban centers to establish their economic supremacy through taxation. Peking itself became the prize of a warlord. In the 1920s the conflict increasingly shifted to urban capitals.

In the PLA, the professionals were greatly influenced by the warlord model. In fact, the most prominent generals had this orientation: Chu Teh, the most senior Chinese military commander and chief of staff until 1956; Ho Lung, senior officer, First Field Army; and Lin Piao, Mao's heir apparent until 1971 and Chinese minister of defense. Mao Tse-tung was a blend of warlord and peasant types. In short, the senior officers of the first three field armies between 1927 and 1937 were warlord-oriented professionals.[20]

The Soviet Model

The first modern professional soldiers in Communist China were either graduates of the Frunze Soviet military academy or men trained by Soviet instructors in the Whampoa Chinese military academy. Whampoa and Soviet professionalism blended to produce the toughest and most brilliant Chinese Communist officers. The USSR was in a state of flux from 1918 to 1927, so the Chinese graduates were guided by the Frunze-Tukhachevsky-Blycher-Trotsky doctrine and political persuasion. General Blycher was sent to Canton in 1923 as head of a Soviet military mission to introduce the Frunze professional orientation to the first Chinese "Soviet" officers. These men were not only the first and second military generations of the PLA but also China's most distinguished soldiers: P'eng Te-huai (Commander of the First Field Army), Hsu Hsiang-chien (senior officer of the First Field Army), Lin Piao (senior officer of the Third and Fourth Armies), Liu Po-ch'eng (commander of the Second Field Army and hero of the Chingkang-shansi campaign of 1928), Nieh Jung-chen (commander of North China PLA Fifth Field Army), Teng Hsiao-p'ing (deputy commander of the Second Field Army), and Yeh Chien-ying (chief of staff, Fourth Corps).[21] The list of military professionals among China's senior and veteran officers who were not necessarily of the warlord or Soviet type but professionals nonetheless is also impressive: Chen Yi (senior officer of the Fourth Field Army), Su Yu (senior officer of the Third Field Army), and Chou En-lai.

The Soviet type of military leader had one important mission—to instill in military cadres a revolutionary and nationalist fervor. Unlike the warlord type, the Soviet-trained leaders had a nationalist orientation. They differed from corporate professionals in believing that the military should be a "party-army"—an instrument for effecting major social and political changes in the fabric of Chinese society.[22] Model professional revolutionary soldiers, they expected authority and command to be subordinate to the party. Political authority, guidance, propaganda, and indoctrination were primary functions of the party, but the revolutionary soldier could also be "the party" in its absence. This orientation formed the basis of a later struggle between Mao and his generals. By instilling the primacy of technocratic organization and order, the Soviet instructors planted the first seeds of modern professionalism. Their most significant contribution to the PLA, however, lay in the area of conventional strategy and tactics, which replaced warlord techniques and stressed communications, mobility, and urban targets.

The Maoist Model

Mao's strategy rested on mobilization of the peasantry through social and economic reforms. Mobilizing the peasantry became a strategic goal and the mark of the professional revolutionary soldier. Mao, more than his generals, captured the imagination of the peasants and under the guise of nationalist mobilization recruited them into the CCP and the PLA and thus ultimately integrated them into the Communist movement. After 1927 Mao became more aware of the realities of Chinese society, and he came to realize that although China *was* a peasant society the peasantry was not equivalent to "rural idiocy" nor was it a monolithic dormant class. Despite these realizations, Mao's attempt to revive historical Chinese peasant warfare, though pragmatically oriented, became counterproductive. The Maoist model was built upon the use of strategem, deception, and bluff by a small roving rebel unit, but this strategy served the PLA only occasionally—from 1927 to 1931 and again from 1937 to 1938. On the whole, Chinese Communist military warfare and strategy between 1927 and 1971 was predicated on the existence of a professional, large-scale peasant army.[23]

The military controversy was not limited to type of warfare; it also involved questions about the proper way to shape the character of the Chinese soldier. Mao was more a molder of men than of military strategists. Though he had a considerable reputation as a military thinker he was no Napoleon, Clausewitz, or Jomini. Mao was a prophet and a philosopher-king who molded the Chinese people according to his world view. As a revolutionary, Mao invested considerable energy in what Benjamin Schwartz calls "the spiritual transformation of the entire Chinese people," including "thought reform," "education through labor," and "peace from the PLA."[24] Spiritual transformation has been linked to "populism" and to "guerrillaism" in the army. Consequently, the Maoist model has played a more important role in Chinese communism as a symbol or ideal type than as an actual military strategy or tactical doctrine.

All three models—warlord, Soviet (professional), and Maoist (peasant)—have been modified through long military struggles. The first military generation, from 1923 to 1937, learned, absorbed, and practiced a combination of all three roles, but the professional model and the professional officer prevailed. Mao's strategy was anachronistic if not archaic; the senior officers, veterans, and juniors subscribed to the modern rational organizational type of warfare. The doctrinal battle over military strategy has been won by the generals, but that between Maoism and its opposition on the future of Chinese communism, China, the CCP, and PLA was not settled by the middle 1970s. Division in

China was not over an "army-party" model (warlord, professional, or Maoist) and not over whether the PLA should become "Maoist" or "professional," but primarily concerned the future of Communist China itself. The PLA, like the CCP, was both Maoist and professional, but the paradigm of the revolutionary soldier that Mao was struggling to create had not yet been worked out.

The evolution of Chinese communism and Maoism has made a deep impact upon the personal orientations, ideological framework, and institutional arrangements of China. The CCP and PLA both have been harnessed to the Chinese Communist ideological chariot. Unquestionably the supreme source of authority, doctrine, and strategy has been the party. The MAC, despite the convulsions it has undergone from 1927 to the Cultural Revolution of 1965–69, has been the supreme military authority, composed as it is of the most senior and influential PLA leaders to whom the lower echelons turn for resolution of key doctrinal, strategic, and ideological issues. The MAC has also represented the Chinese Communist political and military experiences in the sense that it was the high command of the revolution, bringing together senior, veteran, and promising civil and military elites. Formally, the MAC has been a committee of the CCP, not the PLA, even though it has been the informal executive of the dictatorship of mobilization. Because party and army efforts converged, no clear-cut dichotomy of party-army or civil-military functions was meaningful in the Chinese Communist context. The CCP cast its net wide. As early as 1931, it brought under control the MAC (or its predecessor political department of the PLA) and the autonomous four field armies. The PLA never challenged party control although it did dispute Maoist domination. The ensuing debate on professionalism versus guerrillaism centered on the MAC, the link between party and army.

In addition to classifying the three types of Chinese military organizations, William Whitson has devised a generational framework for the Chinese Communist military.[25] Using the term "generation" to mean a classification based on age, he examines the behavior of eleven age groups between 1927 and 1970, noting generational differences in orientation, experience, training, mobility, and, above all, influence over military policy and politics. His analysis converges with my own political generation classification only in terms of their orientations; otherwise, China differs fundamentally from the Afro-Arab praetorian states. Whitson's information on the eleven generations of Chinese

Communist military is used here not so much for what it has to say about age and time as for the light it throws on political orientations and the party-army rivalries over the strategy of the Chinese revolution.

1. *The First Military Generation (Whitson's first three generations, 1923–37)*. This is the first generation to move away from warlord banditry and personal orientation and toward professionalism. The debate over the role of the military in Chinese communism had begun and the pros and cons of guerrillaism versus professionalism were hotly argued. The protagonist of guerrillaism, Mao, was removed from the MAC, and the professionals gained ascendancy.[26] The boundaries between the PLA and CCP were drawn on the basis of a complementary relationship. The PLA and the CCP were assigned different roles. The latter was to effect political and social mobilization within the PLA, whose task was to professionalize the peasantry. Professionalization of the four field armies was accomplished through an extensive peasant reform. All of this was achieved in military campaigns from 1927 to 1934 although coordination of ideology, propaganda, and fighting—the three functions of Chinese communism—was poor.

2. *The Second Military Generation (Whitson's fourth through seventh generations, 1937–49)*. This period saw the rise of the most influential Chinese military leaders. As party and army learned to accommodate each other and honor each other's boundaries, both emerged as stable and highly efficient. Military professionalism was subordinated to the party and guerrilla fighting was abandoned. The civil wars of 1927–49 clearly demonstrated the supremacy of strategic warfare and the effectiveness of large-scale campaigns. As the military expanded the North China Group, which had been recruited after the Long March (1937–49), it emerged as the most educated and professional military elite. Local party organization and a special relationship with the PLA also took shape, as did the office of commissar as a provincial political leader under the supervision of a General Political Department created in the PLA to limit the political jurisdiction of the commander.

3. *The Third Military Generation (Whitson's eighth through eleventh generations, 1950–70)*. By 1976 this generation had not become very influential. The first generation still ran the PLA (96 percent of the high command came from the 1923–37 group), and was dedicated to professionalism, modernization, military expansion, and its own version of corporatism. The first generation was still bent on imperialism, and the impact of P'eng Te-huai continued to be felt. The cumulative

impact of the Sino-Soviet conflict, Korea, and Vietnam had brought about the greatest disruption in the military establishment since 1931— the Great People's Cultural Revolution. According to Whitson, a factional struggle for power was taking place between the CCP and PLA, that is, between the commanders and party apparatchiks on one hand and the Maoists (Red Guards) and commissars on the other.[27] The challenge came from the Red Guards and Mao and from his allies among the PLA commissars and was directed against the CCP elite, middle apparatchiks and military commanders. The senior PLA commanders suffered less than senior CCP leaders, but the PLA toll was significant nevertheless. The PLA was also radicalized, though proportionately less than the Red Guards.

The fall of the two senior officers, Yang Chen-wu, the acting chief of staff, and Lu Jui-ch'ien, demonstrated that a great struggle had been waged not only between the CCP and the PLA but also within them. It seemed to be a struggle between Chinese Communist ruling classes— the CCP-PLA establishment (MAC, the party chiefs, and the first-generation generals) and strategic elites (commanders, commissars, and party apparatchiks). Actually, the struggle can be more accurately depicted as one in which a coalition of about one thousand senior CCP members and an equal number of senior PLA officers were pitted against Mao, the radical Maoists in the PLA led by Lin Piao, and Chou En-lai. The alliance of commanders, commissars, and apparatchiks soon split. Some supported Mao but most continued to support the senior CCP-PLA group. Eventually the military was deradicalized and brought an end to the Red Guard. Meanwhile most of the commissars served as Mao's basic Red Guard, though several joined the commanders and senior CCP-PLA officers in resisting the Maoist onslaught of antiparty radicalism. Again the struggle was over the future of Chinese communism, though in this case it was complicated by institutional, functional, and personal rivalries.

By 1971 no specific, institutionalized third-generation military group had been identified. Whitson offers some tentative conclusions that suggest that the professionals of the third generation (1950–70) were on the rise, that the five field armies were "military-political" networks run by the politicians, and that the professionals prevailed over the Maoists in the greatest crises.[28]

In 1965 Mao Tse-tung, Chen Yi, Teng Hsiao-p'ing, and Li Hsien were still prominent members of the MAC. Although it was dissolved for two years after the end of the Korean War (1952–1954) in order to improve the professionalization of the armed forces, the MAC was soon restored and has since been on the rise. The Cultural Revolution only enhanced its powers. The second echelon of military leadership—the general staff and regional and service army commands—was marked by continuity of office and group cohesiveness. Continuity was particularly impressive in the case of the regional command. In the third echelon of military leadership, which was made up of the commanding officers of provincial military districts, urban garrisons, and divisional branches, the principle of continuity of office also prevailed.[29] On this level the military, like the party (at least until the Cultural Revolution), represented a generational group even though that group was not cohesive. Professionalization, modernization, and functionalism were finally accepted by the Long March veterans and the historical leadership of the CCP. The PLA still seems to be the quintessence of Chinese communism, even if the army, however reluctant to get involved, is now divided. China is led not by just the party, the military, or the commissars, but by all three.

> In our army both military commanders and political commissars are leaders; they are jointly responsible for leadership in the army. However, there is a division of labor between them: military commanders are responsible for the implementation of orders and directives issued by higher authorities and decisions made by the Party committee of the same level so far as they concern military affairs, while political commissars are responsible for the implementation of those concerning political work.[30]

China is no monolith, nor is the USSR, and neither was Nazi Germany. The PLA wielded and continues to wield considerable influence. Most important, continuity of leadership and policy and factionalism are not contradictory facts of politics. In fact, China in its post-Cultural Revolution era is experiencing political struggle between, and within, its bureaucracies, and the PLA is not exempt.[31] Parish argues that the Cultural Revolution broke vertical lines of authority, and when it did impersonal bureaucratic relations were replaced by horizontal personal relationships. Thus, the political conflict between commissars and commanders over the issue of professionalism was on a personal rather than on an institutional level.[32]

Nevertheless, bureaucratic politics, whether they be personal or institutional, demonstrate the polycentrism of Chinese military elites. Meanwhile, continuity on generational, functional, structural, and personal bases explains the dynamics of the PLA, whose elite is divided but more powerful than before the Cultural Revolution.

Is corporate professionalism emerging in the PLA? Superficially it could be argued that the PLA, dominated by veteran professionals, has moved to the right, away from revolutionary action. After so many years of purges and rectification campaigns, the cohesiveness of the senior first-generation PLA is bound to have eroded, and the "balance of power" Whitson speaks of has been achieved between CCP-PLA and the Maoists. But is the warlord nature of the five field army fiefdoms, with its professionalism and accommodation with the CCP, a prelude to the adoption of the principle of exclusivity? Does the first-generation military elite fear erosion because of its age and generational rivalries? Does the Maoist onslaught mean the army must seek protection? It certainly does. But from which institution does the military seek protection? Certainly not from the state machinery or the Maoists and not from itself. So far the CCP has served as the guardian of the guardians, and, during the Maoist attack, the commanders sought an alliance with the CCP and its cadres. The institutional survival of the PLA is not analogous to the case of the military establishments in Brazil or Egypt where praetorian dictatorships have been constructed to protect military corporatism. In China the PLA is as much an embodiment of the Chinese Revolution as the CCP and the Maoists. It needs no corporate shield against a "revolutionary" China. Like all large-scale complex organizations it only seeks organizational autonomy. At the end of the Cultural Revolution in 1971 a CCP-PLA coalition began to emerge on national and regional levels. The PLA was strong, modernizing, and organizationally confident. Authority remained strong even though a political crisis continued. Whitson's conclusion is that party-military personal relations coalesced into five major subelites (the field army groups) whose informal bonds have remained a significant factor, first, in deciding key party and military personnel assignments and, second, in reaching compromises on national and regional policy implementation.[33]

One of the most remarkable institutional aspects of the PLA is that behaviorally it approximates the pure model of a Marxist-Leninist military instrument. The Comintern's manual for armed insurrection deals extensively with the direction of party work in the military. Most if not all of the party rules, constitutional and structural arrangements, and recommendations have been adopted, institutionalized, and sustained by the Chinese. The strict and clear relationship between party and army and the supremacy of the former in China is a textbook example of a Leninist civil-military formula, however modified by the Chinese Communist experiences. Among Communist states, only the PLA, the North Vietnamese, and the Vietcong have allowed so much party interference with the army. (This is not to be confused with Stalin's purge of Red Army personnel, which did not involve *institutional* intervention.) In Communist China the doctrine that "the overall direction of [the] Party's military work throughout the country . . . is the responsibility of the Central Committee"[34] is strictly applied in the PLA. The structure of civil-military domination (MAC) and local military (PLA) subordination still exists in the China of the middle 1970s. The subordination of the PLA to party goals was strictly adhered to by both Mao and his generals, despite their bitter rivalry.

These statements again do not imply that any element—the party, the Maoists, or the military—is monolithic. Ellis Joffe clearly demonstrates that the PLA's intervention in the politics of the Cultural Revolution was *foisted* on it; that this intervention created deep divisions within the PLA that culminated in the Lin Piao affair and the purge in the high command; that political intervention nevertheless consolidated the power of the military with the result that the PLA became the key political power group in the precarious Maoist coalition after 1971.[35]

The PLA got involved as soon as the Cultural Revolution erupted. Its involvement, however, no longer pertained to the revolutionary task of role expansion and nation building, that is, the wide range of nonmilitary activities discussed earlier. The basis for the PLA's involvement was purely political, even though it had no intention of effecting a takeover. The PLA acted as a political broker and a participant in intraparty conflict. "In contrast to the usual pattern of military takeovers, the PLA did not intervene in politics against the wish of the political leadership, but rather was brought into the political arena by this leadership . . . the PLA, moreover, first moved into politics, not in order to pressure, displace, or supplant the political leadership, as represented by the Maoist group, but rather to aid it in an intra-Party conflict."[36] In this sense, the PLA had challenged professionalism "and *had resorted to its revolutionary qualities.*"[37] Joffe writes "There is no doubt that the revolutionary vigor of the PLA in the early 1960's contrasted sharply with increasing bureaucratism and unresponsiveness of the Party apparatus."[38] The military, however, had self-imposed limits to its intraparty interventionism. Even if it were entering into the struggle the military leadership did not lose sight of its role as a national organization[39] nor discard its integrity. It did not intervene "as a radical revolutionary force, but rather as a moderating and stabilizing element."[40] As Joffe states:

> In sum, although the exact balance of forces at the close of the Cultural Revolution was uncertain, one thing was not in doubt: the PLA had become the dominant political and administrative authority in the provinces and a powerful force in national policy-making councils. To the army at least, the Cultural Revolution had indeed brought revolutionary change.[41]

In the Soviet Union the military was depoliticized, professionalized, and separated from party control. The party's military commission lost its raison d'être and importance. In China the preservation of the MAC as the most powerful military organ, although it is strictly an arm of the party, demonstrates the revolutionary nature and role of the PLA. Even the decline or dissolution of the MAC may not necessarily be interpreted as a PLA takeover. Not until a different type of civil-military and party-army relationship has appeared should it be claimed that Soviet-style professionalism, or for that matter the classical West European model, has taken over in China. Thus far the professional PLA adheres to Comintern rules on armed insurrection established in the late 1920s. As an army designed for political mobilization, the PLA has preserved its role as an educator and propagandist, and it is in this area that it differs from the Soviet Red Army. In the USSR the army has never been authorized to act on behalf of the revolution. That has been strictly the party's function. In China the PLA has been an inseparable, even at times primary, representative of the revolution. It certainly has been the most important instrument for political mobilization.

In the middle 1970s the PLA was as resilient as ever despite five decades of protracted warfare and internecine struggle between the Maoists and the professionals and the intra-PLA conflict during the Lin Piao affair. In their defense, the professionals did not take sides in the inner party struggle. Confident of its special role in the rise of a modern Chinese Communist state, the military establishment needed no superior patron. Chinese Communist legitimacy rested within the PLA as it did within the CCP, even if Mao Tse-tung never accepted any other repository for Chinese communism but Maoism.

The effects of intervention have moved the PLA into a pivotal role in the making of Chinese national security policy[42] and thus eventually given it a place in making foreign policy. One result of party reconstruction after 1971 was the PLA's "tightening its grip on the levers of power." The consolidation of power was paralleled by the erosion of the army's internal unity and cohesion.[43] The Lin Piao affair is a good example of the rise of the military to a key role in the structures of the party and the state and the parallel weakening of its ranks, not an unusual outcome of intervention. It differs, however, from the Brazilian or Syrian case, where military fratricide and internal conflict resulted in more pronounced praetorianism—the ruler-type. In China the CCP-PLA symbiosis has remained intact since the 1930s. The internal division within the party increases the unity of the military and its elites.

Both the reconstructed party and the PLA are integral factors in the fulfillment of the Chinese revolution, even if the imperative of long party rule interfered with the PLA's revolutionary momentum and professionalism cut deep into its revolutionary élan. The PLA's anti-radical role did not make it any less a revolutionary force. In fact, acting as the balancer between contending party factions increased its grip over the revolutionary role of CCP-PLA twins. The result was that the PLA has enhanced its role in the determination of national security policy.[44] In the new (post–1971) coalition politics of the Chinese ruling structures, "the army thus remains a central and highly influential element in the coalition that stands on top of China's power structure."[45]

There is little doubt that, once the mist of the Cultural Revolution has lifted and after the death of Mao, the Chinese military will further institutionalize, whatever the nature of the coalition, and act as an arbiter between the warring factions. The professionalism that had emanated from the PLA and Long March veteran cohorts (Whitson's third, my first, generation) will only be enhanced, and it will act as a moderating force on the party's radicals. Mao may have believed the wheel of history has ceased to spin, but the world still aspires to modernity and it can only be achieved with expertise. For China to become a great power once again without a professional army would be unthinkable. China's return to the family of nations would be coupled with aspirations for modernity and military professionalism in competition with the USSR and Japan over Asia. Like the military in the USSR, in a nuclear age the PLA will assert its place in the CCP pyramid. No CCP coalition is feasible without its support.

In the middle 1970s there was little chance for praetorianism in China. In fact, the army was propelled into intraparty conflicts. Its ruling elite is civilian-oriented in the sense that it is not praetorian and it is revolutionary in the sense that its major concern is not corporate integrity. The Chinese military accepts the political supremacy of a civilian and ideological group. It has directed its revolutionary orientation toward modernizing and mobilizing China and toward reasserting China's position as an international actor. However subjective, authoritarian, and controlled, if China were to embark on an imperialistic course after Mao's death like that of the USSR after Stalin's death the military group would certainly gain ascendancy within the party. The system of authority and political procedures for the transfer of power would not be monopolized by the military, of course, nor would the military become a praetorian ruling class as in Egypt, Syria, Brazil, or South Vietnam before 1975. However, if China embarked on an imperialist course the military would play a decisive role in its security and foreign affairs policies.

9

Israel: The Routinized Revolutionary Army

There is only one Israel, a transplanted twentieth-century fragment of Europe. It is one of the most cohesive social systems in modern times and one of the most centralized political systems, analogous to the ancient Greek *polis*. (Israel may be the only modern version of that historic type.) Israel is culturally pluralistic, and it has an orientation toward political institutionalization.[1]

Modern Israel is the only polity in which a colonizing nation-state has combined with a national liberation movement. Ideology played a crucial role in its founding. Unlike other modern national liberation movements, however, the Socialist-Zionist parties opted for voluntary recruitment and mobilization. What binds Israel to the NLM type is the functional similarity between types of warfare and civil-military relations. Marxist NLMs and Israeli political movements both struggle against a brutal enemy: the Marxist NLMs, against colonial forces and internal enemies; Israel, against implacable foes dedicated to its political and even physical annihilation. The expectation of total war and mobilization for it make Israel the link between colonizing and NLM nation-states.

ISRAEL AS A NATION-IN-ARMS

Israel is the twentieth-century model for a nation-in-arms. In this garrison state the military service has become an aspect of virtu or public service, a prerequisite for citizenship. The draft is universal, short of women who object for religious reasons and Arab citizens. Recruitment is egalitarian, and promotion depends on merit.

Among nations-in-arms, Israel is the only representative democratic example. Unlike despotic China, where the nation-in-arms is the very principle behind political organization, Israel exists as a nation-in-arms to maintain the nation's democratic voluntaristic political system. Israel also stands in sharp contrast to late nineteenth-century Germany,

251

where the nation-in-arms was nothing but a policy for the militarization of the middle classes, and revolutionary France, where the nation-
in-arms was a stage along the road to totalitarian democracy.[2]

In the early twentieth century, General von der Goltz equated the
nation-in-arms with militarism and imperialism. The concept was
developed in order to enhance the military mobilization of Germany
and prepare the nation militarily for Weltpolitik activities. General
Friedrich von Bernhardi wrote: "We realize that Prussia's historic
mission is not yet completed, for that mission is to form the core around
which all the *dispersed* elements of the German race will group themselves." Bernhardi's goal was to "guarantee to Germanism the place it
deserves in the world." Goltz "was more concerned than Bernhardi
with purely military terms."[3] For Goltz the nation-in-arms meant the
creation of national unity in war; the Israeli nation-in-arms was developed to meet an external threat. It was necessary for survival, not
chosen to maintain an empire.

There is more resemblance between the Israeli and French concepts
than between the Israeli and the German, but they differ as well. In
France military service was universal and compulsory. The nation-in-
arms was an ideological concept that stemmed from the Jacobin radical tradition of the French Revolution. But in Israel the citizen is not a
professional revolutionary; he is part of a nation struggling for physical
survival. Except for two or three months each year, Israelis are in the
military reserve until they are forty-nine. Thus the military is not a
career, but a system of permanent reserve. The Israeli citizen-conscript
is the backbone of the military, carrying the burden of the nation-in-
arms only when he is in uniform. In France, in contrast, the citizens
were mobilized into revolutionary cadres. The dedication of Israel's
citizen-soldier is demonstrated by the high level of volunteering for
dangerous and difficult military assignments. The paratroops, the air
force and naval commandos, and the Nahal (Fighting Pioneer Youth)
are purely voluntary services. There were no such voluntary services in
the German or the French nation-in-arms. The Israeli nation-in-arms is
a pragmatic instrumental solution to the security problems of Israel,
not a tool for revolutionary or imperialistic purposes. Rapoport observes that "the nation-in-arms does not always need to seek war as the
indispensable stimulant to the vitality of the body politic." In Israel it
is a repository of morale, dedication, and high professionalism.

The Israeli concept of the nation-in-arms was a product of pioneer

Zionism and Arab hostility. By 1936 the Jewish *Yishuv* (community) in Palestine had no choice but to organize its first permanent general staff and a small professional group of staff officers.[4] The organization, structure, and ideology of Haganah, Israel's military and underground movement, were established by pioneer Socialist-Zionists. The Haganah and the Palmach (its commando force) were voluntary organizations except for a few officers who joined the general staff. The system as a whole remained a voluntary military nucleus until 1948.

THE MILITARY AS AN INSTRUMENT OF NATION BUILDING

Israeli society and its political and military structures can be explained only in terms of a constellation of factors. No single factor could possibly explain the creation of a new social system in Israel or the development of its political structures and its army.[5]

The modern army of Israel sprang from the security structures of the pre-independence pioneer movement of the Jews in Palestine. These defense units were created by Socialist-Zionists, the most significant, powerful, and cohesive elements of Jewish colonization. Socialist-Zionism—the House of Labor (HOL)—was embraced by a wide range individuals and organizations in both the Diaspora and Palestine, but only in Palestine was it forged into a movement of great consequence.[6] There it came to represent the interplay between socialist ideological commitments and modifying pragmatic considerations. The result was the gradual transformation of a colonization effort into a program for national liberation. The Socialist-Zionist movement built the nation, mobilized the pioneer revolution, and created a new society. It also founded the Israeli army.

Pioneer Zionists had a genius for organization that enabled them to develop very elaborate institutional frameworks prior to nationhood. To create a new society, the HOL groups consolidated an immigrant-settler movement with a movement for national liberation, based on a socialist and egalitarian ideology. To carry out this task they established three separate but complementary mobilization systems. Beginning in 1920 the workers first organized into an elaborate institutional structure, the Histadrut. The second was the kibbutz movement, which provided support for agricultural settlements. The third structure was made up of the political parties of the HOL led by Mapai, which was created to represent Socialist-Zionist interests and institutions within the Yishuv (the Jewish community in Palestine) and in dealings with the British

Mandate Administration. These three systems were to become the most powerful organizations in Israel. The HOL infused Socialist-Zionist ideology into its political parties, its trade union, and its kibbutz movement, and thus the ideology spread throughout the Yishuv. Thus the HOL created the first comprehensive social, political, and economic structure of the Jewish community in Palestine, independent of both the Mandate and the Palestinian Arab community.[7]

It was within this framework that the HOL created what eventually became the Israeli army. HOL leaders were instrumental in developing military structures, while other Zionist groups firmly implanted in the Israeli army the HOL ideology of "revolutionary constructivism"—the gradual accumulation of functions and powers for an eventually independent Jewish socialist state.[8] Socialist-Zionism left a legacy of fraternity, cohesiveness, egalitarianism, leadership training, and subservience to national and civil authorities that later passed to the Zahal (Israel Defense Force), later to become the major repository of national identity and pride.

In their drive to consolidate and institutionalize the organizational structures of the House of Labor, the HOL leaders overlooked the importance of security. Only the militants in the kibbutzim recognized the need to maintain a permanent defense organization. Eventually, however, the leadership of the Histadrut accepted the recommendation of its committee for defense and organized the Haganah, the first Jewish underground in Palestine, on June 25, 1920.

The turning point for the military organization of the Jewish community in Palestine was the Arab revolt of 1936, which gave those who advocated the establishment of a permanent defense system the evidence they needed to convince the highest Yishuv and Zionist authorities that it was important to form an independent Jewish army. For the duration of the 1936 Arab revolt, the biggest bloc within the Yishuv—the HOL, led by David Ben Gurion—pursued a policy of moderation and restraint (*havlagah*) toward both the Arabs and the Mandate authorities. Realizing the futility of the revolt, the Jews sought to turn it to their advantage. The Jewish leadership knew that adopting the Arabs' strategy against the Mandate authorities would be catastrophic. Rather than be left to fight the Arabs once the Mandate was overthrown, they cooperated with the British.[9]

This policy of restraint eventually proved correct, but it created a division within the Haganah. The first break came in the early 1930s when a militant group called Haganah B was formed. Though its leader did not want to support any political party, no one could remain neutral toward the explosive issues of the day. Haganah B's leaders were inclined toward Jabotinsky's Revisionist-Zionist party, a militant splinter of the World Zionist Organization formed in 1925. Thus, after a series of schisms and splits, Haganah B and Jabotinsky's youth movement united to form a terrorist organization called the Irgun Zvai Léumi (National Military Organization, NMO), led by David Raziel. In 1940 the poet-intellectual Avraham Stern, an independent and also the leader of Jabotinsky's youth movement, took over the split NMO. Under his leadership the organization adopted the doctrine of total military struggle with the British. Within the House of Labor, the advocates of an independent Jewish military force came from the Palestinian-born members of socialist youth movements. Here the United Kibbutz Movement (Ha-Kibbutz ha-Meuchad), which had been formed in 1927, played a key role. It protected, guided, and supported the advocates of resistance, who were to become the next generation of Haganah leaders and the elite of the IDF.[10]

The "Academies" of the Revolutionary Soldier

In 1937, under the leadership of Yitzchak (Sandoberg) Sadeh, the Haganah adopted a new doctrine.[11] Sadeh, clearly, was not neutral. "Don't wait for the Arab marauder. Don't wait to defend the kibbutz," he said. "Go after him, move on to the offensive."[12] This militant stance attracted the rebels of the Hityashvut (the agricultural settlement system) and the kibbutz.

With Sadeh's creation of the patrol (Ha-Nodedet), the first military unit composed of kibbutz youth, Haganah took the offensive and began attacks on centers of Arab terrorism. After 1937, Haganah operated as the general staff or nucleus of a large-scale army that was recruited in the kibbutzim, in the privately owned and operated settlements, and in the cities. It organized centers for officer training, improved communications within the kubbutzim system, and published professional military literature. It organized an intensive Rechesh (a clandestine supply and weaponry purchasing operation), established a small armament industry, and created the nucleus of a navy and air force. Most important, it set up the Shay, a far-flung and efficient intelligence-gathering network. It conducted periodic national fund-raising campaigns and distributed literature to its growing membership, thus combining effective communication with the organizational structures and expertise of Socialist-Zionism.

Sadeh's patrol found ever wider uses in the field. A completely new system of kibbutzim was established between 1937 and 1939 as a result of increasing demands of security. Benefiting from a great influx of youth, the kibbutzim and settlements were transformed into a large-scale defense network. Each kibbutz had its own fortress and tower guarded by patrols patterned after those founded by Sadeh. The kibbutz now became the home, protector, and guide of Haganah's second generation, and the first generation born in Jewish Palestine.

The Special Night Squads (hereafter referred to as SNS), organized and led by Captain Orde Wingate,[13] an irregular British officer, provided another reservoir of Haganah leadership. Wingate, an adventurer of the same stripe as "Chinese" Gordon and Lawrence of Arabia, viewed himself as something of a modern Gideon. Although serving the Mandate authorities, it was he who argued the case for a Jewish army and finally persuaded the moderate Zionist leadership to accept the idea. Then he met with Haganah intelligence officers and proposed the formation of night squads, whose function would be to train Palestinian youth to destroy centers of Arab terrorism and to create the nucleus of a Jewish army. His recruits, like Sadeh's, came chiefly from the agrarian collectives where he was warmly welcomed and eventually regarded as a hero. Among the many of Wingate's volunteers who later became high-ranking officers in the Israel Defense Force, two were outstanding: General Moshe Dayan, who was chief of staff between 1953 and 1957, hero of the Sinai campaign, and defense minister June 1967–March 1974; and General Yigal Allon, commander of the shock platoons and of the southern front during the Israeli War of Liberation, and foreign minister since 1974.

The Palmach: Haganah's Elite Corps

The commanders of Ha-Nodedet and the SNS and the youth in the kubbutzim and agrarian settlements opposed the Haganah's and Yishuv's posture of conciliation and cooperation with the Mandatory. They were bitter that the SNS and other small, independent Jewish military units created in the wake of the Arab revolt had been dissolved when the crisis passed. The United Kibbutz Movement (UKM) and especially Yitzchak Sadeh, commander of Ha-Nodedet and chief security officer of the SNS, resolved to press for the establishment of a permanent and independent Jewish professional elite corps around which a future army could be built. Sadeh prevailed upon and won the support of Eliahu Golomb, the commander of Haganah, and Moshe Sneh, its chief of staff, who appointed him general staff officer for Palmach at Haganah headquarters.

The Palmach was the first full-time professional military unit of Haganah. It soon became the intellectual and organizational training ground for the future elite of the Israel Defense Force. Of the twelve general staff brigadiers during the War of Liberation (there was only one major general, the commander-in-chief, General Ya'aqov Dori), three were from the Palmach—Yigal Allon, Yohanan Ratner, and Yitzchak Sadeh. Allon was the commander of the southern front, which was composed of three Palmach battalions, and one division was headed by a Palmach officer. Out of some forty-five colonels at that time, twenty were Palmach officers. Over forty percent of all major and lieutenant colonels were Palmach officers. The commander of the officers' school was from the Palmach, as was his deputy and several of the senior instructors. General Yitzchak Rabin was Palmach headquarters operations chief in the Negev campaign of 1948 and prime minister of Israel beginning in 1974.

Since 1948, four Palmach officers have become commander in chief —Moshe Dayan (1953–57), Yitzchak Rabin (1963–67), Chaim Bar-Lev (1968–71), and David Elazar (1971–74). Furthermore, at least forty brigadier generals in the Israel Defense Force were former Palmach officers. Three members of the Israeli cabinet (1967–73) were former Palmach commanders: Dayan, who was minister of defense, and Allon, who was minister of labor. Israel Galeeli, one of the Palmach's founders and a former chief of staff of Haganah, was deputy minister of defense in 1948, and after the 1965 elections he became minister of information. The 1974 cabinet included three Palmach officers in key positions: Prime Minister Yitzchak Rabin, Foreign Minister Yigal Allon, and Commerce Minister Chaim Bar-Lev.

The Palmach was the first unit of Haganah composed of Jews born in Palestine. Its members, Israel Galeeli writes, "were followers of the doctrines of Pioneer Zionism—simple, monolithic, and strong." This second generation entered Palestinian and Israeli politics from the Palmach, which had provided a military outlet for the rebels and anti-collaborationists who felt at home in the militant left wing of the HOL. The political and financial support of the Palmach came mainly from the kibbutz movement, which carried the heavy burden of maintaining the Palmach trainees in its settlements. Haganah did contribute to Palmach's maintenance. Still it was apparent that its leader Ben Gurion, the leader of the Haganah, with his growing responsibilities as the chief spokesman for a Jewish state and his opposition to factionalism, supported the Palmach only with reluctance.

The Palmach ideology, which was impressed on volunteers in its training programs and which was subsequently bequeathed to the Israel Defense Force, could be summarized as follows: (a) pride in the nation; (b) devotion to the principles of socialism and the kibbutz movement; (c) self-discipline; (d) egalitarianism; (e) leadership training; and (f) intellectual pursuits and culture. Training for leadership was emphasized above all, and since the Palmach played a key role in determining the sort of leadership training offered by Haganah and later by the Israel Defense Force, this concept of leadership requires some elaboration.

The leadership and cadre programs of the Palmach were designed to produce not only professional but also institutional leaders, men who were trained disseminators of Socialist-Zionist ideology. It aimed to produce officers of the highest caliber.

In some ways (especially in its emphasis on cadre-building), the Palmach's leadership training principles suggested Lenin's ideas on revolutionary leadership. The Palmach's principles of leadership placed great emphasis on the role of the lowest ranking officer, the *mem-mem* (platoon leader). The mem-mem was earmarked to receive the most intensive training because he was the only commander who "has direct relations with his soldiers, and this direct contact is of utmost importance in the process of the creation of the *lohem* (the fighter)."

Leadership programs also de-emphasized punishment as a means of disciplining the cadres. The mem-mem was to be exemplary, always able to withstand the harshest conditions and to serve as an inspiration to his men. Yet discipline could not be surrendered to voluntarism; the two qualities were to be integrated in the mem-mem. "Our war machine," writes a Palmach commander, "must combine freedom and responsibility, discipline and laxity. The leader must be the link between the two. His functions must go beyond mastering technical skills, though he must be dedicated to essential military and professional ethics and standards."

Although the mem-mem course was the highest level of training offered up to 1948, it was so intensive that the Israel Defense Force's present senior officers had little difficulty adjusting to higher command posts. Today, despite the existence of a large-scale army that requires higher as well as more specialized forms of training, the mem-mem course (now called O.T.C.) remains basic and leadership is still stressed as the primary responsibility of the commander.

Since the Palmach numbered no more than 1,300 men in 1941, when Nazi armies were marching toward Egypt and the Middle East, its morale and leadership training was geared to the waging of indirect, close-range warfare. The mobility of the unit and its divisibility into smaller units, sometimes composed of only two or three men, demanded great self-discipline, flexibility, courage, and the ability to make quick, on-the-spot decisions.

The Palmach was based in the kibbutzim under a two-year training-and-work program with most of the training concealed by the kibbutz. This integration of military functions and structural social formations contributed to the development of a high esprit de corps in the Palmach. The Palmach was thus to become the elite of the UKM, its political reservoir and an instrument for institutionalizing the kibbutz's domination over the HOL, the Yishuv, and its security instruments.

According to Yigal Allon the Palmach had four main sources of recruitment. First, the Agricultural Workers' Settlement, led by the kibbutz movement (UKM and the leftist national kibbutz) in coordination with the central (Haganah) recruitment agencies, supplied Palmach with regular quotas. Second, the old private enterprise agricultural settlements bestowed some of their best men upon the Palmach. Third, a constant stream came from the cities' Socialist youth movements as well as the Gadna, a Haganah group for urban young people from thirteen to eighteen years old. Finally, men transferred sporadically from Haganah's city forces to the Palmach.[14]

Out of twenty-eight settlements that served as Palmach bases, seventeen belonged to UKM.[15] Through Palmach's growth in 1941–47, UKM membership in Palmach never dropped to less than 30 percent. Out of six battalions, four (1, 2, 3, and 5) were exclusively composed of recruits from agricultural settlements.

With Sadeh, a UKM left radical, as its commanding officer and Allon, an Israeli-born UKM member, as his deputy, it was only natural that the kibbutz movements and especially UKM should dictate much of the general staff policy, indoctrination, training, and ideology of the

Palmach. Not only did the UKM dominate Palmach's headquarters staff and its battalion commanders, but it also ensured its influence through material and financial support.

When the Palmach found itself in financial difficulties in early 1942 because of inadequate Haganah support (out of the Haganah's total budget of £230,000, the Palmach was alloted only £23,000, and in July received only an additional £7,400), the UKM Executive Committee offered it kibbutzim for training sites. Thus it is little wonder that the UKM viewed the Palmach as its prodigy.

The war years, especially the 1941–45 period, transformed the Haganah from a decentralized, voluntary, and part-time organization into a structure with a permanent headquarters, a general staff headed by a chief of staff, centers for officer training, a clandestine supply and purchasing operation (Rechesh), an extensive and efficient network for gathering intelligence and information (Shay), an organization for clandestine immigration (Ha-Apala), and, of course, the Palmach.[16]

THE FORMATION OF THE ISRAELI ARMY

The single most important factor in civil-military relations in the new state of Israel established in 1948 was Ben Gurion's earlier takeover of the defense structure. "With the end of the Second World War," writes Ben Gurion, "it became clear to us that Britain would not and could not uphold the mandate, and that it could not participate in the creation of a Jewish state, even in that part of the country allotted to the Yishuv under partition."[17] This meant that political solutions to the Palestine problem had to be accompanied by military preparedness. In order to create a unified military command, Ben Gurion found it necessary to bring all military structures under the direction of one political headquarters, the Jewish Agency for Palestine. The years 1945–47, which immediately preceded the establishment of the state of Israel, were thus crucial for the future of the armed forces and their role in the campaign for independence. Left-wing Socialist-Zionists and right-wing Revisionist-Zionists clashed, each aided by the military structures at its disposal. The Haganah headquarters was embroiled in an intense conflict over the destiny of the military structures and their relationships to society and politics. While some Palmach leaders saw in the Palmach the cadres that would produce Israel's people's army, the National Military Organization (NMO) advocated the formation of independent military and terrorist organizations to end British rule in Palestine.

Ben Gurion came to believe that in the struggle for statehood, which meant struggle against the British White Paper policy and against Arab political opposition, the role of the military would be decisive. The army would become the "mailed fist" of the Jewish state. Thus, by October 1947, a month before the United Nations proposed a partition of Palestine that the Arabs rejected, Ben Gurion was ready with an armed Jewish force.

On May 15, 1948, when the Mandate expired, the Jewish forces met the invading troops of five Arab states. The Palmach, numbering just over four thousand men (including reserves), absorbed the first Arab offensive in northern Galilee and in Jerusalem. Palmach units participated on all fronts (it had three battalions in Galilee and three in Jerusalem) and led the major counteroffensive of the liberation campaign, which began in the south in late June 1948. The forces on the southern front were led by the Palmach's chief, General Allon, and the main thrust of the Negev campaign, which repulsed the Egyptian army (the largest organized Arab force), was made almost entirely by Palmach divisions. By January 1949, the Palmach was in Egyptian territory, and in March the new IDF, led by the Palmach, conquered the southernmost tip of Palestine and the port of Eilat. By that time, a political struggle for control of the army had become inevitable.

By late June 1948, Ben Gurion had already ordered a Palmach battalion stationed in Tel Aviv to surrender the *Altalena,* a ship commanded by the NMO, which was attempting to distribute arms to its independent troops waiting on the shores of Natanya on the Mediterranean coast between Haifa and Tel Aviv.[18] After this showdown, the NMO was dissolved. Furthermore, after taking steps to bring military policy under the control of a unified political leadership, on October 29, 1948, the chief of staff, General Ya'aqov Dori, issued an order that Palmach headquarters also be dissolved and that General Allon serve only as commander of the southern front.

The framework for the transformation of voluntary military forces into compulsory military structures was established by Ben Gurion during the debate on the defense service bill in the first Knesset (parliament) in 1949 after he had already successfully nationalized the IDF.[19] The army, he proposed, should be small and professional, with a large reserve system. It should adopt the most recent scientific and technological innovations, inculcate the spirit of the Haganah in new conscripts, and aid in the integration of the new immigrants. Furthermore, the army should participate in agricultural settlement efforts, serve as a model of fraternity, and associate itself with the youth movement. In short, a nation-in-arms must mobilize the public to civic action. These functions of the IDF were conceived after much heated debate in the Knesset and within the IDF's high command. Only when General Dayan assumed the post of chief of staff in November 1953 did the IDF serve both the traditions of the Haganah and Palmach and the demands of a highly professional force.

Depoliticization of the army was calculated to deradicalize it and to eliminate the influence of the United Kibbutz Movement—Palmach leftist officers. The UKM included both militant Zionists and territorialists, that is, those concerned with Jewish agricultural settlement and colonialization of "empty" spaces in the Palestine of the Mandate. To eliminate his political rivals on the left and the militants among the House of Labor, Ben Gurion not only fired and "retired" a considerable number of Palmach officers, but he passed over several senior Palmach officers when he appointed Moshe Dayan to head the Zahal. He also fired Israel Galeeli, the ideological head of UKM who served as deputy defense minister. Thus, Ben Gurion routinized the institutional framework of the defense ministry. No clear bureaucratic and legislative lines of demarcation were established between the minister of defense, the cabinet, and the office of the prime minister (Ben Gurion was both prime minister and minister of defense). Furthermore, the minister's responsibility to parliament was not defined. While the defense ministry was run by Ben Gurion and his inner circle, the Zahal was highly institutionalized. It was to become Israel's most efficient modern bureaucracy and the only structure of government that was almost completely independent from political patronage. Furthermore, although Ben Gurion certainly did not eradicate all the ideological elements in Zahal, he did obliterate its UKM and Palmach orientations. Besides its importance as a maneuver to eliminate political rivals, Ben Gurion's appointment of Dayan, a Mapai loyalist, decisively influenced the course of Israel's national security policy. Dayan and Ben Gurion advocated the same policy: that the next war with the Arabs should be carried into the enemy's territory. Dayan was not only a faithful disciple of Ben Gurion, he was the architect of border raids and retaliation policies that helped to escalate Israel's military confrontation with Egypt-Syria and Jordan.[20]

In the major area of political responsibility the relationship between the minister of defense and the chief of staff, from Ben Gurion's terms

(1947–53, 1955–63) until now (1976), the duties, responsibilities and obligations of each were never institutionalized except on a personal level (Ben Gurion and Dayan, for example).

Although the defense minister had an informal veto over the appointment of the chief of staff, which was usually accepted in a pro forma vote by the cabinet, each defense minister established a different relationship with the chief of staff and Zahal's high command. The revolutionary legacy was extremely pervasive, however. The chief of staff was a highly professional officer, loyal to civilian authorities and to his client, the state, and the regime in power. Nevertheless, most were also active formulators of national security policy. Examples are Generals Yadin, Dayan, Rabin, Bar-Lev, Elazar, and Gur. Others chiefs of staff tended to be oriented more toward a professional role. Generals Makleff, Laskov, and Tsur were examples of this type. In the absence of a formally institutionalized authority, relations between the minister of defense and the chief of staff were eventually routinized, but the revolutionary tradition persisted to the extent that the chief of staff and Zahal's high command wielded extraordinary influence in matters of national security policy. Furthermore, the corporatism played as insignificant a role for the Israeli officer as for the revolutionary soldier. The Israeli officer derived his integrity from military prowess, political influence, and the support of the public. He did not have to resort to exclusivity and corporate defense, because he was not vulnerable to the challenges encountered by the professional and praetorian soldier.

The strategic and organizational revolution of IDF during Dayan's tenure (1953–57) was remarkable and enduring. Under Ben Gurion as political head and Dayan as chief military strategist, the paratroopers (commando troops) organized by Dayan and Colonel (later General) Ariel Sharon, which initiated daring raids and operations behind enemy lines, created a new type of revolutionary warfare. Dayan's transformation of IDF, incorporating the traditions of Haganah and Palmach, produced the unique esprit de corps that characterized Israel twenty years later.

The Haganah, one of the major Jewish national institutions in Palestine, had reflected the patterns of a community that was very active politically but, because of the conditions of the mandate, had no formal state structure to establish set practices, although formal Jewish national institutions—such as the National Committee, the Jewish Agency for Palestine, and the World Zionist Organization—did exist.

The most significant change in political institutions and practices in the new state had been their gradual formalization and bureaucratization, with voluntary civil action groups giving way to formal compulsory units. The professionalization of the Israeli army reflects the fact that the practices, institutions, and behaviors of this colonizing political community were being transformed into a formal political system. The creation of the IDF out of the Haganah shows how a colonizing movement whose social mission was maintained within primary, informal groups was changed into a formal bureaucratic structure.[21]

THE IDF AND THE PLA

A comparison between the Chinese PLA and the Haganah-IDF should be made with caution. Both forces were products of necessity rather than choice. Not until 1927, after the slaughter of the CCP members in Shanghai, did the party in the countryside establish the PLA, a permanent military organization. Not until 1936, when confronted with the Arab-led revolt against Britain and the Jewish community in Palestine, did the Socialist-Zionists found the Haganah's general staff.[22] The PLA and MAC were innovative instruments, as were the Haganah and the Palmach. In both China and Israel, the combination of independent military thinking and the challenge of adversity resulted in the formation of a unique type of modern revolutionary and professional soldier who wields considerable influence upon national security policy. The similarities end here, however.

Whereas the Israeli security system was established to protect a pioneering, colonizing people, the Chinese system emerged out of anticolonial and civil wars. The Israeli revolutionary soldier was strictly an instrument of the colonizing society and in Israel civil-military relations were objective. The Chinese produced a subjective civil-military and revolutionary regime. Furthermore, the Israeli army structure was almost identical to that of the early nineteenth-century nation-in-arms and the Israeli professional soldier also duplicated the nation-in-arms soldier, minus the latter's strong corporate orientations. Except for the Chinese concept of the mass army, the Chinese officer was more like the Soviet professional soldier. Elitism and corporatism were more effective orientations in the PLA in view of the extraordinary role the army played in the Communist regime. In the middle 1970s the military in Israel had a dominant influence in matters of security and defense, yet it still did not equal that of the PLA. (This was true even though the military was heavily represented in Israel's cabinet. In 1976, for example, there were three former senior officers in the cabinet and Prime Minister Yitzchak Rabin was a former chief of staff.) The principle of rotation and turnover of officers, the wide scope given to middle-range officers, and the continual rejuvenation of IDF certainly curtailed the potential power of an institutionalized corporate senior military elite.[23] In the 1970s, the PLA was still dominated by the aged second generation that had come to power between 1931 and 1935. The bureaucratization and depoliticization of IDF between 1948 and 1950 had created new nonpolitical elites of former army officers who in the middle 1970s were among Israel's industrial, business, and intellectual elite. In China the military remained a single career, interchangeable with a career in the CCP.

Although the IDF was not subjected to the direct control that the MAC exercised over the PLA, the Histadrut and Mapai high councils had dominated the Haganah in the past. In fact, the Haganah's general staff was located in the Histadrut's building and was paid by the Socialist-Zionist movement. The creation of the IDF in 1948, however, liberated the military from the political control of a sectarian group. The struggle over the formation of a professionalized high command and the relationships among the minister of defense, the chief of staff, and the IDF represented the turning point for civil-military relations in Israel because the result was objective control over the military.[24] The PLA, in contrast, was still subjectively and heavily controlled by the MAC and the CCP, and it had less autonomy than the IDF. Generals Yadin (1950–52) and Dayan (1953–57) had streamlined the IDF and limited the military to a strictly professional fighting function. Role expansion in the IDF was also curtailed, and by the 1970s had become meager. The PLA still engaged in socioeconomic and propaganda activities and internal CCP politics and actively participated in the regime, while the IDF did not. The IDF was becoming more and more an association of experts and technocrats, whereas the PLA was still an army of generalists. Yet the IDF was closely integrated with its reservists, the people's army of Israel, who made up the bulk of the troops in wartime.

One might expect the IDF to become highly corporate, more than the PLA, in view of the IDF's technocratic orientation. Paradoxically, the policy of the "permanent purge" in the IDF—officer rejuvenation and turnover—constituted a stumbling block to the advancement of corporatism. But the PLA institutionalized military corporatism, and this trend continues after the dust of the Cultural Revolution had settled. Specialization of function had as yet no priority. The PLA was still a partner of the revolution.

The IDF, a highly professional army with considerable political influence, at least in security matters, and dominated by a nationalist elite, had not challenged electoral political power and had remained noninterventionist. Mature professionalization and infant corporatism guaranteed the objective context of the military regime in Israel. The military in Israel was as diverse as its civilian elites. Hawks and doves, moderate and radical nationalists, socialist and liberal officers, all were represented in the high command. In China, the political orientation of social and nationalist thought had been constrained by the ideology and organization of Mao and the CCP. The dynamics of China after 1965 had demonstrated that more than one flower bloomed in the Chinese military.

Formalization and bureaucratization in such groups as the IDF brought about changes in the structure and activities of Israeli elites and in the formation of nonpolitical elites, a rare phenomenon in the pre-independence era.[25] The political consciousness of the IDF's junior officers was rather low, and the whole spectrum of intense ideological pressure had diminished and in some areas been eliminated. In fact, the political consciousness and ideological inclinations of Israel's junior officers (with the exception of those who came from the left-oriented kubbutzim) seemed to be much lower than those of civil servants, legislators, and students. The political ambitions of the senior officers were also restricted. Relatively few senior army officers had joined a political party and most of those had been affiliated with a party before IDF was established. A small number (including Generals Dayan, Allon, Bar Lev, Sharon, Weitzman, and Rabin) had become active in politics, capitalizing on their war exploits and their charismatic appeal. This was not true, however, of the 1967–73 single officers group.

The IDF's elite veterans did play a key role in the industrial and bureaucratic complex in Israel. Many had become prominent in the Israeli civil service, especially in the defense and foreign service, and held important positions in Israel's foreign aid agency, working in Africa, Asia, and Latin America. This "smooth" integration of the IDF elite was crucial for civil-military relations in Israel. On the whole, because of the diverse needs of the Israeli economic and bureaucratic structures, the society was able to absorb and integrate the IDF veterans.

Israel Is not a Praetorian State

In the middle 1970s, Israel, in contrast to the other states in the Middle East—and in fact, to most emerging countries—was not a praetorian state. Its civic culture was not ineffective and army-sustained. In Israel, the civic culture had long been established, and civilian domination over the military had been successfully maintained both before and after independence. Civilian supremacy had not been challenged since 1948—despite twenty-six years of insecurity and border tensions, a state of perpetual military preparedness, and four major wars. Furthermore, there was a high level of political institutionalization and sustained support for political structures.[26] Israel was one of the most complex of the developing or newly developed states, demonstrating a high level of political institutionalization and sustained support.

Unlike praetorian states, Israel did not have weak ineffective political parties. Because of highly cohesive stratified classes, groups, and political parties, no one political section gained predominance. Mapai (now the Labor party) and the Histadrut were themselves confederations of interests, sections, political cleavages, and persons.

Furthermore, there was practically no gap between the ideology of the IDF and that of the state or its major political forces. Since the civilian and military sectors had identical values, it was natural for them to work together. The army's role expansion was no more threatening to civilian supremacy over politics than that of the Histadrut or settlement systems. This did not mean mere absence of constraints; on the contrary, since the formation of the Yishuv, the history of Israel had involved role expansion—the accumulation of many functions to establish an independent Jewish state. Of course, role expansion also meant that each group would take political advantage of its power, position, and influence.

Routinization and the Fruits of Institutionalization, 1967–76

The 1967 war clearly demonstrated the IDF's civilian orientation. During the three weeks of alert and mobilization, between May 15 and June 5, 1967, the high command acted with professional objectivity and with loyalty to the civilian authorities and to the regime. The high command also showed that its influence over Israel's national security and defense policies is of critical importance to the survival of the country. The debate within the military leadership on the timing for initiating the conflict proved once again that Israel's high command has no rival in strategic thinking. No other institution in Israel possessed the information, the machinery, and the instruments for the design, conception, and implementation of Israel's national security policy. This arrangement, whereby the minister of defense deals with grand strategy and decides when to implement national security policy, while the high command executes military policy, had been developed by Ben Gurion. Ben Gurion, however, established no machinery for the development of national security policy. The lines of demarcation between policy and implementation by the high command, especially between the chief of staff and the defense minister, were never clearly drawn.[27] When Ben Gurion took over the defense ministry in 1947, he soon dominated the embryonic machinery of the high command, which was patterned after the Haganah-Palmach structures,[28] but he never established a proper civilian structure for the making and implementation of national security policy.

The 1948 war was conducted in the style of the 1936 struggles.[29] Once he had established civilian control and had formalized and depoliticized the Zahal, Ben Gurion rarely interfered in the area of military doctrine and made no civilian structural innovations. The military domain became the exclusive realm of the Zahal's high command as it has been of the Haganah's high command. The institutionalization of defense also meant that IDF's high command became the sole instrument of Zahal's military doctrines and strategy.[30] It had no rival in the civilian defense establishment except the minister of defense.

Yet, at best, Chief of Staff Moshe Dayan (1953–57) and his officers could only modify Ben Gurion's orientation or accelerate any specific operations about which the defense minister might have had doubts. Ben Gurion, a powerful politician, prevailed, not because the line of demarcation between the minister of defense and the chief of staff was clearly established, but because his own political authority was supreme. The fact remains that until the time of this writing (1976) no formal and legal division of authority has existed between the government, the defense minister, and the chief of staff.[31] Ben Gurion had eliminated all political rivals as well as competing institutional arrangements in and between the ministry and the IDF. Depoliticization of the defense functions and of the Zahal also meant Ben Gurion's total domination over Israel's national security and over the IDF. Thus, no political or other structure was established that might compete with Ben Gurion, except the IDF's chief of staff and the high command. Thus the most that ambitious officers like Generals Yigael Yadin, Moshe Dayan, and Yitzchak Rabin could accomplish were structural changes in the IDF.

In a modern age, particularly in a garrison state, national security policy is as much a preoccupation of officers as is strategy. Thus, when Ben Gurion resigned in 1963, the IDF's high command became the sole arbiter of national security policy, not simply an instrument for its implementation. Prime Minister Levi Eshkol never succeeded in duplicating Ben Gurion's supremacy over national security policy. Moreover, he failed to establish any civilian structure that could compete with the IDF. Eshkol's expertise was in matters of finance, and he became dependent on the high command—especially Chief of Staff Yitzchak Rabin, a brilliant military thinker and analyst—for advice on military policy.

The Haganah tradition of making national security policy had continued during Ben Gurion's first term (1947–50), when it was implemented by an informal group known as the national security inner circle. This tightly knit Socialist-Zionist and Hityashvut group had conducted national security policy before the state was established, but it was abolished by Ben Gurion in 1950. Thereafter, Ben Gurion introduced a built-in adversary system in the high command. Each chief of staff represented a different military tradition and strategic thinking: Yadin, the Haganah; Dayan, the Palmach-commando; Laskov and Tsur, the British Army. Eshkol's high command, although highly professional and totally depoliticized (it possessed no ties with political parties or movements outside the military), was eventually dominated by Palmach graduates (Generals Rabin, Bar-Lev, and Elazar). When Ben Gurion departed, his rotation and adversary systems ceased to function. The conflict over the type of war Israel must conduct was turned over to the generals and to the intelligence branch of the IDF. Eshkol, unlike Ben Gurion, did not conceive of an independent national security decision-making system. This was in part an outcome of the growth of the Zahal, its rapid professionalization, and the pre-emptive blitz strategy IDF conceived after the 1956 war. National security became synonymous with military strategy. The

IDF no longer just influenced national security policy making, it dominated it. The surprise Egyptian mobilization in Sinai on May 15, 1967, left Eshkol at the mercy of the high command and the intelligence branch in handling a critical national security problem, the possibility of war. At first, Eshkol withstood the pressures of the chief of staff and several senior officers to make an immediate pre-emptive move. He tried diplomacy, attempting to use American influence to pressure Egypt to demobilize its forces in Sinai and make them return to the status quo ante. Eshkol's reliance on his chief of staff not only burdened General Rabin with political responsibility, but it also curtailed the prime minister's options. In the end, deprived of advice from the cabinet or the party on national security matters, Eshkol relied on the high command, which was less divided than the cabinet, for a decision on whether to go to war.

Since the 1967 Six Days' War, the national security inner circle system has surfaced again. The IDF's role was again reversed. The new defense minister, Moshe Dayan, a former chief of staff, conceived his role much as Ben Gurion had. He left to the IDF's high command the sole responsibility for military strategy and reserved decisions on national security policy to Prime Minister Golda Meir and himself. Like Ben Gurion, Dayan acted as supreme commander.[32] However, Dayan was not an all-powerful politician who could dictate to cabinets, parties, and the military. He had to share the burden of defense with Prime Minister Eshkol, with whom he had never felt comfortable. After Eshkol's death in 1968, Golda Meir, the new prime minister, re-established a modified version of the inner circle, which was composed of an elite selected by the party and cabinet, a totally different system from that of the pre-Zahal era. The formal distinction between the political and military in the Haganah became blurred in reality: Socialist-Zionist politicians were mixed with professional officers, and some (like Eliahu Golomb, Yitzchak Sadeh, and Israel Galeeli) served in both political and professional capacities.

The new political-military inner circle under Meir, Dayan, and Israel Galeeli clearly was in command of national security and foreign policy. The crucial decision to go to war was always the undisputed prerogative of the civilian politicians; the high command was solely responsible for the execution of military strategy. This arrangement was certainly in the best tradition of objective political control over military professionalism. The inner circle acted as a collective civilian supreme commander in the informal but highly institutionalized tradition of Ben Gurion. Yet the tacit alliance between the three leaders of the inner circle and their political allies in the Labor-dominated cabinet gave the latter tremendous authority over military strategy as well as national security policy.This growth in the inner circle's role was a direct consequence of having an obedient professional officer corps. While Chief of Staff Dayan had constantly challenged Defense Minister Ben Gurion, Generals Bar-Lev and Elazar authored military doctrines that fit with, even enhanced the national security orientation of the inner circle and their political allies in the cabinet.

Between 1967 and 1974, the inner circle was composed of two layers. The innermost layer was the triumvirate of Meir, Dayan, and Galeeli. The second was composed of prominent national security veterans, Deputy Prime Minister Yigal Allon (former commander of the Palmach) and Minister of Justice Ya'aqov S. Shapira. In 1971, when Chief of Staff General Chaim Bar-Lev retired from the military and became minister of commerce, he also joined this group. This group became more powerful than its constitutional role allowed for. The inner trio had ruled supreme since the 1969 formation of the Labor Alignment, which became the most powerful political structure in Israel. In 1969, the three splinter Socialist-Zionist parties (Rafi, Ahdut-Haavoda, and Mapai) joined forces to form the Labor party. At the same time the Labor Alignment—a governmental coalition between the Labor party and the leftist Mapam—strengthened the Labor government to the point of creating an oligarchy. The national security inner circle, too, found itself with a great deal more power.

The division of labor was as follows: Golda Meir was actually foreign minister, assisted by Ambassador Rabin in Washington and General Yariv, while Foreign Minister Abba Eban handled less significant Israeli policy outside the United States and was never given the opportunity to formulate a foreign policy toward the Arabs. Moshe Dayan, the defense minister, became the architect of Israeli policy toward the Arab countries. Between 1967 and 1973, Dayan considered his most important role to be chief in charge of the occupied territories and the author of the successful "open bridges" policy with the Arabs (a policy of open borders between the occupied West Bank and the State of Jordan). Beginning in January 1974, Dayan also intervened as chief negotiator in Geneva and was the only authority other than Meir to deal with Henry Kissinger. The power of Galeeli, a minister without portfolio, can be attributed to the fact that until the 1973 war he was Golda Meir's national security adviser and éminence grise.

Before the October 1973 war, opposition to the trio in the Labor Alignment was meekly led by Finance Minister Pinhas Sapir, who was otherwise Golda Meir's most loyal party ally. The opposition of Allon and Eban was not significant enough to change the national security elite's orientations and actions. The opposition of Mapam, Labor's ally in the government, was nil. The power of the trio was consummated during the 1973 electoral campaign when, in August 1973, the party platform (better known as the Galeeli Document) was changed in favor of policies that Dayan had advocated since 1969. Dayan's proposals were meant to encourage Israeli settlement and gradual integration of the occupied territories and to affirm the status quo; that is, they required military support from the United States and took a militant stance on the absorption of occupied territories and on terrorism.

Both the political misperceptions and military errors of the Mehdal (misdeed) of 1973 stemmed from the national security policy that was adopted by the Meir-Dayan-Galeeli trio[33] and institutionalized in the Galeeli Document. Yet to speak of the politicization of the army or the militarization of Israel is to misperceive the dynamics of civil-military relations in that country. Between 1967 and 1973, Zahal became completely professionalized and highly technocratic. The IDF's strategic doctrine of combined armored and air force power and mobility only strengthened the professionalization and technocratization of the IDF. Since 1948, the IDF tradition held that the high command dominated military strategy; the post-1967 military strategy coverged with the national security policy of the political triumvirate. Under civilian-political control, the policy advocated by the supreme political trio and the IDF's high command prescribed military deterrence, extended lines of supply, and stationing of sparse forces on the Suez Canal and in the Golan Heights.

This policy was the work of the national security inner circle, and the IDF had not forced it upon them. The policy enhanced the rise of a highly professional and technocratic senior officer class. Yet few senior officers since 1948 had meddled in politics, that is, used military prestige while in uniform for partisan politics or identified the military with political party doctrines or interests.[34] General Sharon, an exception, in 1973 aired the view of several retired and active senior officers on the direction of national security policy.

In Israel, professionalism and depoliticization are on the rise. Depoliticization did not, of course, mean that the army elite had no political influence or that the army could not serve as an avenue for attaining political leadership. It only meant that the army's functions were not determined by the internal and parochial politics of labor or any other political organization and that above all the IDF had no political autonomy. The officer corps could not become an ally of one political factor or another, as the Egyptian officers were before 1952 and the Syrian and Iraqi officers have been since 1949. Depoliticization worked to keep the Israeli army and its officers corps from becoming a vehicle for political power.

In 1976, Israel still had no military ideology that was the personal preserve of its officers. It also had no military academy—a military curriculum in the Reali High School in Haifa was the best it could offer. Thus the Israeli military professional could not institutionalize a military or strategic dogma and inculcate it into new generations of officers. This does not mean that IDF is an army lacking rival strategic doctrines, but that strategy does not become dogma and a means to create uniformity among the officers group. The absence of an academy deprived the officers of a special class role and of a foundation for corporate exclusivity, and as such the academy had been consciously rejected in Israel as early as 1952. Veterans' organizations might have provided another source of social exclusivity and political pressure, but organizations of Haganah and IDF veterans were legally restricted to protecting their members' welfare and to helping integrate the veteran into society. Efforts of groups of officers to secure political "representation" in Labor party councils and local party organizations have proved futile, and these organizations have attained little or no political influence.

Except for the IDF's strategic planning department, Israel also lacks think tanks and institutes that are designed to institutionalize military doctrines and indoctrinate officers. IDF officers were given two programs of military professional training. One involved six to nine months in an OTS plus attendance at a specialized technical school (air force, armored division, naval commando, and so forth). The other was Command School (POUM), the training school that prepared middle-ranking officers—major to lieutenant colonel—for senior staff and command roles. Junior officers who had not graduated from POUM could not advance and therefore retired early. The school's professional standards, established by the IDF, were high; but it was not a breeding ground for class, status, or exclusivity orientations, mainly because POUM is simply a short-term professional training school. Military academies, in addition to their prestige, are also schools for gentlemen and breed exclusivity. The cohorts formed in four years of academy study (at West Point or Sandhurst, for example) later become military elites and eventually dominate the senior officer class. Since *all* senior officers of the IDF are graduates of POUM or equivalent training overseas, POUM graduates are not an elite.

The mature Israeli political structures, especially the complex and institutionalized political parties, the kibbutzim, and the Histadrut, would present a formidable challenge to the army should it choose to play independent politics. The identification of the Labor party, the most powerful and popular party, and the kibbutz movement with the state left no room for the kind of maneuvers that occur in praetorian states. The army could not claim that politicians had "betrayed" the nation. No civilian politicians, either as individuals or as organized groups, had meddled in the politics of the army since the dissolution of the Palmach and the NMO in 1948–49. If some former military men, such as Generals Dayan, Allon, Bar-Lev, Rabin, and Sharon played a key role in Israeli politics, it was only because they had resigned from the army and sought power through civilian political parties. Reputations gained in the army may have enhanced their political fortunes, but they did not guarantee political success, as the political failure of Ezer Weitzmann demonstrates. Any attempt to influence politics while in uniform would have been crushed. If army officers wished to become successful in politics, they were obliged to channel their ambitions through civilian and electoral political procedures.

Although no comprehensive study of the political articulation and commitment of the IDF officer corps had been made as of 1976, it had been suggested that political articulation was correlated with the educational level of the officers. Relatively less educated Israeli officers born in the Arab countries were lacking in political consciousness. The better educated were politically articulate but also highly professional.[35] Young officers from the kibbutzim, especially those from small socialist collectives, were highly politically conscious. On the whole, the social isolation (not to be confused with societal isolation) of the professional officers—their tendency to keep to themselves and their apolitical attitude—was greater than that found among the Haganah and Palmach and the IDF officer corps from 1941 to 1950. Because the IDF was a people's army and a reserve organization, its barracks life was short. Its officers were permanently integrated with society, and the chances of an officer's becoming ideologically or professionally independent of the society were meager. A long military career was unlikely in Israel. Because of the age limit on service in the army, the officer corps was constantly changing.

In Israel, a highly professionalized army dependent on a reserve system, with an unusually rapid turnover of officers and men, was harnessed to civilian control, as were the armies of the United States and Western Europe. There was never, therefore, a chance for military coups. There was no political support for the army from the powerful political parties and the effective kibbutz and Histadrut systems. The officer corps as a professional group was removed from political life; officers were prohibited from actively participating in politics, and they showed little interest in politics after retirement.

Again, these restrictions did not prevent elite veterans from actively pressing for and seeking managerial, economic, university, and administrative positions. Neither the size of the Israeli army nor the enormous defense budget (13.1 percent of the total national budget during 1967; estimated at 14.5 percent after the Six Days' War and 40 percent since the October 1973 War) dictated the political and attitudinal behavior of the Israeli army and its high command. Size and budget are determining factors in praetorian states. In nonpraetorian states, however, although the size of the army and the defense budget affects the economic structure, which in turn may bring about structural changes in society and politics, the army's size and budget will not elevate it to a position as the ruling political group. Israel disproved the thesis that in a state under garrison conditions the army is prone to forego the principle of political nonintervention. The values and the ideology of the IDF stemmed from the permanent Arab threat, and the IDF was committed to the nationalism espoused by most Israelis. Though the army elite was differentiated from the social structure it had no more political power than any other elite.

The IDF's high command did grow in stature and political influence, especially after 1967; but this growth led to greater professionalization rather than to corporatism and praetorianism. The drawn-out Arab-Israeli conflict between 1948 and 1967 had not encouraged civilian dependence on permanent military advice. The years 1967–70 (until the cease-fire), however, were a period of constantly escalating war, which meant that the political leadership became more dependent on the military and political judgment of the high command, especially in the areas of strategy and intelligence. The absence of alternative and rival sources of strategic and national security information and advice added to the dependence. At the same time, civilians in charge of defense (including General Moshe Dayan) and the high command did not always speak in unison on policy matters, even though national security policy was their combined responsibility. These periodic controversies divided the IDF's general staff and the senior cabinet in charge of national security on specific issues, but they were nevertheless resolved within their councils.

As the chief of staff and the chief of intelligence grew in influence they exerted considerable pressure upon national security policy. But the political pressures dictated by a permanent state of war did not flow through the usual political channels, such as parties and pressure groups, or through veterans' organizations, which would have been the case in praetorian systems. Nor did they come from outside the political system. Instead pressure was brought to bear by a powerful, autonomous, professional, military structure—the IDF, tightly dominated by senior cabinet officers in charge of national security (Meir, Dayan, and Galeeli). The permanent war of 1967–74 and the accompanying technocratization of the military advanced the routinization of professionalism, and in the aftermath of the 1973 war these changes were only enhanced. Yet they did not touch off a corporate impulse, as one might have expected. The bureaucratization and technocratization of the IDF affected the historical leadership concept of Haganah and Palmach, which became a major internal concern; but they did not enhance the political power of the military or lead it into praetorianism and interventionism. The IDF was a successful, proud, professional organization, highly respected by its own people and independent of the need for a corporate image to rescue it from status decline.

CIVIL-MILITARY RELATIONS IN ISRAEL: AN OVERVIEW

Three decades have demonstrated that the lines of demarcation between civilian and military functions in Israel are integral and fusionist. An analysis of the relationship between the two must cover three areas of interaction: the political-psychological; the institutional-structural; and the personal interaction and perception of elities governing civil and military structures.

The political-psychological, that is, the political and perceptual relationships between the two most authoritative figures in the two systems, the minister of defense and the chief of staff, on the whole were convergent. No minister of defense after David Ben Gurion selected a chief of staff whose political ideology and security perceptions radically diverged from his own. Clearly, it was to the defense minister and his style that the chief of staff would have to adjust. Those who did not resigned, as did Generals Yadin, Makleff, and Laskov under the most authoritative defense minister, David Ben Gurion. Ben Gurion's political philosophy and his concept of the subordinate role of the military were clear, and he did not tolerate deviation from his norms, even if they never formalized. Next, the defense minister was removed from *direct* personal domination over the chief of staff and the IDF, even if Ben Gurion, for instance, was a notorious interventionist and sometimes demanded detailed information on minor military operations. On the whole Dayan succeeded where Yadin and Makleff had failed to radicalize Ben Gurion's policies. Nevertheless, the symbiotic (although clearly unequal) relationship between Ben Gurion and Dayan created one of the most harmonious periods in the IDF–defense ministry relationship.

Structurally, the critical relationship between the two was on the personal level, and much of civil-military relations in Israel was dictated by the following: (1) the degree of the accessibility of the chief of staff to the defense minister and vice versa; (2) the scope and degree of the minister's intervention in the structural and institutional practices of the IDF, especially those of the high command; and (3) the respect of the defense minister for the professionalism of his chief.

Each defense minister attempted to define informally, of course, the role of his chief. Ben Gurion never allowed his chief to become his principal military adviser. The chief of staff seldom participated in cabinet meetings or testified before the Knesset's foreign affairs and security committees, or, for that matter, before the now defunct Mapai military affairs ad hoc committee. Ben Gurion was clearly the commander in chief and acted without much regard for the political views of his chiefs. Lavon, an arrogant man, lacked knowledge of national security matters, and tried in vain to undermine Dayan's military authority. His ouster stemmed precisely from his unsuccessful effort to dethrone the chief of staff and do what Ben Gurion never did—intervene in the chief's realm, the internal conduct of the high command, and his authority over senior subordinates. Lavon's inability to dominate military strategy as Ben Gurion had done led some analysts to assume mistakenly that the chief's authority over his staff and over military operations was only a political ploy by Dayan to oust Lavon. Eshkol, however, clearly saw Rabin as his chief military adviser, and Rabin served in this capacity during the critical days of May-June 1967. As defense minister, Dayan was also dominant in military policy. Yet he did his utmost not to intervene in military operations and to accept the recommendations of the chief and his staff. This was true of both of his subordinates, Bar-Lev and Elazar. General Gur, however, whose military professionalism is greater than that of Defense Minister Peres, is now acting as Peres's chief military adviser.

Clearly, the relationships depended on the personalities of the prime minister, the defense minister, and the chief of staff. An assertive defense minister, Lavon clashed with an ambitious and controversial chief of staff, Moshe Dayan. A domineering and most authoritative David Ben Gurion molded the chiefs to his will, including his protégé Dayan. But Yadin's and Laskov's short tenures demonstrated Ben Gurion's undisputed personal authority. Eshkol, a less assertive person, had a splendid relationship with Rabin, a highly professional and successful staff officer who, with Eshkol's consent, built the IDF's first professional and modern army machine, which was instrumental in the 1967 victory. General Elazar was not Dayan's choice. Nevertheless, the two maintained a correct relationship. Dayan's concept of administration was to maximize the delegation of authority to his subordinates, leaving the IDF to its professionals. Because of this, the Agranat Commission did not find Dayan responsible for the 1973 Mehdal, but placed the full responsibility on the chief of staff and his intelligence officers. General Gur's cordial relationships with Peres and the latter's respect for the chief of staff again leaves the IDF senior command professionally autonomous.

The evolution of the structural relationship among the prime minister, minister of defense, and the chief of staff was cyclical. Ben Gurion, an adherent of formal and institutional authority, exercised authority through his undisputed personal leadership, rather than through his combined offices of prime minister and defense minister, but his successors were unable to duplicate his feat. Lavon, the first defense minister after Ben Gurion, failed not for lack of institutional authority (that is, not because the offices of defense minister and prime minister were no longer combined) but because of his inability in 1954 to exercise sufficient personal authority over the recalcitrant chief of staff and a contemptuous high command in the IDF's already autonomous and institutionalized system. The history of Haganah's and the IDF's high command is a history of three decades of institutionalization. Eshkol, like Ben Gurion, served as prime minister and defense minister at the same time. Thus he technically possessed Ben Gurion's formal authority, but he never enjoyed Ben Gurion's personal authority. His influence over the IDF did not approach Ben Gurion's, and thus Eshkol left Chief of Staff Rabin and the high command on their own. However, despite the growing power of the IDF and its rapid institutionalization between 1963 and 1967 (Eshkol's tenure as defense minister), in the crucial days between May 15 and June 5, 1967, the prime minister, to tame the IDF's high command, succeeded in turning down its recommendations for an immediate resort to force. The IDF, convinced that Israel would win a decisive victory, was pushing for a pre-emptive attack on the Arab states, but it did not persuade Eshkol until early in June when its cabinet was ready to accept this policy. Thus the ultimate decision to go to war rested with Eshkol. Dayan, who served as defense minister in 1973, and whose influence on Golda Meir was considerable, overruled Chief of Staff Elazar's call to mobilize a greater part of the IDF a few days before the Egyptian-Syrian forces were ready for the surprise attack of October 6, 1973. The IDF was thus dominated by Dayan, even if he gave it considerable autonomy.

Chief of Staff Gur commands the largest IDF in history. Now double its 1973 size and the most professional and best equipped army in the Middle East, it is, nevertheless, responsible to the defense minister and the cabinet. In case of a crisis, Gur carries considerable weight in cabinet decisions. But he can be and has been overruled, and thus is no more powerful than key cabinet officers.

In a state enduring garrison conditions, possessing the largest military machine it has ever had, and constantly facing critical decisions on national security policy, it is not possible to demarcate simple formalistic lines between the different functions of national security or between its different structures—or, above all, to establish a type of personality-authority relationship. These combinations are not simple superordination-subordination relationships. Personal, institutional, and structural-bureaucratic relationships dictate civil-military relations as they do in other democratic systems, especially in the United States.

The nature of civil-military relations, the absorbent capacity of the economy, the rapid turnover of officers, the successful integration of IDF veterans, the army's dependence upon the reserve system, the identity of military and national political goals, and the IDF's professionalism precluded the Israeli army's active intervention in politics. Another factor working against intervention was the institutionalized legitimacy of independent civilian control. These conditions, however, did not lead to the formation of a politically docile military. The military in Israel has been a bureaucratic political pressure group similar to those in other nonpraetorian states in which they challenge political authority, especially in the realm of defense and foreign affairs.

The Israeli professional soldier was revolutionary in the sense that his professionalism was untainted by corporatism. The IDF was solely dedicated to the exercise of external violence. Unlike the PLA, it was not a political partner of the regime. It was revolutionary in its professional innovations, mainly because its officer corps was young and its organizational structures suffered constantly from the activities of nonroutinized officers. Nevertheless, the IDF, commanded after 1967 by the last Palmach generation, was a thoroughly bureaucratized and routinized establishment. The 1973 war demonstrated that it too was prone to the dangers of professionalization and routinization. Yet the continual changing of senior officers, the rapid mobility within junior levels, and the internalized awareness that the military was only one career among many created a unique case in the annals of the modern military profession.

The persistence of civilian control over the military in Israel demonstrates the supremacy of its political leadership: the prime minister is supreme commander. The IDF will certainly continue to exert pressure and influence upon national security policy, as the military does in the United States, the USSR, and China. As in those countries, civilian control over the military in Israel has remained consistent and firm, and matters of national security have been given priority in the external politics of the nation-state.

Table 9.1 Types of Revolutionary Professional Orientation over Time, 1918–76

	Revolutionary	Routinized Revolutionary
USSR	1917–18	1918–20
China	1927–49	1949–66
	1966–69	1969–76
Israel	1925–49	1949–76
North Vietnam	1945–65	1965–76

Conclusion: The Challenges of Military Corporatism

Political conditions dictate the nature of civil-military relations. A stable, sustaining, and institutionalized civilian regime can hardly succumb to military pressure and rule. Nor can the military establishment, the most dependent bureaucracy of the modern nation-state, challenge a well-established political order. The military is motivated to intervene only when its corporate or bureaucratic roles seem threatened, a condition that does not usually exist in highly institutionalized and complex political systems. And even if it has such intentions, the military must be aware of the futility of challenging such a regime.

CORPORATE PROFESSIONALISM AND CIVIL ORDER

Compared with other political and bureaucratic elites, the military elite is most closely identified with the political regime and the state, and it is more conscientious than others in its dedication to order.[1] Like all other modern bureaucracies, the military establishment is organized on the basis of skill and function. It is as determined to protect and preserve the integrity and autonomy of military professionalism as it is defensive of the principle of exclusivity. These concerns, however, are not confined to the military. Prussian high civil servants, Bolshevik apparatchiks, and Nazi propagandists have also been zealous to preserve political stability and professional exclusivity. Nevertheless, the military alone can protect itself, make its demands credible, and threaten to use the most violent means at the disposal of the state. The military, in fact, has often dared to challenge an unstable or precarious order. In the absence of authority it has even drawn the sword to influence and dictate the rules for the next regime. Nevertheless, military professionalism in itself is neither a hindrance nor an asset to stable civil-military relations and to the stability of the political order. Both of those depend primarily on the internal strength of the civil order. Only the dynamics of the link between the professional and the client explains military intervention or nonintervention.

Military corporatism has two faces. On one side, the professional integrity and corporate exclusivity of the military have often acted as major obstacles to the growth and development of stable political orders. On the other side, corporatism has sometimes led to military docility; and, in extreme cases, a powerful regime has even kept military corporatism from developing.

The militaries of Prussia-Germany and Japan have both hindered and enhanced the establishment of a stable political order. The German military was led into its alliance with Hitler by "political ineptitude and unpolitical arrogance."[2] The military elites of Latin America, Africa, and the Middle East have challenged the political order and rendered it permanently unstable. Yet the attempt to fulfill corporate aspirations at the expense of political order has been futile. The military's basic purpose—to protect the political order from external and internal threats—has been often defeated by the military's own internal intrigues, fratricide, overambitious programs, and political naiveté. Not only has military intervention failed to defend stable or participatory political systems; it has also inflicted injury upon the military establishment itself and, in the case of Germany and Japan, brought about the demise of corporatism and of two magnificent military traditions.

Each of the Middle Eastern and the African military leaders has led, in his own way, to his own Armageddon, though none so catastrophic as Japan's or Germany's. In 1976 the likelihood that the praetorians would injure or annihilate their own establishments was more than academic. If Israel had not been concerned with world public opinion or fear of intervention by the great powers in 1967 and in 1973, the Egyptian army would have shared the fate of the Nazi-Japanese military establishment. In fact, if it had not been for the Soviet restoration of the Egyptian army after 1967, that army would have ceased to exist. Similarly, in October 1973, had the cease-fire not been imposed, the entire Egyptian army would have been destroyed. Consider the most glaring examples, the Indian and Pakistani militaries. The political intervention of Pakistan's army destroyed its professional ability. Though both the Indian and Pakistani military elites had the same personal, social, intellectual, and military backgrounds, the Indian army demonstrated higher professional skill in the 1970 war on the Indian subcontinent.[3] In another case, the Syrian army has suffered in professional performance because of continuous fratricide among its elites. Its decline was demonstrated not only in the battle with the Israelis over the Golan Heights but in its sorry performance compared with the smaller but noninterventionist Jordanian army. Despite surprise and strategic advantage in October 1973, in three days the Syrian army had been driven back to the outskirts of Damascus. In June 1976 it failed to break the PLO army in Lebanon. If there were measures to assess the professional standards of the Latin American armies, which scarcely engage in warfare other than lengthy but limited guerrilla actions, it would be interesting to evaluate the effects of mass praetorianism in Brazil and Argentina after 1964 and their impact on professional standards.

The case studies of Prussia and Japan in chapter 3 have illustrated in detail the first face of military corporatism—the way in which it has hindered the development of the political order and undermined the integrity of military professionalism. France and the USSR are examples of the other face. In France corporatism has enhanced professional docility and aloofness, while in the USSR a ruthless regime in the past hindered professionalism, and the military, lacking corporate protection, has suffered a heavy toll in men, skill, and performance.

The history of the Prussian state has been closely linked with the emergence of the modern Prussian army. The army played an extraordinary role in a monarchy historically disposed to favor the military, a role that was strengthened by the reforms of 1807. Mutual reinforcement of status and court clientship made the military more powerful politically than any other party or group. The structure of the bureaucratized Prussian state and its autocracy gave the military still greater privilege and power. The influence of the Kriegsakademie outweighed that of the liberal university. Political asymmetry between the military and the civil society and its political groups became more pronounced once the powers of the general staff, the most effective instrument of the Prussian autocracy, far stronger than the bureaucracy, were broadened. Almost a century of military ascendancy (1807–90) and of monarchial and bureaucratic rule, contrasted with the retarded development of democratic, liberal, and group interests, left the military the undisputed power in the realm of defense and foreign policy.

Even after it was tamed by Bismarck, the role of the military in Prussian-German nation building was disproportionately larger than that of the civil authority. From 1890 to 1914 there were conspicuous Weltpolitik orientations, championed by both the kaiser and his politician-bureaucrats, and the military reached its zenith. The middle classes were militarized, and the regime's militarism combined with praetorianism, though both were to collapse in 1919.[4] But again the army "saved" the Vernunftrepublik of Weimar. Von Seeckt, who should have learned from his militaristic predecessors, acted as both kaiser-surrogate and praetorian. Again the civilian system was dependent on military praetorianism, especially upon Germany's key postwar military figures, von Seeckt and Groener. Only Hitler's powerful, Nazi-dominated, civilian regime, outdoing the military in intrigue and violence, could have tamed this privileged group. Hitler used the modern instruments of power, propaganda, mob violence, and the Brown and the Black Shirts of the SA and the SS to overwhelm the military establishment. He destroyed the Reichswehr's exclusive position and oriented its corporate identity toward a new warlord, this time a civilian, who led it into a war that spelled the annihilation of the proudest army in Europe.

The French military establishment, which managed to outlive several regimes of which it disapproved, adopted an apolitical corporate attitude; it was "above the battle" of politics. In actuality it held the view, sometimes covertly but often openly, that republicanism was essentially a depraved form of government, and that only the military could preserve and protect the noble values of eternal France: duty, community, and family integrity. The French version of corporatism claimed to represent the unity and continuity of France. The principle of exclusivity was regarded as noble, historically French, and an integral part of the military elite. The army's special duty was to guide France in those terrible eras of republicanism, democracy, and egalitarianism and to protect France from politics—politics meaning a foreign orientation, a representation of rational and democratic systems.

The French army, the embodiment of the general will, was considered the last corporate and natural form of human bond. Like eternal France it was a community of solidarity where the dependency principle was personal, not structural, where men grew closer to one another, as they could not do in an artificial, "modern" organization. The military was a source of human pride and French integrity. Its ideology remained that of the early nineteenth-century philosopher de Maistre: "Man's characteristic privilege is that the bond he accepts is not physical but moral; that is, social. . . . " As Richard Griffith wrote, "The Vichy motto *Travail, Famille, Patrie* . . . was to replace the Republic's *Liberté, Egalité, Fraternité.*" While French corporatism enhanced military docility, it also encouraged conspiracy against political orders that did not conform to the military's concept of Frenchmen and France. Again in the words of Griffith:

> A claim to be non-political often denotes a political interest. A dislike for "politics" and "politicking" may just mean that one disapproves of the democratic process. It is, in fact, one of the characteristics of a certain kind of Right to make such protestations. The comments are usually sincere; nevertheless they are usually *political*, without those who make them fully realising it. Politics, in its narrower sense (which is the sense such people are using), is the *business* of politics, the wheeling-dealing, the deceit, the agreements, the alliances. Politics, in its wider sense, is the consideration of what is best for a community, and the means to achieve it. Most of those who disapprove of politics in the first sense do so because they have strong ideas in the second area.[5]

Japan demonstrates the futility of military praetorianism. Soldiers without a state created an autonomous military structure, which, after it had been radicalized, became a potent political force in the absence of civilian challengers. It was the professionalization and modernization of the Japanese military that propelled it into a praetorian role. Once the old regime of the Meiji and the Genro declined, the military bureaucracy gained ascendancy, arrogating to itself Meiji legitimacy. The military in Japan did not enjoy the privileges of the Prussian military, but, when the governments of the 1930s opted for militarism, the military establishment proved equal to the task and, like the German army, brought about its own destruction.

Corporate docility would have been no panacea for the Japanese army, however. A tamed, civilian-dominated military in one of the world's most traditional and modernizing societies could still have become interventionist, not because it possessed a high degree of professionalism but because it sought a corporate ideology which, like Prussia's, was colored by romantic nationalism. Corporate docility is a no better guarantee against praetorianism than dynamic corporatism. A civilian order should not depend on the corporate attitude of the military—docile or aggressive—toward the regime, or on the objectivity of military professionalism. Rather, a civilian order must depend upon its own institutional integrity.

In Stalin's day the military of the USSR was a frustrated professional group with no identity of its own. Although its efforts to rise were brutally crushed by Stalin, his successors were unable, even if willing, to tyrannize society or the military. Having embarked on a militaristic policy, they had little choice but to uplift the status of the military, expand its role, and identify it with their own global plans. The modernization, rejuvenation, and professionalization of the military that began in 1965 had by the middle 1970s resulted in military ascendancy. The military did not rule the USSR, but it influenced defense and even foreign policy, which had formerly been the domain of Stalin or the Politburo. Even if the military elites were as divided as the other Russian political elites over global and imperial policies, the politics of militarism, like the German Weltpolitik of the 1890s, was likely to have far-reaching consequences and to increase the newly acquired corporate status of the Red Army.

In the future, if corporate integrity is tied to a policy of militarism, the military establishment could suffer as it has elsewhere. In 1976 civilians were still dictating the policy of militarism in the USSR, and the new Soviet defense minister was a civilian technocrat. In many cases —for example, in Czechoslovakia (1968) and in Egypt (1972)—the Soviet military had apparently recommended restraint, though they might have favored prosecution of the Chinese-Soviet conflict. The military establishment, liberated from the Stalinist yoke and acting in combination with the research and development community in the defense ministry and the Red Army, could assume a role similar to that of the Prussian army much earlier. The Soviet case was not analogous, however, to the situation in the United States, Israel, or the countries of Western Europe, where by 1976 the military had enjoyed a long era of autonomy. Even though five decades of Leninism-Stalinism had produced corporate docility into the Red Army, its newly won independence was not a permanent guarantee of noninterventionism.

In modernizing societies the dual image of the corporate soldier has been evident in the sultanist orientation of the Arab interventionist military and the satrapist orientation of the more docile African armies. In the Middle East and Africa the military has generally been neither progressive nor modern, contrary to the theory presented in the volume edited by John J. Johnson in the early 1960s, according to which a military oligarchy, the most modern and rational organization in a transitional society, serves as the agent of political development and modernization.[6] My analysis has demonstrated that far from being "progressive modernizers," the satrapist and sultanist militaries of Africa and the Middle East have championed corporatism and acted in a praetorian fashion that has not usually advanced economic modernization or political development.

The military in the Middle East has been oriented toward military dictatorship or domination; it seeks a modern regime, to be sure, but one without executive responsiveness to political participation. The major purpose of the military's executive instrument, the Revolutionary Command Council, has been to shield the executive from political pressure and party politics and thus to isolate military rule from societal processes and political life. In Africa the military has been no more responsive politically than in the Middle East. There, however, it has preferred administrative rule to rule by a proxy party. Nevertheless, it is oriented toward autocracy.

But the most remarkable challenge to the theorists of the progressive officer lies in the area of organization. These "progressive officer" theorists have argued that the military is a modern bureaucracy and that military elites in developing countries are inclined to emulate modern organizational forms which ipso facto will rationalize society, institutions, and politics. In actuality the military, however, has failed in the field of modern rational organization, in economic development, and above all in the formation of modern and sustaining political institutions. This failure has stemmed not so much from the military's inability to emulate modern structures as from its inability to internalize, improvise, and orchestrate the fundamentals of modern organization. It is true that in some developing polities the military has scored high on the Weberian scale of rational bureaucracy with its variables of efficiency, honesty, skill, and rational orientation, and hence may be regarded as a representative model of "modern organization." Nevertheless, several "modern" military establishments in developing nations have contributed little toward expanding the political system and widening the political participation of their respective polities. By 1976, not one military establishment in the Arab Middle East had succeeded in creating viable modern political institutions and structures. Political parties and legislative bodies remained weak, fragmented, or virtually nonexistent, and efficient modern bureaucracies had not yet developed. In fact, interventionist actions of the military had served only to foster fragile, infant political systems and had increased the number of bureaucrats but not the efficiency of the bureaucracy.

THE FUTURE OF THE PRAETORIAN AND THE REVOLUTIONARY SOLDIER

In this study I have proposed a theory of praetorianism. I have also presented a taxonomy that explains the dynamics of civil-military relations in developing polities and postulates the conditions contributing to military praetorianism and the extraordinary role that corporatism has played in its development. The Latin American military establishments, I have argued, constitute the most advanced corporate praetorian groups in modern times. They have combined classical praetorianism (protecting the Roman Senate, or, in this case, the Latin American constitution, from invading garrisons) with modern praetorianism (safeguarding the regime's legitimacy). Two general types of praetorian armies have been classified: the ruler and the arbitrator. The ruler type is most advanced in the Middle East; the arbitrator is found generally in Latin America. The Latin American phenomenon is an advanced modern praetorian model from which a projection can be made regarding the future of praetorianism and civil-military relations in non-Western states.

Latin America has gone through a full cycle of praetorianism. Most Latin American states became independent a century and a half before the Middle Eastern and African states. They experimented with military personal rule (caudillismo) and with military reform. In Latin America the military was professionalized at the end of the nineteenth century, and, with the adoption of military reforms, corporate professionalism was institutionalized. The Latin American military accepted various phases—liberal, progressive, fascist, and radical nationalist—and generally succeeded in establishing an arbitrator rule. Yet since the middle 1960s Brazil, Argentina, Chile, and Peru had demonstrated that the military had abandoned its iron law of arbitration. Now it was propelled, despite its mainstream orientation, into the exercise of political dominance and rule. Either to advance mass mobilization or to harness the processes of change, the military had gained an unprecedented ascendancy, even judged by Latin American standards. Though launched as a revolutionary group motivated by the progressive ideas of the times (Comtism, positivism, liberalism, nationalism, and modernization), the military in Latin America had deserted political liberalism, thereby curtailing modernization and restricting mobilization. The military in a few Latin American states was a reactionary force, propelled by anti-socialist, anti-Castro inclinations. The sword was two-edged. Aspiring to the role of ruler on behalf of modernization, serving as an instrument to counter the socialist revolution, the Latin American praetorians were caught in processes of rapid change. They were not necessarily future-oriented, nor did they have a clear conception of their role in the modernization-mobilization revolution, but they did seek to act as a brake on the revolution or confront it pragmatically on a short-term basis.

While the Latin American military was undergoing the challenge of change, the Middle Eastern and African armies were still limited to the narrow concept of a national revolution, for they had not yet had to meet the modernization-mobilization challenge. (In my view, praetorians are most successful in meeting socioeconomic challenges on a short-term, pragmatic basis.) It is likely that, as the forces of modernization and social mobilization gain momentum in the Middle East and Africa, more praetorian rulers will appear. The 1970s and 1980s may become the age of persistent corporate praetorianism in the Middle East and Africa.

On the surface, most Latin American, most Middle Eastern, and some African militaries are revolutionary. Their pronunciamientos approximate the rhetoric of modern revolutions, of nationalism, socialism, and the modernization and mobilization movements. Actually, praetorians are incomplete revolutionary soldiers. Operating in a praetorian environment, they are physically and organizationally a resilient group. They opt for intervention sometimes as a result of their own aspirations, but in the absence of their own power or interest, circumstances may dictate the use of the sword. Their revolutionary aspiration is further mitigated by their corporate orientation, which takes precedence over all other beliefs. And, if corporatism does not supersede their commitment to progressive ideals, the ideals themselves are harnessed to corporate uses. The military may participate in the modernization revolution and social mobilization but it will always view them as potential threats. A comprehensive social and political revolution is considered a danger that might, and in some cases does, annihilate the corporate professional soldier.

Praetorian rule grows in proportion to military intervention and rule. The longer the intervention, the better the chances for praetorianism.

The greater the disenchantment with society, the stronger is the fear of the demise of military corporatism and the wider are the horizons of the ruler type. That has been the case, paradoxically, in both low-mobilization polities such as Syria, South Arabia, and most sub-Saharan and Central American states and in high-mobilization polities like Brazil and Argentina. Thus the corporate orientation fosters the urge to leap into the political culture of the modern revolutionary age. Once the military gains autonomy in a political system and is without serious rivals, it may aspire to fulfill several types of revolutions—nationalist, socialist, and modernization. Dedicated to youth, revolution, action, and anti-establishmentarianism, romantic revolutionary soldiers like the Storm Troopers and the Red Guards have been ultimately unsuccessful in their attempts to destroy all vestiges of political order, including the military establishment itself. The Red Guards were as dedicated to smashing the professional military as the Storm Troopers were dedicated to revolutionalizing the Reichswehr. In short, when the military aspires to dominate politics and be "above the battle," it can also resort to the most violent type of praetorianism, thus bringing about its own demise and sometimes even national disaster.

The only type of soldier that has achieved professional proficiency and pride in addition to high status in his society and state is the professional revolutionary soldier. The revolutionary soldier type demonstrates that professionalism and corporatism are not necessarily linked and that one is not needed to advance the other. A professional stance does not necessarily prevent intervention; nor does a corporate orientation necessarily bring about intervention. High professional performance and corporate pride have been enhanced by the least corporate-oriented of all soldiers—the revolutionaries. The autonomy of the military organization in Israel and China has guaranteed both high professionalism and political subordination. The revolutionary soldier is more value-oriented than the other types. His ability to cope with the revolutionary environment and his influential role in foreign and defense policy are positive factors. He is subordinate to a movement, party, or regime that is certainly more resilient than the military, even if the latter is a major factor in the making of the revolution, as it was in China and North Vietnam. The PLA has been as much a nation-builder as the CCP. The IDF has been not only an instrument of Zionism but a Zionist-oriented military. The civilians and military in China and Israel, however different, have participated in the full life of the revolution, the nation, and the society. An instrumental or mechanical subordination of the military has characterized the status quo powers, the states of Western Europe, the United States, the USSR; but in China, North Vietnam, and Israel the subordination of the military to a higher political authority has not been instrumental but organic.

While the historical professional soldier in the West has been declining, the revolutionary soldier has been on the rise. The classical professional, losing his influence in a complex society, has not inspired the best of the nation to join the military. In Western Europe and the United States, the more industrious and talented citizens have joined the civic society. In China and especially in Israel, the opposite has been true.

In Israel, society has been the army's reservoir. Universal military obligation has required every young man to serve in the armed forces for no less than three years. The officers are the flower of the nation. As a nation-in-arms, the whole society has been in uniform during crises, as in May–June 1967 and in October 1973. The professional army has been small, with less than 100,000 members, but it has been constantly rejuvenated because of the unwritten law that individuals should not make military service their only career. The army's high professionalism, as high among veterans as among junior regulars, combined with a close identification between people and army, has produced one of the world's best and most dedicated military forces whose influence on society and politics has been considerable but reciprocal. In the case of China, the military as a revolutionary leader and the officer as a model personality have contributed to the nation's achievements under the guidance of the CCP. In a sense, the military has been even more autonomous in China than in Israel, and it has served only one aspect, however important, of the revolution. It has not, however, rejuvenated itself. Bizarre as it may sound, the mantle of the historical professional soldier has been placed on the shoulders of Israel and China. This has occurred precisely because their military and society have been *innovative*.

Praetorians on the whole are not innovative. The Latin American military have emulated the Prussian spirit in structure and in form but not in content or in fact. Their Spanish legacy has abetted praetorianism rather than encouraged innovation. In the Middle East and Africa, senior officers of the first generation have modeled themselves after their opposite numbers in Ottoman Turkey, Britain, France, and the USSR. Yet these models and legacies have weighed heavily on the former colonial militaries. The slavish ceremonial emulation of the Nigerian army and the Indian officers' attempts to re-create their British model have produced corporate-seeking, status-seeking officers at the expense of innovation.[7] The "apolitical" Sandhurst type became in Africa an administrative ruler and an interventionist; in Pakistan, he became a praetorian. The second-generation Arab military generally was spared slavish emulation of the British officer; instead, the independent, native military academies of Egypt, Syria, and Iraq strove to duplicate sultanism. The one British-trained military in the Middle East, the Jordanian Legion (later the Jordanian army) has been, with the exception of Lebanon's army, the only noninterventionist military in the area. It has been a native military, however, and the most innovative of all Arab armies. Another successful native military has been the tribal armies in Yemen, which defeated the Egyptian army. Although inspired by nationalism and other modern ideas, the Arab Middle Eastern officers' only legacy, curiously, has been sultanist and Ottoman. They have been less tainted by foreign training and influence than Africans and Latin Americans, but they have become just as praetorian and even less innovative.

The militaries of the Middle East and Africa and the Indian subcontinent have been notoriously unimaginative and parochial. Although the Islamic civilization has proclaimed a legacy of military might and glory, neither quality has been apparent in the Arab failures against Israel and against one another, or in the Pakistani loss to India. Adversity, foreign enemies, and oppression have been insufficient to produce the military innovations found in Israel and China. Praetorianism is the result of political decay and of the decay of a historical political culture. The revolutionary soldier, the product of a new political culture and creator of a new military culture, is the one who has devised an alternative type of military professionalism.

Notes

PREFACE

1. Harold D. Lasswell, "The Garrison State," *American Journal of Sociology* 46 (January 1941): 455–68.

2. Samuel A. Stouffer et al., *The American Soldier* (Princeton, N. J.: Princeton University Press, 1949).

3. Samuel P. Huntington, *The Soldier and the State* (Cambridge, Mass.: Harvard University Press, 1957); Morris Janowitz, *The Professional Soldier* (Chicago: Free Press, 1960).

4. John J. Johnson, ed., *The Role of the Military in Underdeveloped Countries* (Princeton, N. J.: Princeton University Press, 1962). For a description of several of the monographs in this volume, see my article "The Arab Military Elite," in *World Politics* 22, no. 2 (January 1970): 273–74.

5. See Samuel P. Huntington, "The Change to Change: Modernization, Development, and Politics," *Comparative Politics* 3 (April 1971): 294.

CHAPTER 1

1. N. Elias, "Professions," in *A Dictionary of the Social Sciences*, ed. J. Gould and W. Kolb (New York: Free Press, 1964), p. 542.

2. These variables on professional and bureaucratic orientations are borrowed from Peter Blau and Richard Scott, *Formal Organizations* (San Francisco: Chandler, 1962), pp. 60–63.

3. Ibid., p. 62.

4. Ibid., p. 54. Italics mine.

5. Some of these ideas derive from ibid., p. 63.

6. Samuel P. Huntington "Power, Expertise and the Military Profession," *Daedalus* 92 (1963): 785–807.

7. Samuel P. Huntington, *The Soldier and the State* (Cambridge, Mass.: Harvard University Press, 1957), pp. 83–85.

8. R. K. Betts, "Soldiers, Statesmen, and the Resort to Force: American Military in Crisis Decisions; 1945–1975" (Ph. D. diss., Harvard University, 1975), p. 612.

9. D. Waldo, *The Administrative State* (New York: Ronald Press, 1948).

10. Samuel P. Huntington, *The Common Defense* (New York: Columbia University Press, 1961), pp. 1–25.

11. Betts, "Soldiers, Statesmen, and the Resort to Force," pp. 1–47.

12. Huntington, *The Common Defense*, pp. 1–25.

13. D. Yergin, "The National Security State" (Ph. D. diss., Cambridge University, 1974); Harold D. Lasswell, "The Garrison State," *American Journal of Sociology* 46 (January 1941): 455–68; and also his "The Garrison State Hypothesis Today," in *Changing Patterns of Military Politics*, ed. S. P. Huntington (New York: Free Press, 1962), pp. 51–70.

14. Samuel P. Huntington, *Political Order in Changing Societies* (New Haven: Yale University Press, 1968); James B. Crowley, *Japan's Quest for Autonomy* (Princeton, N.J.: Princeton University Press, 1966); Robert O'Neill, *The German Army and the Nazi Party, 1933–1939* (London: Cassell, 1966); Amos Perlmutter, "Israel's Fourth War, October 1973: Political and Military Misperception," *Orbis* (1975), p. 29.

15. Lasswell, "The Garrison State Hypothesis Today," pp. 51–70.

16. Huntington, *The Common Defense*, pp. 3–5.

17. Betts, "Soldiers, Statesmen, and the Resort to Force," pp. 70–253.

18. Philip Selznick, *The Organizational Weapon* (Chicago: Free Press, 1952); Amitai Etzioni, *A Comparative Analysis of Complex Organizations* (New York: Free Press, 1961); and his *Complex Organizations: A Sociological Reader*, 2d ed. (New York: Holt, Rinehart, 1971); H. Simon and J. March, *Organizations* (New York: Wiley, 1957); H. Simon, *Administrative Behavior*, 2d ed. (New York: Macmillan, 1957).

19. Sheldon Wolin, *Politics and Vision* (Boston: Little Brown, 1960), p. 353.

20. A comprehensive bibliography on military organization, sociology, and organizational ideology can be found in Kurt Lang, "Military Organizations," in *Handbook of Organizations*, ed. James March (Chicago: Rand McNally, 1966). The leading exponent of the role of the sociology of the military organization and its organization ideology is Morris Janowitz. See his *The Professional Soldier* (Chicago: Free Press, 1960). See also Lang, "Military Organizations," pp. 838–78; M. D. Feld, "A Typology of Military Organizations," *Yearbook* (School of Public Administration, Harvard University, 1958), pp. 3–40, Morris Janowitz, *Sociology and the Military Establishment* (New York: Russell Sage, 1959); Janowitz, "Changing Patterns of Organizational Authority: The Military Establishment," *Administrative Science Quarterly* 3 (1959): 473–93; Samuel Stouffer et al., *The American Soldier* (Princeton, N.J.: Princeton University Press, 1949).

21. For an analytical explanation, see chapter 4.

22. William Thompson, "Explanations of the Military Coup" (Ph. D. diss., University of Washington, Seattle, 1972), pp. 161–67, esp. table 5.1, which deals with the association between organizational military subsystem strength and coups.

23. Samuel P. Huntington, *The Soldier and the State* (New York: Vintage Books, 1957), pp. 69–72.

24. Ibid., p. 71.

25. See Huntington, *The Common Defense*; Richard Challener, *Admirals, Generals and American Foreign Policy* (Princeton, N.J.: Princeton University Press, 1973); Peter Karsten, *The Naval Aristocracy* (New York: Macmillan, 1972).

26. Huntington, *The Soldier and the State*, p. 79.

27. Ibid., pp. 11–18, and Huntington, *Political Order in Changing Societies*, pp. 192–98.

28. The quotations are from Gerald D. Feldman, *Army, Industry, and Labor in Germany, 1914–1918* (Princeton, N.J.: Princeton University Press, 1966), pp. 3, 41, and 27.

29. Stanislav Andreski, *Military Organization and Society*, 2d ed. (Berkeley and Los Angeles: University of California Press, 1971). Both quotations are on p. 105.

CHAPTER 2

1. For an analysis of subjective-objective regime types, see Samuel P. Huntington,

The Soldier and the State (Cambridge, Mass.: Harvard University Press, 1957), pp. 80–85.

2. David Easton, *A System Analysis of Political Life* (New York: Wiley, 1965), p. 287.

3. Max Weber, *Economy and Society*, ed. Guenther Roth and Claus Wittich, 3 vols. (New York: The Bedminister Press, 1968), 3: 946 (source of quotation), 952–55; Easton, *System Analysis*, pp. 193–210.

4. Easton, *System Analysis*, p. 278 (source of quotation); Robert Bierstedt, "The Problem of Authority," in *Freedom and Control in Modern Society*, ed. Morroe Berger, Theodore Able, and Charles Page (New York: Octagon Books, 1964), p. 70; Weber, *Economy and Society*, 1: 223; Reinhard Bendix, *Max Weber: An Intellectual Portrait* (New York: Doubleday, 1960), pp. 301–02. The ideology of a civic order is that any alternative is unstable and that community population support for civil order is tainted by its civic orientations.

5. Herbert Simon, "Rationality," in *Dictionary of the Social Sciences*, ed. Julius Gould and W. J. Kolb (New York: Free Press, 1964), p. 573.

6. Weber, *Economy and Society* 1:217, 241; 3:976, 981 (source of quotation; my italics), 1005.

7. Ibid., 1: 220; 3: 981; 1: 225 (source of first quotation); 3: 972 (source of second quotation).

8. This point is disputed in the literature. Critics of Weber claim that he failed to differentiate between degrees of bureaucratization in his zeal to explain the inexorable march of rationalization. Alvin Gouldner, in *Patterns of Industrial Bureaucracy* (Glencoe, Ill.: Free Press, 1954), and Helen Constas, in "Max Weber's Two Conceptions of Bureaucracy," *American Journal of Sociology* 63 (1956): 400–09, argue that Weber failed to differentiate between technical (serving) bureaucracies and punishment (authoritarian-ruling) bureaucracies. Thus Weber saw "bureaucracy as a Janus-faced organization. On the one side, it was administration based on expertise; on the other, it was administration based on discipline" (Gouldner, pp. 24–25).

9. Ibid., 3: 959 (source of quotation), 20.

10. Huntington, *The Soldier and the State*, p. 83.

11. Louis B. Hartz, *The Founding of Modern Societies* (New York: Harcourt, Brace & World, 1966), p. 5.

12. Amos Perlmutter, *Military and Politics in Israel: Nation-Building and Role Expansion* (New York: Praeger, 1969), p. 22.

13. Huntington, *The Soldier and the State*, p. 1 (source of quotation). Some of the ideas in this paragraph were discussed with my colleague M. D. Feld at the Center for International Affairs, Harvard University. I have also borrowed here from his unpublished paper "Mass Armies and the Professional Soldier" (Center for International Affairs, Harvard, 1973). The most significant literature dealing with the professional soldier is Huntington, *The Soldier and the State*; Morris Janowitz, *The Professional Soldier* (Glencoe, Ill.: Free Press, 1960); S. E. Finer, *The Man on Horseback* (New York: Praeger, 1962); Gaetano Mosca, *The Ruling Class*, ed. and trans. Arthur Livingston (New York: McGraw-Hill, 1939); Alfred Vagts, *A History of Militarism*, 2d ed. (New York: Meridien, 1959).

14. Feld, "Mass Armies," p. 4 (source of quotation); David C. Rapoport, "A Comparative Theory of Military and Political Types," in *Changing Patterns of Military*

Politics, ed. Samuel P. Huntington (New York: Free Press, 1962), pp. 88–96. The phrase "revolutionary circumstance" is borrowed from Feld, "Mass Armies," p. 8.

15. For the most comprehensive analysis of professional warfare, see Michael Howard, *The Franco-Prussian War* (New York: Macmillan, 1962), pp. 1–40. See also Richard M. Challener, *The French Theory of Nation-in-Arms* (New York: Russell & Russell, 1965), pp. 5–11.

16. Feld, "Mass Armies," p. 15.

17. Huntington, *The Soldier and the State,* pp. 59–79; Feld, "Mass Armies," p. 18 (source of quotation).

18. A. M. Carr-Saunders and P. A. Wilson, *The Professions* (London: Oxford University Press, 1933), pp. 289, 291–94, 295, 300–04. See also Huntington, *The Soldier and the State,* pp. 8–16.

19. Huntington points out that Carr-Saunders and Wilson have omitted the military profession from their analysis "because the service which soldiers are trained to render is one which it is hoped they will never be called upon to perform." Carr-Saunders and Wilson, *The Professions,* p. 3, quoted in Huntington, *The Soldier and the State,* p. 469, n. 1. Huntington's copious but often neglected footnotes should be consulted by all those interested in reviewing the literature on the military in Prussia-Germany, England, and France, from which Huntington's model has been derived. See esp. pp. 469–72, 475–77, 479–80. Janowitz, in his *Professional Soldier* (pp. 1–7), presents an empirical investigation of five military "professional" and "military mind" hypotheses and reaches conclusions that reiterate most of Huntington's theoretical formulations.

20. For the genesis of these and other concepts of corporate professionalism, see Carr-Saunders and Wilson, *The Professions,* pt. 1; N. Elias, "Corporatism," in *Dictionary of the Social Sciences,* ed. Julius Gould and W. J. Kolb (New York: Free Press, 1964); Talcott Parsons, "Professions," *International Encyclopedia of Social Science,* vol. 12 (New York: Macmillan and Free Press, 1968), 536–47; Huntington, *The Soldier and the State,* pp. 7–58; Janowitz, *The Professional Soldier,* pp. 3–20; Talcott Parsons, "The Professions and Social Structure," *Essays in Sociological Theory,* rev. ed. (Chicago: Free Press, 1954); and Bernard Barber, "Some Problems in the Sociology of the Prussians," *Daedalus* 92, no. 4 (fall 1963): 669–88. I have been heavily influenced by the writings of Max Weber in formulating these concepts. See his *Economy and Society,* ed. Guenther Roth and Claus Wittich, 3 vols. (New York; The Bedminister Press, 1968), and *The Protestant Ethic and the Spirit of Capitalism* (New York: Charles Scribner's 1958). See also Stanislaw Andrzejewski, *Military Organization and Society* (London: Routledge & Kegan, Paul, 1954).

21. Talcott Parsons, "Professions," in *International Encyclopedia of Social Science,* 12: 536, 545.

22. Huntington, *The Soldier and the State,* pp. 80–86.

23. See Finer, *Man on Horseback,* pp. 6–71. W. H. Morris-Jones, "Armed Forces and the State," *Public Administration* 35 (winter 1957): 411–16. Finer speaks of the "mood" and "disposition" to intervene (*Man on Horseback,* pp. 61–71).

24. Martin Kitchen, *The German Officer Corps, 1890–1914* (Oxford: Clarendon Press, 1968), p. 30, paraphrased from Colmar von der Goltz, *The Nation in Arms* (London: Macmillan, 1906), p. 51. For an excellent analysis of this type of cere-

monialism and military-organization inelasticity, see Morris Janowitz, "Changing Patterns of Organizational Authority: The Military Establishment," *Administrative Science Quarterly* 3 (March 1969): 473–93.

25. "Military mind" is Huntington's term (*The Soldier and the State*, p. 59). Huntington and Andreski have constructed a civil-military typology and suggested different military and civilian regime types on the basis of the relationship between the military ethic and the social ideology.

26. Huntington, *The Soldier and the State*, p. 15.

27. M. D. Feld has drawn a number of conclusions from his study of military alienation in France, Germany, Great Britain, Russia, Japan, and the United States during the years from 1860 to 1960. I am most grateful to Feld for our conversations and for his stimulating essay "Professionalism, Nationalism, and the Alienation of the Military," in *Armed Forces in Society*, ed. Jacques Van Doorn (The Hague: Mouten, 1969), pp. 55–70, which inspired several of these ideas.

28. In the words of Feld, "since the military policy of a secular society has as its objective the creation of an apolitical armed force and the social policy of the professional soldier has as its objective the creation of an apolitical society, sustained and equal partnership between the two is impossible" (ibid., p. 70).

29. Barber, "Sociology of the Prussians," pp. 676–78.

30. Correlli Barnett, *Britain and Her Army* (London: Allen Lane, Penguin Press, 1970), pp. xviii, xx.

31. Lawrence Stone, *The Crisis of the Aristocracy* (Oxford: Clarendon, 1965), p. 216; Barnett, *Britain and Her Army*, pp. 116–17; Winston Churchill, *Marlborough: His Life and Times* (London: George Harrar, 1947), book 1, pp. 424–65.

32. Philip Abrams, "The Late Profession of Arms," *Archives europeennes de sociologie* 6 (1965): 240–61.

CHAPTER 3

1. The cases of Prussian-Germany, France, Japan, and the USSR are based on my analysis of new monographic literature that in several cases is revisionist in scope and interpretation. My interpretation is also revisionist. The footnotes indicate only the prominent and most suggestive works of a bourgeoning literature on civil-military relations, especially in Germany and France. I have made the selections analytically, in many cases to provide historical and comparative evidence to support my generalizations on corporate professionalism. Thus, I deal only with short periods of military rise and fall, especially in Germany and Japan, and focus on the "oppression" and alienation of the French and Soviet officer class. Far from being a comprehensive overview, this chapter is an analytic kaleidoscope concentrating on the critical years in civil-military relations and their consequences for both the state and the military establishment. The function of the social scientist, in my view, is to focus on what he considers to be the critical points of departure in history and politics.

2. Samuel P. Huntington, *The Soldier and the State* (Cambridge, Mass.: Harvard University Press, 1957), pp. 98–124. The literature on the role of the military in Prussia-Germany is expanding enormously. The most authoritative studies in German, English, and French are Gordon A. Craig, *The Politics of the Prussian Army, 1640–1945* (New York: Oxford University Press, 1956); Benoist-Mechin, *L'Histoire de l'armee*

allemande (Paris: Michel, 1964–66); Harold J. Gordon, *The Reichswehr and the German Republic, 1919–1926* (Princeton, N.J.: Princeton University Press, 1957); J. W. Wheeler-Bennett, *The Nemesis of Power: The German Army in Politics, 1918–1945,* 1st ed. (New York: St. Martin's, 1953); F. L. Carsten, *The Reichswehr and Politics, 1918–1933* (Oxford: Clarendon Press, 1966); and Martin Kitchen, *The German Officer Corps, 1890–1914* (Oxford: Clarendon Press, 1968).

3. Karl Demeter, *The German Officer Corps in Society and State, 1650–1945* (New York: Praeger, 1965), p. 8. Cadets of old Prussian origins in 1860 constituted 89 percent; in 1864, 83.5 percent; and in 1869, 77.8 percent (p. 23). See Craig, *Prussian Army,* pp. 37–81.

4. Bernard Lewis, *The Emergence of Modern Turkey* (London: Oxford University Press, 1958). See also chapter 5 of this book.

5. Craig, *Prussian Army,* p. 80.

6. Ibid.

7. Gerhard Ritter, *The Sword and the Scepter: The Prussian Tradition, 1740–1890,* vol. 1 (Coral Gables, Fla.: University of Miami Press, 1969), p. 161.

8. Ibid., pp. 178–79. On Bismarck's military policy and attitude toward the army, see ibid., pp. 160–232; O. Pflantz, *Bismarck and the Development of Germany, 1815–1871* (Princeton, N.J.: Princeton University Press, 1964); Erich Eyck, *Bismarck and the German Empire* (London: Allen & Unwin, 1950); Ludwig Dehio, "Bismarck und die Heeresubnlangen der Konflikszeitt," in *Heer und Stadt,* ed. Ernst R. Huber (Hamburg, 1938), pp. 220–225.

9. The most recent contribution to the study of social change during the era of German unification is Theodore Hamerow, *The Social Foundations of German Unification, 1858–1871* (Princeton, N.J.: Princeton University Press, 1969); and Hamerow, *Restoration, Revolution, Reaction: Economics and Politics in Germany, 1815–1871* (Princeton, N.J.: Princeton University Press, 1958).

10. Hamerow, *Social Foundations,* pp. 82–83; Bramsted, *Aristocracy and the Middle Classes in Germany* (Chicago: Phoenix Books, University of Chicago Press, 1964) (first published in 1937); Kitchen, *German Officer Corps;* Fritz Stern, *The Failure of Illiberalism* (New York: Knopf, 1972); Walter Struve, *Elites Against Democracy* (Princeton, N.J.: Princeton University Press, 1973).

11. Hamerow, *Social Foundations,* p. 83.

12. Kitchen, *German Officer Corps,* p. 119.

13. Ibid., p. 119.

14. Hamerow, *Social Foundations,* p. 276.

15. Kitchen, *German Officer Corps,* p. 119.

16. Hamerow, *Social Foundations,* p. 278.

17. Ibid., p. 308.

18. Kitchen, *German Officer Corps,* p. 118.

19. Ibid., pp. 30, 120 (source of quotation), 140–42, 115–28.

20. The most elaborate analysis of the militarization of the bourgeoisie is found in Ritter, *The Sword and the Scepter.* See also Kitchen, *German Officer Corps,* pp. 130–42.

21. Hamerow, *Social Foundations,* p. 275.

22. Ibid., p. 230.

23. Ibid., p. 232.

24. Ibid., p. 235.

25. Ibid., p. 237.

26. Ibid., p. 257.

27. Ibid., p. 263.

28. Stern, *The Failure of Illiberalism*, p. xvii; Ralf Dahrendorff, *Society and Democracy in Germany* (Garden City, N.Y.: Doubleday, 1965).

29. Ibid.

30. Ibid., p. 30.

31. Walter Goerlitz, *History of the German General Staff* (New York: Praeger, 1953), pp. 69–102.

32. Craig, *Prussian Army*, pp. 192–93, pp. 204–16; and Goerlitz, *German General Staff*, pp. 89–94. Moltke's resistance to Bismarck in 1870 could have ruined Bismarck's carefully designed diplomacy and his accord in Paris, but Bismarck finally prevailed.

33. Kitchen, *German Officer Corps*, p. xv.

34. Ibid., p. xx.

35. On bureaucratic authoritarianism in Prussia, see Hans Rosenberg, *Bureaucracy, Aristocracy and Autocracy: The Prussian Experience, 1660–1815* (Cambridge, Mass.: Harvard University Press, 1966). The quotation is from Rosenberg, p. 23.

36. Kitchen, *German Officer Corps*, pp. 49–50.

37. Gerald Feldman, *Army, Industry and Labor in Germany, 1914–1918* (Princeton, N.J.: Princeton University Press, 1966), pp. 33–38 (quotation on p. 35).

38. Wolfgang Sauer, "Militarismus," in *Staat und Politik*, ed. Ernst Fraenkel and Karl Bracher (Frankfurt am Main: Fischer Bücher, 1957), pp. 190–91.

39. Kitchen, *German Officer Corps*, p. 227 (source of quotation); Carsten, *Reichswehr*, pp. 4–5. On the mobilization of resources and the political expansion of the military in connection with the war effort, see Feldman, *Army, Industry and Labor*. On the concept of total war, see H. Speier, "Ludendorff: The German Concept of Total War," in *Makers of Modern Strategy*, ed. E. M. Earle (Princeton, N.J.: Princeton University Press, 1952), pp. 306–22.

40. Wilhelm Groener, *Lebenserinnerungen* (Göttingen: Göttingen Verlag, 1957), p. 466, quoted in Carsten, *Reichswehr*, p. 6.

41. Gordon, *Reichswehr*, p. 306.

42. On civil-military relations in Germany since 1918, see the classic studies of Craig (*The Politics of the Prussian Army*) and Wheeler-Bennett (*The Nemesis of Power*). A detailed account of civil-military relations in Weimar is found in Gordon, *Reichswehr*, pp. 307–431. A more recent and critical interpretation of the pre-Nazi policy is in Carsten, *Reichswehr*; see pp. 103–53 and 309–412 on the Nazi army. See also Robert O'Neill, *The German Army and the Nazi Party, 1933–1939* (London: Cassell, 1966). The monumental study by Bracher, Sauer, and Schultz, *Die Nationalsozialistische Machtbegreifung* (Kohls and Opalden: Westdeutsches Verlag, 1960), must be constantly consulted.

43. Quoted in Carsten, *Reichswehr*, p. 405.

44. Carsten, *Reichswehr*, p. 405.

45. O'Neill, *The German Army and the Nazi Party*.

46. Ibid., pp. 8–13.

47. Ibid., p. 30.

48. Ibid., pp. 170–73.

49. Ibid., p. 172.

50. Ibid.

51. Ibid.

52. Ibid., p. 173.

53. Ibid., pp. 174–75.

54. Karl D. Bracher, *The German Dictatorship* (New York: Praeger, 1970), pp. 236–37.

55. For details, see Wheeler-Bennett, *Nemesis of Power*, pp. 3–71 (quotation is from p. 226); Carsten, *Reichswehr*, pp. 335–40; Bracher et al., *Nationalsozialistische Machtbegreifung*; Wheeler-Bennett, *The Wooden Titan: Hindenburg* (London: Anchor Books, 1936).

56. David Ralston, ed., *Soldiers and States* (Boston: Heath, 1966), p. 116.

57. I am grateful to my friend and colleague David Ralston of M.I.T., without whom I could not have threaded my way through the maze of French revolutionary history. He also pointed out to me that the French, rather than the Prussian, army is the classical example of military corporatism. The quotation is from Girardet's *La Societe Militarie*, quoted and translated by Ralston in *Soldiers*, p. 116.

58. For excellent excerpts from Richelieu and Le Tellier, see Ralston, *Soldiers*, pp. 20–30.

59. R. R. Palmer, *Twelve Who Ruled* (Princeton, N. J.: Princeton University Press, 1941), p. 81.

60. I am indebted to David C. Rapoport for this analysis. See his "Comparative Theory of Military and Political Types," in *Changing Patterns of Military Politics*, ed. Samuel P. Huntington (Glencoe, Ill.: Free Press, 1962), pp. 88–96. The quotation from Henry Maine, *Popular Government*, 6th ed. (London: John Murray, 1909), p. 267, is in Rapoport, "Praetorianism: Government without Consensus" (Ph.D. diss., Univerrsity of California, Berkeley, 1960), p. 188.

61. Richard M. Challener, *The French Theory of Nation-in-Arms, 1866–1939* (New York: Russell & Russell, 1965), pp. 4–5; Alexis de Tocqueville, *Democracy in America*, trans. Henry Reeve (New York: Collier & Son, 1900), 2: 759, quoted in Rapoport, "Praetorianism," pp. 184–85.

62. Theodore Zeldin, *France 1849–1945* (Oxford: at Clarendon Press, 1974), 1: 504–05.

63. Ibid., p. 505.

64. Ibid., p. 508.

65. Ibid., p. 518.

66. Ibid., p. 508.

67. Ibid., p. 519.

68. Ibid., p. 519.

69. Ralston, *Soldiers*, pp. 131–200. The best study of the rise of the modern professional French army is Raoul Girardet's *La Société militaire dans la France contemporaine, 1815–1939* (Paris: Plon, 1939).

70. Ralston, *Soldiers*, p. 11.

71. Challener, *French Theory*, pp. 5–6.

72. For a most penetrating analysis, see Michael Howard, *The Franco-Prussian War* (New York: Macmillan, 1962), pp. 1–40.

73. David Ralston, *The Army of the Republic: The Place of the Military in the Political Evolution of France, 1871–1914* (Cambridge, Mass.: M.I.T. Press, 1967), p. 128.

74. Philip C. F. Bankwitz, *Maxime Weygand and Civil-Military Relations in Modern France* (Cambridge, Mass.: Harvard University Press, 1967), pp. 209–89. See also Challener, *French Theory*, chap. 1; and Ralston, *Army of the Republic*, pp. 138–39. Ralston is obviously not responsible for my interpretation of his historical analysis.

75. Ralston, *Army of the Republic*, p. 3. This is corroborated by Challener, *French Theory*, and by John Ambler, *The French Army in Politics, 1945–1962* (Columbus: Ohio State University Press, 1966).

76. Ralston, *Army of the Republic*, pp. 373 (quotation), pp. 374–375.

77. Ibid., p. 372.

78. A typology of republican styles of French generals is found in an unpublished 1967 paper by David Ralston, "From Boulanger to Pétain: Changing Styles of Republic Generalship." On Weygand, see Bankwitz, *Weygand*, pp. 208–89.

79. Judith Hughes, *To the Maginot Line* (Cambridge, Mass.: Harvard University Press, 1971), p. 160.

80. Ibid., pp. 101, 111, 258 (source of quotation). See Marc Bloch, *Strange Defeat* (London: Oxford University Press, 1949).

81. Richard Griffiths, *Pétain* (Garden City, N. Y.: Doubleday, 1972), p. 162.

82. Three authors have covered this period brilliantly. Robert Paton, *Parades and Politics at Vichy* (Princeton, N.J.: Princeton University Press, 1967), pp. 410–27; George A. Kelly, *Lost Soldiers: The French Army and the Empire in Crisis, 1947–1962* (Cambridge, Mass.: M.I.T. Press, 1965); and Ambler, *French Army*. The quotation is from Stanley Hoffmann, "Collaborationism in France during World War II," *The Journal of Modern History* 40 (September 1968): 381.

83. Paxton, *Parades*, pp. 410–22. Ambler, *French Army*, pp. 128–245.

84. Ambler, *French Army*, pp. 132–33.

85. See Paxton's account of the return of the officers of the Armistice Army to dominate the high command and middle echelons of the French army of the 1950s in *Parades*. The leaders of that army, Generals Ely, Teller, Juin, and Rever, the Algerian "rebels" of 1958, and the veterans of the Indo-China War of 1954 (de Lattre), were former Vichy officers. Paxton, *Parades*, pp. 410–32 (quotation on p. 422).

86. Harold D. Lasswell, "The Garrison State," *American Journal of Sociology* 46 (January 1941): 455–68.

87. My analysis of Japanese civil-military relations, like my analyses of Germany and France, is based on those secondary sources that present the balanced judgments of historians, political scientists, and social scientists. In my view, James B. Crowley, *Japan's Quest for Autonomy* (Princeton, N.J.: Princeton University Press, 1966), is a definitive study of the Japanese military of the 1930s, and much of my interpretation is based on it. I have also consulted numerous other studies on the 1930s, of which the following should be mentioned: Akira Iriye, *After Imperialism* (Cambridge, Mass.: Harvard University Press, 1965); the summary essay on Japanese militarism by Roger B. Hackett, "The Military in Japan," in *Political Modernization in Japan and Turkey*, ed.

R. A. Ward and D. A. Rostow (Princeton, N.J.: Princeton University Press, 1964), pp. 283–300; and, above all, "Studies in the Modernization of Japan," 7 vols. (Princeton, N.J.: Princeton University Press, 1965–1972).

88. Marius B. Jansen, *Sakamoto Ryoma and the Meiji Restoration* (Princeton, N.J.: (Princeton University Press, 1961), pp. 3, 8 (source of quotation).

89. Ibid., p. 9.

90. See Hackett, "The Military in Japan," pp. 332–38. On Yamagata's successful introduction of universal military service, see Hackett, "The Meiji Leaders and Modernization: The Case of Yamagata Aritomo," in "Studies in the Modernization of Japan" (Princeton, N.J.: Princeton University Press, 1965–72), vol. 1, *Changing Japanese Attitudes toward Modernization*, ed. Marius Jansen (1965), pp. 253–61.

91. Johannes Hirschmeier, *The Origins of Entrepreneurship in Meiji Japan* (Cambridge, Mass.: Harvard University Press, 1964), p. 3.

92. This analysis is mainly based on a penetrating essay by Herschel Webb: "The Development of an Orthodox Attitude toward an Imperial Institution in the Fifteenth Century," in *Changing Japanese Attitudes*, ed. Marius Jensen, pp. 167–91 (quotation from p. 167).

93. Ibid., pp. 168 (quotation), 189, 190.

94. See Crowley, *Japan's Quest*, pp. xiv–xv.

95. Ibid., pp. 24–25.

96. Ibid., pp. 83–86.

97. Ibid., pp. 82–121, 244–300. James Crowley, "Japanese Army Factionalism in the Early 1930's," *Journal of Asian Studies* 21 (May 1962): 309–26. The quotation is from Akira Iriye, "The Failure of Military Expansionism," in *Dilemmas of Growth in Pre-War Japan*, ed. James W. Morley (Princeton, N.J.: Princeton University Press, 1971), p. 107.

98. Iriye, "Failure of Military Expansionism," p. 237.

99. Huntington, *The Soldier*, p. 83 (emphasis added).

100. The most detailed and comprehensive history of the Soviet army to 1941 is John Erickson, *The Soviet High Command, 1918–1941* (London: Macmillan, 1962). I have greatly benefited from this erudite and scholarly study. See also D. Fedotov-White, *The Growth of the Red Army* (Princeton, N.J.: Princeton University Press, 1944). B. H. Liddell-Hart, *The Red Army* (New York: Harcourt, Brace, 1956), is an excellent compendium. Raymond Garthoff's *The Soviet Military Doctrine* (Glencoe, Ill.: Free Press, 1953) provides an analysis of the Soviet army since 1945. The most comprehensive analysis of army-party relationships is Roman Kolkowicz's *The Soviet Military and the Communist Party* (Princeton, N.J.: Princeton University Press, 1967). See Zbigniew Brzezinski and Samuel P. Huntington, "Cincinnatus and the Apparatchik," in their *Political Power USA/USSR* (New York: Viking, 1962). See also the recent compendium on the army and World War II in Seweryn Bialer, *Stalin and His Generals* (New York: Pegasus, 1969), in which various military revisionist (Soviet) interpretations of the role of the military in World War II are given. H. Dinerstein et al. have provided an excellent translation and interpretation of Marshal V. D. Sokolovsky's *Soviet Military Doctrine* (Englewood Cliffs, N.J.: Prentice-Hall, 1963).

The best analyses of Soviet military power since the death of Stalin are John Erickson, *Soviet Military Power* (London: Royal United Services Institute, 1971), and

Thomas W. Wolfe, *Soviet Power and Europe, 1945–1970* (Baltimore: Johns Hopkins Press, 1970). The latter provides the most extensive bibliography on the subject. Wolfe's footnotes are most useful for the specialist in military affairs. I am also grateful to Professor Erickson for responding to my direct inquiries, and for permitting me to read several of his unpublished papers on Soviet society and military rejuvenation since the death of Stalin.

101. Kolkowicz, *Soviet Military*, p. 12.

102. See the penetrating observation of George Kennan in his *Memoirs* (Boston: Little, Brown, 1967), pp. 313–57; and also Robert Conquest, *The Great Terror* (New York: Macmillan, 1968).

103. For the analysis and history of the Red Army I relied completely on Erickson's monumental study of the Soviet high command, but he bears no responsibility for my interpretation and conceptualizations.

104. For an analysis of L'Armee Nouvelle, see Challener, *French Theory*, pp. 67–69, 71–74, 162–64. On Trotsky's role as commissar of war, see Leon Trotsky, *History of the Russian Revolution* (New York: Simon and Schuster, 1938), 3:88–199, and *My Life* (New York: Grosset, 1959). For an analysis of Trotsky the commissar of war, and of his political trials and tribulations, see Erickson, *Soviet Military Power*, pp. 113–43. On Trotsky's theories of the military and war, see Isaac Deutscher, *The Prophet Armed* (London: Oxford University Press, 1954), pp. 477–85. See also Trotsky, *Military Writings* (New York: Merit Publishers, 1969).

105. On Bonapartism and Bolshevism, see Trotsky, *History*, 1: 248–61; Deutscher, *The Prophet Armed*, pp. 325–45; and Garthoff, *Soviet Military Doctrine*.

106. Erickson, *Soviet Military Power*, p. 22. Kolkowicz summarizes the broad scope of the organs of political control in the military. Their essential functions may be summed up as (a) observation of activities in the units and passing the information to higher levels of the apparatus; (b) "politicalization" of military personnel through intensive indoctrination and political education; (c) regulation of the advancement of officers so that only those who are desirable from the party's point of view are promoted to positions of authority; (d) supervision and control of military as well as political activities within the unit; and (e) prompting of desired action or conduct through intimidation, threats of dismissal, public humiliation, or outright coercion. See Kolkowicz, *Soviet Military*, p. 92.

107. For a most interesting and comprehensive study of the Soviet-German military cooperation, derived from the German war documents, see Erickson, *Soviet Military Power*, pp. 144–63; on the debates over strategy, see pp. 131–43. See also Kolkowicz, *Soviet Military*, p. 36, and Leonard Shapiro, *The Communist Party of the Soviet Union* (New York: Random House, 1960).

108. See Erickson, *Soviet Military Power*, pp. 449–509; Conquest, *The Great Terror*, pp. 201–235; Kolkowicz, *Soviet Military*, pp. 50–57. The quotation is from Erickson, *Soviet Military Power*, p. 509.

109. For the party-army dialogue on professional autonomy between 1953 and 1964, see Kolkowicz, *Soviet Military*, pp. 103–73 (quotation on p. 103). See also Roman Kolkowicz, "Civil-Military Relations in Communist Systems" (Unpublished paper, Conference on Armed Forces and Society, Buffalo, N.Y., October 18, 1974). Kolkowicz, *Soviet Military*, pp. 312–13.

110. Wolfe, *Soviet Power*, p. 430.

111. For details on the Stalingrad Group see Kolkowicz, *Soviet Military*, pp. 220–81.

112. Kolkowicz, *Soviet Military*, pp. 220, 223. Stalin's "politicals," Voroshilov and Budenny, replaced Tukhachevsky and Blycher as the Stalingrad Group emerged with the rise of Khrushchev.

113. Ibid., pp. 221, 225 (source of quotation). Erickson, *Soviet Military Power*, pp. 45–51.

114. Kolkowicz, *Soviet Military*, pp. 324–26.

CHAPTER 4

1. Harold D. Lasswell, "The Garrison State," *American Journal of Sociology* 46 (January 1941), 455–58.

2. I am grateful to M. D. Feld of Harvard University for this analysis.

3. Max Weber, *Economy and Society*, ed. Guenther Roth and Claus Wittich, 3 vols. (New York: The Bedminster Press, 1968), 3:1006–69. The quotation is from p. 1013.

4. Ibid., pp. 1015–17.

5. Ibid., pp. 1020, 1013.

6. Gerhard Lenski, *Power and Privilege* (New York: McGraw-Hill, 1966), p. 243 (source of quotation); Albert H. Lybyer, *The Government of the Ottoman Empire* (New York: Russell & Russell, 1966), pp. 47–62.

7. M. D. Feld, "A Typology of Military Organization," in *Public Policy*, ed. Carl J. Friedrich and Seymour E. Harris (Cambridge, Mass.: Harvard University Press, 1958).

8. For quotations see ibid., pp. 8, 10.

9. Weber recognized that praetorianism might threaten legitimacy in the patrimonial state when the military was an alien professional establishment or when it represented a citizen army, but his analysis does not explain the process of political legitimation and the structural sustenance of praetorian rule. He saw praetorian domination as patrimonial or traditional rather than as an independent type of authority orientation. See S. N. Eisenstadt, *The Political Systems of Empires* (New York: The Free Press, 1963), pp. 172–73: and Weber, *Economy and Society*, 3:1006–69.

10. In the caudillismo case, personalism and violence united to seize the disintegrating patrimonial state apparatus. In the name of republicanism (in Latin America) and liberalism (in nineteenth-century Spain), caudillismo became the driving force of the nation. On personal, patriarchal, and patrimonial types of domination, see Weber, *Economy and Society*, vol. 3.

11. David C. Rapoport, "Praetorianism: Government without Consensus" (Ph.D. diss., University of California, Berkeley, 1960), pp. 14–15, defines praetorianism as a constitutional form of "government without consensus." Rapoport's thesis provides an outstanding theoretical discussion of praetorianism. Although I follow his definition, I emphasize the descriptive aspects of the subject and forego discussions of constitutionalism, consensus, and authority, which he covers at length. This part of my book has been directly influenced by the works of Samuel P. Huntington, especially his essay "Political Development and Political Decay," *World Politics* 18 (April 1965), 386–440. For some time, he and I have carried on an intellectual dialogue. Hopefully, the result has been a more positive approach to a theory of civil-military relations in

developing polities. Especially excellent is Huntington's chapter, "Praetorianism and Political Decay," in *Political Order in Changing Societies* (New Haven: Yale University Press, 1968), pp. 192–263. He argues there that the concept of praetorianism becomes a useful tool to explain the relationship between political development and modernization. In my view Huntington's analysis of the role of political decay in modernizing polities becomes most crucial in the case of praetorianism.

12. Huntington's central thesis in *Political Order* is the gap hypothesis, the idea that modernization breeds both political instability and praetorian order (pp. 32–33, 53–56). See Gino Germani and Kalman H. Silvert, "Politics, Social Structure and Military Intervention in Latin America," *Archives europeennes de sociologie* 2, no. 1 (1961): 62–81. Analysis of the breakdown in modernization is found in S. N. Eisenstadt's extensive studies of the relationships among traditionalism, modernization, and change. See especially his "Breakdown of Modernization," *Economic Development and Cultural Change* 12 (July 1964): 345–67; "Political Modernization: Some Comparative Notes," *International Journal of Comparative Sociology* 5 (March 1964): 3–24; *Modernization: Protest and Change* (Englewood Cliffs, N.J.: Prentice-Hall, 1966)

13. Talcott Parsons, *Structure of Social Action* (Glencoe, Ill: Free Press, 1937), p. 377.

14. See Nadav Safran, *Egypt in Search of Political Community* (Cambridge, Mass.: Harvard University Press, 1961), p. 2.

15. Wyatt MacGaffey and Clifford R. Barnett, *Cuba* (New Haven: Yale University Press, 1962), p. 144.

16. Morroe Berger, "The Middle Class in the Arab World," in *The Middle East in Transition*, ed. Walter Laqueur (New York: Praeger, 1958), pp. 63–65.

17. See Eisenstadt, *Political Systems of Empires*, esp. chaps. 6 and 7. For Eisenstadt, the promotion of "free resources and [the] freeing [of] resources from commitments to particularistic-ascriptive groups" (p. 119) is one of the conditions for the creation and maintenance of autonomous political institutions.

18. Huntington, *Political Order*, pp. 192–98; Amos Perlmutter, "The Arab Military Elite," *World Politics* 22, no. 2 (January 1970): 284–300; Amos Perlmutter, "Israel's Fourth War, October 1973: Political and Military Misperception," *Orbis* 29 (1975): 434–60; S. E. Finer, *The Man on Horseback: The Role of the Military in Politics* (London: Pall Mall Press, 1962), chap. 5.

19. William Thompson, "Explanations of the Military Coup" (Ph.D. diss., University of Washington, Seattle, 1972), pp. 81–124.

20. R. L. Gilmore, *Caudillism and Militarism in Venezuela, 1810–1919* (Athens: Ohio University Press, 1964); E. J. Hobsbawm, *Primitive Rebels* (New York: Norton, 1959); M. Janowitz, *The Military in the Political Development of New Nations: An Essay in Comparative Analysis* (Chicago: University of Chicago Press, 1964); G. W. Grayson, "Portugal and the Armed Forces Movement," *Orbis* 29 (Summer 1975): 335–78; M. C. Needler, *Political Development in Latin America: Instability, Violence, and Evolutionary Change* (New York: Random House, 1968), pp. 157–63;

21. Thompson, "Explanations of the Military Coup," pp. 82–97.

22. Ibid., pp. 99–103. See also M. Halpern, "The Problem of Becoming Conscious of the Salaried New Middle Class," *Comparative Studies in Society and History*, vol. 12, no. 1 (January 1970); Morroe Berger, "Military Elite and Social Change: Egypt Since

Napoleon," Research Monograph no. 6 (Princeton University: Center for International Studies, 1960); J. Nun, "The Middle Class Military Coup," in *The Politics of Conformity in Latin America*, ed. C. Veliz (London: Oxford University Press, 1967); L. North, *Civil-Military Relations in Argentina, Chile, and Peru*, Politics of Modernization Studies (Berkeley: Institute of International Studies, 1966); Huntington, *Political Order*; R. D. Putnam, "Toward Explaining Military Intervention in Latin American Politics," *World Politics*, vol. 20, no. 1 (October 1967); M. Halpern, *The Politics of Social Change in the Middle East and North Africa* (Princeton, N.J.: Princeton University Press, 1963); E. A. Nordlinger, "Soldiers in Mufti: The Impact of Military Rule upon Economic and Social Change in the Non-Western States," *American Political Science Review*, vol. 64, no. 4 (1970); Amos Perlmutter, "The Myth of the Myth of the New Middle Class: Some Lessons in Social and Political Theory," vol. 12, no. 1 (January 1970); and Amos Perlmutter, "The Arab Military Elite."

23. R. A. Hansen, "Military Culture and Organizational Decline: A Study of the Chilean Army" (Ph.D. diss., University of California, Los Angeles, 1967), pp. 127–165; Robert A. Potash, *The Army and Politics in Argentina: 1928–1945*, (Palo Alto, Calif.: Stanford University Press, 1969), pp. 182–200; June Hahner, *Brazilian Civil-Military Relations, 1889–1898* (Ithaca, N.Y.: Cornell University Press, 1966), p. 4; Eliezer Be'eri, *Army Officers in Arab Politics and Society* (New York: Praeger, 1970); H. A. R. Gibb and H. Bowen, *Islamic Society and the West*, vol. 1, pt. 1 (London: Oxford University Press, 1950); A. H. Lybyer, *The Government of the Ottoman Empire*; J. Rothschild, *Pilsudski's Coup d'etat* (New York: Columbia University Press, 1966).

24. Uriel Dann, *Iraq under Qassem: A Political History, 1958–1963* (New York: Praeger, 1969); Potash, *The Army and Politics in Argentina*; Itamar Rabinowitz, *Syrian Army and Ba'th Party, 1963–1966: Army-Party Symbiosis* (Tel Aviv, Israel: Universities Presses, 1973); A. Stepan, *The Military in Politics: Changing Patterns in Brazil* (Princeton, N.J.: Princeton University Press, 1971); W. F. Weiker, *The Turkish Revolution, 1960–1961* (Washington: The Brookings Institution, 1963); D. A. Rostow, "The Army and the Founding of the Turkish Republic," *World Politics*, vol. 11, no. 4 (July 1959); Anwar al-Sadat, *Revolt on the Nile* (New York: John Day, 1957).

25. H. Bienen, "Public Order and the Military in Africa"; E. Lieuwen, *Arms and Politics in Latin America*, rev. ed. (New York: Praeger, 1961); Finer, *The Man on Horseback*; L. N. McAlister, "Civil-Military Relations in Latin America," in *The Dynamics of Change in Latin American Politics*, ed. J. D. Martz (Englewood Cliffs, N.J.: Prentice-Hall, 1966), pp. 5–36; Potash, *The Army and Politics in Argentina*, pp. 182–237; Majid Khadduri, *Independent Iraq: A Study in Iraqi Politics, 1932–1958*, 2d ed. (London: Oxford University Press, 1960), pp. 76–80.

26. Khadduri, *Independent Iraq*; Thompson, "Explanations of the Military Coup," pp. 161–67; Ruth First, *The Barrel of a Gun: Political Power in Africa and the Coup d'Etat* (London: Penguin Press, 1970); P. J. Vatikiotis, *The Egyptian Army in Politics: Pattern for New Nations*, (Bloomington: Indiana University Press, 1961); Carlos A. Astiz, *Pressure Groups and Power Elites in Peruvian Politics* (Ithaca, N. Y., and London: Cornell University Press, 1969); Luigi R. Einaudi, "Peru," in Luigi Einaudi and Alfred Stepan, eds., *Latin American Institutional Development: Changing Military Perspectives in Peru and Brazil* (Rand R-586-DOS, April 1971), pp. 1–70; M. Lissak, "Moderniza-

tion and Role Expansion of the Military in Developing Countries," *Comparative Studies in Society and History*, vol. 9, no. 3 (April, 1967); Bienen, "Public Order and the Military in Africa"; North, *Civil-Military Relations*.

27. See Irving Louis Horowitz, "The Military in Latin America," *Elites in Latin America*, ed. Seymour Martin Lipset and Aldo Solari (London: Oxford University Press, 1965).

28. Martin Kitchen, *The German Officer Corps, 1890–1914* (London: Oxford University Press, 1968), pp. 28–32.

30. Khadduri, *Independent Iraq*, pp. 76–80; Uriel Dann, *Iraq under Qassem* (New York: Praeger, 1969).

31. Khadduri, *Independent Iraq*, pp. 78–80; North, *Civil-Military Relations*, pp. 1–10.

32. North, *Civil-Military Relations*, pp. 34–37. In Turkey the transformation of the army rebels of 1960–61 into permanent senators illustrated once again the persistence of the Kemalist legacy, at least as of 1976. Charles Simmons, "The Rise of the Brazilian Military Class, 1840–1900," *Mid-America* 39 (October 1957): 227–38.

33. Lacouture and Lacouture, *Egypt in Transition*, pp. 144–145; Eliezer Be'eri, *Ha-Kzuna ve-Hashilton Ba-Olam ha-Aravi* (The Officer Class in Politics and Society of the Arab East) (Tel Aviv, Israel: Sifriat Poalim, 1966), pp. 74–80; Shimon Shamir, "Five Years of the Liberation Rally," *The New East (Hamizrah Hehadash)* 8, no. 4 (1957): 274.

34. North, *Civil-Military Relations*, pp. 34–37.

35. Huntington, *The Soldier*, chap. 3, pp. 29–79. See George Blanksten, *Ecuador: Constitutions and Caudillos* (Berkeley and Los Angeles: University of California Press, 1951), pp. 51–54, for a discussion of the "vicious circle" phenomenon. For Latin American cases of this type, see McAlister, "Civil-Military Relations in Latin America."

36. See Weiker, *The Turkish Revolution*, for a complete discussion of this event.

37. North, *Civil-Military Relations*, pp. 52–57.

38. Huntington, *The Soldier*, pp. 93–94, discusses briefly the conservatism of the professional officer. He is dealing with nonpraetorian states, however. See Richard Patch, "The Peruvian Elections of 1962 and Their Annulment," *American Universities Field Staff Reports*, West Coast South America Series, vol. 9 (September 1962), p. 6.

39. Huntington, *The Soldier*, pp. 83–85. The basis of military power in Pakistan was the rural elite and the urban rich. For a parallel analysis that emphasizes the role of the army as the bearer of explicit political norms and images, see Lissak, "Modernization and Role Expansion," pp. 240–255. On Indonesia see Lev, "The Political Role," pp. 349–64.

40. Patrick Seale, *Struggle for Syria: A Study of Post-War Arab Politics: 1945–1958* (London: Oxford University Press, 1965), pp. 124–31.

41. Majid Khadduri, "The Role of the Military in Iraqi Society," in *The Military in the Middle East*, ed. Sydney N. Fisher (Columbus: Ohio State University Press, 1963), p. 47. I am indebted to Daniel S. Lev for most of the points made here on the Indonesian army. See Lev, "The Political Role," pp. 360–64.

42. Gamal Abdel Nasser, *Egypt's Liberation: The Philosophy of the Revolution* (Washington, D.C.: Public Affairs Library, 1955), pp. 32–33, 42–45. See F. L. Carsten,

The Reichswehr and Politics, 1918–1933 (Oxford: Clarendon Press, 1966); Khadduri, *Independent Iraq*, pp. 200–06. See also Col. Salah al-Din al-Sabbagh, *Fursan al-Arab-iyyah fi Iraq* (The Knights of Arabhood in Iraq) (Damascus, 1956), pp. 29–30.

43. David A. Wilson, "The Military in Thai Politics," in *Role of the Military*, ed. Johnson, p. 253 (quotation), pp. 268–69; Fred W. Riggs, *Thailand: The Moderniza-tion of a Bureaucratic Polity* (Honolulu: University of Hawaii Press, 1966).

44. Lucian W. Pye, "Armies in the Process of Political Modernization," in *Role of the Military*, ed. Johnson, p. 75.

CHAPTER 5

1. The first quotation in this paragraph is from Ruth First, *Power in Africa* (New York: Pantheon, 1970), p. 73. I am grateful to Valerie Plave Bennett for some of these ideas. See her "Evolution of Civil-Military Relations in Ghana: 1945–1962" (Ph.D. diss., Boston University, 1972); the second quotation is from p. 50.

2. Professionally frustrated Englishmen and Frenchmen, as well as ambitious young men who could never have risen in their home armies, served in the colonies.

3. Bernard Lewis, *The Emergence of Modern Turkey* (London: Oxford University Press, 1961), p. 23.

4. Eliezer Be'eri, *Army Officers in Arab Politics and Society* (New York: Praeger, 1970), pp. 286–93.

5. Robert Tignor, *Modernization and British Colonial Rule in Egypt, 1882–1914* (Princeton, N.J.: Princeton University Press, 1966), pp. 15–16.

6. Amos Perlmutter, "The Arab Military Elite," *World Politics* 22 (January 1970): 298.

7. A. R. Luckham, "The Nigerian Army: A Case Study on Cohesion" (Ph.D. diss., University of Chicago, 1969). In a challenge to historical determinist and other organizational theories of why the military intervenes, Dowse demonstrates clearly (in the case of Ghana in particular) that the sociology of the military, which centers around the professional performance and social origins of the military elites, as well as the patterns of training and life styles of the armed forces, does not explain why the rule of the military in Africa suddenly became predominant. Robert E. Dowse, "The Military and Political Development," in *Politics and Change in Developing Countries*, ed. Colin Leys (London: Cambridge University Press, 1959). Luckham's exhaustive studies demonstrate only that the collapse of military discipline as a result of organi-zational stress caused the first Nigerian coup in January 1966. This does not explain why the army intervened, but only that it could be expected to intervene.

8. See Dowse, "The Military," p. 227. The quotation is from Samuel P. Hunting-ton, *Political Order in Changing Societies* (New Haven: Yale University Press, 1968), p. 194.

9. See Henry Bienen, ed., *The Military Intervenes* (New York: Russell Sage, 1969), pp. xiv–xvii; and S. E. Finer, *The Man on Horseback* (New York: Praeger, 1962), pp. 23–71. A. A. Afrifa, *The Ghana Coup, 24th February 1966* (London: Frank Cass, 1967), pp. 37–38, 31; see also p. 9.

10. Huntington, *Political Order*, pp. 266 (source of quotation), 277. See the com-prehensive review and analysis of literature on revolution in Isaac Kramnick's "Reflections on Revolution: Definition and Explanation in Recent Scholarship,"

in *History and Theory* 11, no. 1 (1972): 26–63; see esp. his analysis of Huntington's theory of revolution, pp. 35–39.

11. The structural-functional group, including such well-known scholars as Almond, Verba, Apter, and Binder, was influential in American political science during the 1950s. For this school's magnum opus, see the Princeton series on political development and modernization; for its chief critics, read Huntington and Sheldon Wolin.

12. Clifford Geertz, "In Search of North Africa," *New York Review of Books* 16, no. 7 (April 22, 1971): 20.

13. A most interesting study of political generational groups, elites, and political behavior that differs somewhat from mine is William B. Quandt's *Revolution and Political Leadership: Algeria, 1954–1968* (Cambridge, Mass.: M.I.T. Press, 1969), pp. 25–124 (see esp. pp. 108–23). I have made use of his military-intellectual elite analysis. Any misinterpretations are mine. On Egypt, see Nadav Safran, *Egypt in Search of Political Community* (Cambridge, Mass.: Harvard University Press, 1961), p. 192; Gabriel Baer, *A History of Land Ownership in Modern Egypt, 1800–1950* (London: Oxford University Press, 1962); P. J. Vatikiotis, *Egypt since the Revolution* (London: Allen & Unwin, 1968), p. 214; Manfred Halpern, *The Politics of Social Change in the Middle East and North Africa* (Princeton, N.J.: Princeton University Press, 1963), p. 81; R. H. Dekmejian, *Egypt under Nasir* (Albany: State University of New York Press, 1971). On the future of Islam, see Quandt, *Revolution*, pp. 25–65.

14. Malcolm Kerr, *Islamic Reform* (Berkeley and Los Angeles: University of California Press, 1966), p. 1.

15. See Safran, *Egypt*; C. C. Adams, *Islam and Modernism in Egypt* (London: Oxford University Press, 1933); H. A. R. Gibb, *Modern Trends in Islam* (Chicago: University of Chicago Press, 1947); H. A. R. Gibb and Harold Bowen, *Islamic Society and the West* (Oxford: Oxford University Press, 1950), vol. 1, pt. 1; P. M. Holt, ed., *Political and Social Change in Egypt* (London: Oxford University Press, 1966); Bernard Lewis, *The Arabs in History* (New York: Harper Torchbooks, 1960); Albert Hourani, *Arabic Thought in the Liberal Age: 1787–1939* (London: Oxford University Press, 1962). See also David Apter, "Ghana," and Richard Sklar and C. S. Whitaker, Jr., "Nigeria," in *Political Parties and National Integration in Tropical Africa*, ed. James Coleman and Carl Rosberg (Berkeley: University of California Press, 1964).

16. Apter, "Ghana," pp. 292–308; Sklar and Whitaker, "Nigeria," pp. 597–604.

17. See Safran, *Egypt*; Patrick Seale, *The Struggle for Syria: A Study of Post-War Arab Politics 1945–1958* (London: Oxford University Press, 1965); René Lemarchand, "Congo," in Coleman and Rosberg, *Political Parties*, pp. 575–79.

18. Progressive politicians who were active in voluntary associations formalized after independence played an important role in the government coalition. However, the fact that voluntary association was limited in political commitment leaves the distinction between and within political generations ambiguous. Nevertheless, much political interest aggregation and articulation in sub-Saharan Africa took place in these protomodern, limited-participation structures, where both political generations and their various strata, although not yet differentiated, existed.

19. Quandt divides the military into professionals and guerrillas. I doubt the "guerrilla" nature of his guerrillas, and prefer to use the word terrorist (or assassin).

On the military see: Be'eri, *Army Officers*; Perlmutter, "The Arab Military Elite"; Uriel Dann, *Iraq under Qassem* (New York: Praeger, 1969); Morroe Berger, *Military Elite and Social Change: Egypt Since Napoleon* (Princeton: Center for International Studies, 1960), and *The Arab World Today* (New York: Anchor Doubleday, 1963); P. J. Vatikiotis, *The Egyptian Army in Politics* (Bloomington: Indiana University Press, 1961), and *Politics and the Military in Jordan: A Study of the Arab Legion, 1921–1957* (London: Frank Cass & Co., Ltd., 1967); and Quandt, *Revolution*.

20. Be'eri, *Army Officers*, pp. 293–304; William F. Guttridge, "Military and Police Forces in Colonial Africa," in *Colonialism in Africa*, ed. L. H. Gann and Peter Duignan (London: Cambridge University Press, 1970), 2: 257–91; and Quandt, *Revolution*.

21. First, *Power in Africa*, pp. 164–65; Luckham, "Nigerian Army," pp. 508–29; Ali Mazrui, "Soldiers as Traditionalizers," *World Politics* 28, no. 2 (January 1976): 246–72.

22. Quandt, *Revolution*, p. 113.

23. Be'eri, *Army Officers*, p. 79. The Egyptian authorities prohibited uniformed Egyptians from participating in the Palestine conflict until Egypt officially joined the other Arab states' war on Israel in May 1948.

24. Quandt, *Revolution*, p. 113.

25. Yoram Porat, "The Palestinians, the Palestine Issue, and Negotiations toward a British-Hejazi Treary 1920–1925," *The New East* (*Hamizrah Hehadash*), no. 79 (1970), pp. 237–56. On the ideology of Muslim Brotherhood see Richard P. Mitchell, *The Society of the Muslim Brothers* (Oxford: Oxford University Press, 1969). On the assassins see the excellent study by Bernard Lewis, *The Assassins* (New York: Basic Books, 1968). See also E. J. Hobsbawm, *Primitive Rebels* (New York: Norton, 1959).

26. Most of the studies on Arab guerrillas and fedayeen since 1967 are either preliminary or politically tainted. For mainstream and general works see: Yehoshafat Harkabi, *Arab Attitudes to Israel* (Washington, D.C.: Harrar Publications, 1972); Harkabi, "The Arab-Israeli Confrontation," *Jerusalem Post*, December 17, 1965; and Harkabi, *Fedayeen Action and Arab Strategy*, Adelphi Paper no. 53 (London: Institute for Strategic Studies, December 1968); Hisham Sharabi, *Palestine and Israel: The Lethal Dilemma* (New York: Pegasus, 1969); also Fred Khouri, *The Arab-Israeli Dilemma* (Syracuse: Syracuse University Press, 1968). On the radical group see Harkabi, "The Palestinian Concept of Popular Democratic Republic," *Trans-Action* (July 1970); George Habash, "The Popular Front for the Liberation of Palestine" (English translation; published in Arabic in *Tali'ah*, 1959, Cairo).

27. Quandt, *Revolution*, pp. 119–23.

28. This is a revisionist interpretation of the politics of sub-Saharan Africa. See the writings of Aristide Zolberg, Robert Dowse, and Henry Bienen.

29. On African political parties see Ruth Schachter, "Single Party Systems in West Africa," *American Political Science Review* 60, no. 2 (June 1961): 294–307; Thomas Hodgkin, *African Political Parties* (London: Penguin Books, 1961); Martin L. Kilson, "Authoritarian and Single Party Tendencies in African Politics," *World Politics* 14 (January 1963): 262–94.

30. M. Crawford Young, "Rebellion and the Congo," *Protest and Power in Black Africa*, ed. Robert I. Rotberg and Ali A. Mazrui (New York: Oxford University

Press, 1970), p. 970. The quotation is from Aristide Zolberg, *Creating Political Order* (Chicago: Rand, McNally and Co., 1966), p. 3. See Coleman and Rosberg, *Political Parties*, p. 2.

31. Zolberg, *Creating Political Order*, p. 65.

32. For an analysis of group conflict and social change, see Ralf Dahrendorf, *Class and Class Conflict in Industrial Society* (Stanford: Stanford University Press, 1959).

33. Stanislav Andreski, *The African Predicament* (London: Michael Joseph, 1968), pp. 110–33.

34. The first quotation is from Guttridge, "Military and Police Forces," p. 286. The Lugard quotations are from First, *Power in Africa*, p. 34; see also pp. 36, 105, 106.

35. See H. Ehrlich, "Students and Universities in the Political Life of Egypt," *The New East* (*Hamizrah Hehadash*), nos. 73–74 (1969), pp. 50–78.

36. See appendix 1, chapter 5.

37. Amos Perlmutter, "The Praetorian State and the Praetorian Army," *Comparative Politics* 2, no.1 (April 1969): 392–94.

38. I am aware of the century-long debate over "politics" and "administration" and of the progress made by Barnard, Simon, Dahl, March, and others in studying administrative behavior as a political process. The analyses of bureaucratic politics by Lipset, Etzioni, Selznick, Parsons, and Allison have resolved the artificial politics–administration dichotomy. My models are differentiated on the basis of orientation, behavior, and expectations concerning domination. Thus one orientation is "political" and the other "administrative."

39. After designing my own figures to illustrate the types of regimes, I came across Meir Pa'il's essay, "Patterns of Revolutionary Officers' Regimes in Iraq and Syria," *The New East* (*Hamizrah Hehadash*), vol. 19, no. 75 (1969), pp. 181–207 (Hebrew), pp. i–vii (English). Subsequently I modified my charts to follow his designs. I am grateful to Pa'il for our conversations during the summer of 1970.

40. Be'eri, *Army Officers*, pp. 130–70.

41. First, *Power in Africa*, p. 432 (quotation); Luckham, "Nigerian Army," pp. 210–67.

42. Be'eri, *Army Officers*, pp. 97–122.

43. I am grateful to Sarah Lulko of the Shiloah Institute of Tel Aviv University for the use of her excellent seminar paper "The Popular Organization of the Nasserite Regime" (mimeograph, Tel Aviv, 1970).

44. Itamar Rabinowitz, *Syrian Army and Ba'th Party, 1963–1966: Army-Party Symbiosis* (Tel Aviv, Israel: Universities Presses, 1973).

45. First, *Power in Africa*, pp. 388–89, 404–05.

46. Ibid., p. 436.

47. Luckham, "Nigerian Army," pp. 94–95, tables 4 and 5 (pp. 98–99); p. 87, and table 6 (p. 105). On Nigerian military organizational strain, see Luckham, pp. 108–18; and John N. Colas, "The Social and Career Correlates of Military Intervention in Nigeria" (Unpublished paper, Joint Seminar on the Armed Forces and Society, Paris, 1969).

48. Thompson, "Explanations," pp. 21–23.

49. Luckham, "Nigerian Army," pp. 96, 113–23, 182 (source of quotation), 162;

First, *Power in Africa*, pp. 296–300; Colas, "Social and Career Correlates," p. 11.

50. Patrick Seale, *Struggle for Syria*.

51. Amos Perlmutter, "From Obscurity to Rule: The Syrian Army and the Ba'th Party," *Western Political Quarterly* 22, no. 4 (December 1969): 828 (source of quotation), 844–45.

52. Be'eri, *Army Officers*.

53. Dann, *Iraq under Qassem*.

54. David Easton, *A System Analysis of Political Life* (New York: John Wiley, 1965), p. 287.

55. See the pioneer volume, Henry Bienen, ed., *The Military Intervenes* (New York: Russell Sage, 1968); Eric Nordlinger, "Soldiers in Mufti" (Unpublished paper, C.F.I.A., Harvard University, February 1969).

56. Be'eri, *Army Officers*, pp. 63–96.

57. Dann, *Iraq under Qassem*, pp. 62–69.

58. Be'eri, *Army Officers*, pp. 287–312.

59. See Amos Perlmutter, *Egypt: The Praetorian State* (New Brunswick, N.J.: Transaction, 1974).

60. Dann, *Iraq under Qassem*, pp. 1–92, 356–78.

61. Ibid., pp. 108–35.

62. Mitchell, *The Society of Muslim Brothers*, pp. 72–150.

63. The literature on the relation between ideology and organization is growing. See Franz Schurmann, *Ideology and Organization in Communist China* (Berkeley: University of California Press, 1966); Philip Selznick, *Leadership in Administration* (New York: Basic Books, 1954); and Amos Perlmutter, "Ideology and Organization: The Socialist-Zionist Parties in Israel 1896–1959" (Ph.D. diss., University of California, Berkeley, 1957).

64. Thompson, "Explanations," pp. 110–13.

65. Be'eri, pp. 63–96.

66. Gamel Abdul Nasser, *Egypt's Liberation: The Philosophy of the Revolution* (Washington, D.C.: Public Affairs Library, 1955), p. 17.

CHAPTER 6

1. Alfred Stepan, "The New Professionalism of Internal Warfare and Military Role Expansion" in *Authoritarian Brazil*, ed. Alfred Stepan (New Haven: Yale University Press, 1973), pp. 47–65. I do not wish to quarrel with Stepan's profoundly valuable classification of old and new professionalism. In fact, I have incorporated several of his observations into later portions of this chapter. However, corporatism functions and produces the same result whether the military's political weltanschauung is external and imperial (as in the old professionalism of the Prussians, French, and Japanese) or internal (anti-Castro, anti-communist ideology). Both types of professionals are interventionists since they challenge the regime and impose upon it their concept of society and politics, internal or external. Professionalism, that is, the acquisition and manipulation of skill, is not a variable that explains a military's weltanschauung or motivation for intervention. The linkage between the professional, the bureaucrat, and the modern nation-state produces different types of civil-

military relations. The convergence of skill and control produces military corporate intervention. Skills, or their acquisition, result in an occupational, not a *political*, orientation.

2. I am grateful to Jorge R. Dominguez and John D. Powell for sharing their knowledge of Latin America with me. On Latin American military corporatism and the military's role as an arbitrator see: Edwin Lieuwen, *Arms and Politics in Latin America* (New York: Praeger, 1961); Lieuwen, *Generals Versus Presidents* (New York: Praeger, 1964); Liisa North, *Civil-Military Relations in Argentina, Chile, and Peru* (Berkeley: Institute of International Studies, 1966); Samuel E. Finer, *Man on Horseback* (London: Pall Mall Press, 1962); Finer, "Military and Society in Latin America," *Sociological Review Monograph*, no. 11 (Staffordshire, England, 1967); Irving Horowitz, "The Military Elites," *Elites in Latin America*, ed. S. M. Lipset and Aldo Solari (New York: Oxford University Press, 1967); Robert A. Potash, *The Army and Politics in Argentina: 1928–1945* (Palo Alto: Stanford University Press, 1969); John Johnson, ed., *The Role of the Military in Underdeveloped Countries* (Princeton, N. J.: Princeton University Press, 1962); L. N. McAlister, "Recent Research and Writings on the Role of the Military in Latin America," *Latin American Research Review* 2, no. 1 (1966): 5–36.

3. Raymond Carr, "Spain," in *Soldiers and Governments*, ed. Michael Howard (Bloomington: Indiana University Press, 1959), pp. 124, 129 (source of quotation).

4. Ibid., p. 129.

5. Raymond Carr, *Spain* (Oxford: Clarendon Press, 1966), p. 109.

6. Ibid., p. 111.

7. For quotations, see ibid., pp. 105, 109. See also Stanley Payne, *Politics and the Military in Modern Spain* (Palo Alto: Stanford University Press, 1967), p. 7; Robert L. Gilmore, *Caudillism and Militarism in Venezuela* (Athens: Ohio University Press, 1964), p. 131. In volume 1 of his book, *The Age of Democratic Revolution* (Princeton, N. J.: Princeton University Press, 1964), R. R. Palmer used the term "democratic revolution" to describe the experiences, attitudes, and institutional innovations of Europe between 1760 and 1800.

8. See Eric Wolf and Edward Hansen, "Caudillo Politics: A Structural Analysis," *Comparative Studies in Sociology and History* 11, no. 2 (1969): 168–71, 177. See also Gilmore, *Caudillism*, pp. 1–8. Gilmore provides one of the best—and in the absence of any modern monographs on the caudillo system—one of the most comprehensive historical analyses of caudillismo, particularly in Venezuela. See also Hamill's "Caudillismo in the Nineteenth Century," in *Dictatorship in Latin America*, ed. Hugh Hamill, Jr. (New York: Knopf, 1965). The idea contained in the last sentence of this paragraph was suggested by Jorge Dominguez.

9. See North, *Civil-Military Relations*, p. 10; and Victor Alba, "The Stages of Militarism in Latin America," in Johnson, *Role of the Military*, pp. 165–67. For a brilliant analysis of Spanish patrimonialism in Latin America and the demise of the Thomistic model in Spain, see Richard M. Morse, "The Heritage of Latin America," in *The Founding of New Societies*, ed. Louis Hartz (New York: Harcourt, Brace, 1964), pp. 123–77. Gilmore, *Caudillism*, pp. 47, 66.

10. Gilmore, *Caudillism*, p. 33. For a fascinating study of the existence of military

corporatism in Latin America before the revolution, see Lyle N. McAlister, *The 'Fuero Militar' in New Spain: 1764–1800* (Gainesville, Fla.: University of Florida Press, 1957), pp. 6–21, 55–71, 88–89 (source of quotation).

11. Gilmore, *Caudillism*, pp. 11, 157 (italics added).

12. See ibid.; Potash, *Army in Argentina*; North, *Civil-Military Relations*; Carlos A. Astiz, *Pressure Groups and Power Elites in Peruvian Politics* (Ithaca, N.Y., and London: Cornell University Press, 1969); Charles Simmons, "The Rise of the Brazilian Military Class," *Mid-America* 39 (October 1957): 227–38.

13. Samuel P. Huntington, *Political Order in Changing Societies* (New Haven: Yale University Press, 1968), pp. 208–21, 12.

14. North, *Civil-Military Relations*, p. 60.

15. Samuel P. Huntington, *The Soldier and the State* (Cambridge, Mass.: Harvard University Press, 1957), p. 80; North, *Civil-Military Relations*, p. 12. Quotations are from Huntington, *The Soldier*, p. 83.

16. Ernest Greenwood, "Attributes of a Profession," in *Man, Work and Society*, ed. S. Noscow and W. Form (New York: Basic Books, 1962).

17. Generals Orona and Yrigoyen, quoted in Potash, *Army in Argentina*, p. 12. Potash mentions on p. 13 the appointment of civilians to the war ministry. Although the interpretation of its consequences is mine, his general thesis confirms my analysis.

18. Ibid., pp. 16–18, 31 (quotation), 32–35.

19. See Ernst Halperin, *Nationalism and Communism in Chile* (Cambridge, Mass.: M.I.T. Press, 1965), pp. 30–35; and North, *Civil-Military Relations*, pp. 20, 28. On civil-military relations in Chile generally, see Frederick M. Nunn, "Civil-Military Relations in Chile, 1891–1938" (Ph.D. diss., University of New Mexico, 1963); Roy Allen Hansen, "Military Cultures and Organizational Decline, A Study of the Chilean Army" (Ph.D. diss., University of California, Los Angeles, 1967); North, *Civil-Military Relations*; K. H. Silvert, "The Prospects of Chilean Democracy," in *Latin American Politics*, ed. R. D. Tomask (New York: Anchor, 1966); Charles B. Pike, *Chile and the United States, 1880–1902* (Notre Dame, Ind.: Notre Dame University Press, 1963).

20. See Carlos Astiz, "The Military," in *Pressure Groups and Power Elites in Peruvian Politics*, ed. Carlos Astiz (Ithaca, N. Y., and London: Cornell University Press, 1969), pp. 131–35 (2d quotation on 134); North, *Civil-Military Relations*, pp. 21–25, 48–50; Victor Villanueva, *El Militarismo en el Peru* (Lima: Empresa Schenck, 1962). On civil-military relations in Peru, see also Carlos Weisse, *Historia del Peru: La Republica* (Lima: Rasay, 1934).

21. June Hahner, *Brazilian Civil-Military Relations, 1889–1898* (Ithaca, N.Y.: Cornell University Press, 1966), p. 4.

22. Ibid., pp. 184, 185, 47–72, 110–82.

23. The quotations are from Huntington, *The Soldier*, p. 60; from Jacques Ourique, quoted by Hahner, *Brazilian Civil-Military Relations*, p. 84; and from Hahner, pp. 74 and 21.

24. Hahner, *Brazilian Civil-Military Relations*, p. 79–80.

25. Ibid., pp. 86–87 (quotation), 89, 93.

26. I do not accept Jose Nun's interesting proposition that Latin American coups are middle-class coups. It is too all-inclusive an explanation for a phenomenon that

occurred at random in Latin America between 1930 and 1970. Although Nun is aware of the cleavages in the middle class, his conclusions do not reflect this understanding. See his "Latin-American Phenomenon: The Middle Class Military Coup," in *Trends in Social Science Research in Latin America: A Conference Report* (Berkeley: University of California Institute of International Studies, 1965), pp. 55–91.

27. Potash, *Army in Argentina*, pp. 22–25. The quotation, from p. 25, is by General Agustin Justo.

28. Ibid., pp. 4–5, 43 (quotation).

29. Ibid., pp. 55–78. The quotation is from p. 77.

30. North, *Civil-Military Relations*, p. 35; Nunn, "Civil-Military Relations in Chile," p. 205; Hansen, "Military Cultures," pp. 56–58; Nunn, p. 236. The quotation is from Hansen, p. 60.

31. North, *Civil-Military Relations*, p. 48; Astiz, "The Military," pp. 137, 139–41, 145 (source of quotation). On the Center, see Astiz, "The Military," pp. 141–46; on ideology, see North, *Civil-Military Relations*, pp. 53–57.

32. On the growth of military establishments see L. I. Horowitz, "The Military," in Lipset and Solari, *Elites in Latin America*. On their shrinkage see Hansen, "Military Cultures," and North, *Civil-Military Relations*.

33. Potash, *Army in Argentina*, p. 77.

34. Alfredo Colmo, quoted in ibid., p. 78.

35. Ibid., pp. 167–68. In one decade (1930–40) two-thirds of the officer corps were politically involved (ibid., p. 167). On the GOU see ibid., pp. 184–90.

36. For the quotations, see ibid., p. 186.

37. I am grateful to Jorge Dominguez for these valuable facts.

38. See Potash, *Army in Argentina*, pp. 184–91. The officers' coterie was organized by Nasser between 1947 and 1952. Qassam of Iraq followed the same pattern.

39. Ibid., pp. 192–95, 203, 209 (source of quotation), 260–85. Gino Germani indicates Perón's class orientation statistically by analyzing the voting returns of the 1946 elections: middle-class wards in Buenos Aires voted against Perón.

40. Ibid., p. 283.

41. For material concerning the organizational decline of the Chilean military I have depended heavily on Roy Allen Hansen's pioneering study, "Military Cultures," pp. 193–236.

42. Nunn, "Civil-Military Relations in Chile," p. 205; Hansen, "Military Cultures," pp. 14, 198, 208.

43. Hansen, "Military Cultures," pp. 221, 315, 316 (source of quotation).

44. Ibid., p. 303.

45. Ibid.

46. A most informative study of the modern military in Brazil is Alfred Stepan, *The Military in Politics: Changing Patterns in Brazil* (Princeton, N.J.: Princeton University Press, 1971). See also Simmons, "Brazilian Military Class." The quotation is from Stepan, p. 67.

47. Stepan, *Military in Politics*, p. 68.

48. Ibid., tables 5.1 and 5.2, on pp. 108–11, 134–52.

49. Ibid., pp. 191, 193.

50. Ibid., pp. 174–87, 240 (table 11.1). 241 (table 11.2).

51. Ibid., pp. 192–93.

52. Ibid., pp. 69, 188–212.

53. See ibid., pp. 153–71 (quotation on 162).

54. Ibid., pp. 236–52 and esp. tables 11.1, 11.2 (pp. 240–41).

55. Stepan offers some scenarios (see pp. 270–71), but I feel he has not exhausted all the options for civil-military relations in Brazil, or, for that matter, in Argentina.

56. See Luigi R. Einaudi, "Peru," in Luigi Einaudi and Alfred Stepan, *Latin American Institutional Development: Changing Military Perspectives in Peru and Brazil* (Rand R-586-DOS, April 1971), pp. 1–70.

57. Potash, *Army in Argentina*, pp. 283–86; Astiz, "The Military," pp. 141–61.

58. Charles W. Anderson, *Politics and Economic Change in Latin America* (Princeton, N. J.: Van Nostrand, 1967), p. 328, table 16.

59. See Philippe Schmitter, "The 'Portugalization' of Brazil?" in Stepan, *Authoritarian Brazil*, pp. 179–233.

60. See Stepan, *Authoritarian Brazil*.

61. Juan J. Linz, "The Future of an Authoritarian Situation" in Stepan, *Authoritarian Brazil*, p. 235.

62. Ibid.

63. Ibid., Philippe Schmitter, "The 'Portugalization' of Brazil?"   p. 205.

64. Linz, "Future of an Authoritarian Situation," p. 235.

CHAPTER 7

1. Isaac Kramnick, "Reflections on Revolution: Definition and Explanation in Recent Scholarship," *History and Theory* 11, no. 1 (1972): 28.

2. Samuel P. Huntington, *The Soldier and the State* (Cambridge, Mass.: Harvard University Press, 1957), pp. 53–54. Suzanne Keller, *Beyond the Ruling Class* (New York: Random House, 1963), pp. 32, 33.

3. The literature on private and political armies and elite fascist and Nazi groups and youth movements is growing. The following monographs influenced my thinking: George L. Mosse, *Crisis in German Ideology* (New York: Grosset, 1963), is a penetrating study of the myth of German volkish movements and orientations. Walter Z. Laqueur, *Young Germany* (London: Routledge and Kegan Paul, 1962), is the best analysis so far. Robert G. L. Waite, *Vanguard of Nazism* (Cambridge, Mass.: Harvard University Press, 1952; Norton 1969), has endured despite the avalanche of facts with the passage of time. George H. Stein, *The Waffan SS 1939–1945* (Ithaca, N.Y.: Cornell University Press, 1966) is a thorough analysis with some extraordinarily valid conclusions on the subject. Karl D. Bracher's *The German Dictatorship* (New York: Praeger, 1970) is the leading study of Hitler's Germany, including penetrating conclusions on the Nazi youth movement, ideology, and symbols. Hans Buchheim, *SS und Polizei im NS. Staats* (Bonn: Selbstverlag der Studiengesellschaft für Zeitproblem, 1964) is a thorough account. The psychological study by Saul Friendländer, *L'Antisemitisme Nazi* (Paris: Editions du Seuil, 1971), provides some psychoanalytical insight into the Nazi movement. For more complete bibliographies, see the works by Waite and Bracher.

4. Waite, *Vanguard*, pp. 22 (first quotation), 269 (second quotation), 66–79, 169 (third quotation, by Von Salomon), 26, 45–49, 27, 37.

5. Stein, *Waffen SS*, pp. 4–26 (quotation is from p. 9).

6. Ibid., pp. 282, 294 (source of quotation).

7. Ibid., pp. 282, 283, 285.

8. Ibid., pp. 286, 288, 291.

9. The imperialistic designs of Soviet leaders in the early 1960s have changed the nature of civil-military relations in the USSR. The pursuit of militarism and territorial expansion helped the Soviet military professional assert himself against his apparatchiks. Thus the Soviet professional has embarked on a militaristic course to improve his corporate lot and assert his independence. The reforms in the Soviet military since 1965 have raised the reputation of the professional in the USSR, but he is not revolutionary in the Chinese sense, nor does he resemble the Prussian professional of 1807. Instead, the Soviet resembles most closely that of Imperial Germany between Bismarck and World War I.

10. Karl Marx, *Class Struggle in France, 1848–1850* (New York: International Publishers, 1933).

11. Friedrich Engels, *Origin of the Family, Private Property, and the State* (New York: International Publishers, 1937), p. 211.

12. Philip Selznick, *The Organizational Weapon* (Glencoe, Ill.: Free Press, 1952), pp. 2, 6.

13. Ibid., pp. 6 (source of first quotation: emphasis added), 7, 257–58 (second quotation).

14. Shlomo Avineri, *The Social and Political Thought of Karl Marx* (Cambridge: Cambridge University Press, 1968), pp. 185, 187, 190.

15. Lenin, *Revolution and Counterrevolution in Germany*, quoted in A. Neuberg, *Armed Insurrection* (New York: St. Martin's, 1970), p. 59. Eric Wollenberg, a German Communist and insurrectionist, reissued the Comintern's manual for armed insurrection under the pseudonym of A. Neuberg, which stands for the authors Wollenberg, Tukhachevsky, Ho Chi Minh, and Hans Kippenberger. First published in French in 1931, it analyzes the theory and practice of insurrection in Reval, Hamburg, and China.

Insurrection is no putsch, no coup d'etat; it is a an effort by revolutionaries to overthrow a regime, and German and Chinese Communists practiced it to their deteriment in the 1920s and early 1930s. Its impact on Chinese communism was, however, greater than on the Soviet Red Army. But insurrection, armed or otherwise, is not a system of terror qua terror, but an outburst, spontaneous and cathartic, of mobs and frustrated groups or individual anarchists and nihilists. "Insurrection, in the broad sense of the word," write Neuberg (p. 59), "is of course not a purely military operation. It is basically and above all a powerful revolutionary movement, a powerful thrust by the proletarian masses—or at least the active fraction of those masses . . . against the dominant classes."

16. Neuberg, *Armed Insurrection*, p. 59.

17. Ibid., p. 52.

18. Katharine Chorley, *Armies and the Art of Revolution* (London: Faber and Faber, 1943), pp. 184. 233, This original (though disorganized) and thought-provoking comparative analysis is now a classic. I disagree with most, if not all, of Chorley's propositions, but no student of modern military revolution and insurrection could fail to appreciate the historical significance of the book.

CHAPTER 8

1. Franz Schurmann, *Ideology and Organization in Communist China* (Berkeley and Los Angeles: University of California Press, 1966), p. 18.

2. These ideas are borrowed from Chalmers Johnson's *Peasant Nationalism and Communist Power* (Stanford, Calif.: Stanford University Press, 1962), a most interesting study on the exploitation by a Communist party of peasant nationalism. The quotation is from p. 19.

3. See Arslan Harambushi, *Algeria: A Revolution That Failed* (New York: Praeger, 1966).

4. I am greatly indebted to the monumental and thorough research study by Col. William W. Whitson, with Chen-Hsia Huang, *The Chinese High Command: A History of Communist Military Politics, 1927-1971* (New York: Praeger, 1973), on the history of the Chinese army, its military organization, ethics, politics, and purpose. I could not have clarified or supported my theoretical argumentation on the professionalism of the revolutionary soldiers in China without the conclusive evidence of Colonel Whitson's work.

5. For the best bibliography on Chinese Communist military strategy, see H. I. Boorman and Scott Boorman, "Chinese Communist Insurgent Warfare, 1939-1945," *Political Science Quarterly* 81, no. 2 (June 1966): 171-95. On the rise and the essence of Chinese communism and Mao Tse-tung, see Benjamin I. Schwartz's classic, *Chinese Communism and the Rise of Mao* (Cambridge, Mass.: Harvard University Press, 1951). On the CCP and the PLA see Schurmann, *Ideology and Organization*; J. R. Levenson, *Confucian China and Its Modern Fate* (Berkeley: University of California Press, 1958); John Gittings, *The Role of the Chinese Army* (London: Oxford University Press, 1968); C. Johnson, *Peasant Nationalism*; Ellis Joffe, *Party and Army: Professionalism and Political Control in the Chinese Officer Corps, 1949-1964* (Cambridge, Mass.: East Asian Research Center, Harvard University, 1965); Samuel Griffith, *The History of the PLA* (New York: Praeger, 1966).

6. Ralph Powell, "Civil-Military Relations in China," *China Quarterly*, no. 34 (June-July 1968), p. 39.

7. Joffe, *Party and Army*, p. ix.

8. On the military in the USSR, see Thomas W. Wolfe, *Soviet Power and Europe, 1945-1970* (Baltimore: Johns Hopkins University Press, 1970).

9. Barton Whaley, Scott Boorman, and Richard Harris have guided me to this old, yet revolutionary, concept of strategy, human behavior, and method of international interaction. The dearth of literature on stratagem and deception demonstrates its neglect by Western civilization since Napoleon, with the exception of brilliant British and German junior and middle ranking officers in World War II. Consult Barton Whaley, *Stratagem: Deception and Surprise in War* (forthcoming); and Scott Boorman's "Deception in Chinese Strategy," in William W. Whitson, ed., *The Military and Political Power in China in the 1970's* (New York: Praeger, 1972), pp. 313-38.

10. Whaley demonstrates that the art of stratagem practiced by Bonaparte, Jackson, Saxe, and Sherman has developed into the military science of Clausewitz and his successors. The great World War I commanders, Joffre, Foch, Younger, Moltke, Haig, and Falkenhayn, "neither used nor understood surprise much less

deception" (Whaley, *Stratagem*, p. 7). The quotation is from H. I. Boorman and Scott Boorman, "Strategy and National Psychology in China," *The Annals* 370 (1967): 147. See also Scott Boorman, "Deception in Chinese Strategy."

11. Whitson, *Chinese High Command*, pp. 436–39.

12. Ibid., p. 439.

13. Joffe, *Party and Army*, p. x.

14. See Gittings, *Role of the Chinese Army*, pp. 263–302; Joffe, *Party and Army*, pp. 46–100.

15. C. Martin Wilbur, "The Influence of the Past: How the Early Years Helped To Shape the Future of the Chinese Communist Party," *The China Quarterly*, no. 36 (October–December 1968), pp. 23–44, esp. pp. 30, 35, 38–39, 40.

16. For Whitson's classification and analysis, see his introduction to *Chinese High Command*, pp. 3–23. Whitson analyzes the dynamics of the Chinese military "ethic" and "style." He defines "ethic" as the role of the military in society, the authority of the commander, and the system of recruitment and promotions. "Style" is defined as the nature and effectiveness of the military organization, its strategy, tactics, and employment of military power. In this study I am more concerned with "ethic" than "style."

17. James Sheridan, *Chinese Warlord: The Carrer of Feng Yü hsiang* (Stanford, Calif: Stanford University Press, 1966), pp. 1 (source of first quotation), 6, 8 (second quotation).

18. Ibid., pp. 16, 19.

19. Whitson, *Chinese High Command*, pp. 7–13.

20. See ibid., chap. 2–6, pp. 24–363, on the first four and the North China Field armies.

21. For an analysis of the Soviet model see ibid., pp. 14–18.

22. Ibid., p. 17.

23. See Johnson, *Peasant Nationalism*; John Rue, *Mao Tse-tung in Opposition, 1927–1935* (Stanford, Calif.: Stanford University Press, 1966); and Whitson, *Chinese High Command*, pp. 18–22. The foremost analysis of Mao's view of the role of the peasant revolution is still Conrad Brandt et al., *Documentary History of Chinese Communism* (Cambridge, Mass.: Harvard University Press, 1952). See also Schwartz, *Chinese Communism*; and Johnson, *Peasant Nationalism*.

24. Benjamin I. Schwartz, *Communism and China: Ideology in Flux* (Cambridge, Mass.: Harvard University Press, 1968), p. 173. In the case of the PLA one must not interpret China "from the view that China is an inert clay in the hands of the leaders who shape it as they will" (ibid., p. 163).

25. Whitson, *Chinese High Command*, pp. 416–35.

26. Ibid., p. 21.

27. See Whitson, *Chinese High Command*, pp. 436–57, for a thorough description and analysis of the Cultural Revolution and the struggle between party and army factions.

28. Ibid., pp. 518–48.

29. Ibid., pp. 498–517, esp. chart O on p. 499; Gittings, *Role of Army*, pp. 269, 271; Powell, "Civil-Military Relations in China," p. 294.

30. Joffe, *Party and Army*, p. 59.

31. William Parish, "Factions in Chinese Military Politics," *The China Quarterly*, no. 56 (October/December 1973), pp. 667–99, argues that prior to 1967, the Chinese military represented a unified command (not the five army-party factions). Parish contends that there were factions after 1967 but that they were bureaucratic-political and not the type of factions Whitson suggested. Bureaucratic politics in large-scale organization is not a novel phenomenon even in China. Nevertheless types of military orientations take precedence over bureaucratic politics even if they may combine and therefore are solely identified as bureaucratic.

32. Ibid., pp. 695–96.

33. Whitson, *Chinese High Command*, p. 547.

34. A. Neuberg, *Armed Insurrection* (New York: St. Martin's, 1970), p. 183.

35. "The Chinese Army after the Cultural Revolution: The Effects of Intervention," *The China Quarterly*, no. 55 (July-September 1973), pp. 450–77.

36. Ibid., p. 452.

37. Ibid., p. 453. Italics mine.

38. Ibid.

39. Ibid.

40. Ibid., p. 454.

41. Ibid., p. 456.

42. Ibid., p. 463.

43. Ibid., p. 466.

44. Ibid., pp. 471–72.

45. Ibid., p. 477.

CHAPTER 9

1. On the nation-in-arms, see chapter 3. For a more detailed analysis of the evolution of the Israeli army see my *Military and Politics in Israel* (New York: Praeger, 1969).

2. See Martin Kitchen, *The German Officer Corps, 1890–1914* (Oxford: Clarendon Press, 1968); and Gerhard Ritter, *The Sword and the Scepter*, vol. 2, *The European Powers and the Wilhelminian Empire, 1890–1914* (Coral Gables, Fla.: University of Miami Press, 1970).

3. Kitchen, *German Officer Corps*, pp. 99 (italics added), 100.

4. Perlmutter, *Military and Politics*, pp. 3–5.

5. In 1976 no single comprehensive study of the Israeli army existed in Hebrew. However, there was abundant historical, biographical, bibliographical, and oral material dealing with events, personalities, and structures of the pre-1948 underground organizations that were the predecessors of the Israeli army. Moreover, the literature of the 1948 War of Liberation, the Sinai campaign of 1956, and the 1967 war was proliferating. The best historical analysis in Hebrew is Yehuda Bauer's *Diplomacy and Underground in Zionism 1939–1945* (Merchavia, 1966). One chapter of this book appeared in *Middle Eastern Studies* 2 (April 1966): 182–210. Original sources and documents on the Israeli army since its official formation in February 1948 were few and had limited usefulness.

6. "House of Labor" is used to denote all the efforts, the organizational and institutional structures, and the ideology of the Socialist-Zionist movement in Palestine.

7. For a detailed analysis of Socialist-Zionism, see Amos Perlmutter, "Ideology and Organization: The Politics of Socialist Parties in Israel, 1897–1957" (Ph.D. diss., University of California, Berkeley, 1957), pp. 147–58,

8. See Berl Katznelson, *Works* (in Hebrew), 13 vols., (Tel Aviv, 1951–1955). For an interpretation and analysis of Katznelson's ideology, see Perlmutter, "Berl Katznelson, A Socialist Zionist," in *Middle Eastern Studies*, January 1977.

9. Even the militant Jabotinsky was at that time willing to accept some modus vivendi with the Mandate and supported restraint.

10. Ben Zion Dinour et al., *The History of the Haganah* (in Hebrew), vol. 2, pt. 1 (Tel Aviv, 1959), pp. 574, 585, and vol. 2, pt. 2 (Tel Aviv, 1964), pp. 1053–72; David Niv, *Battle for Freedom* (in Hebrew), vol. 2 (Tel Aviv: Klausner Institute, 1965), pp. 74–119, and vol. 3 (Tel Aviv, 1967), 43–52, 161–82. On Stern and the National Military Organization, see Menachem Begin, *The Revolt* (New York: Henry Schuman, 1951); David Niv, *Battle for Freedom*; Ya'aqov Banai, *Unknown Soldiers* (in Hebrew (Tel Aviv: Hug Yedidim, 1958); Nathan Friedman-Yellin and Israel Eldad, eds., *The History of Lehi* (in Hebrew), 2 vols. (Tel Aviv: privately published, 1962).

11. For the historical development of the Palmach, see Zrubavel Gilad, ed., *The Book of the Palmach*, 2 vols. (Tel Aviv: United Kibbutz Movement, 1955); Zrubavel Gilad, ed., *Hidden Shield: The Secret Military Effort of the Yishuv During the War, 1939–1945* (in Hebrew) (Jerusalem: The Jewish Agency, 1951), pp. 14–20, 74–166. In 1942, 41 percent of the Palmach were from the United Kibbutz, whose members dominated the Palmach headquarters. The commander, his deputy, and the entire general staff except for two officers all came from the movement. See Yehudah Bauer, *Diplomacy and Underground* (Merchavia: Sifriat Poalim, 1766). pp. 160–61, 260–64.

12. Dinour, *History of Haganah*, vol. 1, pt. 2, p. 942.

13. On Wingate, see Christopher Sykes, *Orde Wingate* (Cleveland, Ohio: World Publishers, 1959).

14. Yigal Allon, "The Palmach," in Perlmutter, *Military and Politics*, pp. 38–39.

15. Bauer, *Diplomacy*, pp. 161

16. The Ha-Apala was to grow into a large-scale network that illegally brought shiploads of immigrants to Palestine between 1945 and 1948. The Palmach grew from about 900 members in 1942 to over 2,000 by 1945. Perlmutter, *Military and Politics*, pp. 39–10.

17. Much of the material in this section deals with the Israeli army between 1948 and 1972, and it is of a nondocumentary nature. Two important factors hampered research: First, documents deposited with the ministry of defense were still sealed from researchers. Second, neither David Ben Gurion, the central architect of Israel's defense and army policy from 1947 to 1963, nor his biographers had revealed the innermost decision-making processes and factors involved in important defense issues. The key, of course, was Ben Gurion himself, not his biographers. He had written a great deal on these issues in the press and in Mapai, Haganah, and ministry journals and publications and had issued public statements as well. Yet he had not attempted a fully detailed account of factors and motives affecting important security decisions. Most of Ben Gurion's explanations had been offered during controversy and under pressure, and thus consisted of fragmentary, inaccurate, cloudy statements that were often misconstrued. Ben Gurion's own archives at Sdeh-Boker were available only

with his permission. The quotation is from Ben Gurion's autobiography, *In the Battle* (in Hebrew) (Tel Aviv: Ayanot, 1955), 5:135–37. After his death in 1973 the archives were finally opened.

18. Had an internal war occurred—and the *Altalena* affair could have provoked one—it would have crippled the immense defense effort necessary to win against the Arabs. Menachem Begin, in the face of some opposition from other MNO leaders, played a key role in bringing about the MNO's acceptance of the national authority of the Jewish Agency. Recent literature has played down the actual threat presented by the *Altalena* crisis. See Eliahu Lankin, *The Story of the Altalena* (in Hebrew) (Tel Aviv: Hadar, 1967). General Yigael Yadin considers the fall of the Old City of Jerusalem and other military failures in 1948 to have been caused by independent NMO activities in Jerusalem. See the "War of Liberation" interview in *Ma'ariv*, May 14, 1967, pp. 9–11.

19. Debate on the defense service bill of 1949 in *Divrey Ha-Knesset* (in Hebrew), *Parliamentary Debates*, 68th Meeting, August 15, 1949, pp. 1336–41.

20. On Dayan's view, see "Israel's Border and Security Problems," *Foreign Affairs*, vol. 33, no. 2 (January 1955). On the role of Ben Gurion and Dayan in intensifying border raid and retaliation policy, see their chief antagonist, Moshe Sharett, *Memoires*, vol. 3 (Tel Aviv: Am-oved, 1974), pp. B-75.

21. See S. N. Eisenstadt, "Israel," in *The Institutions of Advanced Societies*, ed. Harold M. Rose (Minneapolis: University of Minnesota Press, 1958), pp. 417–30. I am indebted to Eliezer Rosenstein for some of these ideas. See his "Social Change in the Israeli Society" (Ph.D. diss., University of California, Berkeley, 1965), p. 3. See also Eisenstadt, "Israel," p. 422.

22. See Conrad Brandt, *Stalin's Failure in China* (Cambridge, Mass.: Harvard University Press, 1958). On the process of the general staff formation, see Meir Pa'il, "The Evolution of Haganah's High Command from 1920 to the Formation of IDF May–June 1948" (Master's thesis, University of Tel Aviv, 1970).

23. See the case dealing with the French generals' influence on politics between 1919 and 1939 in Judith Hughes, *To the Maginot Line* (Cambridge, Mass.: Harvard University Press, 1971).

24. Perlmutter, *Military and Politics*, pp. 49–68, 80–101; Pa'il, "The Evolution of the Haganah," pp. 54–75.

25. Eisenstadt, "Israel," pp. 427–29.

26. See Samuel P. Huntington, "Political Development and Political Decay," *World Politics* 17 (April 1965): 394.

27. This was written two months before Agranat's investigation committee's interim report was published on April 2, 1974. For an English summary of interim report see *New York Times*, April 3, 1974. The full report was published as *The Agranat Interim Report: Investigation of the Yom Kippur War* (mimeographed, Jerusalem, April, 1, 1974), 33 pp.

28. On the evolution of Haganah into Zahal's high command, see Meir Pa'il, "The Evolution."

29. See Yehudah Bauer, *Diplomacy*, p. 18.

30. Putting the onus for lack of military preparedness and alertness on Chief of Staff David Elazar by the Agranat Committee is based on a similar argument. Ibid., p. 12.

31. This has also been argued in the Agranat Committee Interim Report, ibid., p. 4.

32. My view is contradicted (without proper evidence) by the Agranat Committee Interim Report. The committee argues, "The defense minister was never intended to be a super chief of staff. Nor is the defense minister *ipso facto* a sort of supreme commander" (*New York Times*, p. 12). According to this argument direct responsibility for the Mehdal (misdeed) was shouldered by Chief of Staff Elazar.

33. See Amos Perlmutter, "Israel's Fourth War: Political Misperceptions and Military Errors, *Orbis* 29 (Summer 1975): 434–38.

34. General (Ariel) Sharon has been accused of tacitly campaigning when he was a divisional commander during the December 1973 elections. But even if he did, Sharon's military doctrine is not identical with that of the Likud party, which has no military doctrine. For an account of intervention by Dayan, see Moshe Sharett, *Diaries,* ed. Yaqov Sharett (in Hebrew), vols. 2, 3, 4 (Tel Aviv: Naariv, 1978).

35. Ze'ev Shiff, "The Young Officers of Zahal: Education and Political Consciousness," *Ha-Aretz,* January 23, 1963.

CONCLUSION

1. Obviously in conservative and revolutionary regimes there are times when the bureaucracy and the political party elites, being highly dependent on political order, can be more orthodox than the military in preserving stability. However, the politicians, unlike the military, can "create" another state. No modern state—not even Prussia and Communist China—has been created by and for the military.

2. Karl D. Bracher, *The German Dictatorship* (New York: Praeger, 1970), pp. 245–46.

3. Stephen P. Cohen, *The Indian Army: Its Contribution to the Development of a Nation* (Berkeley: University of California Press, 1971), pp. 169–200. Political intervention was not the *cause célèbre* of the Pakistani defeat in 1970, but it contributed heavily to the military's low performance. The misjudgments of the leader also played an important part. (The Nazi army, although demonstrating to the end the highest professional performance, was defeated because of Hitler's political blunders.) Whatever the cause, the Pakistani military establishment became the chief victim of its praetorianism. This has also been the case in Egypt. On Syria see Itamar Rabinowitz, *The Ba'th Party* (Tel Aviv: Israel University Press, 1973).

4. See Gerhard Ritter's detailed analysis of military praetorianism in Germany between 1890 and 1914, *The Sword and the Scepter: The Problem of Militarism in Germany,* vol. 2 (Coral Gables, Fla.: University of Miami Press, 1970).

5. DeMaistre, quoted by Sheldon Wolin, *Politics and Vision* (Boston: Little, Brown, 1960), p. 399. Richard Griffith, *Pétain* (New York: Doubleday, 1972), p. 160 (italics added).

6. John J. Johnson, ed., *The Role of the Military in Underdeveloped Countries* (Princeton, N.J.: Princeton University Press, 1962).

7. On the Nigerian army, see A. R. Luckham, "The Nigerian Army: A Case Study on Cohesion" (Ph.D. diss., University of Chicago, 1969). On India, see Cohen, *Indian Army.*

Index

Administration: in Africa, 134, 135–36, 140, 141; classical, 3, 4; in Europe, 22; fusionist, 4–5

Africa: elites in, 122–32; guerrillas in, 126, 129–31, 143; and innovation, 291–92; interventionism in, 115, 120–22, 138–39, 151, 153–54, 282; military professionals in, 127–28, 130, 143; military regimes in, 109, 132–46, 151; and modernization, 289; political parties in, 124–26, 129–36, 145, 151; satrapism in, 117–18, 286–87

Afrifa, A. A., 121

'Alawi officers, 150, 151, 155

Algeria: intellectuals in, 132; military in, 109, 127–28, 129, 130, 143; political parties in, 124, 125, 130

Ali, Muhammed, 151

Alianza Popular Revolucionaria Americana (APRA), 180–81, 186–87

Allende, Salvador, 191, 192

Allon, Yigal, 274; as deputy prime minister, 271, 272; as military commander, 256, 257; and Palmach, 257, 259, 261

Americas, colonizing nation-states in, 27–28. *See also* Latin America; United States

Amin, Idi, 128

Andreski, Stanislav, xiii, 7, 12, 135

Antitraditionalist, 108

Apter, David, 125

Arab Liberation Movement (ALM), 111, 142

Arab Socialist Union (ASU), 125, 135, 147–49, 159

Argentina: arbitrator praetorianism in, 105, 178, 185–86; latent praetorianism in, 174; politics in, 178–79; professionalism in, 103, 172, 173, 190, 283; ruler praetorianism in, 109, 110, 187–90, 288; social forces in, 97, 184, 185, 198

Armies: antitraditionalist radical, 108–09; antitraditionalist reformer, 108, 109; conservative antiradical, 108, 109; mass, 30, 40; national liberation, 208, 216–17, 231–37, 240–50, 254–80 passim; praetorian, 102–14, 136–41, 166–67, 198–99

Atatürk, 109, 111, 163

Australia, 27–28

Authoritarianism: of Communist regimes, 220, 228; in Germany, 46, 47; in Latin America, 177, 182–83, 199, 201; in Middle East, 141, 182–83; and politics, 8–9; and praetorianism, 95, 201

Authority, 22–23; decline of, 99; legal-rational, 93; legitimacy of, 13, 21–23, 35, 93, 156; and military skills, 4–6, 13. *See also* Control, civilian; Regimes

Autocracies, 22, 95, 145, 287

Autonomy: bureaucratic, 24; political, 177, 200

—corporate, 24, 38, 205; in China, 290–91; in Europe, 38, 40, 44, 59; in Latin America, 13, 177, 190, 198, 201; in Middle East, 13, 147, 290–91; and politics, 31, 34, 42, 177, 201, 290–91; in USSR, 75–85

Avineri, Shlomo, 222

Awolowo, Obafemi, 125

Azikiwe, Nmandi, 125

Bar-Lev, Chaim, 257, 263, 271, 274, 278

Ba'th Arab Socialist party, 124, 132, 135, 151, 152, 182–83; conquest of, 134, 149–50, 160; rule by, 111–12, 142, 154–55, 163

Be'eri, Eliezer, 155–56, 161

Belletrists, 131

Ben Bella, Ahmed, 109–10

Ben Gurion, David, 271; and British, 254, 260–61; as minister of defense, 262–63, 268–69, 277, 278, 279; and Palmach, 258